TWENTIETH-CENTURY NEWFOUNDLAND: EXPLORATIONS

TWENTIETH-CENTURY NEWFOUNDLAND: EXPLORATIONS

EDITED BY
JAMES HILLER AND PETER NEARY

BREAKWATER

Breakwater
100 Water Street
P.O. Box 2188
St. John's, NF
A1C 6E6

The Publisher gratefully acknowledges the financial assistance of the Canada Council.

Cover photo: Group of children examining anti-aircraft guns of HMS *Newfoundland*, St. John's, Newfoundland, 10 August 1944 (National Archives of Canada, PA116991).

Canadian Cataloguing in Publication Data
　　Main entry under title:

　Twentieth century Newfoundland

　　　Includes bibliographical references and index.
　　　ISBN 1-55081-072-3
　1. Newfoundland — History. 2. Newfoundland — Social conditions. 3. Newfoundland — Politics and government. I. Hiller, J.K. (James K.), 1942-
II. Neary, Peter, 1938-

FC2161.7.T93　1993	971.8	C93-098717-9
F1122.5.T93　1993		

Printed in Canada

CONTENTS

Newfoundland History Series

General Editors
Peter Neary/Patrick O'Flaherty

1 Part of the Main:
An Illustrated History of Newfoundland and Labrador
Peter Neary/Patrick O'Flaherty

2 Fish Out of Water:
The Newfoundland Saltfish Trade 1814-1914
Shannon Ryan

3 Corner Brook:
A Social History of a Paper Town
Harold Horwood

4 Lectures on the History of Newfoundland: 1500-1830
Keith Matthews

5 Out of Mind, Out of Sight: A History
of the Waterford Hospital
Patricia O'Brien

6 Soe longe as there comes noe women:
Origins of English Settlement in Newfoundland
W. Gordon Handcock

PREFACE

IN 1980 WE PUBLISHED *Newfoundland in the Nineteenth and Twentieth Centuries: Essays in Interpretation*, a collection of ten papers by six authors. We were pleased with the reception this book received and we are gratified that it is still widely used. Our purpose in bringing out the present collection of papers is to build upon and supplement our earlier work. Our second volume covers a broad range of topics and indicates the vigour and diversity of the present day writing on the past of Newfoundland and Labrador. We do not claim that the subject matter of the book is comprehensive but we trust that the papers we have brought together will help to fill some important gaps in existing knowledge. Our aim is to be informative rather than definitive. We also hope that the papers will point the way to new topics for research and to new approaches in what is a rapidly expanding and developing field of scholarly interest. Melvin Baker's bibliography, which closes the volume, should be useful to a wide variety of readers but will be of special interest, we believe, to undergraduate students of Canadian history.

As the essays in this book clearly show, Newfoundland and Labrador have experienced in this century a series of political, economic and social shocks. In his essay on the career of Sir Robert Bond, James Hiller notes that the century began promisingly. The railway had been built across the island and new industry was being attracted to the country. Bond eventually became the symbol of a progressive and harmonious time, though more was read into his career by hard pressed later generations than the facts justified. Nevertheless, Newfoundland looked outward with uncommon confidence in the 1900-14 period and, as Gerald L. Pocius relates, became in time an attractive destination for Americans in search of adventure in travel. World War I, however, shook the country to its foundations and the 1920s was a decade of disarray. The motives of those who sought to reform Newfoundland's social services in that period are explored in James Overton's essay on the origins of the charity organization movement in Newfoundland. Worse followed, for the Great Depression of the 1930s led to the suspension of self-government and from 1934 to 1949 Newfoundland was administered by a British appointed Commission of Government. One of the main policies of that government was to diversify the economy by settling more people on the land. This effort, which brought mixed results, is the subject of Gordon Handcock's essay. World War II restored Newfoundland financially and brought unprecedented prosperity but it also intensified some underlying differences between the native born, who constituted an overwhelming majority of the population, and a small number of foreign born residents. Newfoundland's immigration policy before 1949 is the topic of Gerhard P. Bassler's essay, which extends and enriches his work on a neglected but important subject. Societies can be judged by how they treat their minorities and Newfoundland is no exception.

After World War II, Newfoundlanders and Labradorians—the latter group achieved separate political representation for the first time in the National Convention elected in 1946—were caught up in an intense debate on the constitutional future of their country. This culminated in the July 1948 referendum which resulted in a vote for union with Canada. Confederation then took effect on 31 March 1949. The influence of the United States on this outcome is Peter Neary's first subject in this volume. Given the terms of the Anglo-American leased bases agreement of March 1941, United States policy makers considered Newfoundland 'a mortgaged property' and acted accordingly. Neary's second essay explores the impact of confederation on a large and well organized group, the veterans of World Wars I and II. Raymond Blake moves the volume into the post-confederation period. His topic is the interplay of federal and provincial policy with respect to the Newfoundland fishing industry in the first decade of union. If, as he demonstrates, the 1950s marked a period of rapid decline for the saltfish industry, it was also a time of burgeoning opportunity in other parts of the economy. In his paper Melvin Baker discusses how the government of Joseph R. Smallwood, Newfoundlands's first post-confederation premier, pushed ahead with ambitious schemes of hydroelectric development that revolutionized daily life in the province. Before 1949 the production of electricity had been a private concern; after 1949, in order to meet rising expectations, the province had to take the lead. Newfoundland changed remarkably in the Smallwood era but the prolonged political and constitutional crisis that marked the end of his administration resembled the factionalism of the 1920s. This episode, the subject of Peter Neary's final contribution to the volume, raises interesting questions about the nature of party politics in the Canadian province and invites reflection on the interplay of past and present in Newfoundland's modern history.

We are grateful to A.M.J. Hyatt of the Department of History, University of Western Ontario, for providing us with needed facilities and to Glenda Hunt of that Department for expert word processing assistance. We thank A.P. Bates of London, Ontario, for acute editorial advice and Memorial University for the map of Newfoundland and Labrador we have included.

CONTRIBUTORS

MELVIN BAKER. A graduate of Memorial University and the University of Western Ontario. One of the authors of *The Illustrated History of Newfoundland Light & Power* (1990) and one of the editors of the *Dictionary of Newfoundland and Labrador Biography* (1990). Archivist-Historian for Memorial University.

GERHARD P. BASSLER. Professor of History at Memorial University. Author of *Sanctuary Denied: Refugees from the Third Reich and Newfoundland Immigration Policy, 1906-1949* (1992) and of numerous articles on ethnic relations in Newfoundland and Canada.

RAYMOND BLAKE. A 1991 PH D graduate of York University. His doctoral thesis is entitled 'The Making of a Province: The Integration of Newfoundland into Canada, 1948-57.'

GORDON HANDCOCK. A graduate of Memorial University and the University of Birmingham and currently Professor of Geography at Memorial University. He has written extensively on the historical geography of Newfoundland, and is the author of *So longe as there comes noe women: Origins of English Settlement in Newfoundland* (1989).

JAMES HILLER. Professor of History at Memorial University and author of a number of articles on Newfoundland in the nineteenth and twentieth centuries.

PETER NEARY. Professor of History at the University of Western Ontario and the author of *Newfoundland in the North Atlantic World, 1929-1949* (1988).

JAMES OVERTON. A graduate of the University of Hull and the University of Western Ontario and a member of the Department of Sociology, Memorial University. He has written extensively on Newfoundland society and culture and has a book in progress on 'Poverty and the State in Newfoundland Between the Wars.'

GERALD L. POCIUS. A graduate of the University of Pennsylvania, he is a member of the Memorial University Folklore Department, and director of that University's Centre for Material Culture Studies. He has written numerous articles on Newfoundland subjects, and in 1991 published *A Place to Belong: Community Order and Community Space in Calvert, Newfoundland.*

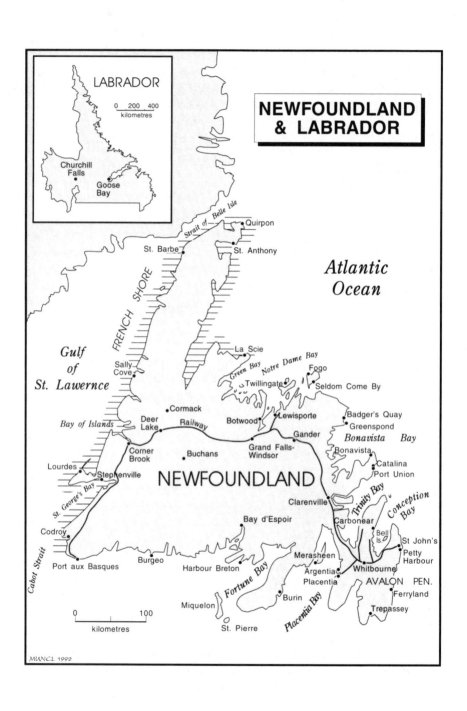

The Political Career of
Robert Bond

James Hiller

I N THE COURSE of its brief review of Newfoundland's history, the *Report* of the 1933 Newfoundland Royal Commission, chaired by Lord Amulree, gave this assessment of the premiership of Sir Robert Bond (1900-09):

> [He] left behind him a reputation of far-sighted devotion to the interests of the Island and is generally regarded as the most statesmanlike figure in the line of Newfoundland Prime Ministers. To-day, a disillusioned people, looking back on the past, single out the years of his premiership as a period of orthodox finance and sane government when the fortunes of the island were at their zenith; there was almost unanimous agreement among witnesses that the present period of misfortune might be regarded as having originated with his fall from power in 1908.[1]

Bond had died only six years earlier, and his obituaries referred even then to his ability, patriotism and his qualities as a statesman.[2] It is a view that still prevails, reinforced after 1949 by Premier Joseph R. Smallwood, who saw himself as part of 'a great Liberal tradition' stretching back through Richard Squires and Edward Morris to Bond, and beyond him to William Whiteway and others. In the first volume of Smallwood's *Encyclopedia of Newfoundland and Labrador*, Bond alone received the accolade of a full-page photograph.[3]

This paper reviews Bond's career, concentrating on his premiership, with the intention of testing the received wisdom. In so doing, the paper amplifies the account given by S.J.R. Noel, which deals mainly with the colony's external affairs, and with the unusual and dramatic circumstances surrounding Bond's downfall.[4] Noel's is the only study of Bond's premiership currently available—a curious circumstance, given Bond's apparent importance and high reputation, but understandable when one considers the recent development of academic studies of Newfoundland's modern history, and a prevailing bias against political narrative.

Robert Bond was born in 1857 into a wealthy St. John's merchant family. His father died in 1872, leaving a widow and three sons amply provided for. Robert, the second child, was educated in England and then returned to live with his mother in St. John's. He never married, and never practiced a profession, though he had some legal training.[5] Unlike all other contemporary Newfoundland politicians, Bond could devote time and energy to politics and government alone. His peers had to climb the greasy pole to financial security and political success, and either could not afford, or were unwilling to abandon their law offices and counting houses. They entered public life conditioned by the rough and tumble of everyday business in the colony, driven by ambitions that did not diminish with achievement. William Whiteway, Bond's political mentor, had started life as a merchant's clerk; his rival and eventual nemesis, Edward Morris, came from an Irish immigrant family of insubstantial means. In contrast, Bond started at the top, unscarred by the climb. He never knew financial or social insecurity.

His entry into politics was likewise smooth and untroubled. Adopted as his protege by Sir William Whiteway, the Conservative leader, Bond ran as Whiteway's partner in the Trinity Bay election of 1882. It was the start of a political career that was to last over 30 years. The choice of party affiliation was significant. The overriding issue in the election was the building of a railway, which Whiteway and his Conservative party—in alliance with the predominantly Roman Catholic Liberals—touted as the solution to Newfoundland's economic ills. By opening up the interior, by bringing its valuable resources into productive use, the railway would help create a balanced, self-sufficient economy. It was a seductive vision, which those who had doubts, represented in the election by the merchant-oriented New party, found it hard to counter.[6] From the beginning, Bond was a firm supporter of the railway and all it represented, and optimistic about the colony's resource potential. 'Why should this country be looked on as a barren fishing station, or as a mere chip that was thrown out into the Atlantic as completely useless when the world was created?' he once asked. The interior would in time provide for agriculture, mining and manufacturing[7]—it was there 'that the people...would have to look for future prosperity.'[8] Backwardness, he was convinced, could be conquered. As if to set an example, Bond bought land near the railway line at Whitbourne, some 60 miles from St. John's, built himself a country house, laid out formal gardens and started a small farm.[9]

The young nationalist achieved rapid prominence. A political crisis brought on by an Orange-Catholic riot at Harbour Grace in December 1883 led to the break-up, early in 1885, of Whiteway's coalition with the Liberals, who went into opposition. Their leader, R.J. Kent, resigned as Speaker. Bond replaced him; and when Whiteway retired temporarily from public life that autumn, Bond found himself the leader of a small Whitewayite opposition to the Reform party government led by Robert Thorburn and James Winter.[10]

The next few years saw the emergence of other central features of Bond's political philosophy. First, Bond demonstrated his opposition to confederation with Canada. The issue arose when his colleague Alfred B. Morine, an ambitious Nova Scotian adventurer with contacts in high places in Ottawa, began a series of clandestine manoeuvres designed to join the Whitewayites and the Winter faction of Reform party in confederate wedlock. Whiteway had been a confederate in the 1860s, but defeat on the issue had taught him caution, and he was unwilling to risk a reviving political career. Thus he listened to Bond rather than Morine, and when a Newfoundland delegation was invited to Ottawa, the Whitewayites refused to participate. To cement his position as Whiteway's lieutenant, Bond then forced Morine out of the party.[11]

Bond was convinced that while confederation made little economic or political sense, Newfoundland would be well served by a separate reciprocity treaty with the United States. The whole question of relations between British North America and the republic was very much in the air in the mid to late 1880s, and Bond believed that Newfoundland's chances of a satisfactory agreement should not be jeopardized by having to join with Canada, whose quarrels with the United States were not Newfoundland's affair. Moreover, since Canada produced more fish and was nearer the market, it could dominate the trade.[12] Bond envisaged an arrangement whereby American bank fishermen would be granted access to Newfoundland waters for supplies of bait, in return for free access to the United States market for Newfoundland fish and mineral ores. Attracted by the size of the potential American market, and by the possibility of American investment in Newfoundland, Bond argued that this option would encourage economic development while preserving political independence. The problem, of course, was that Canada strongly opposed Newfoundland negotiating an independent reciprocity treaty, and London was more likely to listen to the former than the latter—a fact of political life which Bond found very difficult to accept.

Bond's emphasis on political independence, economic diversification, and close relations with the USA, was combined with a growing frustration at the French presence in the Newfoundland fisheries. Ambiguously worded eighteenth-century treaties allowed French fishermen the seasonal use of the so-called French or Treaty Shore, and the islands of St. Pierre and Miquelon provided a base for a large deep-sea fleet. These fisheries were supported by government bounties, and much of the saltfish produced competed with Newfoundland exports in traditional Mediterranean and Iberian markets. Moreover, French claims to a privileged position on the Treaty Shore created legal and diplomatic uncertainties that impeded the economic development of the island's west coast, a region which was thought to have considerable potential. Like many Newfoundlanders, Bond thought that the French presence had held the country back. 'This...Question has retarded Newfoundland's progress to a very marked extent,' he wrote in 1902. 'If [it] were cleared up emigration would immediately flow in, with capital to develop the natural resources of our soil and forests, which are very great.'[13] The British government, he believed, had been— and remained—all too ready to sacrifice Newfoundland in the interest of good relations with France. His nationalism was coloured with francopho- bia and with mistrust of the imperial authorities. If Newfoundland was backward, he told the House of Assembly in 1900, it was not the colony's fault.[14]

> The contrast that exists today between this, the oldest British colony and the other colony [Canada] that borders us, is a national disgrace to England. There is not a traveller to our shores...who has not imposed this conviction on the world. We blush at the contrast but not on our own account. We have no need to do so for we could not alter it one iota. We have been handicapped in the march of progress by imperial interdiction on the one hand, and French aggression on the other, and have thus been subjected to the imputation of an inferiority we neither merit nor feel.

In 1889 Whiteway returned to active politics, and led his party—now calling itself Liberal—to victory in the election that autumn. Bond entered the government as Colonial Secretary, rapidly establishing himself as one of its most influential members. True to its platform, the new administration resumed railway work—the first contractor having gone bankrupt in 1885 —by signing a contract with Robert G. Reid of Montreal, who had had considerable experience with the Canadian Pacific Railway (CPR). For the next seven years the line pushed steadily forward to its terminus at Port aux Basques, and the public debt climbed in proportion. It was external affairs, however, which preoccupied the government. Bond's performance was true to his principles, but showed a stubbornness and inflexibility which should have given his supporters pause.

The situation that developed was extremely complex. In 1890 the British government allowed Bond to go to Washington to explore the possibility of a reciprocity treaty. No harm could come of this, it was thought, since the mission would almost certainly fail. There was great consternation in London and Ottawa when, late in the year, it was learned that Bond and the American Secretary of State, the mischievous James Blaine, had agreed on a draft treaty. Faced with Canadian protests the British refused to allow matters to proceed any further. The Newfoundland government was angry; Bond felt personally humiliated, and in the 1891 session of the legislature launched fierce attacks against the imperial gov- ernment for its willingness to subordinate Newfoundland's interests to those of Canada. He persuaded the government to retaliate against Canada by refusing to issue bait licences to Canadian fishing vessels.[15]

At the same time as this dispute was brewing, the Colonial Office was trying to persuade the Newfoundland government to pass legislation en- forcing the hated French Shore treaties, the old imperial statutes having been repealed (by mistake) or allowed to expire. This coincided with a highly charged quarrel over the legality of the French taking and canning lobsters on the Shore, Newfoundland claiming they could do no more than take and salt codfish. An Anglo-French *modus vivendi* on this matter in 1890 was greeted with howls of outrage in St. John's, particularly from opposition politicians trying to embarrass Whiteway, who was seen as soft on the French question.

The English born premier was, in fact, prepared to make a deal. His view had always been that a compromise on the French Shore was necessary in order to complete the railway and open the west coast to economic development, and that more was to be gained by negotiation than by confrontation—particularly for a politician with an eye on imperial preferment. Bond, on the other hand, hurt and angered by the rejection of the United States convention, saw in Britain's attitude yet another example of its readiness to sacrifice Newfoundland; and in Whiteway's practical willingness to negotiate on the issue of treaty legislation, a lamentable sell-out. The imperial government had announced that if Newfoundland did not pass the necessary bill, the deed would be done in London. While Whiteway wanted to avoid this, Bond appears to have preferred the prospect of imperial coercion. In the end, the legislature passed temporary enforcement legislation, and Whiteway negotiated the terms of a permanent bill. When this was presented to the Assembly in 1892, Bond deserted Whiteway and led the opposition to the bill, which was overwhelmingly defeated. Understandably, Whiteway saw this as a betrayal. Relations between the two became embittered, distant and cold, and the stability and effectiveness of the government suffered.

For instance, at a conference with Canadian government representatives at Halifax in November 1892, the Newfoundland delegation was noticeably disunited, with Whiteway, Bond and Augustus W. Harvey each seeming on occasion to take divergent positions. Called to settle the differences then existing between the two countries, the Canadian representatives first floated the idea of confederation. When the bait was refused, they made it plain that they would not withdraw Canadian objections to the Bond-Blaine convention, stressing that Newfoundland could not legally discriminate against Canadian vessels in its coastal waters—by, for instance, refusing bait licences. Knowing that Canadian interests and arguments would generally have precedence in London over those of Newfoundland, the Canadians in effect demonstrated that equality of status did not imply equality of stature, and that Newfoundland's future relations with the United States depended on Canadian policy. Whiteway understood the moral, even if he did not like it.[16] Bond refused to discuss union at Halifax, and apparently found it difficult to accept that his country ranked lower than Canada. One of his objects in public life, he said, 'was to secure for this colony that dignity, recognition and right that had been accorded to the other colonies of the Empire,'[17] to ensure that Newfoundland should 'maintain an honourable and independent position as part of the British Empire.'[18] This implied resisting Canadian pretensions rather than recognizing the reality.

For all the government's internal difficulties—in July 1893 Bond went so far as to submit his resignation[19]—the Liberals won the 1893 election and seemed almost impregnable, their success fuelled by railway building, utopian promises, and a popular leader. But they had not counted on the resourcefulness of the expelled Morine, now a leading spirit in the Tory party. Under his guidance the Tories filed election petitions alleging corrupt practice against seventeen Liberals, including Bond and Whiteway, all of whom eventually lost their seats. This process caused the Liberal government's resignation in April 1894, and a period of serious political instability which precipitated the crash of the two local banks in December. The catastrophe left the colony on the edge of bankruptcy, and the Tories crept out of office. Newfoundland's saviour was to be Robert Bond, once the old firm had replaced an interim Liberal government early in 1895.

Since Whiteway was ill, it was the anti-confederate Bond who led a delegation to Ottawa in March 1895 in an attempt to negotiate satisfactory terms of union—his view being that confederation was preferable to the indignities which would surround a receivership managed by the Colonial Office. The failure of these talks had more to do with Canadian and British inflexibility than with Bond and his colleagues, who showed—*in extremis*—a remarkable ability to compromise.[20] With default fast approaching, Bond next set off with Robert G. Reid—who had close links to the Bank of Montreal, and was being paid in Newfoundland government bonds—to try and raise loans to salvage both the colony and the government's Savings Bank. To everyone's surprise, and to the chagrin of some, Bond succeeded, an achievement which won him immense local prestige. The fact that he gave his personal guarantee on part of the Savings Bank loan entered into folklore: Bond was the incorruptible patriot who had pledged his fortune to save his country.[21] 'In campaign after campaign', grumbled the St. John's *Daily News* in 1909, 'the people have been told of it, and Bond has been magnified into a demi-god.'[22]

Bond's personal popularity could not save the Liberals, however, who were defeated in the 1897 election by a revived Tory party led by Winter (who became premier) and Morine. Since Whiteway lost his seat, Bond led the opposition. The major issue with which he had to deal was a new contract which the government signed with Robert G. Reid in 1898, and forced through the legislature. In 1893 the railway construction contract had been supplemented with an agreement whereby Reid undertook to operate the line for ten years in return for fee simple land grants of 5,000 acres per mile. In 1898 the Tory government decided that it would be best to dispose of the now completed railway altogether. The new deal provided that Reid would operate the railway for fifty years (until 1945) in return for additional land grants which would bring his total holdings to about four million acres. At the end of that period the railway would become the property of his successors, and for that reversionary interest Reid would pay the colony $1 million. He agreed to operate a coastal steamship service and the Gulf of St. Lawrence ferry, providing his own vessels, in return for subsidy payments. Further, Reid agreed to take over the government's telegraph lines and to purchase the St. John's dry dock. Other clauses awarded Reid the right to build a street railway in St. John's, and to supply the town with electricity from a power plant at Petty Harbour.[23]

The new contract split the Liberal party. Edward Morris, a prominent St. John's politician who had joined the 1889 Liberal government, supported the Tory argument that the deal represented immediate and long-term financial savings. The colony got rid of what Morine described as 'an octopus, an old man of the sea'[24] by transferring it to Reid and his successors, who would have to make substantial outlays to create traffic for the railway and to make their lands profitable. The result would be the development of the interior at the Reids' expense and risk. The sale, Morris thought, was irrelevant: 'What is all this sentimental nonsense about [Reid] owning the road? Nothing could be more false. We only gave him the rails and sleepers. What do I care who owns my carriage and horse if I can still ride in it always and get someone to keep it in repair [?].'[25]

Bond the nationalist thought the deal 'immoral and dishonest,' the 'betrayal of a country's trust.' There was no good reason to sell the railway and other assets to a Canadian for a fraction of their cost:'If there is money in our railways, telegraphs and docks for Mr. Reid, there is also money in them for the people of this colony.' Beyond that was the question of control and responsibility:

> Sell out that railway to Mr. Reid, grant him the further concessions named, and he, as sole owner and proprietor of both the lands of the interior and of the railway can bid defiance to the Legislature and do as he pleases with those lands...I am not prepared to thus barter away the property of the people of this country and of those who shall come after us. I have full faith in the brighter future that is in store for us, the gleam of which is already apparent...The crisis is a great one. The whole complexion of the destinies of the country depends on the action of the Government. By whom, by what influence, from what quarter, are its rich resources, its hopes, its fortunes to be controlled? That is the question we have now to decide.[26]

The contract's critics were supported by the governor, the opinionated Sir Herbert Murray; by the Roman Catholic bishop (later archbishop), M.F. Howley; and by officials at the Colonial Office, who saw the deal as a humiliating confession of incompetence.[27]

The unpopularity of the contract, the effectiveness of the criticism mounted by Bond and his allies, and the active hostility of the governor, weakened a Tory government already suffering from rivalry between

Winter and Morine and their respective factions. The opposition was in no better condition. The members of the old Whiteway party, wrote Bond, were 'like the scattered leaves of autumn,' some 'buried beneath treachery and fraud,' others under the influence of the government or of Reid. He hoped the remainder would form the nucleus of a new Liberal party.[28] In March 1899, Winter proposed that their groups form an alliance. Serious negotiations resulted, since both men wished to prevent Morine becoming premier, and Bond could avoid dealing with Morris. They failed because Bond insisted that the coalition be on his terms: in summary, Winter would be found a safe berth, and Bond would lead a new government which would include several Winterites, but which would adopt Bond's policies. The new arrangements would be ratified by an early election.[29] With the failure of these talks, anti-contract Liberals bestirred themselves. Later in the year Bond officially took over the party leadership from Whiteway in somewhat confused circumstances—some claimed that the old man went willingly, others that he had been knifed—and set about bringing down the Tory government.[30]

In February 1900, at the request of Governor Henry Edward McCallum, Winter called a special session of the legislature to renew the legislation enforcing the French Shore treaties, other business being postponed to the spring. Bond gave Winter the impression that he would reluctantly agree to this. However, Morris apparently sensed that the government might collapse, carrying the contract and its supporters into political oblivion. To save himself, and to salvage the essence of the contract, Morris offered to join Bond in bringing down the Winter government. Bond accepted, and moved a no confidence motion which was carried with the help of the Morris group and three Tory defectors. Winter resigned on 5 March.[31] When asked to form a government, Bond, who owed his political advantage and his majority to Morris, now faced the problem of disentangling himself from a disagreeable alliance. He requested an immediate dissolution. McCallum refused. Bond therefore proposed that Morris enter the cabinet, but that future policy be left undecided until the House was dissolved, which Bond hoped would be in the spring. In effect, Bond wanted to form a provisional government.[32] However, McCallum adamantly refused to allow an election to take place until the autumn, and Morris insisted on a clear and distinct understanding on the contract issue.[33] In these circumstances Bond had no alternative but to negotiate an agreement with Morris. This took the form of a compromise paragraph for a future election manifesto pledging that the 1898 contract would be 'modified'—rather than repealed as Bond would have wished, or maintained intact as Morris would have preferred.[34] On this basis a government was formed with an effective majority of two seats.

Having unwisely allied with Morris, was there any way in which Bond could have ditched him while keeping the premiership? Given the governor's rigid views on early dissolutions—of which Winter had warned

Bond—it would not have been easy. His only solution would have been to insist that the governor accept the advice of his premier and to get concerted pressure on the governor from Bishop Howley and others, and perhaps as well from the Colonial Office. Given the state of public opinion and the collapse of the Tories, Bond was in fact in a strong position. He was the only possible premier at this juncture, and persistence might well have succeeded. But Bond chose to accept the governor's decision, probably counting it a victory that McCallum had retreated from his original position that no election could take place until 1901. The result, though, was that Bond found himself in the uncomfortable position of leading an apparently anti-contract government which contained one of the contract's most prominent supporters, and a number of others who had voted for it in the Assembly.

The Reid deal was, of course, the central issue in the fall election. Now led by Morine, the Tories campaigned on Reid's behalf and with his money. The St. John's *Daily News*, which Reid controlled, sang his praises. His railway cars and steamers carried Tory posters and colours. Thirteen Tory candidates were either employed by, or were connected with the Reid empire.[35] The Liberals (with Morris and the compromise in the background) mounted a nationalistic crusade: was Newfoundland to be sold to a monopolistic Canadian contractor and his political hirelings? The answer was resoundingly in the negative, and Bond swept to victory with a twenty-eight seat majority. 'I feel *deeply grateful to God* for having saved our poor old Country,' wrote Bishop Howley. 'And I had no scruple in having the prayers of the Church offered up in sincere thanksgiving.'[36] He went on to advise Bond to beware of Morris: 'I cannot see how you can in justice or with safety to your policy, admit [him] to your Executive Council.'[37] It was sound advice, but impractical. It was now too late for Bond part with Morris; he could not risk splitting the party again, and losing the chance even to modify the Reid deal.

At this time Bond was very much the dominant, and the more attractive figure. The public saw him standing at the dawn of a new century, relatively young, native born, well-educated, untainted by scandal (the St. John's *Evening Telegram* liked to call him the 'incorruptible commoner'), his patriotism clearly shown by the 1895 loan negotiations and his campaigns against Reid and monopoly. Further back were his attempts to save the country from French aggression, and to obtain reciprocal trade with the United States. Less savoury episodes tended to be forgotten, to be resurrected only as his popularity diminished. In the same way, the less admirable traits of his character eventually received more attention. Bond lived a protected and solitary life, with his mother in St. John's until her death in 1903, thereafter at Whitbourne, where he spent as much time as possible—the opposition press frequently referred to 'the recluse of Whitbourne,' and the 'Whitbourne hermitage.'[38] When he had to be in St. John's, he stayed at a hotel. His most frequent companions were books. On the whole, his solitariness probably enhanced his reputation.[39] Something of a valetudinarian, reserved in manner,[40] Bond was nevertheless a dreamer attracted to dramatic, large-scale developments—his enemies called them 'Bond's fads'—and was both impervious to, and resentful of criticism. He became deeply involved with such projects, and pursued them with determination and inflexibility. Bond had a very high opinion of himself. An opposition newspaper was not being unfair when it remarked that Bond would have done well to have knocked about the world a bit, 'meeting men who would take him at their valuation instead of his own...instead of being wrapped up, figuratively, in cotton wool and listening only to the incense offered by a small, but admiring circle of dependents, he realised that the men he meets in life are his equals, not his inferiors.'[41]

His first test as premier was the renegotiation of the Reid contract. Agreement was not easily concluded. The Reid family was resentful of the way it had been vilified in the election campaign, and of Bond's reluctance to allow them to incorporate, an essential precondition to raising the capital to finance an elaborate development scheme.[42] For his part, Bond's experience of the Reids since he became premier had only intensified his mistrust and suspicion, and he had no intention of allowing the Reids an overly dominant role in future economic development. A new contract modifying that of 1898 was eventually signed in July 1901. Robert G. Reid gave up the reversionary interest in the railway, and was returned his $1 million with interest. He handed back the government telegraph system, agreeing that compensation should be settled by arbitration. For an additional payment of $850,000 he gave up his entitlement to roughly 1.5 million acres, and agreed so to adjust his lot boundaries as to exclude occupied and claimed areas. For its part, the government now allowed him to form the Reid Newfoundland Company, which was to retain the responsibility for operating the railway, the coastal steamship services, the dry dock, and the St. John's streetcar and electrical systems, as well as managing the extensive Reid landholdings.

The revised contract pleased neither side. Bond had managed to reduce the potentially enormous power of the Reids to more manageable proportions, and had regained control of major public services, but had been unable to go as far as he would have liked, being constrained both by the Morris agreement and by the need to keep the Reids in Newfoundland with an operation large enough to have the chance of making a profit: hence an attitude which Morine described as being 'a mixture of Dick Turpin and Uriah Heep.'[43] Moreover, Bond had been persuaded to arbitrate various Reid claims, which was to prove expensive and contentious. For their part, the Reids had been forced to give up some important parts of their empire, which made the implementation of their grand development scheme uncertain. But they had gained incorporation; and they obviously expected that in time their lands would bring them wealth, and that a less hostile government would be elected. They were not prepared to walk away from what was already a considerable investment. Relations between Bond and the company appear to have been relatively cordial until 1903. Thereafter the two parties became embroiled in endemic warfare, and Reids began actively to work against the Liberal government. For most of Bond's first government, however, the they were not an immediate political threat. The Tory party was weak and discredited, and in fomenting anti-Reid prejudice Bond had clearly found a winning ploy. Without effective allies there was little the Reids could do to improve their position, and Bond was able to devote a considerable amount of energy to external affairs. He was once again preoccupied with those two familiar issues, the French Shore and reciprocity with the United States.

Bond assumed office at the start of the diplomatic manoevering that was to culminate in the 1904 *entente cordiale*. At the request of the British government, Bond and Morris went to London in late February 1901, where they were faced with the predictable French demand that an essential part of any agreement would be French access to bait purchase on Newfoundland's south coast. Equally predictably, the delegates responded that this could be done only if the French modified their fishery bounty system, or the British government gave Newfoundland financial compensation.[44] The Colonial Secretary, Joseph Chamberlain, rejected these proposals—'Mr. Bond is even less reasonable than Mr. Cambon'—and the talks got no further.[45]

Frustrated as Chamberlain was by this impasse, he nevertheless sympathized with Bond's application to renew separate trade negotiations with the United States. Before going any further, he asked Bond to discuss the question with Sir Wilfrid Laurier. The latter was prepared. He had foreseen that if there was no general trade agreement between British North America and the United States, Newfoundland would once again try to act alone, and like his Conservative predecessors, he understood that confederation was the only effective way to prevent it. But the French Shore question seemed to pose a great difficulty—Laurier had gone so far as to discuss possible avenues of settlement with the French consul at Montreal, and to send a note to Delcassé, the French foreign minister[46]—and in 1901 it was still an active issue. Laurier therefore does not seem to have raised the question of confederation. Instead he simply refused to withdraw Canada's objections to an independent Newfoundland treaty, though assuring Bond that he would reconsider the matter.[47] But Laurier knew that his objections would not automatically be sustained at the Colonial Office, where officials hoped, as in 1890, that permission to negotiate in Washington would make the Newfoundland government more flexible on French Shore issues; and in any case, Chamberlain noted acidly, 'Sir W. Laurier who is so strong an adherent of Home Rule that he must pay special attention to Mr. Redmond, cannot complain if the principle of Home Rule is followed in the case of N[ew]f[oun]dland.'[48] Canada was informed that Newfoundland would be allowed to negotiate. Laurier asked Bond to postpone any action until they had met at the 1902 Colonial Conference. It is possible that he hoped to make a last effort to prevent the talks, and may have intended to raise confederation.[49] But there were no Canada-Newfoundland negotiations in London, and soon after the conference ended, Bond set off for Washington.

On 8 November 1902 a draft reciprocity treaty was signed by John Hay, the Secretary of State, and the British ambassador, Sir Michael Herbert. It was virtually identical to that of 1890. United States fishermen would be allowed to obtain bait in Newfoundland waters without paying a licence fee, and to touch and trade at Newfoundland ports. In return the United States would allow the free entry of salted and other fish, seal products and mineral ores. Newfoundland also accorded the United States most favoured nation status. This last provision effectively prevented Newfoundland from granting an imperial preference, much to the satisfaction of John Hay but to the annoyance of the British government.[50] The latter should not have been surprised, since Bond had made it quite clear at the Colonial Conference that Newfoundland would and could not implement a preferential tariff.[51] Nevertheless Chamberlain angrily declared that since the treaty was at variance 'with the declared policy of H.M.G.' it should never have been signed, and heaped blame on Herbert for having failed to spot the offending clause.[52] However, official chagrin was tempered by the knowledge that the treaty faced a difficult passage in the Senate.

Even before the draft treaty had been signed, the Gloucester fishing interests had indicated that they wanted it destroyed. Concerned by a downturn in its fisheries, Gloucester was determined that its dominance in the United States salt codfish and herring markets should continue to be protected by a high tariff.[53] Pressure was exerted on the Massachusetts senators, the senior of whom, Henry Cabot Lodge, chaired the Foreign Relations Committee. As the treaty disappeared into the Senate it was generally assumed that it was virtually dead, in spite of support from the administration, Boston and New York fish importers, and much of the press. There was nothing Bond could do until Lodge's committee reported. Chamberlain and Laurier were content that the convention was moribund, and that they were not responsible.[54]

As the Colonial Office had hoped, permission to negotiate in Washington had made Bond more flexible on French Shore issues. He proved willing to continue renewing the treaty enforcement legislation in spite of increasing opposition from the Legislative Council, and by mid-1902 was personally willing to concede bait privileges.[55] But since he was unable to persuade his colleagues, the British government had to bargain on another basis. In January 1904, therefore, it proposed an agreement whereby the French would give up their fishing rights under the Treaty of Utrecht but retain a concurrent seasonal fishery, compensation being paid to French owners of shore establishments.[56] Since such a deal did not remove the French from the Newfoundland coast altogether, Bond did not respond with the enthusiasm expected of him. He was worried, not unreasonably, by the prospect of a joint fishery and wanted more details. After clarifications from London the government finally agreed to obtain the legislation necessary to police the new fishery, providing that the French received no new rights, left the coast by 20 October annually, and gave up rights of landing and drying. Newfoundland also wanted an assurance that its use and exploitation of the French Shore would henceforth be unrestricted.[57] The Colonial Office thought this very grudging; but Bond's caution was justified. As he explained, he had 'to feel [his] way very carefully so as to be certain of a united Council and party in dealing with this matter later on.'[58] Premiers before him had sustained political damage as a result of their handling of French Shore issues; Bond wanted to avoid trouble if he could.

The Anglo-French Convention was signed in London on 8 April. The island of Newfoundland, Bond told the Assembly, 'may henceforth be hailed...as our native land, freed from every foreign claim, and the blasting influence of foreign oppression—ours in entirety—solely ours.'[59] It was not an achievement for which he could take much credit, but he could plausibly argue that he had kept concessions to a minimum. There were a few final snags. In order to make the most of an historic event in an election year, Bond claimed that the convention would have to be approved by the legislature, citing in support of this contention the dog-eared Labouchere despatch of 1857 and the draft convention of 1885.[60] The novel idea that a colony should have the power to ratify rather than concur in an imperial treaty was soon demolished, and Bond had to content himself with moving resolutions which recorded the Assembly's endorsement.[61] An attack on the settlement was led by Morine and, outside the legislature, by Sir William Whiteway. Their carping had little impact, and most Newfoundlanders welcomed the end of an interminable and frustrating dispute.

The settlement was a good one for Newfoundland, in that it removed all remaining obstacles to the economic development of the Treaty Shore while denying French fishermen access to the south coast bait supplies which they had always wanted. But Bond had not been able to damage the French bank fishery, which was a far more serious competitor than the Treaty Shore fishery had ever been. The French fleet now made relatively little use of St. Pierre and Miquelon, which were experiencing a severe economic crisis, with the result that Bond's continued enforcement of the Bait Act, his refusal to allow the export of firewood to the islands, and his obsession with what had become much smaller smuggling operations, seemed petty and vindictive.[62] Attacking the French, however, like attacking the Reid family, had never done a Newfoundland politician any harm;

and Bond sincerely believed that the French presence had been, and remained a genuine threat to Newfoundland's ability to prosper.

Besides the French settlement, the Liberals could also by 1904 boast to the electorate of the imminent establishment of a large newsprint mill in the interior. The approach had come from Harmsworth publishing empire in England, which had decided that it needed its own source of paper. By the spring of 1903 the Harmsworths had decided to build a mill in Newfoundland, subject to satisfactory local arrangements, either at the Grand Falls on the Exploits River, or at Grand Lake in the western interior.[63] Either development depended vitally on the Reid Newfoundland Company, which owned much of the timber land that would be needed, and controlled both the railway and important water-power sources (including the Grand Falls). The Reids were at this time deeply involved in promoting forest industries in eastern Newfoundland, and had been planning a Grand Lake development for some years. They resented the arrival of the Harmsworths, and quickly put together an application to the government for loan guarantees and other financial assistance to enable them to fund a giant scheme which envisaged branch railways, hotels, cold storage plants, refrigerator cars, a flour mill, coal mines, and a paper mill at Grand Lake. The government turned the proposal down in May 1903 on financial grounds.

Bond was a financial conservative who recoiled from the idea of loan guarantees; but the rejection was also consistent with his policy of limiting Reid power and influence. Certainly, the rejection signalled the resumption of warfare. As if to rebuke the government, in October 1903 the Reid Company filed a claim for $3,488,000 to compensate for losses associated with its brief management of the telegraph system. Bond was outraged, having already paid out $853,000 in 1902 for railway improvements,[64] and himself retaliated by advertising for tenders for a coastal steamship service to supplement that provided by Reids under the 1898 contract. The company was infuriated, but could not prevent the conclusion of a contract with Bowring Brothers in February 1904.[65]

Against this background, the Harmsworth agreement could not quickly be concluded. But during 1904 the parties managed to work out a deal which would allow a mill to be built at Grand Falls. Bond proved willing to grant very generous concessions to obtain the development, which could be seen as a justification for the railway policy he had supported since entering public life. The Harmsworth subsidiary undertaking the new enterprise was to receive about 2,300 square miles of timber lands—some Crown, some from the Reids and other private owners—on ninety-nine year renewable leases at an annual rental of $2 per square mile. Mineral and water rights were thrown in, with low royalties on mineral developments only. Pulpwood could be cut free of stumpage. This financial regime was unprecedented. Had its terms been widely known during the 1904 election campaign, the opposition might have had an issue of genuine importance with which to belabour the erstwhile scourge of the 1898 Reid contract. But nothing was then in final form, and the government could point to less controversial achievements.

Besides the French and American agreements, and the general promise of interior developments, the Bond government had profited from a general economic upturn which, by increasing revenues, had allowed not only a current account surplus, but increased expenditures and a revision of the tariff which provided free entry for such essentials as flour, salt, lines and twines. The contrast with the bleak 1890s was startling. The value of the country's annual total trade increased by 42 per cent (1900-05 over 1895-1900), average annual exports by 59 per cent, imports by 33 per cent. 'We have passed through a crucible of misfortune,' declaimed the Minister of Finance in 1902, 'and we rise out of our difficulties clad in the full garb of civilisation, and moving straight ahead in the van of progress and development.'[66] Against this background the government increased spending on education and marine works, extended the telegraph system, encouraged the exploration of coal deposits in central Newfoundland and supported the development of agriculture. Optimism and unreality combined in 1903, when Bond brought in a bill providing bounties to encourage the establishment of an iron and steel industry. Clearly, the government envisaged a replication of the Cape Breton development, using Bell Island iron ore at home. The dream was never realized, since Newfoundland lacks the necessary supplies of coal, and investors were hardly likely to take risks east of Sydney.[67] More realistic were the government's attempts to promote the use of cold storage in the fisheries, the ultimate objectives being the production of fresh frozen fish and vastly increased sales to the American market. This tied in with the negotiations for reciprocity. At first, financial support was provided to independent operators of bait depots, most of whom found it impossible to make money; but in 1903, Morris—a keen advocate of cold storage—introduced a bill to subsidise an American company which promised to build a depot in each electoral district. Though there was a significant amount of conservative opposition to this attempt to stimulate a fresh fish industry, the legislation eventually passed in 1904. Nothing ever came of it: but failure had not been demonstrated by the time the elections took place that fall.[68]

The government was full of self-congratulation at being so blessed by Providence. Morine was right to warn that 'our prosperity was built upon shifting sands,'[69] but the country was in no mood to listen to such forebodings. The newspapers reflect pride, optimism, confidence and patriotism; it is no coincidence that the country's two national anthems were written in this period—the now forgotten 'Flag of Newfoundland' by Bishop Howley (1902), and the still sung 'Ode to Newfoundland' (1903) by Governor Sir Cavendish Boyle.[70] All this was to Bond's advantage, when combined with the disorganisation of his opponents.

Defeat in 1900 had left the Tories in disarray. Morine led a tiny opposition of four members, joined in 1902 by two by-election victors, and in 1903 by a pair of Liberal dissidents. Though intelligent and industrious, Morine was anathema to those Tories who had sided with Winter in the crisis that had wrecked the Tory government in the wake of the 1898 Reid contract. This group anxiously sought another leader. They found one in Sir William Whiteway who, late in 1901, indicated his readiness to return to public life in opposition to Bond.[71] Embittered, vindictive, unable to retire with dignity, Whiteway claimed that Bond was no longer a true Liberal, and had bungled the 1901 railway contract. He allied himself with Donald Morison, a former Winterite Tory who in April 1902 resigned from the Supreme Court bench. By the autumn of 1903 there was talk of a new party supported by the *Free Press*, a new journal edited by J.A. Robinson, another former Winter loyalist.[72] There was no chance of the two opposition groups joining forces until Morine was gone. Widely unpopular within the party, and among the electorate because of his close association with the Reids— he was the company's lawyer—and his confederate sympathies, he had become a political albatross. Perhaps sensing this, or perhaps nudged by his employers, Morine submitted his resignation as Tory leader in the autumn of 1902. In the absence of a successor it was not accepted, but he put it about that he was retiring from active politics and absented himself from the 1903 session. In January 1904 the party stalwarts offered the leadership to Whiteway, clearly hoping to unite the anti-Bond forces. When he refused it, they turned to A.F. Goodridge, who had been premier for eight months in 1894.[73] Morine still remained active in party affairs, and this may have been a factor in Whiteway's decision. In any event, he must have been reluctant to become closely associated with men who had bitterly opposed his party and policies in the past. It would also have meant abandoning the pretence that he represented true Liberalism. It was not until September 1904, not long before the election, that he agreed to amalgamate his small following with the Tories under the name of the 'United Opposition.' It was too late. The Liberal press delightedly ridiculed the motley coalition: Goodridge, the bank crash premier; Morine, Reids' hireling; Morison, the devious Orangeman; Whiteway, back in politics out of personal spite; and even Winter, dusted off to run in his old district of Burin. These were yesterday's men. Old gossip and scandals were resurrected, and voters were warned that while a vote for the government was a vote for 'Bond, Prosperity and Home Rule,' the United Opposition would bring national ruin. The main Liberal tactic, as in 1900, was to raise a scare, this time by branding the Opposition as covert, Reid-backed confederates. There was virtually no debate on the issues and promises made in the rival manifestos. The fabricated confederation scare, plus the smokescreen of charge and countercharge effectively obscured them. It was a bitter campaign, which the Liberals eventually won with a handsome majority of 22 seats, and 60 per cent of the popular vote. The ex-premiers fared badly: all were defeated, even Whiteway, who had once dominated the political stage.[74] Once again a Tory rump graced the Assembly, once again led by Morine. But Bond's second ministry was not to be a repeat of his first, and his political position soon began to crumble.

The two forces that were to undermine the second Bond government were evident during 1905, though somewhat obscured by the passage of the Harmsworth pulp and paper deal, a controversial issue which dominated the legislative session. The first of these was the Reid company. In February the government learned that the abitrators appointed to settle the telegraph claim had awarded the company $1.5 million plus interest. Though the sum was considerably less than that claimed, the government was shocked and outraged.[75] Since the company had operated the lines for only three years, and had received an annual subsidy of $10,000, it looked like 'public plunder.'[76] Morine took the opportunity to criticise once again Bond's handling of the 1901 contract revisions, and took particular aim at his policy of creating a comprehensive government telegraph system. This policy involved an attack on the Anglo-American Telegraph Company (managed by a stalwart Tory),[77] which had hitherto controlled the telegraph lines on the Avalon Peninsula in addition to all international cables. Anglo made no public complaint until the government in 1905 imposed taxes on private telegraph, wireless and telephone companies. Its outraged complaints were echoed by the Reids, who found themselves hit by new taxes on express companies and on coal imported for business purposes. The companies charged that they were being subjected to discriminatory taxation, but even a petition to the King (from the Reid company) brought no results. It is likely, though, that Bond was taxing Anglo to pay for the new government cable under the Cabot Strait, and the Reid company to pay the telegraph award.[78]

It was during 1905 that the Reids concluded that their battle with the Bond administration had to be brought to a head. In April, Robert G. Reid offered to sell the railway and steamship operations for $3 million, the company retaining the dock and its lands.[79] The government decided not to buy,[80] whereupon the Reids began a series of manoeuvres designed to install a friendly administration. The first step was to strengthen the opposition by ridding it of Morine. Though no longer official party leader, he retained great influence as house leader, and as owner of the *Daily News*. In September 1905, William D. Reid—Robert G.'s eldest son and the company's general manager—sacked Morine's brother from his job with the railway, and successfully defended an action for wrongful dismissal.[81] At the same time, W.D. started an action against Morine and the *News*, claiming repayment of money advanced in 1898 to enable Morine to buy the paper. The case was heard and decided in Reid's favour early in 1906. It aired plenty of dirty Tory linen, and temporarily ended Morine's political career.[82] In May 1906 he sold his interest in the paper to Morison and left for Ontario. For his part, Robert G. Reid agreed to continue to pay Morine an annual salary of $10,000 until his contract expired in 1912—on condition that he stayed away.

Morison jumped into Morine's seat at Bonavista, and clearly aspired to the Tory leadership. But when Goodridge resigned in September the leadership passed to Captain Charles Dawe of Bay Roberts, a worthy but uninspired sealing skipper and exporter of Labrador fish. He was a stop-gap. The party was looking for someone more energetic and experienced; and by 1907 the question of who should lead Bond's opponents was of more than local interest. By this time the premier had handed the Reids an array of distinguished allies outside the colony, all of them anxious that a new government be installed. The issue which had created this situation was Bond's handling of the draft reciprocity treaty with the United States.

Early in 1905 the Senate Foreign Relations Committee finally reported the treaty, so drastically changed that it bore little resemblance to the original. Bond's immediate response, as in 1890-91, was to retaliate. The government decided to end the privileges which American fisherman had been enjoying in colonial waters under the 1888 *modus vivendi*, and apply a strict and contentious interpretation of the 1818 convention, which defined American rights in the British North American fisheries.[83] The precise target was the Bay of Islands winter herring fishery. American schooners arrived each season either to buy, or to hire Newfoundlanders to catch herring, which was then shipped home to enter duty free as an American product.[84] By enforcing the Bait Act and a new Foreign Fishing Vessels Act, Bond hoped to ruin this trade. His narrow interpretation of American rights was intended to reinforce the legislation by keeping American vessels out of bays altogether, thus allowing Newfoundlanders access to a larger share of the herring export business.[85] The Colonial Office braced for an explosion: 'Who sups with Uncle Sam needs a long spoon,' commented Cox, 'and I expect they will come off second best and give us no end of diplomatic trouble.'[86] Morine was even more to the point: 'You cannot conquer the Senate,' he said, 'by attacking the people.'[87]

Bond's policy was based on three dubious assumptions. The first was that since the American administration supported the treaty, it would allow Gloucester fishermen to be harassed in foreign waters. The second was that the British government would either condone or support Newfoundland's actions. The third was that though some Newfoundlanders would be hurt by the disruption of the American fishery, they would nevertheless support a crusade to obtain the treaty's ratification. The *Free Press* not unreasonably thought Bond had been 'carried away by his imagination.'[88] He seemed to have learned nothing from the events of the early 1890s, and his failure in this respect was to be a major cause of his downfall.

The crisis broke in October with the arrival of American schooners for the herring fishery. The government announced it would prevent Newfoundlanders both from selling herring to the Americans, and from engaging as crew members.[89] This filtered back to Washington as a report that Americans were being forbidden to fish within the 1818 limits. Elihu Root, the new Secretary of State, thereupon made a formal protest claiming that US vessels had the right to a free fishery on their treaty coast: that is, they were not subject to any local laws that were inconsistent with the 1818 convention. Thus US vessels did not have to obtain bait licences, did not have to report at customs houses (unless they intended to trade), and could disregard the sections of the 1905 Foreign Fishing Vessels Act which authorized local officers to stop and search foreign vessels.[90]

As the American reaction became clear, the British government moved to contain the dispute: it was not prepared to allow Newfoundland herring to disrupt Anglo-American concord. In summary, the Newfoundland government was told that although its interpretation of the 1818 convention was untenable, it did have the right to prevent Newfoundlanders from assisting the American fishery. However, there were to be no seizures of American vessels, as such actions would cause political difficulties out of all proportion to the interests at stake.[91] Bond, of course, wanted to order wholesale arrests of both Americans and Newfoundlanders, since the former were evading the law by hiring the latter outside the three-mile limit, and then bringing them into the bays to catch herring. It needed all Governor Sir William MacGregor's skill to dissuade Bond from taking such action, though it is likely he was helped by cabinet members queasy about the political reprecussions.[92] The unfortunate result for Bond was that having announced a bold, defiant policy, he was now unable to enforce it. Aided by the US government vessel *Grampus* and watched by HMS *Latona*, American schooners continued to ship crews at sea, refuse payment of light dues, and in general to ignore local laws. It was an embarrassing situation. When the fishery ended in January 1906, there had been no arrests and no incidents; and local fishermen had made as much money as usual.

Bond was not prepared to give up. In the 1906 session the Foreign Fishing Vessels Act was tightened to ensure that American fishermen received no assistance from Newfoundlanders.[93] The Colonial Office asked for a suspending clause to allow for the giving of notice, but instead—inexplicably and unusually—got a clause providing for confirmation by King in Council. This had the effect of giving the British government a more direct control over the legislation than would otherwise have been the case, which Bond cannot have intended. It was a control which the British were prepared to exercise, since serious concerns were emerging over the Newfoundland confrontation. 'This may become a very serious matter if it is not carefully handled,' wrote Sir Edward Grey, Foreign Secretary in the new Liberal administration, to Lord Elgin at the Colonial Office. 'On its merits it is a small question, but it may lead to a very big row.'[94] Elgin himself thought Newfoundland was indulging in 'gratuitous mischief';[95] and

MacGregor likewise thought it ridiculous to start a conflict with the United States 'over a fishery of the value of £45,000 a year.'[96]

For all his misgivings, Grey was prepared to go some way to defend the Newfoundland position. In February 1906 he told Root that American vessels on their treaty coast should have American crews, since the 1818 convention granted privileges not to vessels, but to American citizens; and since it was a common, regulated fishery, Americans should observe local law.[97] Root responded that Newfoundland could not question the nationality of crews, or in any way interfere with Americans exercising their rights on their treaty coast. The phrase 'in common' did not mean that American rights were subject to local law, but that the liberty to take fish was held in common.[98] In view of this wide divergence of opinion, the only solution appeared to be an arbitration and, pending the result, a *modus vivendi*.[99]

The colonial government protested angrily, and demanded the confirmation and proclamation of the 1906 act. But the British government had made its decision. Concluded in October, the *modus* suspended both the 1906 act and the objectionable sections of the 1905 act. Though forbidden by local law, purse seines could be used by Americans, since they feared they might not be able to ship local crews. For their part, the Americans agreed not to fish on Sundays, to pay light dues, and to ship Newfoundlanders at sea only when necessary.[100] The *modus* effectively destroyed the credibility of Bond's policy. As a result the government refused its consent, arguing that the *modus* was 'subversive of the Colony's constitutional rights, calculated to work severe injury to the fisheries of the Colony,' and of dubious legality since it suspended colonial statute law which had received royal assent.[101] Bond insisted that only the imperial parliament could suspend colonial laws, and that Americans were subject to local regulation. He found the imperial action 'most humiliating and unjust...as well as a menace to every Colony possessing Responsible Government.'[102]

In order to test the *modus*, the government decided to arrest two Newfoundlanders out of the 300-400 who had shipped with American schooners at sea, and charge them with breaches of the Bait Act by selling herring to Americans without a licence. Thus in November 1906, George Crane and Alexander Dubois were hauled before the magistrate at Birchy Cove and duly convicted.[103] An appeal was lodged. If the Supreme Court upheld the conviction, then fishermen such as Crane and Dubois were not protected by the *modus* and the government could frustrate it. The case was of such importance that the Colonial Office secretly arranged to pay the defendants' legal costs, and supplied advice to defence lawyers.

On the herring grounds the *modus* was not unpopular, and the fishery went on peaceably. In St. John's, the Liberal press tried to work up patriotic excitement, claiming that once again Newfoundland had been sacrificed on the altar of imperial expediency by the 'Little Englanders of Downing Street,' and that the country was passing through 'the gravest crisis which

[had] ever arisen in [its] constitutional history.'[104] Archbishop Howley recalled the successful popular opposition to the 1857 Anglo-French Convention, and urged his countrymen to be 'up and doing at once.'[105] But there were no public meetings, no demonstrations, no rallying to the colours of old Terra Nova. The outcries of 1857 and 1890 were not repeated, simply because the Americans were not the French. The latter had been the colony's traditional scapegoat. The Americans, on the other hand, had always been popular, and many of their captains and crewmen were either Newfoundland born or of Newfoundland ancestry.[106] 'For the past thirty years,' said Michael P. Cashin, a member for Ferryland who left the Liberals over the 1905 legislation, 'they have fished in amity and good fellowship side by side with our people...they have never injured our markets...or unfairly competed with us.'[107] Apart from this, the questions at issue were complicated and remote. To the average voter, it must have been incomprehensible that Bond should want to prevent Newfoundlanders carrying on a traditional and lucrative trade, not only in Bay of Islands, but also in those areas—like Ferryland—where American bankers could no longer come in to purchase bait and supplies. Small wonder that the Tories christened the 1905 act 'the Premier's bill to punish and pauperise the people of Newfoundland.'[108]

In spite of the lack of public enthusiasm for its anti-American policy, the government appeared united and determined to continue the battle. In May 1907 Bond went to London where, at the Colonial Conference, he came under intense pressure from Grey and Elgin to modify his stand. Though the treaty was effectively lost, Bond was unwilling to bend. He put his case to the English public, and demanded, and was reluctantly allowed, to raise the fisheries question at the conference.[109] Though other colonial premiers appear to have sympathized with Newfoundland,[110] the imperial government did not feel obliged to change its position. Only Laurier's active intervention might have had this effect, and he was unwilling to become deeply involved. He opposed Bond's treaty, and objected to the prospect of an arbitration on the 1818 convention since (like Bond) he thought that many of the points that would be raised were not open to dispute.[111] Bond finally agreed that Newfoundland fishery regulations applicable to the treaty coast should be sent to Washington for comment, and that the interpretation of the 1818 convention should be submitted to the Hague Tribunal.[112] But the question of continuing the *modus* for another season remained in dispute.

Bond held that this was unnecessary, and that pending the arbitration Americans should conform to local laws amended in the light of American criticism, his government guaranteeing that there would be no breaches of the peace.[113] The British government rejected the proposition.[114] Rather than contest the point, Bond then offered to return to the *status quo ante* by licencing American vessels to purchase herring for export.[115] This was as great a concession as the British government could have reasonably expected. It marked the abandonment of any attempt to harass American vessels, while maintaining the principle of the colony's sovereignty within its territorial waters. But the American government was not prepared to accept Newfoundland regulation in any form and insisted on a renewal of the *modus*. The British government did not argue, accepting that pending a formal settlement, an Anglo-American agreement was inescapable.

In May the Newfoundland Supreme Court had upheld the conviction of Crane and Dubois.[116] It was feared as a result that wholesale prosecutions might follow—unreasonably, given Bond's obvious desire to avoid imperial dictation, his offer to licence American vessels, and the imminence of a general election. But if there was to be a *modus* it had to be enforced; and if Newfoundland was not prepared to pass local legislation, what might be done? After some debate the British government decided to promulgate an order in council under the authority of 59 Geo. III c. 38, providing that legal process could not be served on Newfoundlanders when on board American vessels, and that such vessels and their gear were immune from seizure.[117] Humiliated and angry, the Newfoundland government argued that the order was unjust, illegal, and in view of the concessions offered, unnecessary. It refused to publish the order—Governor MacGregor had to do so on his own authority—and immediately gave permission for west coast fishermen to sell herring, so long as they did not ship on American vessels.[118] A local compromise then emerged in the Bay of Islands, whereby American vessels entered at customs, paid duty on the nets and gear which they sold to local men, who in turn sold the Americans their catch. Newfoundland could now claim that it was controlling the fishery in a manner beneficial to the fishermen of both countries, and asked in vain for the cancellation of the now irrelevant *modus* and order in council.[119]

Bond claimed that the precedent set by the order in council was 'a menace to Responsible Government in the Colonies,'[120] but he received scant support either from other colonial premiers—to whom he appealed— or from within Newfoundland. Indeed, Archbishop Howley, who compared the order to the revival of penal laws in Ireland, regretted the absence of the 'old-time spirit of patriotism' which would have set the country aflame.[121] Sir James Winter told the London *Morning Post* that the feeling in the colony was 'one either of total indifference to and even ignorance of the whole question, or, among a very small fraction of the population, of strong antagonism.'[122] Critics argued that the order was Bond's fault alone; it could have been avoided had he accepted a negotiated settlement once the arbitration was agreed. In any case, if he felt so strongly that the colony's rights had been abused, why had he not followed the example of the Natal ministry in 1906, and threatened resignation?[123] These were fair points. Had Bond offered to return to the *status quo ante* in June rather than August 1907, there is little doubt that a formal arrangement with the Americans to replace the *modus* could have been negotiated in time for the 1907-08 season. As it was, his stubbornness, and his unrealistic determination that the colony should control a treaty fishery, delayed and aggravated an already difficult situation. But why had he not resigned, or at least threatened to? The answer is that he could not be sure of emerging victorious.

A year earlier, the Governor General of Canada, Earl Grey, had paid a private visit to Newfoundland. He was a keen proponent of imperial federation, favoured Newfoundland's joining Canada, and saw Bond as an imperial nuisance whose actions imperilled smooth Canadian-American relations.[124] He stayed with MacGregor, by then very hostile to Bond, and spent most of his time in the company of the governor and the Reid clan. He left the colony with a very slanted view of the situation, and with the conviction that the most effective political leader apart from Bond was that good friend of MacGregor and the Reids, the amiable Sir Edward Morris.[125] Whether or not Morris was a confederate, or could be so persuaded, was uncertain. But it seemed likely that he would eventually split with Bond.[126] In July 1907 Morris made his move, resigning from the government and the Liberal party on a transparent pretext.[127] There was applause from Earl Grey, the Colonial Office and MacGregor. The latter was a valuable ally. A contemporary observed that the governor was 'never too busy...to listen to and smile at his ample supply of well-worn jokes and witticisms,' acting from this point as Morris' 'guide, philosopher and friend.'[128] Bond no doubt realized that were he to resign, MacGregor would refuse a dissolution, and help Charles Dawe and Morris cobble together a government. If defeated in the Assembly, the new administration could then go to the country with the advantage of controlling the machinery of government.[129] In these circumstances, and despising Morris as an untrustworthy hireling of the Reid interests, Bond decided to ride out the storm, confident he could win the 1908 election.[130] This was a serious misjudgment. The anti-American policy had alienated voters in western and southern districts, and Morris' defection weakened the party in St. John's and Conception Bay. Bond could still count on Archbishop Howley's support, and the influence of his own reputation. But he had been such a dominant and intolerant party leader that able supporters had bolted government ranks; and his second term had been so obsessively dominated by the fisheries dispute that domestic legislation had been neglected. The current account remained in surplus, and there were judicious, but careful increases in expenditure, especially on education. But there was insufficient courting of the voters with those small but vital expenditures so necessary to political survival. Instead there were failed initiatives in fisheries development, and another visionary promotion.

As cold storage schemes fizzled, the government turned to the development of the herring fishery through the encouragement of drift-net fishing and the export of Scotch cured herring. This was part of Bond's attempt to take the herring trade from the Americans and Nova Scotians,

but like cold storage, it failed, and gave live ammunition to his enemies.[131]
The iron and steel scheme of the first term was paralleled in 1907 by an even
more bizarre proposal, to build a railway from Green Bay across to Bay of
Islands, designed to carry transatlantic express traffic. The link to the
mainland would be either by ferry, or through a tunnel under the Strait of
Belle Isle. The approach from the east was to be through an allegedly fog
free zone, a proposition which caused mirth among Opposition mariners.
This concept was not new; Sandford Fleming had enthused about such a
line in the 1870s, the legislature had approved one in 1884, and in 1894 Bond
had told the House that such a connecting link was part of Newfoundland's
destiny.[132] Immediately branded as another of Bond's fads, the new version
stimulated little enthusiasm and considerable scepticism. The English promoters—a lawyer and a firm of diamond merchants—soon faded from the
scene.[133]

The pre-election 1908 legislative session was remarkably short, and
bereft of vote winning legislation. Bond introduced legislation to create a
model farm, and increased education spending; but Morris—who effectively led the opposition, since Dawe was terminally ill—gained many more
points by arguing for land clearing bonuses, a branch railway to Bonavista,
and tax reductions. Cleverly, he forced the government to defeat a motion
to place tea and sugar on the free list.[134] By the end of February, the
legislature closed, it was clear that all opposition groups were prepared to
unite behind Morris. In early March, when sealers from the outports con-
gregated in St. John's, he launched a new People's party with an address
containing a long list of promises; his policy was to be 'broad enough...to
take in every interest and meet the general requirements of the whole
people of the country.'[135] 'For the last eight years the present Government
has not built a road to a cabbage garden'[136]—the People's party promised
plenty of them, as well as branch railways.

Though the new party was a catch-all coalition of personal followers,
disaffected Liberals and former Tories, Morris' challenge posed a serious
threat to the Bond government. He was generously financed by the Reid
family, and his propaganda was managed by P.T. McGrath, a mercenary
but extremely skilful journalist, who resigned the editorship of the Liberal
St. John's *Evening Herald* in order to start a pro-Morris newspaper. Morris
himself was an experienced and supple politician with a firm base in the
west end of St. John's, and with a reputation as a tolerant Catholic of
independent mind. In contrast to the aloof, patrician Bond, he was seen as
sensitive to the needs of the ordinary person, willing to spend money rather
than save it, to create jobs and to be practical, rather than promote personal
'fads,' whether these were fog-free zones or campaigns against American
fishermen. Though there was more similarity in terms of basic assumptions
and policies between Bond and Morris than either would have cared to
admit, it was obscured by radically different styles, both personal and

political. Their major policy dispute had been illustrated during the debate over the 1898 contract. Both men believed in the rich potential of the interior. But while Bond wanted to ensure that control over its development rested ultimately with the government, given his intense concern with Newfoundland's status and integrity, Morris thought ends more important than means, jobs more important than constitutional niceties, the fact of development more important than how it was done, or by whom. Thus Morris had no difficulty with allowing the Reids to dominate economic development. Bond saw them as potential destroyers of his country's independence. In 1908, Bond's defensive caution faced Morris' expansive confidence.

Bond made no special efforts to resist Morris' onslaught. The Liberal manifesto in effect stated that the government stood on its record.[137] The People's party, in contrast, promised much, and made great play with a St. John's grand jury report which denounced the condition of the poor house, calling it 'the saddest place in Newfoundland.'[138] Why, then, was Bond building a new museum and tucking money away into a reserve fund? That Morris had so recently been a member of the government was conveniently overlooked. Bond spent most of the campaign in his own district (Twillingate), refusing to assist Liberal candidates facing hard fights, which was especially the case in Conception Bay. It is as if Bond did not want to do Morris the compliment of trying to outbid him, taking the lofty approach that the voters were sure to agree that the country was in good condition and in competent hands. Morris not only campaigned hard, but he gained from the discontent caused by a 35-40 per cent collapse in fish prices, which gave sudden relevance to his promises of fisheries reform, and his championing the formation of a Board of Trade.[139] The result of the 2 November election was a tie.

Bond took the view that since he had not been defeated, he could say in office until he ascertained whether he had the confidence of the new House of Assembly.[140] MacGregor agreed, but insisted that the legislature meet in February 1909, refused to say what he would do if Bond asked for a dissolution, and would not accept that the government had full authority to make any and all decisions. In the time that elapsed before the legislature met both parties made extensive but unsuccessful attempts to persuade or bribe members to change sides, and political conspirators worked long hours. The most exotic among them was one Harry Crowe, a Nova Scotian sawmill operator with extensive interests in Newfoundland, and a keen proponent of the colony's joining Canada. He thought that a coalition between the two parties might be arranged under Bond's leadership on the basis of confederation. Morris would be swung into line by the Reids, who in turn would be pressured by Sir Edward Clouston of the Bank of Montreal and Sir Thomas Shaughnessy of the CPR, both of whom had close connections with the Reid company. Bond would be persuaded by pressure from his ally Archbishop Howley (a confederate), the promise of a peerage, and an appeal to his patriotism—his desire to save Newfoundland from the corrupt rule of the Reid-Morris combination. Earl Grey, to whom this scheme was put, was delighted at the idea, and despatched Chief Justice Charles Fitzpatrick to talk to Shaughnessy and Clouston. In the event the whole fantastic plot collapsed because William D. Reid refused to be diverted from his major object, the destruction of Bond; and because Bond, when he got wind of it, angrily made it clear that he was not prepared to hold office by permission of Morris and his handlers. Bond did say, however, that if the Canadians were prepared to help him stay on, he would hold a plebiscite on confederation. There was no response.[141]

On 18 February 1909, with the parties still tied, Bond advised MacGregor to dissolve the legislature immediately it met, since it would be impossible to elect a Speaker.[142] Predictably enough, MacGregor rejected this advice—after all, Bond himself had argued the previous November that the legislature had to meet and attempt to transact business before a dissolution could be considered.[143] As a result, Bond resigned on 22 February, claiming that the inevitable dissolution should be awarded to him, since he had first advised it, and since he had not been, and would not be defeated in the House of Assembly.[144] Whatever the merits of the constitutional arguments involved, Bond had made a serious tactical mistake, losing the advantage to an unsympathetic governor and the pliable Morris.

When MacGregor asked Morris whether he could 'form a Ministry that would meet the House at an early date with a reasonable prospect of being able to induce Parliament to pass supply,'[145] Morris brazenly replied that he could.[146] Both the governor and the new premier, who took over on 3 March, must have known that they were playing charades. When the House finally met on 30 March, it indeed proved impossible to elect a Speaker, but because Bond made yet another tactical mistake. Morris' candidate did not vote, and was defeated; but the Liberal candidate voted against himself, supported by his colleagues. In order to show MacGregor that he had been right all along, Bond had departed from usual procedures; far better if he had had the patience to allow Morris to elect a Speaker, and then defeated him on a confidence vote. For although Bond had demonstrated that Morris had obtained power under false pretences, he had again placed himself in a weaker tactical position. When Morris went to see his friend the governor to ask for a dissolution, he could say that—unlike Bond—he had at least met the House and tried to carry on business.[147] MacGregor felt under no obligation to recall Bond and give him the dissolution, and in this he was supported by Colonial Office officials, who had had enough of Bond, and thought questions of fairness irrelevant.[148] The *Free Press* correctly called the Speakership fiasco 'One of the most extraordinary blunders that Sir Robert Bond has ever committed.'[149]

The election date was set for Morris' birthday, 8 May. The campaign was nasty, short, and vituperative. This time Bond fought hard for his

Conception Bay candidates, showing some courage in the process. At Western Bay he refused to be intimidated by a hostile crowd when landing at the wharf, only to be kicked—a non-swimmer—into the icy water. The humilation was to no avail. The Liberals lost eight more seats, and Morris obtained a comfortable majority. To paraphrase the contemporary election slogan, Bond's day seemed to be done.

Morris remained premier until 1917 when, as isolated and unpopular as Bond had once been, he escaped to England, a Lloyd George peerage and a clutch of directorships. Branch railway building and the costs of participating in the war had driven up the debt. The People's party had been plagued by a succession of scandals, and its management of the war effort had proved controversial and divisive. Moreover, its power was threatened by the dramatic growth of William F. Coaker's Fishermen's Protective Union (FPU), which had successfully run candidates in the 1913 election, and tarnished the party's reputation as the friend of the common man. With the end of the war and the collapse of the national government, it seemed as if Newfoundland political life would collapse into endemic skirmishing between rival chieftains. The economic collapse presaged by falling fish prices emphasized the how bleak a place post-war Newfoundland might be. Eyes therefore turned to Whitbourne.[150]

After his 1909 defeat, Bond had unenthusiastically led the Liberals in opposition, leaving much of the responsibility to J.M. Kent. When he did attend the house, there were frequent and heated quarrels with Morris, and with Michael P. Cashin, who attacked Bond with bitter ferocity. Bond was absent for the entire 1913 session. As that year's election approached, he faced the unpleasant necessity of having to come to terms with the FPU, which was powerful in the Liberal heartland of the northeast coast. Eventually he swallowed his pride and negotiated a deal with Coaker (once a Liberal heeler) in order to avoid the virtual extinction of his party. But when the election gave the Liberals fewer seats than the FPU, and some of those by union permission, Bond resigned from political life. Just has he had refused in 1908-09 to hold power by consent of Morris and his backers, so now he refused to be beholden to the FPU, whose leader he disliked, and whose philosophy and tactics he found distasteful. Efforts to bring him back into political life began in 1917, as Liberals sought to revive their party, and as the new Roman Catholic Archbishop, E.P. Roche, sought a leader strong enough to form a government without FPU support. The courtship ended late in 1918, when Bond unequivocally refused the invitation. The state of the country was so bad, and the quality of its public life so low, he wrote, that there was nothing anyone could do to avoid the inevitable debacle: 'I turn from the dirty business with contempt and loathing.'[151]

Within four years of his political retirement, then, Bond was widely seen as a potential saviour. His was still a name to conjure with, associated with the prosperous years of the earlier twentieth century, with the establishment of the newsprint industry, and with a patriotic stance in external affairs. Untainted by scandal, educated and upright, he seemed to represent the best of the past at a time when Newfoundlanders faced the future with uncertainty and pessimism. To those who found it difficult to accept the legitimacy of Coaker and the FPU, and who found other potential leaders at best unimpressive, Bond seemed the perfect, almost symbolic figure to forge unity and stability. That the elite should have been so powerfully attracted to a sixtyish, conservative ex-politician says much about its members. They were being nostalgic and unrealistic. In refusing to play the national deliverer, Bond was for once being practical.

Similarly, the witnesses who spoke of Bond to the 1933 Newfoundland Royal Commission were indulging in nostalgia for a pre-war golden age. To see Bond as a great man laid low by the wily machinations of corrupt and spendthrift opponents is to caricature the reality. Bond possessed real and acknowledged talents, genuine patriotism, and a clear vision of what his country might be. What he lacked was the detached objectivity that would have allowed him to see his country for what it was in the larger scheme of things, and act accordingly; and which would have caused him to avoid the more curious 'fads' which gave such ammunition to his critics. He might well have achieved more, and had a longer political life, had he been less certain of the correctness of his opinions, less inflexible and dictatorial, and less socially isolated—and a better political tactician. Nevertheless, the witnesses had a point. In comparison to almost all his successors as premier, Bond does indeed stand out as as an attractive figure; but it is improbable that he could have prevented the eventual suspension of responsible government. The Newfoundland of the 1920s called for leaders with agile, radical, imaginative minds. Cautious, conservative, his attitudes set in another age, Bond would have had no more success than those who did try, and who the Amulree royal commission so severely criticized. He was wise to remain at Whitbourne, allowing isolation and inaccessibility to inflate his reputation, and so to wreak subtle revenge on Morris and his allies, who are remembered (if at all) with little respect. It is a situation which Bond would have found very satisfying.

NOTES

1   United Kingdom, Parliamentary Papers, Cmd. 4480, 1933, *Newfoundland Royal Commission 1933: Report.*

2   *Evening Telegram* (St. John's), 18 March 1927; *Daily News* (St. John's) 18 March 1927.

3   J.R. Smallwood (ed.), *Encyclopedia of Newfoundland and Labrador*, vol. 1 (St. John's 1981), 219.

4   S.J.R. Noel, *Politics in Newfoundland* (Toronto, 1971).

5   In later years, a rumour spread that Bond had failed his law exams. He claimed in response that he had never taken a law exam, his physician having advised against it (*Proceedings of the House of Assembly (PHA), 1911, 185*).

6   On this period in general, see James Hiller, 'The Railway and Local Politics in Newfoundland, 1870-1901,' in James Hiller and Peter Neary (eds.), *Newfoundland in the Nineteenth and Twentieth Centuries: Essays in Interpretation* (Toronto 1980), 123-47.

7   Bond in Assembly debate, 24 March 1897 (*Evening Telegram*, 1 April 1897).

8   Bond in Assembly debate, 16 March 1893 (*Evening Telegram*, 3 April 1893).

9   There is a description of the property, called 'The Grange,' in J.R. Smallwood (ed.), *Encyclopedia of Newfoundland and Labrador*, vol. 2 (St. John's 1984), 695.

10   The Reform party was the successor to the New party. For a narrative of these events, see James Hiller, 'A History of Newfoundland, 1874-1901' (unpublished PH D. thesis, Cambridge University 1971), ch. 4.

11   Hiller, 'History,' ch. 5; Harvey Mitchell, 'Canada's Negotiations with Newfoundland, 1887-1895,' in G.A. Rawlyk (ed.), *Historical Essays on the Atlantic Provinces* (Toronto 1967), 242-59.

12   *PHA*, 1911, 4l.

13   'Newfoundland's Hopes and Trials', *The Independent 54* (1902), 2337-8.

14   Bond in Assembly debate, 10 March 1900 (*Evening Herald* (St. John's), 19 March 1900). The standard work on the French question is F.F. Thompson, *The French Shore Problem in Newfoundland: An Imperial Study* (Toronto 1961). See also Peter Neary, 'The French and American Shore Questions in Newfoundland History,' in Hiller and Neary (eds.), *Newfoundland*, 95-122. On the codfishery and French competition, see Shannon Ryan, *Fish Out Of Water: The Newfoundland Saltfish Trade, 1814-1914* (St. John's 1986).

15   For the American negotiations and aftermath, see D.J. Davis, 'The Bond-Blaine Negotiations, 1890-91' (unpublished MA thesis, Memorial University 1970); Hiller, 'History,' ch. 6.

16   For an account of the Halifax conference, see Hiller, 'History,' 256-9.

17   Bond in Assembly debate, 24 April 1903 (*Evening Telegram*, 11 June 1903).

18   Quotation printed in Bond's entry in *Canadian Men and Women of the Time* (Toronto 1912), 118. In the Assembly in 1911 he spoke of 'the honour and dignity of Newfoundland as a self-governing state of the Empire' (*PHA*, 1911, 41).

19   Sir Robert Bond papers, Bond to Whiteway, 29 July 1893. The Bond papers are privately owned; at the time of writing this essay, the collection was closed to scholars.

20   See Hiller, 'History,' 302-08; and Mitchell, 'Negotiations,' 253-9.

21   Hiller, 'History,' 308-12.

22   Quoted in the *Free Press* (St. John's), 30 March 1909.

23   The text of the contract can be found as an encl. to Public Record Office, Kew, CO 194/240, Murray to Chamberlain, conf., 25 Feb. 1898. All subsequent CO (Colonial Office) references are to documents in this archive. Transcripts of crown copyright records in the Public Record Office appear by permission of the controller of H.M. Stationery Office.

24   Morine in Assembly debate, 13 July 1898 (*Evening Herald*, 27 July 1898).

25   *PHA*, 1911, 158.

26   Bond in Assembly debate, 25 Feb. 1898 (*Evening Telegram*, 1 March 1898). For a more formal statement of Bond's position, see the Opposition's memorial to the Colonial Secretary, 22 March 1898, CO 194/240, encl. in Murray to Chamberlain, conf., 22 March 1898.

27   CO 194/240, minutes by Anderson, 23 Feb. and 5 March 1898. For an account of the controversy, see Hiller, 'History,' 343-9.

28   Bond papers, Bond to Parsons, 16 Feb. 1899.

29   Correspondence on the proposed coalition is in the Bond papers, 'Meeting with Sir James Winter, March 11/99. Re the Political Crisis,' and letters between Bond and Winter from that date to 1 April.

30   Evening Herald, 30 October 1899; W.V. Whiteway, *Duty's Call* (St. John's 1904), 1.

31   The collapse of the Winter administration is described in Hiller, 'History,' 351-7. Morris stated that he initiated the negotiations which led to the no-confidence vote. Since Bond did not dispute this claim, it is almost certainly accurate (see *PHA*, 1910, 157).

32   Bond papers, Bond to Morris, 7 March 1900. This letter and other relevant correspondence is printed in E.B. Foran, 'Battle of the Giants: Bond and Morris,' in J.R. Smallwood (ed.), *The Book of Newfoundland*, vol. 3 (St. John's 1967), 153-70. Bishop Howley also urged the necessity of a provisional government (see Bond papers, Howley to Bond, 6 March 1900)

.33   Bond papers, Morris to Bond, 7 March 1900. McCallum's account of these events can be found in CO 194/245, McCallum to Chamberlain, 16 March 1900. The correspondence between Morris and Bond was tabled by Morris in the Assembly in 1910.

34   Foran, 'Giants,' 157. See also CO 194/245, McCallum to Chamberlain, 2 April 1900. The correspondence between Bond and McCallum is in the Provincial Archives of Newfoundland and Labrador (PANL), GN 3/27.

35   *Evening Herald, Evening Telegram*, Oct. 1900, various references.

36   Bond papers, Howley to Bond, 16 Nov. 1900. For an account of the 1900 election, see Hiller, 'History,' 361-3.

37   Bond papers, Howley to Bond, 28 Nov. 1900.

38   For example, *Free Press*, 6, 13 Aug. 1907.

39   See PANL, MG 271 (A.B. Morine papers), A.B. Morine, draft history of Newfoundland.

40   The *Free Press*, 23 July 1907, referred to Bond's 'stiff, stand offishness, and "noli me tangere" attitude.'

41   *Free Press*, 18 June 1907.

42   See CO 194/245, McCallum to Chamberlain, 10 Oct. 1900.

43   Morine in Assembly debate, 24 July 1901 (*Daily News*, 26 July 1901).

44   Thompson, *French Shore*, 176-7; CO 194/249, memo by Bond, 26 March 1901; minute by Ommanney, 23 March 1901; memo by McCallum, 1 April 1901.

45   Thompson, *French Shore*, 177; CO 194/249, minute by Chamberlain, 23 March 1901.

46   National Archives of Canada (NAC), MG 26, E (Sir Wilfrid Laurier papers), Laurier to Willison, 16 Sept. 1899; to Mulock, 21 Jan. 1900; Minto to Chamber-

lain, private, 18 Jan. 1899, encl. in Minto to Laurier, 4 Feb.; Laurier to Delcassé, 20 Dec. 1900; NAC, MG 27, II 13 1 (4th Earl of Minto papers), 'Interview with Sir Wilfrid Laurier...3 June '02.'

47 CO 194/248, Bond to Ommanney, 7 June 1901, encl. in Boyle to Chamberlain, 18 Dec. 1901.

48 CO 194/248, minute by Anderson 8 Jan. 1902; CO 194/250, minute by Anderson, 7 April 1902; CO 194/248, Chamberlain to Boyle, 22 Jan. 1902; minute by Chamberlain, 7 Jan. 1902. John Redmond was leader of the home rule for Ireland party in the British House of Commons.

49 CO 194/250, Boyle to Chamberlain, tel., 16 May 1902. C.S. Campbell in *Anglo-American Understanding, 1898-1903* (Baltimore 1957) suggests that Laurier made concessions on the Alaska boundary problem in a last attempt to prevent the Newfoundland-US trade negotiations, and that by 1903 he was willing to discuss confederation (262-4).

50 CO 194/251, Foreign Office to CO, 29 Dec. 1902; C.C. Tansill *Canadian-American Relations, 1875-1911* (Gloucester, Mass. 1964), 93.

51 Bond's statement can be found in CO 885/8, no. 144, *Conferences between the Secretary of State for the Colonies and the Premiers of Self-Governing Colonies. Minutes and Papers.*

52 CO 194/251, Ommanney to Horwood, 9 Jan. 1903.

53 W.G. Reeves, "Our Yankee Cousins": Modernization and the Newfoundland-American Relationship, 1898-1910' (unpublished PH D thesis, University of Maine 1987), 117.

54 Tansill, *Canadian-American Relations*, 93; Bond papers, Herbert to Bond, conf., 31 Dec. 1902.

55 CO 194/250, Boyle to Chamberlain, secret, 30 May 1902.

56 CO 194/255, Lyttleton to Boyle, tel., secret and conf., 14 Jan. 1904.

57 CO 194/254, 255, Boyle to Lyttleton, tel., 18 Jan. 1904; to Anderson, private, 21 Jan. 1904; minute of council, 26 Jan. 1904, encl. in Boyle to Lyttleton, tel., 27 Jan. 1904.

58 CO 194/254, Bond to Anderson, 26 Jan. 1904.

59 Bond in Assembly debate, 21 April 1904 (*Evening Telegram*, 22 April 1904).

60 The Labouchere despatch had conceded that 'the consent of the community of Newfoundland is regarded...as the essential preliminary to any modification of their territorial or maritime rights' (see Thompson, *French Shore*, 36-7). The text of the draft 1885 Anglo-French agreement provided for the consent of the Newfoundland legislature.

61 CO 194/254 contains the exchange of tels. on this issue.

62 CO 194/265, Consul Woodhouse to Grey, 1 Aug. 1906, encl. in Foreign Office to CO, 29 Aug. 1906.

63 James Hiller, 'The Origins of the Pulp and Paper Industry in Newfoundland,' *Acadiensis* 11, no. 2 (1982): 42-68; Reeves, 'Yankee Cousins,'402-16.

64 '...a further index as to the kind of men we have to deal with,' Bond told Governor Boyle (PANL, GN 1/3, 1903/38, Bond to Boyle, 23 Oct. 1903).

65 CO 194/254, Boyle to Lyttleton, secret, 9 Feb. 1904; Assembly debates 16, 18 March 1904 (*Evening Telegram*, 31 March, 2, 12 April 1904).

66 Budget speech, 25 March 1902, *Evening Telegram*, 29 March 1902.

67   Reeves, 'Yankee Cousins,' 338-9, 372-4; Bond's speech on the proposal, 15
      April 1903 (*Evening Telegram*, 17 April 1903). The Legislative Council debate
      is in the *Free Press*, 5 May 1903.

68   Reeves, 'Yankee Cousins,' 279-99.

69   Morine in Assembly debate, 29 March 1904 (*Evening Telegram*, 20 April 1904).

70   It is interesting that the anthem which has survived is that by the British
      governor, rather than that by the native-born bishop. Boyle's verses had no
      sectarian or political associations, suitably woolly language, and were cham-
      pioned by Bond. In any event the Ode had the better tune, written by Boyle's
      old school friend Sir Hubert Parry.

71   *Daily News*, 23 Nov. 1901.

72   *Daily News*, 22 Jan.; 4, 23 Nov. 1903.

73   *Evening Telegram, Daily News*, 19 Jan. 1904.

74   Some material on the 1904 election has been drawn from a graduate seminar
      paper written by Jeff A. Webb, Department of History, Memorial University,
      St. John's, in 1984.

75   *Evening Telegram*, 3, 4 Feb. 1905; CO 194/256, MacGregor to Lyttleton, tel., 3
      Feb. 1905.

76   E.M. Jackman in Assembly debate, 13 April 1905 (*Evening Telegram*, 19 April
      1905).

77   In 1854 the Anglo-American Telegraph Co. had been given a 50-year monop-
      oly on landing transatlantic lines, and on building and working certain land
      lines. The government's network fed into the Anglo lines on the Avalon
      Peninsula, and used Anglo's international lines. When the monopoly expired
      in 1904, Bond attempted to take over the Anglo lines. When this strategy
      failed, the government built a competing line across the Avalon, and in 1905
      arranged for its own cable to be laid under the Cabot Strait.

78   On the Anglo affair, see CO 194/257, MacGregor to Lyttleton, tel., 9 June 1905;
      to Lyttleton, conf., 29 July 1905; memo of a meeting at the CO with Anglo
      directors; Horwood to Lyttleton, conf., 24 Aug. 1905.

79   Bond papers, Bond to MacGregor, 3 May 1905; *Evening Telegram*, 20 May 1905.

80   *Daily News*, 11, 31 July 1905.

81   *Daily News*, 8 Sept. 1905. H.A. Morine vs. Reid Newfoundland Co. was
      reported in *Evening Telegram*, 13-24 Dec. 1905.

82   The case was reported in *Evening Telegram*, 16-20 Feb. 1906.

83   Bond argued that since the convention mentioned American access to 'har-
      bours, creeks and coves' only in connection with the Labrador coast, Ameri-
      cans had no right to enter 'harbours, creeks and coves' on the Newfoundland
      American treaty shore (Ramea to Quirpon), but should stay outside a line
      drawn from headland to headland (Bond in Assembly debate, 7 April 1905,
      Evening Telegram, 10 April 1905). For more detailed accounts of the ensuing
      fisheries crisis see Noel, *Politics in Newfoundland*, 36-50; and A.M. Fraser, 'The
      Foreign Fishing Vessels Act of 1905' in R.A. MacKay (ed.), *Newfoundland:
      Economic, Diplomatic and Strategic Studies* (Toronto 1946), 387-99. For a con-
      venient summary of the historical background, see Peter Neary, 'The French
      and American Shore Questions,' in Hiller and Neary (eds.), *Newfoundland*,
      95-122.

84   Reeves, 'Yankee Cousins,' 167-89.

85   Bond in Assembly debate, 7 April 1905 (*Evening Telegram*, 10 April 1905); CO 194/261, Bond to Ommanney, 4 Oct. 1905.

86   CO 194/259, minute, 13 April 1905.

87   Morine in Assembly debate, 7 April 1905 (*Evening Telegram*, 11 April 1905).

88   *Free Press*, 17 Oct. 1905.

89   CO 194/257, MacGregor to Lyttleton, tel., 5 Oct. 1905.

90   Tansill, *Canadian-American Relations*, 100.

91   CO 194/261, Law Officers to CO, 24 Oct. 1905; Lyttleton to MacGregor, tel., 25 Oct. 1905; CO 194/257, MacGregor to Lyttleton, tel., 26 Oct. 1905; Lyttleton to MacGregor, tel., 27 Oct. 1905.

92   R.B. Joyce, *Sir William MacGregor* (Melbourne 1971), 317. MacGregor found Bond 'ambitious and vindictive.'

93   Bond in Assembly debate, 4 May 1906 (*Evening Telegram*, 5 May 1906). The amendments provided that no British subject was to fish on or for a foreign vessel in Newfoundland waters, leave Newfoundland to hire onto such a vessel, or sell, lend or hire any equipment.

94   CO 194/265, Grey to Elgin, private, 27 July 1906.

95   Ronald Hyam, *Elgin and Churchill at the Colonial Office 1905-1908: The Watershed of the Empire-Commonwealth* (London 1968), 294.

96   Quoted in Joyce, *MacGregor*, 318. Ironically, Bond had requested that MacGregor be appointed to the Newfoundland governorship.

97   Tansill, *Canadian-American Relations*, 104-05.

98   Ibid., 106-07; CO 194/265, Foreign Office to CO, 30 July 1906.

99   CO 194/265, Elgin to MacGregor, tel., 8 Aug. 1906.

100   Tansill, *Canadian-American Relations*, 111.

101   CO 194/266, MacGregor to Elgin, tel., 12 Oct. 1906. Bond elaborated the argument in a speech reported in the *Evening Telegram*, 13 Feb. 1907.

102   *Evening Telegram*, 13 Feb. 1907. 'It was not a mere question of the taking or purchasing of a few herring that was involved, it was one of jurisdiction and sovereignty' (Bond, *PHA*, 1911, 30).

103   Now Curling, Bay of Islands. It was later claimed that Morris had been instrumental in preventing a larger number of arrests, and that the magistrate, a confirmed Liberal, had been provided with his judgement before the trial, neatly typewritten. Since Morris was by this time Minister of Justice, he probably wrote it.

104   *Evening Telegram*, 10 Oct. 1906, and Oct.-Nov. 1906, various references.

105   Ibid., 10 Oct. 1906, 4 Jan. 1907.

106   Reeves, 'Yankee Cousins,' 188-9.

107   Cashin in Assembly debate, 14 Feb. 1907 (*Evening Telegram*, 25 Feb. 1907).

108   *Daily News*, 11 April 1905.

109   CO 880/18, 'Minutes of Proceedings of the Colonial Conference, 1907; 13th, 14th and 15th Days'; Hyam, *Elgin*, 295-6.

110   Lyttleton in House of Commons, 17 June 1907 (United Kingdom, *Parliamentary Debates*, 4th series, vol. 176, col. 151).

111   MG 26, E, Laurier to Grey, 20 May 1907. The 1818 convention applied to both Canadian and Newfoundland waters.

112   CO 194/270, Elgin to Grey, private, 17 May 1907; Bond to Elgin, 10, 15 June 1907; Hyam, *Elgin*, 295-6.

113   CO 194/270, Bond to Elgin, 10 June 1907; CO 194/269, MacGregor to Elgin, tel., 2 Aug. 1907.

114   CO 194/269, minute by Cox, 4 Aug. 1907.

115   CO 194/269, MacGregor to Elgin, tel., 22 Aug. 1907.

116   *Evening Telegram*, 7 May 1907.

117   CO 194/270, Loreburn to CO, 22 June 1907; minute by Elgin, 6 July 1907; Noel, *Politics in Newfoundland*, 47.

118   *Evening Telegram*, 25-8 Sept. 1907.

119   CO 194/271, Bryce to Grey, conf., 1 Nov. 1907, encl. in Foreign Office to CO, 14 Nov. 1907; CO 194/270, MacGregor to Elgin, tel., 1 Nov. 1907.

120   *Evening Telegram*, 10 Sept. 1907.

121   Ibid., 7 Oct. 1907.

122   Printed in the *Free Press*, 8 Oct. 1907.

123   *Times* (London), 26 Sept. 1907, printed in *Daily News*, 11 Oct. 1907; P.T. McGrath in *Evening Telegram*, 29 Oct., 4 Nov. 1907.

124   M.E. Hallett, 'The Fourth Earl Grey as Governor-General of Canada' (unpublished PH D thesis, London University 1969), 179; Noel, *Politics in Newfoundland*, 41-2.

125   MacGregor even lobbied for Morris to receive an English K.C. (Joyce, *MacGregor*, 322).

126   Hallett, 'Grey,' 188; NAC, MG 27, II B 2 (4th Earl Grey papers), Grey to Laurier, 8 Aug. 1906; to Elgin, 8 Aug. 1906.

127   *Evening Telegram*, 27 July 1907.

128   *Newfoundland Quarterly* 21, no. 2 (1920): 4.

129   MG 27, II B 2, MacGregor to Grey, personal and conf., 11 Nov. 1907.

130   Ibid., MacGregor to Grey, personal, 29 Nov. 1907.

131   On the unsuccessful operations carried out by the Scottish firm of Flett and Co., see Reeves, 'Yankee Cousins,' 299-304.

132   Bond in Assembly debate, 22 Feb. 1894 (*Evening Telegram*, 24 Feb. 1894).

133   Bond in Assembly debate, 27 Feb. 1907 (*Evening Telegram*, 1 March 1907); *Free Press*, 5 March 1907.

134   For Morris' tactics, see *Free Press*, 4, 11, 18 Feb. 1908.

135   *Daily News*, 7 March 1908.

136   Ibid.

137   *Evening Telegram*, 29 Sept. 1908. For a fuller account of the campaign, see Noel, *Politics in Newfoundland*, 51-67.

138   *Free Press* 17 March 1908. The People's Party manifesto is printed in the *Free Press*, 13 Oct. 1908.

139   Ian McDonald claims the fish price collapse largely explains the election result (*"To Each His Own": William Coaker and the Fishermen's Protective Union in Newfoundland Politics, 1908-1925* (St. John's 1987), 14).

140   CO 194/273, Bond to MacGregor, 17 Nov. 1908, encl. in MacGregor to Crewe, conf., 25 Nov. 1908. Morris took the opposite view that since Bond had failed to obtain a majority, he had suffered a moral if not an actual defeat and should be asked to resign (CO 194/273, Morris to MacGregor, 12 Nov. 1908, encl. in

MacGregor to Crewe, secret, 13 Nov. 1908). When shown the letter, Bond acidly remarked that he of course dismissed the thought that Morris was motivated by 'selfish ambition, morbid cupidity or vanity' (CO 194/273, Bond to MacGregor, 17 Nov. 1908). See also Noel, *Politics in Newfoundland*, 68-76.

141 The correspondence generated by this plot can be found in the Grey and Bond papers. A certain amount of it was published in the *Evening Chronicle* (St. John's) and the *Evening Telegram* in April and May 1909. See also CO 124/275.

142 CO 194/275, Bond to MacGregor, 18 Feb. 1909, encl. in MacGregor to Crewe, conf., 25 Feb. 1909; MacGregor to Crewe, tel., 19 Feb. 1909.

143 CO 194/275, MacGregor to Bond, 20 Feb. 1909.

144 CO 194/275, Bond to MacGregor, 22 Feb. 1909, encl. in MacGregor to Crewe, conf., 25 Feb. 1909.

145 CO 194/275, MacGregor to Morris, 25 Feb. 1909, encl. in MacGregor to Crewe, conf., 25 Feb. 1909.

146 CO 194/275, MacGregor to Morris, 25 Feb. 1909; Morris to MacGregor, 26 Feb.; 'Points to be shewn to Sir Edward Morris, 25th Feb. 1909,' encl. in MacGregor to Crewe, conf., 26 Feb. 1909.

147 The documentation on these events can be found in CO 194/275, 276, encls. in MacGregor to Crewe, conf., 31 March 1909; and conf., 9 April 1909.

148 MacGregor had decided to give Morris the dissolution soon after the latter took office (CO 194/275, MacGregor to Crewe, secret, 6 March 1909). At the CO, A.B. Keith—the future expert on the constitutional law of the dominions—was the only official who thought Bond ill treated.

149 *Free Press*, 6 April 1909.

150 Noel, *Politics in Newfoundland*, 77-148; McDonald, "To Each His Own," 34-85.

151 Quoted in Noel, *Politics in Newfoundland*, 140. See also McDonald, "To Each His Own," 73-85.

Tourists, Health Seekers and Sportsmen: Luring Americans to Newfoundland in the Early Twentieth Century*

Gerald L. Pocius

A BRIEF PUBLICITY BROCHURE (figure 1), published around 1910, announced on its first page: 'During the last few years Newfoundland and Labrador have been appealing to the tourist, health seeker and sportsman, and every year witnesses an increasing number of tourists in search of the picturesque. Travellers, explorers, health seekers, anglers and hunters carry back glowing reports of the wonderful attractions of Newfoundland and Labrador, and all have pronounced them the "Gems of the Western World," and [a] "Sportsman's Paradise."'[1] This sales pitch was put forward by the Reid Newfoundland Company, which owned the major transportation links—the railway and steamship lines—in the colony. It was primarily through the activities of the Reid company, with other private entrepreneurs, that Newfoundland attempted to diversify its economy during the first decades of the twentieth century, adding tourism as one other alternative to the fishery.

As was often the case in North America, private transportation ventures with only limited support from governments were the first to bring tourists and their cash to new lands. In Canada, the Canadian Pacific Railway (CPR) directed much of its promotional effort between 1885 and 1900 toward attracting tourists to its routes. Hotels were built along the line, and advertising campaigns were launched which presented images geared to particular groups of tourists. The CPR's efforts were aimed largely at Great Britain, in part because of Canada's desire to lure immigrants as well as tourists from the motherland. In the process the CPR produced some of the first images of Canada for a public at large outside the country, images which have contributed to the enduring stereotypes associated with the nation.[2] It was the same with Newfoundland.

Newfoundland—like Canada—owes its first mass influx of tourists to the promotional efforts of a railway company, in this case the Reid Newfoundland Company. One local writer, realizing the similarities of railroad development in Canada and Newfoundland, commented: 'It has been said

Figure 1—Publicity brochure of the Reid Newfoundland Company, c. 1910.

that the "Canadian Pacific Railway made Canada;" we might almost venture to slightly alter the expression and say that the "Reid Newfoundland Company made Newfoundland."[3] Unlike the CPR, the Reid company targeted its market largely at the northeastern United States, hoping to draw rich American tourists and their dollars north of the border. During the first two decades of the twentieth century, the Reids, co-operating with private entrepreneurs and the government, attempted to lure Americans to Newfoundland through a series of images that depicted what were perceived to be the colony's selling points: the attractions of scenery, climate and wildlife. While few historical studies of tourism exist for Newfoundland, Canada, or elsewhere,[4] it is clear that the early tourist imagery promoted in Newfoundland fits into greater overall trends pervasive in North America. As in Canada, the railway was the key player in this development.

Tourism itself takes many forms. Broadly speaking, tourism is centred either on the natural landscape, or on the activities of a particular people—in short on what can be called nature tourism or cultural tourism.[5] Certainly in Newfoundland—like other areas of Canada—the earliest tourism developments were concerned mainly with the lure of nature, and attracted tourists who came to experience various aspects of the natural environment. These experiences could be simply ecological (enjoying scenery and climate) or more intensive—of a hunter/gatherer variety (sportsmen). Newfoundlanders were there to serve these visitors, and their task was largely one of providing amenities. In sum, they were cast in the role of striving to create the kind of surroundings that they thought their guests wanted. Locals were usually not expected consciously to display any unique culture and only in recent years, as cultural tourism has grown, have staged displays (such as folk festivals) become important.[6] Indeed, the early lack of historical or cultural tourism shows how railway operators viewed tourist development.

Tourism usually occurs in situations where groups of people from more affluent places travel to destinations where the economies are much less developed. Rarely does tourism occur among peoples who are not financially well off; with such groups permanent migration is more likely. Tourism by the affluent to a poorer region is possible only when methods of transportation have developed sufficiently to permit reasonably easy access. Tourist destinations also rise and fall in popularity; as certain places become more congested, new places are sought.[7] All of these factors played a role in the development of Newfoundland in the early twentieth century.

A tourist destination is socially constructed; the needs of a certain tourist group require certain landscapes. Sometimes these landscapes need to be filled with other tourists, sometimes with modern amenities considered necessary, and sometimes with surroundings only slightly different from those of home. Regions become tourist destinations not because there is anything inherently 'tourist' about them that is waiting to be discovered, but rather because they fill the need of a particular guest group. How Newfoundland was portrayed in promotional literature such as travel guides and publicity brochures, and how the actual tourist trade developed, was shaped specifically by a particular American tourist market.[8]

At the beginning of the twentieth century, Americans increasingly felt that their frontier had vanished, that no longer were there vast unconquered spaces in their own country left to explore. As in other countries, the perceived disappearance of the frontier led to a developing cult of the wilderness. People became concerned with the quest for the wild—both animals and land. With increasing urbanization and industrialization, stimulated by the writings of wilderness lovers such as Frederick Jackson Turner, Americans more and more turned to the primitive for inspiration and rejuvenation, be it primitive man or primitive land. An increasing number of books appeared on Indians, whom anthropologists studied in great detail; likewise, popular primitives were created, of whom Edgar Rice Burroughs' 'Tarzan' was the most famous.[9] The wild land, too, was praised, and by the end of the century Americans believed that their own wilderness was both threatened and in need of preservation (a major change from the feelings of the first pioneers). National parks such as Yellowstone (1872), as well as regional reserves such as the 'Forest Preserve' in the Adirondacks (1885) were created. It was not long before Americans realized that while their wilderness was becoming increasingly endangered, Canada and New-foundland had plenty to spare. Indeed, Patrick O'Flaherty, commenting on the number of travel writers describing Newfoundland in the 1890s and the 1900s, noted that 'It may not be an exaggeration to say that the island and Labrador became in some sense an imaginative outpost of the eastern United States, with authors recreating in this sparsely populated and primitive territory an image of their own diminishing frontier.'[10] O'Flaherty also points out that the American fascination with the North (as witnessed by writers like Jack London and Robert Service) found a ready topic in Labrador, through the writings of the social and medical missionary Wilfred Grenfell, and the travel adventures of writers like Dillon Wallace.[11]

For American culture, freedom has always meant freedom to move.[12] Some leading New England writers travelled across the border into Canada in the mid-nineteenth century, and created at first hand an impression of a vast and unsettled wilderness. Henry David Thoreau, for example, journeyed from his increasingly crowded Concord to Maine and then into Canada, excited by being 'on the verge of the uninhabited, and, for the most part, unexploited wilderness stretching toward Hudson's Bay.'[13] In a similar vein, the future explorer of the Oregon Trail, the Bostonian Francis Parkman, Jr., made a series of summer journeys into northern New England and Canada in the 1840s. During one of his trips near the Canadian border in 1841 he noted that 'My chief object in coming so far was merely to have a taste of the half-savage kind of life necessary to be led, and to see the wilderness where it was as yet uninvaded by the hand of man.'[14]

Newfoundland and Canada had rarely taken notice of their wilderness spaces, since until recently they had been so abundant. Unlike Americans, who were developing a cult of wilderness by the turn of the century, Canadians generally did not regard vast uninhabited spaces as anything to be appreciated. Wilderness is not a commodity in need of the cultural act of preservation until it is in danger of extinction.[15] The landscape existed not to be preserved in some type of ecological museum, but rather to be used for whatever purposes humans saw fit. Thus, no schemes were proposed to enshrine areas of wilderness for simple enjoyment, but rather it was quickly realized that wilderness could be marketed. When national parks were established in Canada, private enterprise played an integral role; the primary goal was to lure tourists, no matter how the landscape had to be altered, or what tourist landscapes had to be fabricated.[16] This would also be the case in Newfoundland, where the private concerns of the railway spearheaded the tourist campaign.

Coinciding with a growing American thirst for the wild was a major period in Newfoundland of economic hopes and dreams, closely associated with the building of the trans-island railway. All nations at the time equated the building of railways as a sign of progress, whether necessary or not.[17] The construction of the railway from the east coast to the west took place largely through the island's interior, primarily to develop previously inaccessible natural resources. The Reids and their political supporters looked upon the railway as a way to diversify Newfoundland's economy, and to develop industries such as mining, agriculture and paper manufacturing that would both bring needed cash into the colony and promote settlement in the interior. The Reids soon became involved in various development schemes involving these resources, with their railway as a prime ingredient in the planning.[18]

Robert G. Reid had worked for the CPR as a bridge and railway builder, and it is certain that he was familiar with the early promotional efforts of that company. He obviously realized that in Newfoundland he could market landscape as well, but to a different clientele than the CPR. He sensed that his route might draw from a geographically closer group than the British, namely, wilderness-hungry Americans who could hunt or fish anywhere along the 546-mile stretch of track. The Reids began to market the island, leading to a series of hotels and sports camps operated by private entrepreneurs, all catering to the wilderness appetite that was increasingly unsatisfied in the northeastern United States. The company obviously realized that as many users as possible were necessary to make the railway profitable, and tourists could be one more group who would use the line.

By the end of the nineteenth century, popular guidebooks and brochures were being produced by these entrepreneurs, and Newfoundland apologists were aware that wealthy tourists could be lured to their shores if they sold the right commodities. Indeed, the Reids had planned as early as 1890 to build a luxury hotel in St. John's: 'A number of Americans visited the Colony last year, and a much larger contingent is expected the coming season. They have lots of money to spend, are willing to spend it, and want the best accommodations to be had.'[19] Tourism required not just means of transportation to the island itself (the steamship line), and to travel across it to see the sights (the railway), but also a series of hotels, sports camps and bungalows along the route.

Contemporary promotional guides and brochures indicate that entrepreneurs believed that Newfoundland could be sold to Americans using three drawing cards: as a health resort; as a place where unlimited fish and game could be caught; and as a wilderness area. A guide book distributed by the Reid Newfoundland Company highlighted to the visiting tourist the island's major attractions. As a sportsman's paradise, there were 'hundreds of lakes—all pretty and inviting,' with what was touted as the 'best salmon and trout fishing in North America.' As well, the island was 'an ideal health resort' with a 'good, dry, bracing climate,' where a person could 'build up mind and body.' And just in case physical misfortune might occur, there were 'physicians in nearly every resort.'[20]

The discovery of Newfoundland wilderness—and that of Canada generally—occurred at a time when available wilderness areas on the American northeast coast had certainly declined. Geographically, Canada was just as close as the preserves of the American west such as Yellowstone or Yosemite. Some tourist advertisements deliberately played on the notion that lands in the eastern United States were becoming overcrowded. One Reid publication quoted Walter Hammitt, writing in *The Brooklyn Times* of September 15, 1901:

> To the vacationer who would deviate from the beaten track, to whom such forests as Sullivan County possesses have lost their attractiveness, to whom even the beauties of the Adirondacks and the wildness fastnesses of the Maine Woods have taken on a atmosphere of tameness, and who wants 'something different,' I would say,'pack your trunk with your oldest clothes, gather your trout tackle together, provide yourself with salmon tackle if you haven't it, look to the re-provisioning of your rifle or shot gun, and go to Newfoundland.'[21]

Newfoundland obviously had become more accessible to the east coast of the United States as railway lines provided links between New England and the Maritime Provinces.[22] By 1898 the New Brunswick and Canadian Railway had reached Presque Isle, Maine, bringing American tourists eastward. Much of the Nova Scotia tourist promotion of this period focused on the pastoral landscape of Evangeline, aimed as much at markets in Britain as America. However, as early as 1908 the Intercolonial Railway's advertising did cater to the American sportsman, using many of the arguments found in Newfoundland promotions.[23] By 1902, the Reid Newfoundland Company had advertising and travel links with the Intercolonial Railway (Moncton), Prince Edward Island Railway and Steam Navigation Company (Charlottetown), Maine Central Railroad (Portland), and Boston and Maine Railroad (Boston).[24]

With developing railway connections, Newfoundland obviously attempted to draw to its shores those American tourists who in the past had frequented the Maine wilderness. The Maine Central Railroad issued a guide in the early 1900s entitled 'To Hunt and Fish in Maine, New Brunswick and Newfoundland' (figure 2).[25] One of the Reid company's employees, C. M. Beane, who seems to have been involved with the publication, may have written the Newfoundland section, and certainly did issue a Newfoundland edition.[26] While only a few pages are devoted to Newfoundland, the railways throughout New England and Atlantic Canada obviously realized that they all could benefit by selling these wilderness lands to Americans searching for the hunting or fishing Garden of Eden. One writer even quoted a poem drawing on this imagery to describe Newfoundland: 'regions where, in spite of sin and woe / Traces of Eden are still seen below / Where mountain, river, forest, field and grove / Remind him of his Maker's power and love.'[27] To reach this paradise, one merely had to buy a railway ticket, so the pamphlet claimed, and one could take the choice of any number of fish and game trophies throughout the region—nothing

Figure 2—Publicity brochure of the Maine Central Railroad, c. 1910.

could be easier. The Reid company itself launched direct efforts to lure Americans to the colony. One apologist for the company claimed:

> Throughout every town and city in the United States and Canada, as well as in many English cities, by means of well-organized and competent systems of advertising, Newfoundland has been brought into a prominence she never before occupied. Already the foundation for the tourist traffic, of which we hear so much, has been well laid; for not a trip of the *Bruce* passes during the hunting and fishing seasons without the coming of these 'seekers of recreation,' brought hither through the instrumentality of the Reid Newfoundland Company, who have so well laid bare the natural charms and advantages of our island in the folder boxes of the hotel and transportation offices outside.[28]

In 1908 the Reid Newfoundland Company cooperated with the Newfoundlanders' Mutual Benefit Association in Boston to present a lecture by the publicist, C. M. Beane, on the merits of travelling to Newfoundland.[29]

W. J. Carroll, writing in 1905, made a direct comparison between Maine and Newfoundland, pointing out the monies to be gained if rich Americans could be lured northward. He wrote:

> It was estimated that there were between eight and twelve million dollars spent in Maine last year by tourists. There have been lately dozens of articles written by visitors of repute in the British and American sporting journals that prove that our shooting and fishing facilities are peerless in the world to-day, and as far as Maine is concerned for deer, salmon, grilse, sea and brook trout, it is not the same class at all as Newfoundland...The time has now come when we should make an intelligent effort, to turn these grand assets to good account. If Maine earns ten million dollars yearly, in the next decade we should earn as much. We have everything that Maine has to offer visitors, and more. We only lack good hotels and boarding houses. But these will

follow. If our own people don't cater in this respect, there are others
who will see the possibilities, and erect summer hotels in favoured
regions along the railway.[30]

In 1911, Carroll noted that 'competent authorities compute that the State of
Maine last season netted over ten millions of dollars from its visitors, and
that the American people spent over one hundred million dollars in travelling expenses.'[31] And another American state provided Carroll with a
model for Newfoundland:

> While New Hampshire supplies beautiful scenery, a healthy climate
> and other attractions, it has nothing to compare with our salmon and
> sea-trou[t] fishing, and our herds of noble caribou. It is a simple sum in
> proportion to find how much we ought to make yearly out of the
> attractions we possess in common with New Hampshire, plus our
> peerless fishing and shooting (which are worth millions in themselves)
> if that State can earn from this source over $620,000 in one year.[32]

Tourist resorts and hotels for Americans began opening up all along
the railway line. This especially happened on the west coast of the island,
where the scenery was dramatic, salmon rivers were plentiful, and the
tourist would be only an hour or so from the ferry terminal at Port aux
Basques. With a ferry connecting Nova Scotia with the western terminus of
the Newfoundland railway, advertisements began to boast that Newfoundland could be reached from any city in the United States in a few short hours
or days. One visitor noted the former inaccessibility of Newfoundland to
tourists. 'Then,' she explained, 'came a new era, when the Reid Newfoundland Company spanned the Straits of Cabot with the rapid ocean-going
steamers, and traversed Newfoundland with the luxuriously equipped
railroad, the comforts and service of which are not to be outdone by any
similar system in America. Thus were the doors of the colony opened.'[33]
The trip from New York to Newfoundland took fifty-four hours, and travel
information could be obtained from all railway offices and tourist agencies
throughout the United States.[34] Visitors could travel direct to St. John's, with
the railway then carrying them westward. The Red Cross Line travelled
between New York and St. John's in five and a half days, while the Allan
Steamship Company connected St. John's with Philadelphia.[35]

Wealthy Americans, then, were searching for new exotic lands to
explore as the northeast part of their country became more congested.
Newfoundland might not necessarily be a new destination, but it could
offer a new tourist experience with the railroad having opened up the
interior. The Reid company therefore focused on the three attractions
related to its railway route that it felt would draw Americans: the lure of
health, sport and wilderness.

Health

The very nature of the tourist experience involves a structured break from
ordinary life, a kind of ritual that reverses daily routine. As Nelson Graburn
notes, 'It is no wonder, then, that tourism is often identified with "re-crea-
tion"—the renewal of life, the recharging of run-down elements—so necessary for the maintenance of mental and bodily health which characterize a
balanced life style.'[36] While all tourism can have such a physical impact, the
health effects of travelling to Newfoundland were often argued to be much
more direct.

To the American tourist, Newfoundland was portrayed as a kind of
giant health sanatorium, where people weary from the hustle and bustle of
major American cities could come. Certainly a Reid guidebook made one
of the most forceful claims for the benefits of Newfoundland's climate:

> In the sea-girt isle, the citizens of the United States and Canada will find
> a welcome escape from the burning heat of their summers; scenery
> novel and attractive; and a bracing exhilarating air which imparts new
> vigour to the frame and sends back the smoke-dried denizens of the
> great cities with the tide of health coursing through their veins, and life
> made incomparably better worth living...As a pleasant health resort,
> Newfoundland takes a high place. In fine summer days the heat is never
> oppressive and the nights are always cool, so that after the day's ramble,
> sleep comes sweet and refreshing. There is something peculiarly balmy,
> soothing and yet invigorating in the summer breezes, whether on sea
> or land, cooling the fevered brain and soothing the wrinkled brow of
> care. After a few weeks near the coast, inhaling the salt sea breezes and
> exposed to the life-giving sun's rays, the invalid who has come with
> shattered nerves and fluttering pulse, returns with a new supply of iron
> in his blood and a sense of well-being that makes it a luxury to live and
> breath the pure air of Terra Nova.[37]

And sportswriter F. C. Selous argued: 'I feel sure that many a man whose
health has been impaired by the strain on body and mind of modern
civilized life would reap far more benefit from a trip into the interior of
Newfoundland than he could derive from a German watering-place. Plain
food, hard exercise, and the pure invigorating air of the northern wilderness
will cure most ailments, and it would have to be a very bad case that could
not find an appetite for a fat caribou steak a fortnight after leaving St.
John's.'[38] James Davis of Summerside on the west coast had begun building
a new hotel in Curling in 1916, partly to draw tourists to the health giving
climate of the colony. The discussion of his resort plans and of the health
benefits of the island closed with the somewhat religious exhortation: 'If
perchance this should fall into the hands of any who are looking for healthy
pleasure and prosperity we extend the invitation to arise; gird thyself; come
and enjoy its blessings!'[39] When the Governor General of Canada, Lord
Grey, visited the west coast early in the century, one report claimed that 'he

could never forget the beautiful scenery through which he had passed, or the delightfulness of the climate.' 'The illuminated glory of the Bay of Islands in the radiance of the setting sun,' this same report continued, 'left him with a lovely recollection, which, like Wordsworth's daffodil, would never fade from his memory, and [which] had enabled him to foresee the ever increasing stream of humanity which would one day seek in the unregarding air, and in the healing waters and mountains of their beautiful fiords, the rest and refreshment of which its tired spirit would stand so sorely in need.'[40] In fact, during the late nineteenth century a form of medical treatment known as the 'wilderness cure' enjoyed considerable popularity in the United States. This treatment simply involved exposure to what was perceived to be wilderness areas; the particular climate and landscape would then enhance the curative powers of the body.[41]

With regard to health, two characteristics were mentioned again and again in Newfoundland tourist promotions: the quality of the air, and the cool temperatures. However, the reality of Newfoundland's weather meant that tourist promotions emphasized only one aspect of the annual climate: the short cool summer, a summer that contrasted so greatly with that of other parts of North America. In truth, for much of the year, the Newfoundland climate is 'notorious,' and marked by fog and strong and quickly changing winds.[42] But the cool summers were often contrasted with conditions in the hot urban centres of the northeastern mainland, where the air was becoming increasingly polluted by industrialization. As the Newfoundland historian and publicist D.W. Prowse argued, 'To the heat-stricken New Yorker or citizen of the United States, stifling in June or July, the cool, refreshing breezes and the salubrious airs act as the most bracing tonic.'[43] W. J. Carroll claimed that 'in comparison with the deadly heat of the American and Canadian cities, especially in the night-time, when, no matter how jaded one may be, refreshing sleep is out of the question, the bracing sea-searched air of this Island in the summer is like champagne.'[44] And a later railway promotional brochure noted: 'The salt breezes wafted across the island from the ambient waters are charged with invigorating ozone that quickly brings back the glow of health to the invalid's pallid cheek and puts new vigor into the constitution sapped by the arduous routine of social duties or the cares of business life.'[45] The Maine Central Railroad pamphlet argued that the environment in all of Atlantic Canada was healthful for different reasons: 'The air then breathed is full of oxygen, with its nerve-tissue strengthening qualities; the odor of pine and fir is on every hand, building up the lungs, renewing the blood, and girding the muscles for a better struggle in this world of existence.'[46]

Although Newfoundlanders were often portrayed as a hardy race—partly because of this climate—one writer did note that consumption was found amongst the population. However, he noted that this did not detract from the healthy environment: 'The purity of the air of Newfoundland is without doubt due to the fact that the people of the outports never open their windows.'[47]

Sport

Much of the early tourist promotional literature spoke of the vast quantities of game waiting for the sportsman; a Reid pamphlet boasted that 'It would be like painting the lily or gilding refined gold to exaggerate the sporting attractions of Newfoundland and Labrador.'[48] Beyond the railway lay 'the trackless waste, with its preserves of game—fin, fur and feather—to tempt the sportsman and angler.'[49] Prowse claimed that the island was 'one vast deer park';[50] another advertisement boasted that streams were filled with 'gamey fish.'[51] W. F. Cormack, Vice-President of the Bank of Florida, pointed out that tuna he saw along the shore in the Bay of Islands were 'without exception...the gamiest fish in the world.'[52] The Reid Newfoundland Company succinctly boasted the colony had the 'best salmon and trout streams that have yet been discovered.'[53] Entire books were written about bountiful hunting and fishing expeditions on the island; numerous articles appeared in American sporting and outdoor magazines such as *Forest and Stream, Recreation of New York*, and the *New York Shooting and Fishing Magazine*, as well as newspapers like the *New York Herald, Brooklyn Standard Union* and *Boston Journal Gazette*.[54] Articles began to appear in local Newfoundland publications written by American sportsmen such as Wakeman Holberton, billed as 'Famous Deer Stalker, residing in Ithaca, N.Y.'[55] Syndicated writers publicized a land where fish caught were counted not individually, but by dozens, and caribou could be shot daily. One writer explained Newfoundland's bounty thus: 'One American gentleman who has fished all Canada and from Maine to California, in an American magazine for this month, says, talking about brook trout and brown trout: "They are more common than perch and sun fish in the States. Catching them will soon surfeit the angler....Such catches are *counted by the dozen*, one lot of seventy-two dozen being brought aboard the train."'[56] Col. Blair from Scranton, Pennsylvania, spent several weeks in Newfoundland with three sporting friends; he remarked that 'We had all the shooting we desired, and to all legitimate sportsmen would say, go up to Newfoundland and enjoy a two month outing.'[57] Americans obviously were coming in increasing numbers; in 1908, Lord Howick, son of Earl Grey, fishing on the west coast, remarked: 'Most of the "Sports" as the visitors who come to shoot and fish, are called, are Americans, and their numbers are increasing every year.'[58]

Caribou could be shot easily along the railway, particularly since they migrated across the line near Howley every year. Lord Morris (the former Sir Edward Morris) remarked that 'I myself at Howley Station saw thousands pass in an afternoon,' and a photograph from around 1910 shows what was described as one of the 'canvas towns'—dozens of tents—'that appeared at Howley during the sporting season.'[59] The migration of the caribou herd in this area led to a vast number being shot there, as well as at other spots along the track. This 'railway sport' was despised by many hunters who considered it merely a form of slaughter. Real hunting had to involve travel from the rail line into the interior.[60] Yet wherever the hunt took place, a number of trophies—'good heads'—were brought back to civilization.[61] William R. Philler, Secretary of the Real Estate Trust Company of Philadelphia, noted: 'We secured five heads, the smallest thirty-two points and the largest thirty-five points, of the heavy, wide variety of horns.' And the sportswriter H. Hesketh Pritchard, described the problem of hunting in Newfoundland: 'It would almost seem that the art of hunting in Newfoundland lies in knowing what stags not to shoot, and it is the man who is bold enough to let a good head slip, in the hope of getting a better one, who secures the finest trophies.'[62] Trophies were not just brought back for the wealthy hunter's den. Col. Cecil Clay from Washington D. C. had collected a number of 'fine specimens' of moose for the 'National Museum,' and travelled to Newfoundland in 1899 to furnish the same museum with a group of caribou that were also exhibited at the Chicago World's Columbia Exposition of 1893.[63] Likewise, in 1900 at a sportsmen's show at Madison Square Garden in New York, twenty-one caribou heads and two mounted stags were exhibited from Newfoundland.[64]

Robert G. Reid himself proudly displayed his caribou trophies to visitors, and may well have been a hunter.[65] His son, William D. Reid, accompanied 'His serene Highness, Prince Louis of [Battenburg]' on a visit in 1905, where they 'spent a most enjoyable time deer stalking and salmon fishing near the Humber, accompanied by His Excellency, Governor MacGregor.'[66]

In any case, the Reids obviously did all they could to assist visiting sportsmen and paid special attention to sportsmen-writers who could praise in print the abundance of fish and game in the colony. H. Hesketh Prichard, who wrote several essays on hunting in Newfoundland, noted: 'One thing, however, I cannot pass without remark, and that is the kindness I met with at the hands of Mr. W. D. Reid, and of the Reid Newfoundland Company. Everything that could be done to make my trip pleasant and successful was ungrudgingly done.'[67]

Hunting and camping was 'all very primitive, but it has a strong appeal to the man with good red blood in his veins';[68] the machismo of the hunt was clear. Sportswriter J.G. Millais mentioned the connections between love and the hunt:

> Since the beginning of things, man has had three dominant passions: to make love, to go to war, and to hunt wild beasts. Whilst time is teaching us that the second of these is not always an unmixed blessing nor an advantage, although we must ever be prepared for it, the first and third will remain with us until the crack of doom.[69]

W. K. Vanderbilt from New York spent a season hunting caribou in 1903 and claimed that 'Newfoundland was a veritable Sportsman's Paradise.' He brought back a number of trophy heads, and planned to return the next year with a larger party.[70] This male activity was filled with the typical metaphors of pursuit and conquest, whether it was for fish or game. For example:

> The spirit of the most enthusiastic angler rises with the elevating influence of the scene, for his trained eye can take in at a glance the increasing activity existing beneath the trembling, transparent bosom of the matchless waters that are found within the confines of this extensive tract of pleasure grounds, where myriads of the finny tribe, unmolested, disport themselves.[71]

Another writer, in an account too lengthy to quote in its entirety, described the pleasures of midnight fishing, setting a scene that would rival any moonlit romantic stroll taken by starry-eyed lovers:

> The sun was setting, and its warm declining rays were calling every insect and animal out to bask and enjoy to the full the beauty and warmth of the late evening. Little streaks of gold were wandering through the greenery of the trees, dancing between the branches and lighting up the deeper recesses of the forest with thousands of golden sparks, tripping from branch to branch, until they disappeared and were lost in the shadows of the deeper woods...The silence, every now and again, was broken by a breaching trout, and I waited in contemplative mood for the moon to rise to give sufficient light to enable me to indulge in my favourite sport of moonlight fishing...The light gone, I slowly wended my way through the darkness back to the fishing shack, and there in the smoke of the camp-fire's glow, I told of my catch. And all through the night I dreamed that Paradise was filled not with angelic women, but with perfect trout streams, and the 'feeding rise' was always on; and the moon never set.[72]

The hunt was primarily a male pursuit, and the clientele of many of the hunting hotels was mainly composed of men. The Log Cabin Hotel at Spruce Brook, for example, specifically mentioned that it catered to tourists with ladies in their party, an obvious exception to the norm.[73] Many of the hunting narratives describe the desire to conquer—in this case, to shoot large numbers of caribou or moose each day, and to bring back a number of trophies. As with other sports, the preoccupation of the hunt was the quest; J. G. Millais likened the beauty of the caribou to that of an attractive woman:

> Like some beautiful women, whose charms are undeniable, you can take every individual point of the caribou stag, and tear it to bits piece by piece. The nose is positively Hebraic, the eyes small and insignificant, the feet are large and out of all proportion, while its whole body is stumpy and movements the reverse of graceful. And yet—the 'tout ensemble' is palpitating life—what is it? Something indefinable, and with all its imperfections a sum-total that is magnificent.[74]

Wilderness

While Newfoundland's climate was argued to be healthy, and its ponds, streams and forests abounding with wildlife, the colony above all was promoted to tourists as wilderness.[75] But, as Roderick Nash points out, 'there is no specific material object that is wilderness.' Indeed, local business and government officials had to convince the potential visitor that the Newfoundland landscape was the type to satisfy the thirst for the wild, for unspoiled space, that it was free from crowds, and at least reasonably similar to that of America's pioneer east coast.

In terms of its wilderness qualities *per se*, Newfoundland was described as one vast tract devoid of habitation, excelling in raw beauty. Since most of the settlement had occurred around the coasts, the railway itself travelled largely through wilderness. Much of the promotional literature gave little hint that Newfoundlanders themselves actually lived in the colony. Writers pictured the island as 'virgin ground,' 'wholly unexplored,' 'where the foot of the white man has never trod.'[76] The travel writer F. G. Selous claimed that 'The wild, primeval desolation of the country and the vast voiceless solitudes—where the silence is never broken save by the cry of some wild creature—have an inexpressible charm all their own. You feel that you stand on a portion of the earth's surface which has known no change for countless centuries, a land which may remain in its natural condition for centuries yet to come.'[77] And it was the railway that permitted this 'discovery' of a new wilderness, for an area untouched by Europeans had been created. James F. Faunce of Philadelphia wrote: 'It was back in June, 1899, that we landed for the first time on the Newfoundland shore, with virgin country as our objective. We had learned of a railroad having been opened up across the country, offering easy access to rivers never fished with rod and fly, and forests unmarred by the lumberman's axe.'[78]

The Reids promoted Newfoundland as the 'Norway of the New World,' although many guidebooks illustrated the often monotonous bogs and scrub forests that characterized much of the railway's route. Newfoundland had 'deep fiords,' which indented 'the shores everywhere, guarded by lofty cliffs whose forms' were 'reflected in the clear, bright waters of the bays.' These fiords had 'a remarkable resemblance to those of Norway,' and were not less magnificent in their scenery.' 'Many of these great watery ravines,' this account continued, 'running inland for eighty or ninety miles, exhibit a wonderful variety of scenery along the great arms which they project in all directions, and in the islands which stud their bosoms, are on a much grander scale than the famous Norwegian fiords.'[79] Another writer, obviously focusing on other landscape features, felt that Newfoundland would become 'the Switzerland of the new world.'[80]

Wild landscape was there to be enjoyed, and could also form the subject for the leisured people who travelled to exotic lands to paint and sketch.

One American visitor in 1895 explained that 'The banks of the Humber River were quite as picturesque as those of the Hudson or the Saint John, and would make a most attractive and still unhackyned [sic] field for landscape painting.' And the City Engineer of St. John's, after travelling to the Bay of Islands in the early nineties, commented: 'I feel the Creator was almost prodigious in his distribution of beauty here, some aesthetical English ladies with a mania for sketching would go into raptures over landscapes that open up fresh magnificence at every step you take.'[81] The art critic of the New York *Century Magazine*, S. J. W. Benjamin, declared that 'The Coast scenery of Bay of Islands was the finest in North America.'[82] However, it was obvious that foreign visitors were searching for landscapes different from their own: 'Space will not permit of a detailed description of the scenic gems I saw during my recent visit to Newfoundland...There are places where forest fires have stripped the leaves and bark from the trees and painted them in a silvery beauty that defies description.'[83]

William D. Reid planned to build hotels in St. John's, Bay of Islands and at Notre Dame Bay to encourage the tourist trade. His most 'palatial' hotel would be the model: an 83 room facility in St. John's at the eastern terminus of the railway, luring tourists across the island. The cornerstone for his Avalon Hotel was actually laid in 1900 by Governor McCallum, on the site where the Newfoundland Hotel was eventually constructed, but contract squabbles with the government meant that only the foundation was completed.[84]

Other tourist hotels and lodges were built following the fad for 'rustic' architecture and furniture prevalent in the northeastern United States.[85] The creation of a rustic artifact world catering to American notions of the pioneer obviously added to Newfoundland's wilderness appeal. In contrast, the British clientele being lured by the CPR were looking for images of a new Swiss alpine wilderness, and CPR hotels were influenced by chalets built in a European style.[86] Newfoundland hotels such as the Log Cabin at Spruce Brook, near St. George's (figure 3), did not borrow from any longstanding vernacular tradition in the area (tourists at the time were not interested in anything vernacular, be it speech or buildings); instead, these structures played upon the American preoccupation with the romantic log cabin image as the essence of frontier life.[87] Rustic log buildings, designed to concur with American taste, were clearly the appropriate structures for a region where all things wild and rustic were expected. This construction style was not unique to Newfoundland, and similar buildings were erected in all regions where rustic wilderness was being marketed to tourists. Writing about similar structures in Maine, Mia Boynton has noted that 'They are architectural hybrids, born of a combination of national influences and local know-how. They partake of a somewhat mythologized "pioneer" imagery which is national rather than strictly local.'[88]

Courtesy of the Centre for Newfoundland Studies Archives, Memorial University, St. John's, NF.

Figure 3—The Log Cabin at Spruce Brook, c. 1925.

Besides Spruce Brook, a log hotel was built at Grand Falls (the Log Cabin Hotel), and another at St. George's;[89] in later years, the Gleneagles Hotel at Gander, operated by one of the Reid family, also consisted of a main log cabin building with private sleeping cabins grouped around it.[90] All these log hotels have disappeared, but their atmosphere can be judged from a description, written about 1900, of the Log Cabin at Spruce Brook, which had twenty-one bedrooms as well as tennis courts and other facilities:

> It is built of logs, which are finished on the inside and give a primitive effect to the general appearance of the rooms. Access to the rooms is had by a number of doors leading from rustic verandas. The windows give enough light to produce a subdued effect, and when open lead to the verandas. The columns, balustrades and furnishings are all of rustic work and native woods. The main entrance opens in the reception room, and the visitor is at once arrested by the noble proportions of an old-fashioned chimney and its enormous hearth, a solid mantel appropriately decorated and the whole surmounted by a magnificent pair of caribou horns, combine to make a picture not easily forgotten. Upon the floors are attractive rugs, including some skins of our famed caribou shot quite near the cabin. In the reading and smoking rooms a good stock of up-to-date literature is always available. In the dining-room, where meals are served at any hour to suit the convenience of the guests, the visitor is confronted with a bountiful supply of good things that would put many pretentious hotels to the blush and served in a manner that cannot help winning admiration. The building is a handsome roomy structure, admirably arranged for the purposes intended. It is literally embowered with shade trees, among which it is delightful to stroll; whose odours fill the air with incense, and whose gentle sighing in the summer breeze lulls tired souls to sweet repose.[91]

Besides these main hotel buildings, many proprietors built a series of small log cabins along the banks of particular fishing rivers (figure 4). These could be rented, and guides hired with complete provisioning, creating the

necessary social arrange-
ments for the recreational
tourist in what was now an
institutionalized natural
landscape.[92] The proprietors of the Spruce Brook
Log Cabin, for example,
supervised a series of log
cabins 'on all the best rivers on the West Coast—
Crabbes, Middle Bara-
chois, Fischells, Harrys
Brook, Loch Levan (on

Figure 4—Small overnight rustic cabins.

Highlands River), etc.'[93] On Crabbes River, the proprietor had 'three log
cabins' which could be 'hired by parties,' while Harrys Brook had 'many
small log cabins.'[94] They were usually one room structures, intended primarily to provide shelter, places where lunch could be easily prepared and
overnight accommodation occasionally obtained. The railway made arrangements with the hotel operators to provide transportation to the fishing
pools, either by freight train or by speeders—small hand-cars that made
special trips specifically to drop off hunters and fishermen (figure 5). There
was also a daily 'accommodation train' that catered to these sportsmen;
Selous noted that 'It travels slowly, time is of no object to it, and on being
hailed it will obligingly stop anywhere, independently of stations, and take
up passengers or deer carcases.'[95]

There were also private dwellings that fell clearly within this early
twentieth century fascination with rustic life in the wilderness. The presi-

Figure 5—Sportsmen on a railroad speeder.

dent of the Anglo-Newfoundland Development Company, which manufactured newsprint at Grand Falls, lived when in town at 'The Loghouse,' a horizontal log structure similar to the Log Cabin at Spruce Brook.[96] Probably the best example was the home of Victor Campbell, a British naval officer who came to Black Duck Brook in 1923 as a gentleman farmer.[97] His house design (figures 6 and 7) was probably influenced by the rustic

Courtesy of Photographic Services, Memorial University, St. John's, NF.

Figure 6—Exterior of the Victor Campbell house, Black Duck Brook.

architecture of buildings like the Log Cabin at Spruce Brook, but the plan may have originated elsewhere. Campbell owned a copy of William S. Wicks' widely-known *Log Cabins and Cottages: How to Build and Furnish Them*, which contained plans for both private dwellings and hotels (figure 8).[98] In his copy there are a series of pencilled sketches of a house (figure 9) closely resembling the one he finally built, and he may well have followed many of the book's suggestions.[99]

Courtesy of Photographic Services, Memorial University, St. John's, NF.

Figure 7—Interior of the Victor Campbell house, Black Duck Brook.

At times, as Nelson Graburn points out, 'Nature in the "raw" is nice but somewhat boring because there is no dialogue.' As he claims, 'Another way to get close to Nature's bosom is through her children, the people of Nature, once labelled Peasant and Primitive peoples and considered creatures of instinct. Interaction with them is possible and their naturalness and simplicity exemplifies all that is good in Nature herself.'[100] Tourists did not come to Newfoundland to experience local culture; instead, Newfoundlanders exhibiting the characteristics that Graburn mentions were there to

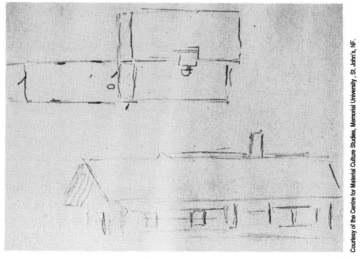

Figures 8 and 9—Plate from Victor Campbell's copy of Wicks' *Log Cabins and Cottages*, with pencil drawing below.

facilitate wilderness experiences. One tourist from Trenton, New Jersey, who visited in 1899 remarked that 'The guides and other assistants were willing, good natured fellows, and we were pleased with them very much.'[101] Another noted that wherever you went, the Newfoundland guide would be standing by, 'gaff in hand—eager to lay on the river's bank the result of your skill.'[102] Numerous accounts mention the stamina and skill of Newfoundlanders who guided sportsmen through the wilderness, their ability to improvise, to withstand any hardship and to answer any challenge. In the words of one tourist brochure, 'Inheriting the sterling traits of their English, Irish and Scotch ancestors, Newfoundlanders still exemplify their pioneering spirit which is amply borne out by the hardship they are called upon to endure in search of their livelihood in reaping the harvest of the sea.'[103]

What was often perceived as a lack of civilization enabled the New-foundlander to interact with the wilderness in ways that Americans could imagine having happened in their pioneer past. Thus the Newfoundlander was perceived as happy, energetic and somewhat childlike; one American, observing his guide kneeling in prayer, remarked: 'It touched me very deeply. I thought if this simple child of the forest had so much to be thankful for, how much we, a happy, prosperous people.'[104] This primitive happiness was apparently so pervasive that another writer remarked that 'no people in the world maintain a more comfortable and contented existence than the Newfoundland fishermen.'[105] A visitor, arriving in Port aux Basques, re-marked on the 'politeness of "the natives"'; 'beautiful flaxen-haired chil-dren...smile, but do not stare, and without exception, the boys lift their caps to you, it matters not whether you are man or woman.' And echoing the common image of the healthy Newfoundlander, the same visitor remarked that childrens' faces were 'like flowers, wind-blown, with cheeks of roses, skins like cream, and hair like a curly maze of yellow floss.' 'On a recent trip through Michigan,' she continued, 'I observed that out of every twenty school children, about twelve wore glasses and eight had weak eyes. In the six weeks I spent in Newfoundland, I never saw one single child who wore glasses, and only one with weak eyes, and he was a tiny cripple.'[106]

However, with increasing attention from outside tourists, visitors be-gan to comment on the differences in speech and customs of the local inhabitants. During this time period, both outsiders and upper class St. John's residents increasingly wrote about what was thought to be different about Newfoundlanders. This combination of interest by the outside visitor and the urban intelligentsia led to the creation of the image of the 'hardy Newfoundlander,' an image which in turn was then quickly appropriated by the local entrepreneur to be marketed to tourists looking for simple uncorrupted peoples.

The image of this sturdy Newfoundlander would be important to sportsmen looking for competent and ingenious guides. On the other hand, locals could point to certain characteristics as evidence of an emerging nation peopled by a unique genius. Thus, while most aspects of local culture (except for survival abilities related to the environment) were not marketed to tourists, outsiders did become intrigued by a number of daily behaviours which were considered different, and these often became symbolic of Newfoundland culture generally. Much like the custom of mummering in recent years, local speech, customs and beliefs were singled out as 'genuine' Newfoundland, and local residents themselves assumed these items as authentically local and unique.[107] In keeping with this, Moses Harvey, a prominent local writer and clergyman, suggested, for example, that a short visit to a small outport community might be of interest to the tourist in order to observe local curiosities; at Quidi Vidi, for example, visitors could 'enjoy a chat with the sturdy fishermen and their wives' whose 'insular peculiarities, linguistic oddities, and quaint views of things' formed 'an interesting study.'[108]

In was during this late nineteenth and early twentieth century period that a local interest in the study of folk culture began to develop. With comments by visitors on differences in speech or custom, local folk culture became the domain of the idle rich (either non-native Newfoundland residents or members of the monied classes)—a common development in many other countries—and the St. John's elite began to advocate the recording of unique Newfoundland customs in local newspapers and magazines. As one of them noted, the folk culture of the common person outside of St. John's was 'comparatively unknown to the entire world, and *even to ourselves.*'[109] Several writers—usually outsiders who had visited or settled in Newfoundland—documented local folklore items, and some were published in scholarly journals such as the *Journal of American Folklore*.[110] However, tourist guidebooks and sports travelogues appearing in places like Boston and New York rarely contained such material. If a tourist publication suggested that a local community should be visited, it would only be for picturesque reasons, an afternoon of photographs or sketching—certainly not to learn about the locals.

Increasingly interested in antiques, Americans were also drawn to the colony by the news that supposedly naive Newfoundlanders were oblivious to the value of local artifacts. Again, it was Newfoundland writers who promoted myths about the locals, pointing out that Newfoundlanders were neither aware of nor appreciative of their material heritage, and antiques were there for the taking. As P.T. McGrath noted, 'Curiosities, in the shape of old furniture, old silver and other articles of this kind, are often to be secured.'[111] Another writer hinted that even local merchants were not always aware of what they had: 'The lover of the antique will find in St. John's an answer to his prayer and no doubt hidden away in some of the shops are treasures awaiting those experts who know.'[112]

The Newfoundlander was often painted as the epitome of virtue, a guarantee that there would be little friction with the tourists he was guiding. The local population enjoyed its pleasures, but Newfoundland was a place free from many social ills; only when confronted with obvious improprieties by the visitor would a Newfoundlander become troublesome. As the expatriate Newfoundland Roman Catholic priest Richard Howley wrote in 1887:

> The Newfoundland fisherman undoubtedly drinks hard, at times of a less harmless liquid. Rum, and only rum, straight from the West Indies in Spanish and native bottoms, is his beloved invigorator. He is not however a persistent drinker...but he drinks thoroughly when about it. He becomes noisy but not usually quarrelsome. No country is more free

from acts of crime or violence than Newfoundland. Yet with all his soft
'slobbishness' of temperament the Newfoundlander is not a safe animal
to exasperate. Like the dog of the country he will bear any amount of
teazing and tantalizing from a kind master or a trusty friend, but is a
decidedly ugly customer for a recognized foe to deal with.[113]

One writer noted that Newfoundland was 'the most temperate portion of
the world'—free from the problems of drinking—and that most natives
'were hard-working and good-natured, and never swore.'[114] Even as late as
1950, one local writer, L.E.F. English, continued much of the imagery used
by Howley years earlier when portraying the hardy Newfoundlander;
English produced a collage of various folk with a Newfoundland dog as
the central image. Newfoundlanders, he wrote, are 'somewhat like the great
native canine that bears his name, kind and gentle and patient to a degree,
suffering ill-treatment stolidly until his patience is exhausted.'[115]

Much of this portrayal of the hardy Newfoundlander was curiously
one-sided, obviously aimed at impressing outsiders with the ability of local
residents to handle any physical difficulties of the visiting tourist, while at
the same time giving the local populace a distinctive nationalistic myth.
While much of the tourist literature portrayed the romantic image of the
noble Newfoundlander, other writers focused on the poverty, disease and
illiteracy prevalent at the time. For some—like Wilfred Grenfell—these
issues promoted their own particular reformist causes, while others—such
as Millais—simply were chronicling the many complex components of
everyday Newfoundland life. Indeed, local Newfoundland intellectuals
and apologists were sometimes disturbed at outsiders writing about the
negative aspects of their culture.[116]

Visitors began to arrive in increasing numbers, literally an invasion by
the 'army of tourists' that the Reids had worked hard to attract.[117] Over a
ten year period, the number of tourists had almost quadrupled (table 1),
although one apologist made the exaggerated claim that by 1913 some 7,000
tourists were visiting the island annually.[118] W. J. Carroll wrote of a 'coming
invasion,' an 'ever-increasing army,' in which all classes would be represented. However, the poem he used to describe the tourists who actually
arrived indicates that most came from the wealthier classes: 'The statesman,
lawyer, merchant, man of trade / Pants for the refuge of some rural shade
/ Where all his long anxieties forgot / Amid the charms of a sequestered
spot.'[119] The few visitors' lists that were printed show a liberal sprinkling
of leading American families of the time—Vanderbilts, Duponts, Biddels,
and the like.[120] The American Secretary of State and the Assistant Secretary
of War came to hunt caribou in 1904 and 1905; around the same time,
Senator Redfield Proctor of Vermont, Secretary of War in President Harri-
son's cabinet, fished at Codroy and Harrys Brook.[121] 'In the summer of 1900,
100 guests were at the "Log Cabin." Natives of many lands, Madras, India,
Savannah, Georgia, New York, Baltimore, Providence, R.I., New Haven,

TABLE 1
Number of Sportsmen or Tourists arriving in Newfoundland, 1903-13.

Year	Sportsmen or Tourists
1903	1,046
1904	1,029
1905	1,611
1906	1,862
1907	1,804
1908	2,086
1909	2,412
1910	2,372
1911	3,899
1912	3,677
1913	4,072

Source: *Royal Commission on the Natural Resources, Trade and Legislation of Certain Portions of His Majesty's Dominions: Minutes of Evidence Taken in Newfoundland in 1914.* Cd. 7898 (London 1915), 1.

Connecticut, Boston, Massachusetts, Chicago, and a number of Professors from Princeton University and fourteen doctors.'[122] Even in the twenties and thirties, tourist hotels like Afton Farm House in Tompkins were still catering to the gentleman tourist: he dressed properly, even when hunting or fishing, and although not demanding the luxuries of home, he did expect the occasional treat of special food or drink. As Graburn notes, 'tourists only choose to switch a *few* of their behavioral parameters at any one time, while retaining the vast majority of normal repertoires.'[123] Accordingly, the cuisine on the Newfoundland railway was weighed down with steaks (sirloin or tenderloin—with or without mushrooms), and accompanied by a wide liquor selection.[124]

As this rich upper class discovered the growing number of sports hotels in Newfoundland, many came back to the same establishment summer after summer. Particular areas became associated with Americans—the Little Codroy, for instance, 'was a favourite river with American anglers.'[125] According to Don Tompkins, two Connecticut senators returned to the hotel at South Branch owned by his father every summer for eight to ten years and knew everyone in the community by their first names. Tompkins remembers that most of the visitors were 'doctors, lawyers, professionals, clergymen, and millionaires.' One wealthy American bachelor came to South Branch to fish salmon for years, and when he became too old to fish, he returned just to sit and watch the other anglers. When he died, he specified that his ashes should be returned to his old fishing spot on the Codroy and scattered there, a wish that two of his old guides carried out.[126] And in 1919, Lord Morris noted that friends of his, 'a leading lawyer of Boston, and his wife,' had come to the Little River for the previous twenty years, and that the lawyer had had 'the distinction of having one of the pools on the river called after him.'[127]

Selling Newfoundland as a vast sports and health preserve peopled by childlike natives eager to act as guides and servants soon began to produce results, and as the twentieth century progressed a growing entrepreneurial class began to cash in on the influx of visitors. A wide variety of tourist hotels was constructed. Some of them were merely adaptations of existing homes, with additions for increased sleeping quarters. On the west coast, Afton Farm House in Tompkins was a leading hotel grafted onto an existing dwelling. Newer buildings were also constructed along the standard house forms of the day. The bungalow seemed to be one of the most popular, and Tompkins' hotel in South Branch was known specifically as 'The Bungalow.' Smaller versions were built as private lodges, such as Woodfords, also in South Branch. Such bungalows were also constructed near the railway for hunters; as one tourist advertisement explained, there were: 'Shooting bungalows within easy reach of the lordly caribou, the finest game in the new world.'[128]

As the twentieth century continued, wealthy Americans still travelled to Newfoundland, but the face of the colony's tourism was gradually to change. In 1923 the Newfoundland government took over the railway from the financially troubled Reid company. Traffic on the line was too light—even with the tourist trade—to make a profit.[129] With the takeover, tourist promotion was appropriated by different interest groups, and new themes were soon to appear. Tourism was no longer tied directly to a rail line, most of which travelled through a vast uninhabited wilderness, and therefore its promotion did not have to concentrate on forms of nature tourism. As early as 1906 calls had come for some type of tourist association, based on models found in the northeastern United States and the Maritimes.[130] The Newfoundland Tourist and Publicity Association, an organization representing private tourism entrepreneurs was eventually founded in 1925.[131] While this new association realized that health, sport and wilderness would still draw visitors—as much of its publicity proclaimed—it now added a new theme: historical and cultural tourism.

The argument that Newfoundland could be promoted through its history and culture had been made before. H. F. Shortis, involved with the Newfoundland Historical Society during the early years of the twentieth century, wrote an article in 1910 that pointed out that Americans might well be drawn to the island if common historical connections were promoted. He used as examples the ties between Ferryland and Maryland. He also noted that it was 'not generally known that one of our oldest and most noted families, the Pinns, of Mosquito...were cousins of the Penns of Pennsylvania.' Besides sharing much common heritage, Americans would be interested in 'military relics' if excavations could be conducted at Castle Hill in Placentia. According to Shortis, if 'a few of these old records' were 'published in American magazines,' such publicity 'would bring thousands of their tourists to visit Newfoundland.'[132] However, Shortis' arguments seem to have fallen on deaf ears, for it was not until the Reid Newfoundland Company handed the railway back to the government, and tourist promotion was taken over by other agencies, that history and culture were seen as marketable commodities. The Reids may well have decided that the historical tourism that would center largely on the island's east coast would not be lucrative enough. Obviously influenced by the success of museums like Williamsburg, government and private promoters began to realize that visitors were interested in seeing the past and were willing to pay to do so. Brochures began to provide brief, not always accurate sketches of the vast panorama of the island's history. Writers were careful to mention that Newfoundland was indeed older than the United States. If Americans enjoyed their 'settler days,' then Newfoundland had something even older to offer. It was claimed that people were living in Newfoundland long before Jamestown, or before 'Plymouth Rock felt the touch of the Pilgrims' feet.' Tourists were advised to 'linger among its historical regions where Cabot, Cartier, Lord Baltimore, Captain John Mason and Sir W. Alexander pioneered.' In the same brochure, the Newfoundland Tourist and Publicity Commission, a government agency, hedging its bets, prefaced the old tourist themes of health, sport and wilderness with the comment: 'Historical facts and figures are sometimes dull but such is not the case where Nature is concerned.'[133]

In subsequent years historical and cultural themes were increasingly promoted, so that today, coming to experience 'authentic' Newfoundland culture is as important as is the enjoyment of the natural environment. The legacy of the Reid Newfoundland Company's promotion of tourism may well partly explain, however, why both the government and private entrepreneurs were so late in selling the 'heritage' of the island to the outsider. While New England was opening historic homes and museums to draw tourists in the early twentieth century, Newfoundland has moved in this direction only in the past twenty years. The real impact of the promotion of early tourist Newfoundland as one vast uninhabited nature preserve may still be felt today. Historical and cultural attractions are often underfunded, poor second cousins still to those attractions of scenery, fin, fur and feather promoted by the Reids.

NOTES

*This paper was initially presented as part of the Canada Week Series sponsored by the Canadian Studies Center, University of Maine, Orono, Maine, April, 1984; I would like to thank Edward D. Ives for inviting me to speak. Later versions were given at the Folklore Studies Association of Canada meeting, Ottawa, Ontario, June, 1984, and the joint meeting of the American Folklore Society and the Folklore Studies Association of Canada, St. John's, Newfoundland, October, 1991. Those who helped with this essay in numerous ways include: Gerhard P. Bassler, Gilbert Higgins, Richard MacKinnon, David Taylor and Don Tompkins. Iona Bulgin, James Hiller, Peter Neary and Shane O'Dea offered comments on several drafts.

1   Reid Newfoundland Company, *Newfoundland and Labrador: Unrivalled Resorts for the Tourist, Health Seeker and Sportsman* (St. John's c. 1910), 3.

2   See E.J. Hart, *The Selling of Canada: The CPR and the Beginnings of Canadian Tourism* (Banff 1983), 7, 22, 176; James B. Hedges, *Building the Canadian West: The Land and Colonization Policies of the Canadian Pacific Railway* (New York 1939), 94.

3   'Our Great Developer,' *Christmas Annual* (St. John's), 1909, 6.

4   For an overview of historical studies of tourism, see John Towner and Geoffrey Wall, 'History and Tourism,' *Annals of Tourism Research* 18, no. 1 (1991): 71-84.

5   Valerie L. Smith, 'Introduction,' 2-3, and Nelson H.H. Graburn, 'Tourism: The Sacred Journey,' 26-8, both in Valerie L. Smith (ed.), *Hosts and Guests: The Anthropology of Tourism* (Philadelphia 1977).

6   Dean MacCannell has argued that the touristic search for 'authentic' cultural experiences is the primary defining characteristic of modern culture. See his *The Tourist: A New Theory of the Leisure Class* (New York 1976).

7   Dennison Nash, 'Tourism as a Form of Imperialism' in Smith (ed.), *Hosts and Guests*, 36-8.

8   An overview of this promotional literature can be found in Susan T. Williams, 'Images of Newfoundland in Promotional Literature, 1890-1914' (unpublished MA thesis, McGill University 1980). See also George M. Story, 'Guides to Newfoundland,' *Newfoundland Quarterly* 75, no.4 (1980): 17-23.

9   For such popular fictional heroes see Roderick Nash, *The Call of the Wild, (1900-1916)* (New York 1970), 240-55.

10   Patrick O'Flaherty, *The Rock Observed: Studies in the Literature of Newfoundland* (Toronto 1979), 83.

11   Ibid., 85-6, 102-10.

12   Jean Baudrillard, *America*, translated by Chris Turner (London 1988), 94. See also Roger D. Abrahams, 'Moving in America,' *Prospects* 3 (1977): 63-82.

13   Henry David Thoreau, *A Yankee in Canada, with Anti-Slavery and Reform Papers* (New York 1969), reprint of 1892 original, 39. See also Roderick Nash, *Wilderness and the American Mind* (New Haven 1967).

14   Francis Parkman, *Journals*, ed. by Mason Wade (New York 1947), vol. 1, 31.

15 Roderick Nash, 'Wilderness and Man in North America,' in J.G. Nelson and R.C. Scace (eds.), *The Canadian National Parks: Today and Tomorrow* (Calgary 1968), vol. 1, 73. Nash points out that 'the Canadian public's sensitivity to and enthusiasm for wilderness values lags at least two generations behind opinion in the United States' (75).

16 For the cooperation of government and private enterprise in Canada's national parks, see J.G. Nelson, 'Canada's National Parks: Past, Present and Future,' in Geoffrey Wall and John Marsh (eds.), *Recreational Land Use: Perspectives on its Evolution in Canada* (Ottawa 1982), 43-4, 52-8.

17 James Hiller, *The Newfoundland Railway, 1881-1949*, pamphlet (St. John's 1981), 26.

18 James Hiller, 'The Railway and Local Politics in Newfoundland, 1870-1901' in James Hiller and Peter Neary (eds.), *Newfoundland in the Nineteenth and Twentieth Centuries: Essays in Interpretation* (Toronto 1980), 123, 128-9: James Hiller, 'The Origins of the Pulp and Paper Industry in Newfoundland,' *Acadiensis* 11, no. 2 (1982): 42-68.

19 *Daily News* (St. John's), 23 Jan. 1890.

20 Reid Newfoundland Company, *Newfoundland and Labrador*, 2.

21 Reid Newfoundland Company, *Fishing and Shooting in Newfoundland and Labrador* (St. John's 1903), 16.

22 Nathan Lowrey, 'Tales of the Northern Woods: The History and Traditions of the Maine Guide,' *Northeast Folklore* 28 (1989): 75.

23 Ian McKay, 'Tartanism Triumphant: The Construction and Uses of Scottishness in Nova Scotia, 1933-54,' unpublished manuscript; 'Among the Fisherfolk: J.F.B. Livesay and the Invention of Peggy's Cove,' *Journal of Canadian Studies*, 23, nos. 1-2 (1988), 29-31; 'The Five Ages of Nova Scotia Tourism,' *New Maritimes* 5, nos. 11-12 (July-Aug., 1987), 8.

24 *Newfoundland Illustrated Tribune Xmas Number* (St. John's), 1902, 22.

25 Maine Central Railroad, *To Hunt and Fish in Maine, New Brunswick and Newfoundland* (Portland n.d.).

26 *Daily News*, 19 March 1908.

27 W.J. Carroll, 'The Coming Invasion,' *Newfoundland Illustrated Tribune Christmas Number*, 1906, 17.

28 'Our Great Developer,' 6.

29 W.G. Reeves, 'Newfoundlanders in the "Boston States": a Study in Early Twentieth-Century Community and Counterpoint,' *Newfoundland Studies* 6, no. 1 (1990): 48.

30 W.J. Carroll, 'Newfoundland: A Sportsman's Paradise,' *Newfoundland Quarterly* 5, no. 1 (1905): 1.

31 W.J. Carroll, 'The Future Recreation Ground of America,' *Newfoundland Illustrated Tribune Christmas Number*, 1911, 16.

32 Carroll, 'The Coming Invasion,' 17.

33 E. Pauline Johnson, 'Rhapsodies About Newfoundland,' *Newfoundland Illustrated Tribune Christmas Number*, 1906, 16.

34 Reid Newfoundland Company, *Newfoundland and Labrador*, 74.

35   Moses Harvey, 'Newfoundland,' in Karl Baedeker, *The Dominion of Canada with Newfoundland and an Excursion to Alaska: Handbook for Travellers* (Leipzig 1894), 99.

36   Nelson H.H. Graburn, 'The Anthropology of Tourism,' *Annals of Tourism Research* 10, no. 1 (1983): 11.

37   Reid Newfoundland Company, *Newfoundland and Labrador*, 4-5.

38   F.C. Selous, 'The Woodland Caribou in Newfoundland,' in D.W. Prowse (ed.), *The Newfoundland Guide Book, 1905: Including Labrador and St. Pierre* (London 1905), 56.

39   'Bay of Islands World Famous Pleasure Resort,' *Western Star* (Corner Brook), 19 July 1916.

40   Johnson, 'Rhapsodies about Newfoundland,' 17.

41   See Kenneth Thompson, 'Wilderness and Health in the Nineteenth Century,' *Journal of Historical Geography* 2, no. 2 (1976), 145-61.

42   See 'Climate,' in J.R. Smallwood (ed.), *Encyclopedia of Newfoundland and Labrador*, vol. 1 (St. John's 1981), 452-3.

43   Prowse, *Newfoundland Guide Book, 1905*, 32.

44   Carroll, 'The Future Recreation Ground,' 16.

45   Newfoundland Railway, *Dominion of Newfoundland: Britain's Oldest Colony* (St. John's c. 1926), 2.

46   Maine Central Railroad, *To Hunt and Fish*, 4.

47   J.G. Millais, *Newfoundland and Its Untrodden Ways* (New York 1967), reprint of 1907 original, 150.

48   Reid Newfoundland Company, *Fishing and Shooting*, 8.

49   Reid Newfoundland Company, *Golden Age of Newfoundland's Advancement: Striking Portrayal of Its Progress the Past Fifteen Years* (St. John's 1910), 6.

50   Prowse, *Newfoundland Guide Book, 1905*, 3.

51   'Newfoundland, The Sportsman's Paradise,' *Western Star*, 22 Dec. 1915.

52   Lord Morris, 'Rod and Gun in Newfoundland,' *Commercial Annual* (St. John's), 1919, 12.

53   *Christmas Chimes* (St. John's), 1913, advertisement opposite p.1.

54   Richard Hibbs, *Newfoundland for Business and Pleasure* (St. John's 1925), 182-3, 186-8.

55   Wakeman Holberton, 'Newfoundland Caribou,' *Newfoundland Illustrated Tribune Holiday Number*, 1899, 1.

56   Carroll, 'Newfoundland,' 1.

57   Reid Newfoundland Company, *Fishing and Shooting*, 17.

58   Quoted in D.W. Prowse (ed.), *The Newfoundland Guide Book, 1911: Including Labrador and St. Pierre*, 3rd ed. (London 1911), 73.

59   Morris, 'Rod and Gun,' 10. See also the photograph of 'A Group of Sports at Howley' which shows a number of hunters waiting at the station with their kill in S.H. Parsons, 'With Rod, Gun and Camera,' *Parsons' Xmas Annual* (St. John's), 1900, 17. The photograph of sportsmens' tents near Howley appears in *Christmas Bells* (St. John's), 1911, opposite p. 10.

60   H. Hesketh Prichard, *Hunting Camps in Wood and Wilderness* (London 1910), 83.

61 There are numerous illustrations of such 'good heads' in the various promotional guides. For examples see Millais, *Newfoundland and its Untrodden Ways.*

62 Both quoted in Morris, 'Rod and Gun,' 10-11.

63 Holberton, 'Newfoundland Caribou,' 11.

64 Hibbs, *Newfoundland for Business and Pleasure*, 186-7.

65 See Prowse, *Newfoundland Guide Book, 1905*, plate opposite page 36.

66 Hibbs, *Newfoundland for Business and Pleasure*, 182.

67 H. Hesketh Prichard, 'Caribou Shooting in Newfoundland' in Prowse, *Newfoundland Guide Book, 1905*, 47.

68 C.H. Palmer, *The Salmon Rivers of Newfoundland: A Descriptive Account of the Various Rivers of the Island* (Boston 1928), 264.

69 Millais, *Newfoundland and Its Untrodden Ways*, 295.

70 Robert E. Holloway, *Through Newfoundland with the Camera* (St. John's 1905), 144.

71 Reid Newfoundland Company, *Newfoundland and Labrador*, 3-4.

72 Palmer, *Salmon Rivers*, 250.

73 Karl Baedeker, *The Dominion of Canada with Newfoundland and an Excursion to Alaska*, 3rd ed. (Leipzig 1907), 123.

74 J.G. Millais, 'The Natural History of the Newfoundland Caribou,' in Prowse, *Newfoundland Guide Book, 1905*, 35-6.

75 Nash, *Wilderness*, 1.

76 Reid Newfoundland Company, *Newfoundland and Labrador*, 5.

77 F.C. Selous, *Recent Hunting Trips in British North America* (London 1907), 134.

78 Quoted in Newfoundland Railway, *Dominion of Newfoundland*, 22.

79 Reid Newfoundland Company, *Newfoundland and Labrador*, 4.

80 'No Longer Terra Incognita,' *Newfoundland Illustrated Tribune Xmas Number*, 1900, 2.

81 Hibbs, *Newfoundland for Business and Pleasure*, 185.

82 Quoted in Morris, 'Rod and Gun,' 13.

83 Hibbs, *Newfoundland for Business and Pleasure*, 190.

84 P.K. Devine, *Ye Olde St. John's* (St. John's 1936), 170-1; 'The Atlantic Hotel Played Important Role in St. John's,' *Evening Telegram* (St. John's), 3 April 1972; J.W. McGrath, 'R.G. Reid and the Newfoundland Railway' (Newfoundland Historical Society lecture, 1971); P.T. McGrath, *Newfoundland in 1911* (London 1911), 57; Alfred R. Penney, 'The Newfoundland Railway: Newfoundland Epic,' in J.R. Smallwood (ed.), *The Book of Newfoundland*, vol. 3 (St. John's 1967), 491.

85 See Craig Gilborn, 'Adirondack Hickory,' in Mary Jean Madigan (ed.), *Nineteenth Century Furniture: Innovation, Revival and Reform* (New York 1982), 148-53; Craig Gilborn, *Adirondack Furniture and the Rustic Tradition* (New York 1987); Ralph Kylloe, *Rustic Furniture* (Lexington 1989).

86 John A. Jakle, *The Tourist: Travel in Twentieth-Century North America* (Lincoln 1985), 81; Hart, *Selling of Canada*, 81-95.

87 See Mac E. Barrick, 'The Log House as Cultural Symbol,' *Material Culture* 18, no. 1 (1986): 1-19.

88 Mia Boynton, 'A Gift of Native Knowledge: The History of Russell's Motor Camps in Rangeley, Maine,' *Northeast Folklore* 28 (1989): 4.

89 Prowse, *Guide* (1911), 3, 73; Baedeker, *Dominion* (1907), 123; 'Popular West Coast Summer Resort for Sale,' *Western Star*, 31 Oct. 1917.

90 R.H. Tait, *Newfoundland: A Summary of the History and Development of Britain's Oldest Colony from 1497 to 1939* (New York 1939), 176.

91 Mrs. W.S. March, 'The Coronation Year Should See a Tourist Association in Newfoundland,' *Newfoundland Quarterly* 2, no. 1 (1902): 18.

92 See MacCannell, *The Tourist*, 82.

93 Newfoundland Railway, *Dominion of Newfoundland*, 21.

94 Newfoundland Tourist and Publicity Commission, *Newfoundland Invites You* (St. John's n.d.), 14, 16.

95 Selous, *Recent Hunting Trips*, 78.

96 *Christmas Bells*, 1909, 1, and photograph opposite 11.

97 Robert H. Cuff, Melvin Baker and Robert D.W. Pitt (eds.), *Dictionary of Newfoundland and Labrador Biography* (St. John's 1990), 47; Smallwood (ed.), *Encyclopedia of Newfoundland and Labrador*, 318.

98 William S. Wicks, *Log Cabins and Cottages: How to Build and Furnish Them*, 8th ed. (New York [1909]). For its impact on the rustic architecture tradition, see Gilborn, *Adirondack Furniture*, 43, 57.

99 Campbell's copy was deposited in the Queen Elizabeth II Library, Memorial University, St. John's, around 1980; it is now missing. Slides of the pencil sketches are on deposit in the Centre for Material Culture Studies, Memorial University.

100 Graburn, 'Tourism,' 27.

101 Maine Central Railroad, *To Hunt and Fish*, 53.

102 Palmer, *Salmon Rivers*, 12.

103 Newfoundland Tourist and Publicity Commission, *Newfoundland Invites You*, 4.

104 William S. Thomas, *Trails and Tramps in Alaska and Newfoundland* (New York 1913), 210.

105 *Golden Age*, 8.

106 Johnson, 'Rhapsodies,' 16.

107 For a discussion of attempts to isolate 'genuine' Newfoundland culture see Gerald L. Pocius, *A Place to Belong: Community Order and Everyday Space in Calvert, Newfoundland* (Montreal and Kingston 1991), 24-5, 274-9; for the recent fixation on mummering as distinctively Newfoundland see Gerald L. Pocius, 'The Mummers Song in Newfoundland: Intellectuals, Revivalists and Cultural Nativism,' *Newfoundland Studies* 4, no. 1 (1988): 57-85.

108 Harvey, 'Newfoundland,' 108.

109 Isaac C. Morris, 'The Old Fisher-Folk,' *Newfoundland Quarterly* 1, no. 3 (1901): 20.

110 For example, Arthur C. Waghorne, 'Christmas Customs in Newfoundland'; William Whittle, 'Christmas "Fools" and "Mummers" in Newfoundland'; Arthur Waghorne, 'Hunting the Wren,' all in the *Journal of American Folklore* 6, no. 20 (1893): 63-5; no. 21 (1893): 143-4. See also in this same journal George Patterson, 'Notes on the Dialect of the People of Newfoundland,' 8, no. 28 (1895): 27-40; 9, no. 32 (1896): 19-37; 10, no. 38 (1897): 203-13; 'Superstitions in Newfoundland,' 9, no. 34 (1896): 222-3; 'Folk-Lore in Newfoundland,' 10, no.

38 (1897): 214-15; A.F. Waghorne, 'Death Signs and Weather Signs from Newfoundland and Labrador,' 13, no. 51 (1900): 297-9.

111 McGrath, *Newfoundland in 1911*, 208.

112 Newfoundland Tourist and Publicity Commission, *Newfoundland* (St. John's, n.d.).

113 Quoted in O'Flaherty, *The Rock Observed*, 90-1.

114 McGrath, *Newfoundland*, 206; Millais, *Newfoundland*, 81.

115 L.E.F. English, *Newfoundland Past and Present* (Toronto 1950), 118.

116 For Grenfell's focus on poverty and starvation see Ronald Rompkey, *Grenfell of Labrador: A Biography* (Toronto 1991), 85-8.

117 'The Great Sir Robert Reid: The Man Who Built the Railway,' reprinted in Smallwood (ed.), *The Book of Newfoundland*, 573. For comments about tourism as a kind of 'secondary invasion' similar to a military invasion, see Louis Turner and John Ash, *The Golden Hordes: International Tourism and the Pleasure Periphery* (New York 1976), 30.

118 Hibbs, *Newfoundland for Business and Pleasure*, 199.

119 Carroll, 'Coming Invasion,' 17.

120 For example Reid Newfoundland Company, *Newfoundland and Labrador*, 67-9.

121 Carroll, 'Coming Invasion,' 17.

122 Hibbs, *Newfoundland for Business and Pleasure*, 181

123 Graburn, 'Anthropology of Tourism,' 22.

124 Reid Newfoundland Company, *Fishing and Shooting*, 45.

125 Prowse, *Newfoundland Guide Book, 1905*, 123.

126 Interview with Don Tompkins, Stephenville, Newfoundland, March, 1984.

127 Morris, 'Rod and Gun,' 12.

128 'Newfoundland, The Tourists' Paradise,' *Christmas Bells*, 1909, 15.

129 See Hiller, 'The Railway and Local Politics,' 141-2.

130 Carroll, 'Coming Invasion,' 17.

131 Douglas J. Wheeler, 'The Boom in Tourism,' in Smallwood (ed.), *The Book of Newfoundland*, 578.

132 H.F. Shortis, 'The Tourist Traffic,' *Christmas Chimes*, 1910, 10-11. This was reprinted in 1911 in the *Newfoundland Illustrated Tribune Christmas Number*.

133 Newfoundland Tourist and Publicity Commission, *Come to Britain's Oldest Colony* (St. John's n.d.), 3.

Self-Help, Charity, and Individual Responsibility: the Political Economy of Social Policy in Newfoundland in the 1920s

James Overton

The Ignorant Masses (1928)[1]

The Social Uplifters, those eminent sifters
Of merit and poor people's needs,
Went down to the slums to regenerate bums
And do meritorious deeds.
We washed them, we dressed them, with libraries blessed them,
We prayed with those ignorant mobs;
And the wretches were hateful, and vilely ungrateful,
And said what they wanted was jobs.

Our noble Committee then searched through the City
To find all the fallen and lost;
We learned how they came to be living in shame—
This, mind you, at no little cost.
We swamped them with tracts and statistical facts,
But the creatures were terribly rude;
They acknowledged 'twas nice to be free from all vice,
But they said what they wanted was food.

They're just as God made them—It's useless to aid them,
The brutes do not ask for reform;
Intellectual feasts are all wasted on beasts
Who want to be fed or kept warm.
Let them keep their allotted position besotted
And blind! When you bid them advance,
These ignorant asses, the underworld classes
Will say all they want is a chance.

THE DEVELOPMENT OF social policy in Newfoundland has received little attention from academics.[2] Even the details of the development of policy in some areas remain sketchy. More neglected still has been the question of how and why particular social problems became the focus of attention and action. Few studies do more than touch on the politics of social policy, and even fewer allow those who are the objects of policy to appear in accounts as anything more than 'problems.'[3] Therefore, one of the aims of this paper is to outline an approach to social policy which places the development of such policy in its historical and political context.

What developed in the first quarter of the twentieth century in New-foundland was a fairly wide-ranging, if limited, reform movement which focused its attention on medical and social problems. An early concern was with tuberculosis and health, but by the 1920s attention was also being directed towards child welfare, youth, housing, and poverty. It is with this phase of the reform movement that this paper is concerned. The movement was led by philanthropically minded members of the business and profes-sional classes of St. John's and emphasized self-help, individual responsi-bility, and, to a limited extent, charity, as the solutions to social problems, rather than an expanded role for the state.

This study investigates the political and economic climate in which this conservative movement emerged, and examines its ideas and practices by focusing on health care, and relief to the destitute. Particular attention is given to the activities of the Charity Organization Bureau (COB) established in 1925 in St. John's, following the disturbing revelations about public relief administration contained in the report, discussed below, of the Hollis Walker enquiry.

Paths to reform

Well before the end of World War I the labouring classes of Newfoundland had organized to improve their conditions of life. As in Britain and most other self-governing British colonies, the early twentieth century saw the rise of a 'mass-organized and politically conscious labour movement.'[4] The most spectacular organization to emerge was the Fishermen's Protective Union (FPU) led by William F. Coaker.[5] Founded in 1908, the union had over 20,000 members at the peak of its power. The FPU aimed to improve the lot of producers in the fishery and to 'rationalize and modernize' the industry.[6] It sought to weaken the hold of the credit system by establishing a trading company with forty branch stores, and tried to improve working conditions for loggers and sealers. It campaigned as well for old age pensions, improved education, small rural hospitals, work for the unem-ployed, and industrial development. With its move into formal politics, the union adopted a balance of power strategy, supporting the party which would do the most for Newfoundland's 'toilers.'[7] With a maximum of thirteen members in the House of Assembly, the FPU was able to exert some influence, and gain some concessions for those it represented. Union mem-bers of the Assembly joined the wartime national governments of Edward

Morris and William Lloyd. Coaker was a minister without portfolio, and George Grimes, who had an explicitly socialist orientation, was appointed to the Food Control Board.[8]

Another ambitious union undertaking was the formation of the New-foundland Industrial Workers' Association (NIWA) in April 1917.[9] This was a general union which sought both to organize 'all classes of workers from clerks to manual labourers,' and to act as a national labour federation.[10] It aimed to organize new unions and to act as a legislative lobby. The association was based in St. John's, but had branches in Port aux Basques, Botwood, Grand Falls and Whitbourne. In 1918 the NIWA claimed a membership of 3,500. It published a weekly paper (*The Industrial Worker*), operated a co-operative store, and became increasingly influential.[11] The membership of the NIWA was diverse. Railway employees formed the core of the organization, but it was supported by many St. John's unions. It also attracted the support of some reform minded members of the middle class and 'socialists' such as Joseph R. Smallwood and George Grimes.[12] The NIWA also established a women's branch with Julia Salter Earle, an em-ployee of the House of Assembly, as president.[13] The NIWA took up important issues such as the cost of living, the eight hour day, a minimum wage, and the control of child labour. It pressed for a labour department to deal with such issues, and to act as a kind of employment exchange. The NIWA was also a self-help organization, and attempted a programme of land development (allotment gardens) during World War I.[14] Like the FPU, the NIWA moved into electoral politics. In 1919 a new workingman's party contested elections in St. John's, but without success. NIWA members, including E.J. Whitty, the leader of protests by the unemployed in St. John's in the early 1920s, and Julia Salter Earle, also ran in municipal elections in St. John's, but again without success.[15]

Wartime inflation, resulting in part from merchant profiteering, was one of the first concerns of the NIWA. The establishment of a Food Control Board in 1917 and some limited control of food prices was an early if minor victory. Another was the official recognition signalled by representation both on the board, and on a post-war commission enquiring into the high cost of living.[16] All in all the war saw the strengthening of organized labour and some acknowledgement that its voice should be heard. Other move-ments for reform emerged in the period. The women's suffrage movement gained momentum during and immediately after the war, and the Great War Veterans' Association of Newfoundland (GWVA) was formed in 1918. This grew out of an association of returned soldiers and rejected volunteers, and with the NIWA's help the GWVA eventually gained official recogni-tion.[17]

Immediately following the war there was an atmosphere of radicalism and optimism in the countries involved in the conflict. The mood in New-foundland was typical. Working class organizations actively sought reforms, women demanded the vote, and groups like the GWVA pressed for government attention to the problems of those they represented. An *Evening Telegram* editorial captures well the mood early in 1919:

> A feeling of general unrest is beginning to manifest itself throughout this Colony, and unconfined to any particular class is spreading and developing...While the great conflict was raging every person was doing their best to help the Allied cause to Victory. That victory has now been won, and the thoughts which were directed towards that end are now moving towards conditions at home...The West has awakened; the North is awakening. The masses of the people are throwing off the lethargy of the past and are beginning to ask questions...Newfoundland is not going to be permitted to shirk the new responsibilities which have come to her because of the new order of things...to carry out certain measures for the betterment of those who fought our battles...Promises have been listened to in the past. Performance is needed to-day.[18]

The masses were on the move and unrest was in the air. In the wake of the Russian revolution this caused a great deal of unease. The threat of Bolshevism hung like a dark cloud over the middle class and in the Newfoundland press the Bolshevik 'disease or...mania' was regularly denounced.[19] Indeed, the post-war world was a threatening place for many middle class people, who thought themselves surounded by 'social, economic and industrial disturbances, socialistic outbreaks and similar evidences of retrogressive social and political movements.'[20]

Returning veterans were the focus of much public concern, and many suggestions for reform were linked with the broad question of rewarding the sacrifices made by those who, in the rhetoric of the time, had fought for freedom. But there was also an awareness that reform might be necessary in order to counter any tendency toward dissatisfaction or even radicalism on the part of this group. In Newfoundland, as elsewhere, a home fit for heroes would have to be one with substantial improvements in material conditions. If the war had been fought for democracy, now it was time for democracy to become a reality. It was argued that those who had survived had a special responsibility to those who had selflessly sacrificed themselves. No doubt feelings of guilt among the survivors reinforced this sense of responsibility.[21] For Liberal politician and newspaper editor H.M. Mosdell—the top official of the Department of Public Health and Welfare from 1932-44—the government of the country was a sacred trust. It was the duty of those who held the trust to ensure that the nation became a monument worthy of those who had sacrificed themselves.[22] This impetus towards reform was supported by the lobbying efforts of the GWVA under the leadership of its founding president Harold Mitchell, managing director of a firm of brokers and customs agents, and Major Bertram Butler, its vice-president.[23]

There were other pressures towards reform. The poor physical condition of the population had been dramatically revealed by wartime recruiting. Some 47 per cent of volunteers and 57 per cent of conscripts had been rejected as medically unfit,[24] and those concerned about national vitality felt an urgent need to do something to improve the quality of the country's manpower. A movement promoting the conservation of human life pre-dated the Great War,[25] fuelled by concerns about national and imperial efficiency. In Newfoundland it had led to the establishment of an anti-tu-berculosis campaign and the beginnings of a public health movement. But it was the war which really stimulated the human conservation movement. Newfoundland's Medical Health Officer, Dr. Robert A. Brehm, put it this way in his report for 1916:

> In every enlightened country great attention has been paid during recent years to the saving of infant and and child life, and this move-ment has lately received a great impetus on account of the terrible sacrifice of life in the war.[26]

The child welfare movement emerged as a major force for reform in 1917,[27] the offspring of the elite, which both started and supported it. Public health nurses from New York were hired to work in St. John's. The Women's Patriotic Association, organized in 1914 to help the war effort on the home front, became involved at the end of the war. It collected money to pay the salaries of three nurses and provided free milk for children, and food and clothing for the needy.[28] The movement led to the more efficient registration of births, the training of midwives, and eventually to the opening of the Child Welfare Centre.

The war also stimulated limited action on the medical front. However, much of what was done was undertaken by volunteers and charitable organizations, and progress was slow and halting. New hospitals and centres for treating tuberculosis were opened to cater to the needs of sick and injured servicemen.[29] The Board of Health moved forward with a disinfection program, and a start was made on sanitary and food inspection. Vital statistics were collected and analysed, and measures for the reporting and control of infectious diseases were improved.[30] But health reformers recognized that much more state involvement would be needed to solve the country's health problems. Brehm, for instance, argued that the key to improvement was the replacement of an obsolete health system with one more suited to 'modern requirements.'[31] He recognized that hospitaliza-tion played a key role in keeping down the death rate from many infectious diseases—those who had access to medical facilities were less at risk than those who did not.[32] Since there were few rural hospitals and a limited number of doctors, Brehm advocated the creation of a district nurse system as a feasible way to provide minimal health care for many Newfoundlan-ders.

Most of what was done during the war to improve health conditions was confined to St. John's. In rural areas there was virtually no change, and there was no real sign that the state was prepared now to take a more active role in promoting health. Some small rural hospitals were opened, but these were mainly financed by public subscription. And a scheme was developed to provide nursing services, the impetus coming from Lady Constance Harris, the wife of Governor Sir Charles A. Harris (1917-22).[33] With government endorsement, influential St. John's people organized an outport nursing scheme in 1919 with nurses recruited in Great Britain.

Concerns about national efficiency came together with other anxieties after the war. In particular, it was the threat of unrest which gave arguments for reform an urgency and importance, and the need for 'reconstruction' was widely recognized and supported. The *Evening Telegram* spoke of 'the new order of things' and the need to 'make provision for the men...returning from "over there."'[34] A prominent businessman writing in the same paper argued for 'a thorough systematic business governmental programme of reconstruction' in order to 'build up a new dominion.'[35] He went on to talk of 'a gigantic Housing Scheme'—'homes fit for heroes' in Britain should have their parallel in Newfoundland with 'the building of one thousand houses for our workingmen and industrial workers, at a fair and reasonable rent. Comfortable, pure homes.' He also advocated a scheme to ensure that ex-servicemen would 'become producers of the country, and not a barnacle upon the state':

> A new start in life, money to be advanced at reasonable rates of interest, grants of land and houses built. Motor fishing boats fully equipped with traps, lines and twines, a fit out such as the above to every soldier fisherman and fisherman of the navy who has volunteered and fought for their country.[36]

Soldiers should be given 'first claim' on civil service jobs, a national shipyard should be constructed, and new industries started. Such a programme would be both a 'blessing to the living' and 'an everlasting memorial to the dead.' Such proposals as this were given added force by the criticism of the government's treatment of war veterans, already being voiced in early 1919. There was much talk of change, and impatience for action. A poem, 'The Old "Ding Dong",' printed in the *Evening Telegram*, conveyed this well:

> *We are tired of the same old talking,*
> *We are tired of the old ding dong.*
> *Our eyes are weak and weary,*
> *From reading those letters long.*
> *All telling the same old story,*
> *All promising glorious things*
> *Of the housing schemes quite hoary, hoary,*
> *They've been promised for several springs.*
>
> *Oh quit the writing and talking,*
> *And take up the shovel and pick.*
> *Let us hear the sound of a hammer*
> *A making a sill from a stick.*

Let us see one upright-erected,
'Twill banish our trouble and care.
Do something for truth I will tell you
We are sick of this blooming hot air.[37]

The Newfoundland Board of Trade joined in the call for a new New-foundland. At a special meeting in January 1919, Walter B. Grieve (of Baine Johnston and Co.) and Reuben F. Horwood (of the Horwood Lumber Co.) discussed 'our obligations to those who delivered us from the perils that threatened us.'[38] Both men were philanthopists and had been involved in the Newfoundland Patriotic Association, formed during the war. They now advocated improved education, better housing and 'the care of child life.' Soldiers and sailors did 'not want charity, but rather a helping hand.' And this, they suggested, should be offered. Horwood argued that 'labor is the most important problem that we have to face.' Acknowledging that 'labor discontent is, and has been, evident,' he thought that this might be solved by capital and labour studying each other's business. Again, change was on the agenda:

> Capital should recognize labor's right to organize...Snobbery and pa-tronage must end. Arbitrary adjustment of wages must end. What right has a business man to raise or lower the wages of labor? Labor is the one to raise or lower its wages.

Labour and capital should work together in the future and, to achieve this, Horwood suggested the establishment of an industrial council, consisting of business and union representatives. Support was offered for the building of technical schools, for an institute of scientific research, for agricultural development, for some means to deal with profiteering, and for a fund to assist victims of marine disasters.

There were some limited reforms during and immediately after the war. The first efforts to provide public housing for the working poor of St. John's and returning war veterans were made in 1919-20 by the St. John's Municipal Council and the business community with government, church, and labour support.[39] Other reforms included the passing of a new Work-men's Compensation Act and an Industrial and Provident Societies Act. But much of the impetus for reform disappeared in the economic crisis that engulfed Newfoundland after the war. Expectations were not met and even the limited promises that had been made were not fulfilled. The resulting disillusion haunted the new government formed in November 1919 by the FPU, still led by Coaker, and the Liberal Reform party of Richard Squires. Their election pledge to 'Make Newfoundland Safe for Democracy'[40] was to seem increasingly hollow.

Unemployment and relief in the post-war crisis

It was not until the passing of the Health and Public Welfare Act in 1931 that there was anything close to a systematic approach to providing public relief. [41] Until this time Newfoundland did not have a coherent and comprehensive system of state provision of support for the poor. The central government took direct responsibility for public relief, but the system, administered by the Department of Public Charities and headed by a commissioner responsible to the Colonial Secretary, was rudimentary in nature and provided very limited assistance. A few old age pensions were provided for worn-out fishermen, there was a pension system for widows, and there was some support for the permanent and casual poor—those unable to work because of infirmity, old age, or sickness. At the turn of the century, when the total population was about 225,000, just under than 50 cents per capita—about $100,000 altogether—was spent on relief. By the early 1920s the population has increased to about 270,000 and per capita spending on the permanent and casual poor had risen to almost 80 cents. [42] By this time it had become standard practice to grant each of the ninety or so relieving officers about $1 per head of the total population in their jurisdictions. They were subject to only minimal controls. In the mid-1920s the officers had to deal with between 6,000-7,000 people classed as permanent poor, and 11,000-12,000 classed as casual poor. [43]

With money distributed on a per capita basis and with wide variations in levels of poverty, the poor relief system was badly organized to deal with destitution. In addition, able-bodied relief was not provided as a matter of course, even in the early 1920s. Governments had developed the practice of spending some money on direct relief—groceries, not work—for the able-bodied, but the amount spent varied from year to year and from district to district. Able-bodied, or 'extra,' relief amounted to about $10,000 a year during World War I, but in the immediate post-war period it rose dramatically to over $200,000. Expenditure varied considerably from district to district, and it seems that need often played a less significant role in determining disbursements than politics. In the mid-1920s spending on able-bodied relief in Harbour Grace district was $1.70 per capita. In Fogo distict it was just one cent. [44]

The government did provide indirect relief to the able-bodied. Occasionally, it arranged supplies for fishermen denied credit by merchants. There were bonus schemes to encourage employment in schooner building and cooperage. People were employed on road construction and other public works, and employment was arranged for able-bodied destitute men in wood cutting operations run by contractors. Seed potatoes were sometimes distributed. Overall, the able-bodied poor were provided for on an *ad hoc* basis at the government's pleasure. Free medical aid was provided, but this was rationed and applicants were investigated by relieving officers.

The system of poor relief was unusual in that it was centrally operated, funded, and controlled. Lacking the machinery of local government, there was no system for charging poor relief expenditures to local rates, as in England. The system was unwieldy and often slow to respond to problems of destitution, in part because there was continuous tension between the desire to control spending and the pressure to give relief. Periodically, relieving officers were instructed to cut all assistance to the able-bodied poor and to refer all requests for assistance to the central government. Not surprisingly in such a system, politics played a considerable role. By and large the government did not provide aid to the able-bodied unless this was requested by politicians, lobbied for by local residents, or extracted by threats and direct action.

Apart from the public relief system, there existed various charitable organizations which provided food, clothing and sometimes medical aid. These were concentrated in St. John's, but also had a presence in the other large towns and in some rural areas. Most of these charities were run by the major churches. Other organizations also played a role in providing for the welfare of specific sections of the population. For example, the GWVA provided assistance to ex-servicemen. Labour unions and associations provided assistance to their members. In the mid-1920s private charities were supported financially by the state, but this was gradually withdrawn.

In 1919 the economic situation was still superficially healthy. The cost of living continued to be very high, but so did the price of fish. The value of salt codfish exported during the 1919-20 season was $23,260,000, only slightly below the previous year's value. But an international economic crisis was brewing and in 1920-21 exports of salt cod were valued at a mere $13,500,000.[45] Rising state revenues and balanced budgets became a thing of the past. A budget deficit of almost $4,300,000, equal to half the total revenue for the year, was recorded in 1920-1.[46]

As unemployment and poverty mounted the Squires government came under increasing pressure to provide relief. It was seldom if ever moved to provide assistance by evidence of distress alone. Rather it was protests, strikes, violence and threats of violence, which moved the government to provide relief to the able-bodied on an unprecedented scale. St. John's soon emerged as the centre of protest over poverty and unemployment. The NIWA under the leadership of E.J. Whitty forged the unemployed into a fighting force whose essential purpose was explained by one of its leaders as follows:

> This is a question of work or bread. There is plenty of grub in the stores on Water Street and if there is no work and it is not given to us we will not be long in placing men in those stores who will hand it out to the needy men.[47]

When confronted, the government reluctantly responded to the demands of the unemployed, adopting a twofold strategy. First, limited relief and work was provided when absolutely necessary. Second, military force was employed both to maintain law and order and to discourage agitation. The government's strategy here was to back up the use of the Constabulary and the Naval Reserve with carefully timed visits by British warships. The Constabulary was expanded, and a small mounted section added. This was no doubt intended to reassure the many middle class observers who were not slow to link the problematic political situation with the rise of lower class organization, arguing that perhaps the time was ripe to roll back the evil of 'Coakerism' which seemed to have taken over the country.[48]

Governor Harris took an active interest in the serious economic situation, and attempted to develop a community approach to dealing with the problem of unemployment. Anxious about increasing evidence of destitution, he organized a conference at Government House in May 1921 attended by the heads of religious bodies and charitable organizations,[49] who described the increasing distress in St. John's. However, the governor was of the opinion that the situation did 'not demand hasty exceptional treatment.' At least some of the problem could be put down to 'improvidence and thriftlessness.' Nevertheless, he argued that some government action might be needed, either in the form of 'supplies for the new fishery, including such maintenance as would support life' or of seed potatoes. It might be 'proper to pledge the credit of the future for a longer or shorter period' in order to keep people going who were engaged in 'productive operations,' but such efforts would have to be carefully controlled. Supplies should *only* be issued where it could be shown that a man had no savings and he had proved unable to 'get any sort of help from those around him.' The government should also 'reject cases of notorious laziness or incompetence.'

But as conditions worsened, the governor's position changed. He became anxious to avoid a major outbreak of violence.[50] In the fall of 1921 he proposed to the government that the community should be involved in supporting the unemployed through the creation of a wages fund:

> I would appeal to everyone to tax themselves for this purpose. I should think that out of 30,000 families in Newfoundland some 10,000 families could average $12.50 each. This would make $125,000, and this would give 1,000 families some $8 a week for 15 weeks of the winter—say from Dec. to March. A wage of $1 a day should more than support life, if properly spent. I am willing myself to make a substantial payment to such a fund.

The 'refusal of such a wage' would be 'proof of an absence of real need.' If the provision of work was one prong of the attack on unemployment, the other would be the harsh treatment of trouble-makers:

> It is necessary to face those who are out to agitate and give trouble under pretence of wanting employment. However weak-kneed others have been in England and elsewhere—we have to hoe our own road and do it well. In the last resort—though I hope it may not come to that—there is the riot act and an armed constabulary.

Harris devoted considerable time and energy to his scheme. He aimed for wide representation on a committee, arguing that 'all classes of the Colony should realize the necessity for sympathetic cooperation.'[51] The wages fund would 'bind the community together in facing adverse fortunes' and help the unemployed by providing work, not charity. It was also presented as a possible way of ending poor relief:

> The whole system should as far as possible be directed to getting rid of the present system of poor relief and if properly administered there ought to be considerable saving in the funds at present placed at the disposal of the Commissioner of Public Charities.

In early November Harris tried to sell his scheme to the Board of Trade,[52] proposing the creation of an organization which would register both those needing employment and any work which could be found. He also outlined a plan to establish 'a fund for employing labour' by getting $10 subscriptions from families in St. John's. The proposal was, then, for a labour exchange which would allocate work only to 'men who really need it,' and perhaps also to women and girls. It was 'essential,' Harris said, 'to be in a position to divide the man who really is unemployed from the man who is merely holding up the community because he does not want to work. It is also essential that when the genuine cases are found they should be put upon work which is genuinely useful to the community.' Low wages would be the 'test of a man's desire to work.' The governor anticipated opposition to his proposal from those who advocated union rates of pay in all conditions, and from 'that minority of men who want disturbance rather than work.' He hoped to limit this opposition and undermine the influence of 'hooligans' by including labour unions on the unemployment committee.

Following these initiatives, Harris drew up a 'general sketch' of action to deal with the situation in St. John's.[53] He suggested the formation of 'a strong general committee' consisting of people nominated by the Board of Trade, religious bodies, charities, the GWVA and unions. The committee would provide wide community support for his efforts, and also to 'get as near as possible to the malcontents or those likely to be personally affected.' It would be the work of the committee to canvass the city to find what items of work, and what contributions, citizens might be prepared to provide for the unemployed. The results of the canvass would be lodged with the employment registry opened by Major Butler of the GWVA at the government's request earlier in 1921.

While some ex-servicemen were trying to gain concessions by militant action, the GWVA became heavily involved from the outset in these moves to organize charity in St. John's. At the end of November 1921, the GWVA offered to hand over to the government its store on Water Street for the first three months of 1922 for the distribution of wares made by the destitute.[54] The GWVA also suggested that the government bring together in the building all charity organizations, so that central control might be established. This, it was argued, would prevent overlapping in the provision of assistance. All veterans and their dependents would be kept on a separate register which would be looked after by the Ladies Khaki Guild of which Lady Squires was a member. They also suggested that the motto of the Guild, 'to help those in need to help themselves,' be applied to all charity organizations so that the word 'charity' might be replaced with 'self-help.' The GWVA endorsed the idea of an employment bureau. Both in philosophy and organizational structure this proposal clearly followed Harris' suggestions, and anticipated the establishment of the COB later in the decade. The GWVA's emphasis on self-help was also useful to a government anxious to deflect demands that it provide jobs and support for the unemployed and destitute. It is significant that Harold Mitchell, the GWVA president, was a strong promoter of the patriotic 'back to the land' movement which was one of the main responses of the concerned middle class to the problem of unemployment and poverty during the crisis of the early 1930s. It seems likely that this proposal for organizing charity in part reflects the concerns and thinking of the middle class reformers involved in the GWVA, which was itself dispensing relief to its destitute members.

But self-help for the unemployed and destitute was not simply a middle class idea imposed on the working class. There were also deep wells of support for self-help within the working class itself. It was partly a case of necessity becoming a virtue. But there was also a populist anti-statism which emphasized the importance of self-help as a means by which working people could maintain their independence both from the state, and from the fickle and degrading charity of others. It is easy to underestimate the extent to which the dole and charity were feared and hated by the working classes.

The GWVA's attempt to forge a close relationship with the government was part of a strategy to gain recognition for the special status of veterans. A consistent theme in GWVA statements was that the ex-serviceman should be treated preferentially. Even when the organization pressed in 1923 for the establishment of a civil service commission in order to eliminate patronage from government appointments, it argued that ex-servicemen should be given equal representation on the commission and that the ex-service applicant should be treated preferentially.[55]

At the behest of the governor, the systematic organization of charity in St. John's was slowly and surely emerging. Without using the name, a charity organization bureau was being established. The aim of the governor's unemployment committee was, like that of charity organization bureaus everywhere, to put assistance to the destitute on a systematic basis. Aid would be provided, but only to 'the deserving poor.' As far as possible relief would be provided only in exchange for work, and acceptance of the very low wages offered would distinguish the destitute *and* deserving from the slackers and trouble makers. The organization of charity and the handling of work through the employment exchange run by Major Butler would prevent overlapping in the distribution of assistance, and ensure that aid was provided only to those judged to be worthy of support. It was Major Butler's task to maintain the central bank of information about the destitute. Charitable organizations, such as the St Vincent de Paul Society, were given the names of the 'genuinely unemployed,' and instructed not 'to accept cases without investigation.'[56]

The governor's plan was in the final analysis dependent on the charity of private citizens. For this reason it was a plan which failed. The committee did not succeed in its efforts to establish the proposed wages fund,[57] and early in 1922 the government was forced to fund relief work in St. John's. Some of this spending was, in Harris' opinion, unproductive, though he thought that it might be 'looked upon as...an insurance of the other citizens against extreme poverty, unrest, etc.'[58] He was concerned about the government's special employment projects[59] on the grounds that they would undermine efforts to reduce able-bodied relief exenditures,[60] and were not effectively controlled. These suspicions were heightened by the report of the Auditor General in December 1921,[61] which attacked excessive spending on relief projects, their high rates of pay, and their poor administration. When his wages fund collapsed, Harris did what he could to get the government to adopt a 'broad and businesslike' approach to the relief question, and continued to play an important role in managing the unemployment problem in St. John's. In February 1922, for example, he received a deputation from the unemployed, which asked for representation on the citizens' committee.[62] The governor thought that this might diffuse some of the discontent, and he suggested to Major Butler of the GWVA that it might also be useful and prudent to employ a member of the Unemployed Committee as 'a sort of foreman or supervisor' on relief projects. E.J. Whitty, the main leader of the unemployed, was given this job.

By the end of March 1922 Harris thought it likely to that Newfoundland would make it through another winter without a major confrontation. Various initiatives had helped to quieten the 'restless anxiety' in the country.[63] As the immediate crisis passed, thoughts turned to the future. The governor's thinking was made clear in a public statement issued in April:

> Conditions are such that all workers must be content to go back to more primitive and harder times; for instance, it may be necessary to lay up the expensive motor boats and stick to oars and sails. It may also be desirable that, instead of joining to cure fish on a large scale, men should be encouraged as in the old days to make more individual efforts; in other words, it is not a time for waiting on Providence and it should be remembered that 'God helps those who help themselves.'[64]

If state aid was limited and indeed undesirable, if charity had proved inadequate, then people would have to provide for themselves. Fish should be caught and vegetables cultivated. By May efforts were being made to encourage the cultivation of allotment gardens in St. John's,[65] and it was announced that there would be no money for relief work during the fishing season 'in any district at all...to encourage those who can to get to work on fishing or agriculture.'[66]

Respite and reaction

Throughout the 1920s, all Newfoundland governments saw industrial development as the solution to the country's pressing economic and political problems. Thus there were persistent attempts to encourage the expansion of existing staple industries and to assist the development of new ones, though it was the Liberal party which led the quest. There existed a broad base of support for such a programme. Joseph R. Smallwood and the Newfoundland Federation of Labour, which he formed in 1925, were solidly behind it. In his optimistic book *The New Newfoundland* (1931), Smallwood argued strongly that the country was 'upon a new march...towards modern, large-scale industrialism'; the strides already taken had been 'giant ones' and the whole country had become 'industrial minded.'[67] Such support for industrial expansion was boosted by the fact that, early in 1923, arrangements were made to establish a new paper mill on the Humber River.[68] Industrialization had been one of Squires' 1919 campaign slogans and the $20 million project, promising to employ 2,500 men, came as a godsend to the struggling Liberal government.[69] A snap election led to its return in 1923.

The development of the west coast mill was a significant step in the continuing trend away from reliance on the fishing industry. The value of fishery and marine products had risen during the war years to almost 85 per cent of all exports, but fell to 64 per cent in the early 1920s and 46 per cent in the second half of the decade. This was a trend which continued throughout the 1930s.[70] It was the development of the forest sector which was the main factor in the diversification of the country's economic base in the 1920s. By the end of the decade the export value of forest products had more than tripled to equal the export value—and the export share—of marine products. Thanks to the opening of the Buchans mine, mineral exports also expanded in the 1920s. As a result, the annual value of total exports, which hovered at around $20 million between 1921 and 1925, increased to an average of $33.7 million in the second half of the decade.

But such figures are deceptive. The declining fishery remained the largest employer, and its problems, together with continued high commodity prices, made life particularly difficult in the early 1920s. In 1921, products of the sea accounted for $16 million out of a total export trade worth only $22 million. Such a heavy dependence on the fishery meant that any fluctuation in the fortunes of that industry had far-reaching effects. The relative decline in the importance of the fishing industry, its stagnation in the 1920s and its complete collapse in the 1930s, measured in terms of value of exports, is a crucial feature of the interwar period. For this reason the doubling of export values in the 1920s did not translate into a substantial improvement in material well-being for the majority of Newfoundlanders who were still directly or indirectly dependent on fishing. Newfoundland's growth centres were the mill and mine towns. In fishing areas and in places like St. John's, heavily dependent on the fish trade, the 1920s were far from boom years.

The decline in the significance of fishing is reflected in the relative weakening of the FPU's importance both as a union and a political force. The most active centres of union growth in the period were Newfoundland's industrial centres. Moreover, the problems of the fishing industry led to substantial emigration from rural areas. This was uneven in duration and geography. Some people left only to return later. But St. John's received a steady stream of migrants in the 1920s, and this undoubtedly contributed to the city's severe housing and unemployment problems.

In 1923 the Liberal government of Richard Squires was re-elected in spite of public criticism of the administration of the public works and other relief efforts employed during the crisis. The projects had proved inefficient, unproductive, difficult to control, and a major drain on the public purse during a period of continued budget deficits. Pressure mounted for the government to rethink the whole question of support for the destitute. But however much the government might want to cut spending on relief, it could not do so without risking a major confrontation with the unemployed. The unrest which had forced the government to expand relief spending in the early 1920s had eased, but the situation remained quite volatile, though masked in 1923 by what has been described as a 'wild election binge' of spending, which bought the government relative social quiet and political support. [71]

Evidence of corruption and laxity in the handling of public relief became so overwhelming in the summer of 1923 that Squires was faced with a party revolt. He resigned as leader in late July and was replaced by William Warren. One of the first tasks of the new ministry was to arrange for an impartial enquiry into the allegations of wrongdoing. This was carried out by T. Hollis Walker, the Recorder of Derby. [72] He was instructed, among other things, to examine the relief expenditures made by the Departments of Public Works and of Public Charities during 1922 and 1923.

Even before the enquiry was established the government had announced that it intended to revise relief policy. The change was signalled in the 1923 budget speech:

> The experience which the Colony has had in relief work during recent years has been very unsatisfactory. It has been difficult, often quite impossible, to secure value in labour for money expended in connection with such operations. I consequently desire to take this opportunity of

expressing the firm conviction that the policy of this Administration in discontinuing relief operations is wise, and that such works should not be undertaken, but that, on the other hand, such permanent works as are imperatively necessary for the well-being and development of the resources of the country should be undertaken on the basis of contract, subject to rigid inspection. Such a course would give employment to those who are able and willing to give value for money expended, and those who for physical or mental reasons are unable to give value in work for the money expended, should be handled through the various religious and philanthropic charitable organizations, assisted where necessary by the Department of Public Charities in precisely the same manner as such assistance was given prior to the post-War turmoil, which so upset labour conditions and reduced efficiency.[73]

This change in direction was made possible by increasing employment on the Humber project,[74] and other signs of an improvement in economic conditions. The cod fishery was successful in 1924 and fish prices improved. In 1925 construction of a new dry dock started in St. John's. Efforts to develop the tourist trade involved both road improvement and the construction of the Newfoundland Hotel. The railway was repaired. Because more money was being spent, local factories were well employed. The budget situation eased slightly before large deficits were again recorded in the 1926-27 fiscal year. The employment situation was such that the government decided to cut relief work and close the Employment Bureau in November 1925.[75] Nevertheless, the Warren government and its mid-decade successors still faced serious problems.[76]

The publication of Hollis Walker's report in March 1924 provided additional support for moves to rework relief policy.[77] The report recognized that the need to relieve the unemployed in the post-war period had been 'great and urgent' and that the means to dispense assistance were 'novel and experimental.' Nevertheless, Hollis Walker argued that 'generosity to those in need of relief did not necessarily exclude justice to those who had to pay for it.' Public money had been 'wantonly wasted.' There had been 'gross mismanagement' of relief projects. 'Politics' had played a key role in deciding the distribution of relief and the awarding of contracts. The operation of the Department of Public Charities was 'slovenly and unbusinesslike.' This amounted to a powerful indictment of the Squires government and a call to put assistance to the destitute on a more business-like basis. It was in this context that those interested in rolling back state involvement in providing aid to the poor came into their own.

Retrenchment and reorganization

Following the release of the Hollis Walker report, and during the short period of relative economic improvement, an attempt was made to redirect relief policy. This coincided with the election in June 1924 of a what the political scientist S.J.R. Noel has described as 'another merchant junta' under the leadership of Walter Monroe.[78] The new regime's stated commitment to clean, stable government and 'wise economy and retrenchment' must have been appealing to many of the electorate in the wake of the political scandal which unseated the Liberals.[79] The movement to both re-establish what were seen as the principles of true charity in the provision of relief, and to base its distribution on 'scientific' principles came into its own in the mid-1920s. The movement was most powerful in St. John's where the main result was the establishment of the COB.[80] There is no evidence that attempts were made to organize charity along similar lines outside St. John's.

Charity organization

As noted above, the systematic provision of charity had been debated during the post-war crisis, and the first steps in forming a charity organization bureau had followed Governor Harris' initiative in 1921. The disturbing revelations of the Hollis Walker enquiry stimulated further efforts along these lines. They signalled that an attempt was being made to rethink the whole question of relief for the destitute.

Early in December 1924 the *Daily News* added its support to the cause of 'co-ordinating charity.'[81] Acknowledging the need for charity, the *News* argued that 'the methods in vogue' for providing assistance were wasteful. In particular, 'overlapping'—people obtaining charity from more than one source—was described as 'an unmixed evil' which 'robs the silent sufferers of that which is intended for them' and those who received the charity of 'their manhood and womanhood.' The main focus of concern was the 'professional beggars' of the city, those who 'exhaust the charities of one Church or Society, and then proceed to exploit those of another.' The co-ordination of charity would prevent such evils by establishing a central information bank which would provide donors with basic information about those requesting assistance. By eliminating overlapping it would also be a means of cutting expenditures. The formation of the St. John's COB was announced in early May 1925.[82] Like its counterparts elsewhere, the new organization was the child of a powerful business and professional elite concerned not only with efficiency, but also with attacking the moral degradation which it assumed to be a major cause of poverty.[83]

Attempts at charity organization through the formation of societies and bureaus had a long history on both sides of the Atlantic as well as in Australia. The nineteenth century was the heyday of charity organization, but it enjoyed a resurgence in the 1920s in some places. At the heart of the movement was *laissez-faire* ideology. Self-help was the key to the welfare of the individual. Through thrift and industriousness, individuals should strive to secure their own welfare. This did not mean, however, that

individuals should be solely responsible for their own well-being. Voluntary organizations could help individuals to help themselves, and were
therefore a vital link in the chain of social welfare. By using volunteers, the
intervention of the state could be minimized or avoided altogether. By the
same token, networks of family and friends constituted a 'natural'—that is
to say private—backup system which would provide mutual assistance in
times of stress. Hence it was quite legitimate for the state to enforce the
principle of family responsibility in dealing with the problem of destitution
or the provision of medical attention to the poor. Where people failed to
provide support for their relatives, they should be required to provide this
assistance by law.[84] Where self-help and family responsibility failed, voluntary effort might be necessary to provide for the welfare of the individual.
But the aim of charity must be the reinforcement and restoration of self-
help. In this process social workers would play a key role. They would
assess the moral character of those who applied for assistance and separate
the deserving from the undeserving. A basic assumption of charity organization was that a large proportion of those applying for relief were either
not destitute at all, or had been made poor because of thriftlessness, mismanagement and unemployment which they had brought on themselves.
The picture of the poor was of two groups, one destitute and deserving of
support, the other whose poverty was either uncertain or self-induced. The
latter group was morally questionable and degenerate. It was against the
cunning beggar who took advantage of a lax charity system that the charity
organizers marched into battle. In such 'undeserving' cases relief should
not be provided because it would only encourage pauperism (permanent
dependence) rather than a reduction of poverty.

In the ideal *laissez faire* state there would be no public relief system at
all. Instead the relief of the unfortunate would be 'attained by a more perfect
development of the natural benevolence...inherent in family, social and
industrial relationships.'[85] In practice, however, a poor law system could
not be avoided. But this must play a very restricted role and be operated
according to the principle of 'less eligibility,' so as to make the claiming of
public relief as unattractive as possible. People dependent on the poor law
must be provided with minimal support, and must be kept less eligible for
society's benefits than those at the bottom of the wage scale. They might
also be deprived of their civil rights and be required to undergo a 'work
test' to qualify for support:

> If a work test is to have any value it must combine three features: First,
> it must be simple so that no one can pretend to lack the skill to do it.
> Second, it must be reasonably severe, and yet not too severe for the
> ordinary strength. Third, it must be for 'a fair wage and under condi-
> tions which do not tend to destroy a man's self-respect.'[86]

The state must play a minimum role in the relief of poverty and collectivist solutions involving more and more government intervention were anathema.

The charity organizers stood for the 'natural community' against 'government' as an 'artificial institution,' for 'individualism' against 'collectivism,' for 'charity' rather than the 'right' to relief, and for 'voluntarism' against state provision of services. The movement was more concerned to reduce pauperism than poverty. It aimed at freedom, but what it sought was freedom from dependence on the state rather than freedom from want. Accordingly the movement saw social democracy and socialism, with their reformist orientation and their talk of rights, as a threat. What the charity reformers really wanted was to preserve the class system but encourage 'social intercourse' between the rich and poor. *Noblesse oblige* would remain the core philosophy governing the relationship of rich and poor, but in a reworked form. Paternalism would now be combined with 'flexibility, experimentation, pragmatism, careful study, and expert advice.'[87] This in turn meant an emphasis on decentralization, on communities dealing with 'their' own problems, on establishing working relationships between donors and professionals, on de-institutionalization and on forming a network of personal ties with the poor. Charity organizers wanted 'benevolent ladies' and 'Christian Gentlemen' to exercise 'civic stewardship' and they were enthusiastic supporters of professionalization in social service. The stewardship they had in mind was presented as an alternative to state welfare which the stewards often fought with great vigour. The charity organization movement preached self-reliance and individual responsibility but the 'urban gentry' who everywhere formed the core of the movement practiced an extreme form of paternalism. Newfoundland was but a case in point. Thus it was no accident that it was Leonard Outerbridge, a prominent St. John's businessman and the first president of the COB, who took a leading role in advocating the disenfranchisement of paupers in the year before the introduction of Commission of Government.

For many middle class people the involvement of women in the social reform movement of the 1920s was a continuation and development of the part they had played in fighting World War I on the home front. Inspired by patriotism and a commitment to national efficiency, women were the frontline workers in the fight to transform everyday life. In this work they carved out a new public role for themselves as organizers and administrators, enhancing their self-confidence and supporting their demands for political rights.

In Newfoundland the furore over public works and relief in the early 1920s provided fertile ground for the arguments of the charity organizers. Against a background of allegations of corruption, lax administration and political interference, the charity organizers sought to put charity on a scientific basis. There would be no indiscriminate, unregulated and thoughtless alms-giving. The *method* of charity was to be the method of business, and it was to be subordinate to the principles of self-help which were such an important part of both middle and respectable working class thinking. Relief must never undermine the responsibility of individuals for their own welfare. But the organizers also wished to educate the giver by developing the 'sentiment of charity' along scientific lines. To this end the *Daily News* made clear the 'interpretation' of charity which it found acceptable.[88] 'True charity,' it was suggested, often found 'its expression in alms-giving,' but 'not all alms-giving' was charity. If given without knowledge, and therefore unwisely, charity 'might work more harm than good'— it might even give the 'gift of laziness to laziness.' Charity organizers set out to educate the public about charity in the belief that it could be transformed from a 'simple and primitive emotion' into a science.

The philosophy of the COB in St. John's was no different from that of similar organizations elsewhere. Its initial aim was to collect information and statistics which would be distributed to charitable agencies thereby 'ensuring more effective work and a closer co-ordination of effort.'[89] As elsewhere, the nerve centre of the COB was its central file where information about the city's poor was 'systematically accumulated, arranged, and stored.'[90] The fundamental law of charity was expressed in the word, INVESTIGATE, and this is what the COB did. The 'friendly visitor' was, in fact, Janus-faced.

The bureau created a 'repository of accurate records' about destitute people in St. John's,[91] meaning a detailed dossier on every person who had ever had cause to claim assistance. Each claimant was individually investigated, and the bureau listed the names and addresses of all who were considered to be 'suitable candidates for charitable relief.' This enabled private citizens and charitable organizations to decide whether people were both destitute and deserving of their support. The system aimed to prevent overlapping and waste, and to eliminate 'parasites.' It would 'repress as far as possible...unseemly and degrading mendicity' while directing the 'largesse of citizens...towards the really needy.'[92] Here is an argument which has become very familiar in recent years, namely, that the broad coverage of state programmes must be restricted in order to allow the really needy to be given the assistance they require. The intent of charity organization, then, was to 'co-operate and co-ordinate' but 'never to substitute or usurp the services already being rendered.'[93] It also assumed the educational role of enlightening the public about the community's social needs, and about existing and recommended measures intended to meet them.

Outerbridge's vice-president at the COB was Alice Brehm, wife of the Medical Health Officer. The board was made up of businessmen and representatives of charitable organizations. Supported by voluntary donations, the bureau began its work in May 1925 in an office in the GWVA building with Jean Crawford (she later married Gordon Muir) as its secretary.[94] Educated at the Presbyterian and Spencer colleges, Crawford had then attended McGill University.[95] After two years in charge of a diet dispensary in Montreal, work which involved record keeping, visiting, and the 'full investigation of every case assisted,' she returned to Newfoundland in 1925 and was immediately hired by the COB. A 'busy woman,' she proved totally dedicated to the 'tiring business' of investigating relief applicants, issuing relief orders and work tickets.

The COB's establishment had caused problems. The drive to establish a bureau began at a public meeting held on 12 December 1924, at which a committee was established to approach the government for financial assistance to cover the costs of administration and propaganda.[96] At the same time it was proposed that the bureau be 'composed of sufficient members to represent every avenue or agency of active charity in the City.'[97] Thus 'the five churches and Salvation Army, together with the Department of Public Charities, and the six Organizations of the City with charitable aims' should all be involved. However, the Monroe government, in spite of its close links to many of those involved, was reluctant to provide support. While the government may have been uncertain about the organization's effectiveness, it also seems to have been unwilling to increase the limited amount of money it made available to private charities. In the event, the government agreed to provide financial support on condition that all the other groups involved in the organization also contributed.[98]

Some churches were uncertain about giving their support. The Salvation Army at first opposed the COB altogether. Colonel Thomas Cloud, the Territorial Commander, objected to the creation and financial support of an organization which would have as its sole object the investigation of poverty and the poor. There would be duplication of services, and the cost of the bureau would take money away from those who really needed it. The Salvation Army also objected to the kind of investigation that was proposed:

> The penalizing of poverty is too sad and we as an Army can never countenance this; the poor in this City are suffering enough now because of circumstances over which they have no control, and to rob them of their self respect and penalize them for their poverty would add to their sorrow...The Parasites of Society are well known to Societies that dispense Charities, but it is the deserving poor that must be helped.

Cloud argued that if every charitable society would investigate and assist its 'own cases,' there would be no overlapping. Other cases should be the responsibility of the government, handled possibly through a statutory distress committee. In Cloud's view, any payment for service to the poor was 'robbing [them] of what they ought to have.' All charitable work should be voluntary.[99]

The dispute between the Salvation Army and the COB, and the initial uneasiness of the Methodists, were examples of the kind of difficulties which had emerged wherever attempts had been made to challenge church control over charity. Two philosophies of charity were in conflict, but it is also possible that the Salvation Army felt that the bureau would undermine its control over 'its poor.'

The attitude of the Salvation Army and the Methodists caused a minor crisis, since the government's agreement to help finance the bureau was conditional on its representing all charititable agencies. On 1 May 1925, the organizers announced the formation of the COB.[100] Business supporters had already subscribed $1,000 and the government's promised support was requested. But since neither the Salvation Army nor the Methodists had yet been persuaded to participate the promised funds were denied; the COB, it was pointed out, did 'not comprise the charitable organizations of...[the] city.'[101] By early June the COB could report that all major charitable organizations 'of a permanent nature' were within the fold except the Salvation Army.[102] And even here some success was reported: 'We have approached them and when it was learned that we were not endeavouring to collect funds for distribution Staff Captain Sainsbury expressed willingness to co-operate.' Further, the Methodist clergy had also expressed their willingness to co-operate. Obtaining the support of all churches in a society deeply divided on denominational lines was a remarkable achievement; but the government continued to deny support. It was not until the bureau was able, in late August, to demonstrate the nature and effectiveness of its work—tabulating information, conducting interviews and home visits, cautioning child beggars[103]—that a $1,500 grant was given for one year on an experimental basis.

In November 1926 the COB again requested government assistance reporting that it was 'very strapped,'[104] and that its work had 'saved the Government many thousands of dollars.' In support of the COB's case, Outerbridge cited the report of the Auditor General for 1924-25:[105]

> The vote for Permanent and Casual Poor amounts to $242,619.00 per annum. This sum is divided at the rate of One Dollar per capita, between the several Districts, regardless of actual requirements. About $200,000 is required for permanent poor, i.e. Widows, Orphans, Aged and Infirm. The balance is used for 'casual' poor. In addition to the latter $3,321.00 is granted for Charitable Societies. I am quite confident that the money does not effectively achieve the purposes for which it is granted. If it were judiciously administered it should, combined with private contributions, be ample for our requirements. Lack of proper investigation, overlapping and other causes operate in minimizing its full utility. To my mind the cure exists in the organization of a scheme which could embrace all the charitable societies in our midst, and coordinate their activities. If properly encouraged and assisted as to funds its potential value to Newfoundland would be incalculable.

The report went on to suggest official recognition and financial support for the organization of charity. It was even suggested that such a scheme might be applied to the whole country. The Colonial Secretary consulted H.J. Brownrigg, the Commissioner of Public Charities, who reported favourably on the COB.[106] It had aided in the issuing of relief orders by conducting investigations and Jean Crawford had proved 'most attentive and indefatigable' in her service to the Department of Public Charities. Brownrigg noted that in 1924-25, over $89,000 had been distributed for relief in St. John's; the following year, while Miss Crawford was 'acting as an investigator,' less than $4,000 had been disbursed. Brownrigg was 'strongly of the opinion' that 'if Miss Crawford had been investigating the previous year the expenditures would not have been so heavy.' In fact, Brownrigg was endorsing Jean Crawford rather than the bureau, but his letter did persuade the government to renew funding for another year.

In spite of financial uncertainties, the COB was well established by November 1925, when it issued its first report.[107] In the first six months of its operation the COB had enjoyed the active co-operation of the Child Welfare Association, the Employment Office, the GWVA, the charitable St. Vincent de Paul and Dorcas Societies, the General Hospital, the Patriotic Association, the Girls' Industrial Home and all the churches. Over 1,500 cases had been investigated and several hundred visits had been made to societies, employers and homes. As a result of COB reports, seventeen grocery and five coal orders had been distributed, clothing had been provided to eighty-nine people, and medical attention given to twelve. Employment had been found for eighteen persons and one mother and her child had been given a holiday. Sixteen children had been given warnings about begging on the streets. The *Evening Telegram* thought that the COB had proved its value: it was well on the way to making the work of relief in St. John's 'as systematic as possible.'[108]

In time the bureau assumed a central role in investigating those who applied for relief work. During the early spring of 1927 it assisted the City Clerk by investigating and recommending men for relief work—some 2,687 'cases' were interviewed and investigated, and 875 men recommended. In the bureau's opinion, their work was responsible for saving the government 'many thousands of dollars.'[109] However, the move towards complete and effective control of relief work was limited by lack of staff and by the activities of politicians. Outerbridge's comment on the latter problem is instructive:

> In spite of the assurance that no members of the Government would interfere, nevertheless Miss Crawford was constantly communicated with endeavours to get work for special parties in whom certain members were interested. As an example we might cite the case of four men who were sent to her with a letter from a member of the Government advising her that they had not received any relief work and asking her to see that they were given employment. The letter further stated that the writer had personal knowledge of their circumstances. On referring to her records Miss Crawford found that those men had been on the

> relief work and had just been taken off the day before. During the same
> day, later in the afternoon, another member of the Government rang
> her up in a most indignant manner about the same four men, who he
> stated had not had any unemployed work.[110]

The system was being circumvented. Gangs of men were being given work
without a COB recommendation. In addition, the work was inefficiently
done, and time was wasted because timekeepers and foremen were not well
selected.

Subsequently, the involvement of the bureau in investigations for relief
work continued to expand as did its involvement in overseeing the distribution of the dole and the feeding of hungry children. The COB, moreover,
gradually took on the wider role which its promoters had envisaged. This
was to investigate the conditions giving rise to poverty and to arrange
meetings and lectures for the study of social questions.

Health policy and the poor

The COB only affected St. John's. But the principles which underlay its
foundation and its work also conditioned the government's response to the
provision of health care to the destitute, and this had island wide implications. The aim was, once again, to reduce expenditure to a minimum, to roll
back state involvement, and to reassert the principles of self-help, and
individual and family responsibility for providing care.

The provision of health care for the destitute was potentially very
costly. Since only those who were financially able were expected to pay for
medical attention, the government faced an almost open-ended demand for
services. In practice, hospital services for the destitute were rationed. The
number of doctors was limited and medical services were strictly supervised by government officials. The effect was to limit the use of services. A
great deal of power lay in the hands of doctors, relieving officers, magistrates and the other officials. Access to medical services was virtually
denied to the poor by some officials, while others were more lenient. At the
same time, if the government decided that spending on medical services
was too great, it could exert pressure on doctors and officials to limit access.

The Monroe government was concerned to cut medical expenditures
by means of economy measures and improved efficiency.[111] It initiated
discussion of this issue at a medical convention held in St. John's in 1924.
Both the payment of doctors for attending paupers, and the desirability of
continuing to use magistrates as outport health officers were discussed.
What emerged as a key issue was the question of how to exert effective
control over doctors. One magistrate responded to the suggestion that
magistrates cease to be health officers as follows:

> I think I am safe in saying that there is not one magistrate but what
> would like to get clear of this work, because it is nothing more or less

than a source of worry and discontent, without reward or pay. On the other hand looking back over the past with my experience of the outport doctor one is duty bound to ask if there is not a grave doubt but what history would repeat itself, and we would find Boards of Health spending a good deal more money than the country could afford.[112]

The magistrates controlled health expenditures; if this control were removed it might prove 'very difficult...to keep some doctors within bounds.' From late November 1924, meetings were arranged with the Newfoundland Medical Association to examine the question of expenditures.

As matters developed, the government did not wait for the results of the investigation. The immediate target was the level of spending in Placentia and Trinity Bays.[113] According to the Auditor General spending in these areas had been 'very considerable,' averaging between $400 and $500 a month. On the basis of this report, the Colonial Secretary ordered immediate action to 'bring this expenditure under control':

> At the present time the people have got into the habit of wiring their representative or the Colonial Secretary, and we have been issuing instructions to Dr. Chisholm to attend these cases. This procedure is not correct...The Government desire that, in the areas touched by Dr. Chisholm, as well as any other localities where cases requiring medical attendance arise, the applications, in the case of persons unable to pay for the services of a Doctor, should be made by such persons to the Relieving Officer for that section.[114]

The relieving officer would ascertain whether the applicant could pay for the doctor, and if not, whether the case required 'special attendance by a medical man.' If the officer decided in favour of medical attention, he would then contact the Commissioner of Public Charities, who would then take 'necessary action.' For his part the errant Dr. Chisholm heard directly from the Colonial Secretary about the new arrangement:

> I thought it well to let you know this so that you may be able to tell the people what to do in cases of illness. It is no use wiring to the Colonial Secretary, nor to their Member, nor will it be any use communicating with their Clergyman. They must see the Relieving Officer and convince him of the worthiness of their case, and of their inability to pay.[115]

The new system came into force on 15 December 1924. The government's circulated instructions concerning the use of hospitals outlined and justified the new policy. Since 'the expenditure of public money upon Hospitals and similar Charitable Organizations, the care of outside patients, and transportation to and from...[had] grown to alarming proportions,'[116] anyone able to pay for medical services was required to do so. Public money was only available to help those who, after investigation, were found to be absolutely destitute. A doctor would have to decide whether or not the medical problem required treatment, and the relieving officer had the authority to send patients, at public expense, for treatment in the public wards of hospitals.

The introduction of the new regulations was not without its problems. Some confusion developed over the correct way to treat domestic servants resident in St. John's. Some domestics who applied for admission to hospital were referred to the Commissioner of Public Charities for investigation.[117] Public Charities refused to investigate on the grounds that these cases should be handled by the relieving officers 'at their homes in the Outports.' It was ruled eventually that such persons were city residents. But the approach taken by the commissioner did make some sense. He argued that St. John's was not in a position to know the circumstances of domestic servants; and the principle of family responsibility meant that it was not just the individual's ability to pay which was the subject of investigation in a claim for medical aid.

A central assumption behind the new regulations was that the high cost of medical care for the destitute was the result of slack investigations and disregard of the approved procedures for sending patients to be treated in St. John's. To reduce expenditures, more effective control over those dealing with the sick poor would have to be exercised. Savings had certainly been made by February 1925, when it was reported that over $10,000 in claims had been disallowed.[118]

Just as it approved of the COB, the *Daily News* heralded the new instructions as 'a much needed reform' which would bring the provision of health care to the destitute back to the principles of 'charity' from which, it was thought, state policy had strayed.[119] Charity should never be provided to those 'able to help themselves'; such persons were guilty of fraud and dishonesty, forfeiting their self-respect. The *Daily News* was firmly behind the government's attempts to roll back the boundaries of state involvement in providing medical assistance, arguing that the Department of Public Charities should only be concerned with the 'sick and helpless.' To this end, regulations should be 'fearlessly and impartially enforced' and 'pressure from outside sources'—politicians—ignored.

The government's reform policy received a stimulus from the publication early in 1925 of expenditures on medical services in the year 1923-24.[120] Payments to doctors for providing medical services to the 'so-called helpless poor' had amounted to $70,000. The figures also showed tremendous variation from district to district. St. John's and Conception Bay had both spent well over $10,000, while the 'places of honour on the list' were held by Fortune Bay, and by Burgeo-LaPoile, which had been allocated just $38 for medical aid to the poor. According to the *Evening Telegram*, this record did not suggest that government provision was inadequate in most of Newfoundland; rather it revealed extravagance and improper discrimination in the distribution of aid. The newspaper used the statistics to beat both the public service and the 'old regime.' The former was accused of 'prostitution' and 'the squandering of public funds...under the sacred name of charity.' But officials were simply the tools of the former Liberal government which had encouraged the move away from the good old days of pure charity. Like the *Daily News*, the *Evening Telegram* called for reform. A 'public uprising' had swept the 'old regime' out of power; now it was up to the new government to continue the 'sweeping process' so that 'order will be restored out of chaos.' A new era of clean politics and controlled expenditure was being heralded and the *Telegram* asked:

> How many...will regret the passing of a system, whereby the minimum of assistance was given to the sick and afflicted at a maximum of cost—a system which relegated to the background the officials directly responsible for the expenditure, and in fact compelled them to confine their efforts, regardless of their judgement, to the manipulation of a rubber stamp?[121]

The *Evening Telegram*'s judgement that $70,000 constituted 'riotous expenditure' on medical aid to the poor is debatable. Certainly, spending had increased in the early 1920s, and no doubt some laxity in administration existed, as well as some inequalities in allocation. But an increase in spending did not necessarily indicate inefficient control, nor can it be assumed that because more money was being spent, the medical needs of people were being fully or even adequately met. The *Evening Telegram* noted that 'public health cost the most where there were the greatest number of doctors.' Where doctors did not exist or were few in number, spending was, for the most part, minimal. This simply suggests that lack of access was an effective way of preventing people from obtaining medical aid. The *Telegram* acknowledged that the patterns of spending raised questions about the health of the population in areas without doctors—in some of which spending on medical aid was high. But wherever this occurred, it was usually assumed to indicate a problem of 'little or very indifferent control over services.' Certainly, some relieving officers were more sympathetic to the plight of the destitute than others. There is ample evidence that some officials were harsh to the point of cruelty and inhumanity. Why, therefore, should inequalities in spending on health not be taken as indicating that in some areas it was virtually impossible for the poor to obtain medical aid for any reason? Politicians clearly did intervene to support some claims to medical aid. However, it may be that in the absence of such support people who were sick and destitute might have been denied aid. Just as there is no way of gauging how many people who were not strictly destitute did receive aid, there is no way of determining how much political interference took place. There is also no way of determining what would have been a 'reasonable' level of spending on medical aid to the poor. Accordingly, the statements of the *Evening Telegram* and the *Daily News* can only be understood as part of a propaganda campaign designed to justify the limiting or rationing of aid. And it is clear that those arguing for reform started from the premise that virtually any use of medical services by the poor was an abuse of the system.

The desire to limit state expenditures ran through virtually every discussion of health care in the 1920s. It could even be woven into arguments for an improvement in living standards. A delegation of British members of parliament visited Newfoundland in 1925. One of their number noted the extent of 'under-development and under-nourishment' amongst children, and was alarmed by the prevalence of tuberculosis. The solution he suggested was a general improvement in the standard of living. The *Evening Telegram* argued that this question should be carefully examined.[122] In the United States, 'sub-standard health' cost $30 for every man, woman and child without including public expenditure. Similar costs for Newfoundland were impossible to estimate, but the public expenditures made necessary by ill health were quite considerable. The newspaper thought that the 'high cost of ill-health' might be due in large part to the high cost of living. If the standard diet was low, then this was because of the high price of 'the more nourishing foods.' If shoddy clothing was purchased, it was because better quality clothes were too expensive. Much of the blame for this situation might be laid at the door of the tariff. It might increase public revenue, but in doing so it might be 'working in a vicious circle' by increasing the demands placed on the public purse for health care. Such a far-sighted, cost-benefit approach to public policy was rare, however; and acknowledging the existence of severe social problems did not cause the *Evening Telegram* to back away from its central concern, the need to limit public spending. For both government and private citizen the lesson for 'hard times' was 'ECONOMY!'[123] 'Necessities rather than...non essentials' were to be purchased. Thrift was to become the guide for all actions. This meant that any action to improve conditions would involve only a limited role for the state. Much would rest on the voluntary efforts of philanthropically minded citizens and on the poor themselves. It is clear, in fact, that reforms to the health care system in this period were aimed at limiting expenditures.[124] The need to improve medical services for the poor paid *no part* in shaping policy.

The need for improved control was a major reason for the formation in mid-1925 of a Board of Health attached to the Department of Public Charities, which was given responsibility for the administration of medical services for the sick poor through local boards of health with broad powers. The central board moved quickly to control spending. It decided that doctors should no longer be allowed to act as magistrates and relieving officers, and that the jurisdiction of magistrates should be cleared up. A fixed scale of medical charges was promulgated so as 'to materially reduce the Doctors bills,'[125] and rates for transportating patients to medical services were also fixed. The board began to force doctors and other officials to use approved channels by, for example, refusing to pay transportation bills where these had not been approved by the appropriate authority. This issue precipitated a dispute with the International Grenfell Association, which ran medical services in northern Newfoundland and Labrador,[126] and signalled a much tougher approach than before. A system of district surgeons was introduced in 1926, whereby a doctor was given a fixed salary to look after all the sick poor in a particular district, thus eliminating the incentive to make more visits than were absolutely necessary. In 1927 the government even discussed having a layman as chairman of the Board of Health, since a medical man would 'not be of much use in respect of the control of expenditures and the checking of accounts.'[127]

Not surprisingly, this enthusiastic pursuit of parsimony produced severe hardship for the sick poor. Inevitably, some officials placed their concern with the health of the poor below their search for economy. In April 1926, for example, the relieving officer at Harbour Grace refused to allow Dr. Charles Cron to attend a woman during childbirth because her husband was able-bodied 'and presumably able to pay the doctor himself.'[128] It was shown subsequently that the man was in fact destitute, sick and on relief. This case was further complicated by friction between the relieving officer and the doctor; according to the former, the latter was 'inclined to be reckless.' The case forced the Colonial Secretary to caution the Board of Health about its duties and responsibilities:

> Whilst it is the aim of the Government, and I am sure of your Board, to cut down expenditure, at the same time it appears as though the thing may be overdone, and undue hardship may be brought upon those deserving of assistance.[129]

Tension between the doctor and the relieving officer at Harbour Grace continued. In late 1927 the doctor again attended a case without authorization. The Board was unsure whether to pay the doctor for the case, but was eventually ordered to do so by the Colonial Secretary: 'I think you will admit that Dr. Cron, or any other medical practitioner, would not be justified in permitting any unnecessary delay to occur in dealing with serious cases possibly involving human life.'[130]

The limited provision of hospital services for paupers also had the effect of rationing medical care. In August 1925 the Board of Health requested full control over admissions to the General Hospital in St. John's, where there were a limited number of free beds for the sick poor. Most poor people had to wait for hospital care. Some patients could be allocated to government subsidized beds in private hospitals—the Grace Hospital, for example, had eight such beds—but there was still a shortage of accommodation. The situation presented the Board of Health with a severe problem, in that the flow of patients coming to St. John's for medical attention had to be regulated so as to minimize the expense of keeping people in boarding houses while they awaited admission to hospital.

Efforts to limit spending often came into conflict with the demands put on the health care system. The Sudbury Hospital had originally been for ex-servicemen, and its closure had been considered as early as 1922; however, congestion at the General Hospital had led to its being used for civilian patients. In 1927 some 172 in-patients, of whom only 45 were ex-servicemen, were treated at a cost of $2.33 per patient day. The government was advised to close the Sudbury in 1927 as an economy measure. What would be called 'privatization' was adopted, because it was cheaper. In 1928 the Board found a private 'hospital' that was 'quite suitable' for 'charity cases.' The cost was only $1.50 per person per day.[131]

Even before the establishment of the COB, the movement's philosophy was well entrenched amongst Newfoundland's ruling elite. Its members recognized the need for reform in order to deal with problems of poverty and poor health, yet for the most part they were against the state enlarging its role in this area. In Newfoundland, as elsewhere, the impetus was to roll back the limited extension of state intervention which was an outcome of the war.[132] During a time of retrenchment, improvements would have to be the result of people's efforts to help themselves. A brief discussion of one key health issue, housing improvement, will set the stage for a broader discussion of the promotion of self-help approaches to health improvement.

A 1923 comment by the *Evening Telegram* on 'enlightenment and responsibility' in connection with 'the housing problem' provides a good starting point for discussion.[133] The newspaper acknowledged that there existed a serious problem in St. John's which represented a great danger. Urgent action was needed. The solution lay in a 'systematic campaign' of education. The schools, it was argued, offered 'the best fields in which to plant the seed' of improvement. The object was to create in people an awareness of the 'dangers to which they are exposed by reason of their surroundings.' This would lead people to agitate for improvements and to use the franchise to secure them. The *Telegram* recognized that the state had some responsibility to deal with the housing problem, but it went to great lengths to outline the course of action which should *not* be taken:

> Assistance to ameliorate conditions will be rendered useless—worse than that, harmful, if it is confused with charity. Individual effort must be encouraged and independence fostered. Charity in exceptional cases is unfortunately necessary, but used indiscriminately it is capable of causing far more injury than any other agency. The dole has been responsible for incalculable harm to the public morale, and a governing body which permits its use as an easy way out of a difficulty, or to secure votes is deliberately inflicting injury upon the community.

What was needed was a system of state housing loans for those with low incomes, the whole transaction being maintained on a business basis.[134]

The *Telegram* also supported efforts to do something about the 'rookeries' and 'tenements' of St. John's,[135] a central concern of the child welfare movement. 1 May 1925 had been declared Child's Health Day in the United States. In an editorial entitled 'The Slaughter of the Innocents,'[136] the *Telegram* pleaded for greater public interest in 'the nation's most precious

assets, its little citizens.' The St. John's death rate of 1 in 7 during the first
year after birth was the cause of much of the concern. This compared with
a rate of 1 in 20 in New Zealand and 1 in 13 in the United States. The high
infant mortality rate was linked to poor housing. Half the babies born in St.
John's in 1924 were living in houses with no water and sewer connection.
According to the Child Welfare Association, one-sixth were born in overcrowded conditions and over half with no doctor in attendance. The *Evening
Telegram* made this plea:

> Let us consider if the careless manner in which our foods are handled,
> the fetid cobble drains, the open ash cans and dust carts, the crude and
> reeking night cars, the deplorable conditions of many of the tenement
> buildings into which our citizens are herded are not each and all of them
> far more fatal in their effect than the baby killers' bombs or the poison-
> ous fumes resorted to by a barbarous race in order to cause terror and
> demoralization.

The housing question became a key one for middle class reformers in
the mid-1920s. The Child Welfare Association and the COB, aided by the
St. John's Rotary Club, initiated a major study of the whole problem in 1926,
carried out by Arthur G. Dalzell, a consulting engineer from Toronto. His
report was published by the COB in November.[137] Dalzell pointed out how
the city was virtually unplanned and housing construction unregulated.
Many houses showed the 'serious structural defects' which resulted from
rapid construction with cheap materials on poor foundations. Leaking
roofs, defective and uneven floors, bulging walls and cracked and dangerous chimneys were everywhere. Many houses were without either a water
supply or any form of sanitary convenience. Over 56 per cent of the children
born in the city in 1925 were in such homes. Many of these homes were
seriously overcrowded and this gave rise to what Dalzell called 'promiscu-
ous living.' The night soil collection system was a rarity among cities and
dangerous to everyone.

Dalzell disputed the argument that many houses were 'unsuited for
water services' because they were inadequately heated. He suggested that
insulation be used, though he did not recommend heating the houses
adequately. Dalzell also suggested that property owners should be forced
to fulfil their obligation to provide sanitary appliances—if they refused, the
properties in question should be 'condemned as public nuisances.' The 1921
St. John's Municipal Act authorized such action, but the acute shortage of
housing prevented its implementation. Clearly, the construction of more
housing in areas close to places of work was a priority, but this would have
to be done under proper controls. The Municipal Act already provided for
the establishment of a town planning commission. Its appointment would
be the 'first step' towards the solution of the housing problem in St. John's.
A town plan would follow.

The housing shortage was not a problem unique to St. John's. In many cities it was being found that 'private enterprise' would 'not now provide homes suitable for the poorer classes of the community.' Governments had been forced to step in with loan programmes. This could be done under the Municipal Act and 'thrifty citizens' could be helped to house themselves. Employers might also assist their employees to become house owners. Where it had been possible to build splendid churches, parks, memorials and monuments, should it not be possible to see that social justice was done by enabling the poor and unfortunate to live under better conditions? But in case this appeal to justice and civic pride did not succeed, Dalzell presented improved housing as 'a business proposition,' that is, a way of cutting the public health bill:

> No modern community can afford to neglect the element of health. A community can buy means if it wants to, but it has to pay the deficit on poor health whether it wants to or not. It has to make the distinction between the cost of prevention of the disease, and the costs of the results of the disease. There is no escape from the cost of the care of the indigent, the insane, the feeble-minded, the chronically sick, those afflicted with infectious diseases, the very old and the very young: but these costs can be greatly reduced by attention to health, the provision of pure water supply, proper systems for the disposal of human wastes, and decent housing.

In the introduction to the Dalzell report the COB made clear its concern with the link between poor housing and unemployment:

> Poor housing conditions beget infectious disease, intemperance and unemployment, and are a danger to the health and prosperity of not only the occupants but of the whole community.[138]

Improvements in housing were seen as one step in the fight against unemployment and to this end a Town Planning Commission was soon formed in St. John's.[139]

Further insights into the promotion of self-help solutions to health care problems can be gained by a brief discussion of the Newfoundland Outport Nursing and Industrial Association (NONIA).[140] Formed in 1924, NONIA grew out of the outport nursing scheme organized in 1919, which had been partly financed by grants and donations, but also charged fees for service. This proved to be a shaky foundation, and Lady Allardyce, wife of Governor Sir William Allardyce, set about reorganizing the nursing service. The idea was to establish local committees in rural areas to oversee the provision of nursing services. These committees would be responsible for looking after the salaries and welfare of nurses, raising funds through the establishment of 'home industrial centres' for knitting and weaving. Volunteers provided instruction, and by the end of 1923 six industrial centres had been established. NONIA was formed the next year, and by 1926 employed twleve nurses. In 1934 nursing services were placed under government control, and NONIA became a non-profit home industries organization.

NONIA's purpose was to send fully trained nurses to live in the outports. As part of their job, The nurses were to stimulate those activities which would raise the local standard of living and so help pay their own salaries. The whole scheme was, therefore, an attempt to provide minimal health services in rural areas without any cost to the government. It was in essence an attempt by middle class philanthropists to encourage a self-help solution to the health care problems of outport residents. It is no accident that the foundation and growth of NONIA coincided with efforts to curtail expenditures on medical aid to the poor. That the lower orders should improve themselves through self-help was axiomatic in most middle class circles in the 1920s, and from Governor and Lady Allardyce down there was no shortage of 'ladies and gentlemen' who were willing to work tirelessly to stimulate self-help and independence. From St. John's to the outports, the lower orders became the objects of intensive betterment work.

NONIA's went far beyond the medical sphere, as Governor Allardyce made clear in a 1926 address.[141] He found the large increase in relief disbursements in 1923 'little less than astounding,' and action was urgently needed both to reduce poverty and dependence on the state. The solution being pursued by NONIA was, for him, the ideal one. The establishment of home industry would encourage people to become self-reliant and self-supporting:

> Anything that...strengthens or re-awakens the spirit of independence of which bygone generations were so proud; anything that inspires hope and confidence in the future, that relieves the dull monotony of their all too restricted and isolated lives and extends to them at the same time the priceless gift of human kindness; anything indeed that discourages them from accepting 'relief' until ill-health or old age necessitates such acceptance, is assuredly to the good.

Increased 'industry and thrift' would reduce relief payments; this was of particular importance, given that attempts were being made to cut spending on all social services.

NONIA, then, was another attempt by Newfoundland's ruling elite to deal with the country's severe social problems without substantially expanding the role of the state. The core members of NONIA were leading citizens of St. John's. Governor and Lady Allardyce had played a key role in starting NONIA, and in 1925-26 Premier Walter Monroe and his wife were made honourary vice-presidents. In fact, most of the service organizations which were active in the this period were the product of the philanthropic efforts of the Newfoundland oligarchy.

The COB and relief policy in the late 1920s

In 1925 the government, perhaps reluctantly, had become involved in the COB. However, the nature of this involvement was shifting and limited. Initially, the bureau was given the task of investigating the sick poor, aged and infirm (the 'unfortunate') and advising the Department of Public Charities as to their suitability for assistance. In 1927 the bureau was given responsibility for relief investigations in St. John's and its work extended to include the investigation of applicants for city relief work. In 1928, however, the government handled able-bodied relief directly, while the bureau dealt with widows, orphans and applicants for medical assistance. Even after a Liberal government returned to power late in 1928, the bureau continued to investigate relief work applicants. The COB's role expanded from July 1931 when the government was forced to increase provision for public assistance.

Following the passing of the 1931 Health and Public Welfare Act, the Squires government attempted to reorganize relief. This involved an attempt to issue a standard food ration for all those on relief.[142] It was during this reorganization that the full effects of the Great Depression began to be felt. When the Civic Relief Committee was organized in the winter of 1931-32 to provide charitable assistance to the destitute, the COB undertook investigations. The assistance provided consisted of fuel (mainly coal)— something not made available by the government. This attempt to organize the citizens to provide aid for the destitute was, as with the efforts of the early 1920s, less than successful. In the spring of 1932 the COB offices were raided during protests by the St. John's unemployed. That year the organization was taken over by the government. It continued operations under Commission of Government as the City Relief Office.

The late 1920s saw continued and active discussion in government circles of the problems of public health and relief. As always, the main concerns were rising costs and the need to control spending. All political parties advocated retrenchment, and all governments retrenched as far as was politically feasible. For example, when relief issues were discussed in the Assembly in 1928, the Liberal opposition accused the government of 'reckless expenditure' and 'extravagance.'[143] As with expenditures on health, the evidence for this was rising expenditures and substantial variations in spending from district to district. Although it was recognized that this was in part due to variations in need, it was suggested that both political patronage and administrative laxity were major causes of unnecessary spending. Under the prevailing system considerable discretion lay in the hands of relieving officers. While some were harsh, others were clearly more sympathetic to the poor. Not surprisingly, alleged 'abuses' in the system were used as an argument for tightening up the distribution of relief and systematizing administration. The fact that some districts received very little relief was not taken as insensitivity to acute hardship, but as proof that independence could be fostered. If some districts could do without relief, then why not all? The statement by the Colonial Secretary on a two-thirds cut in relief provision to Harbour Grace is revealing:

> The relieving officer in Harbour Grace is about the best man in the country for the job as far as public funds are concerned. He does not give out one dollar's worth more than is necessary. In fact sometimes he is too harsh, and, therefore, errs on the right side; and I may point out too, the people of Harbour Grace are better off now than they were when they were getting $27,000.00 a year relief.[144]

All the arguments led inexorably towards the same conclusion. In the words of the Minister of Justice:

> I do think we should give serious consideration to the stopping of the dole. We are ruining the morals of the people of the country by continuing this system of relief.[145]

This conclusion was reached in spite of the recognition that expenditure had been related to 'hard conditions.'[146]

It was the rise in demand for able-bodied relief which created alarm in government circles. That people who were capable of working should apply for relief was, from the government's point of view, deplorable. This was taken not as evidence of worsening economic conditions, but of a decline in morals. What had happened to the individual's sense of personal and family responsibility? The line of argument was a familiar one:

> The people now are making use of things that our forefathers would have been ashamed to use. In my time a man that worked on the road was looked upon with a certain amount of disapproval, because he had no greater ambition than to go to the government to get a day's work. But today our competent, intelligent, strong men have no hesitation whatever in going to the relieving officer and getting a dole ticket and going down and bringing home relief.[147]

The notion of the self-sufficient, independent Newfoundlander of the past was used as a stick to beat the unemployed and as a justification for cutting relief:

> No man in this world today can excel the Newfoundlander when put to his own resources. He can go out and make his way as well as any man in it and he can make his way in this country if he is industrious and inclined to work.[148]

Efforts to 'inculcate a more independent spirit into the people' might take various forms. They could include the limiting of able-bodied relief, preaching 'from the pulpit,' and the enforcement of the principle of 'family responsibility' for the destitute.[149] They might also include providing migrants to the city with a ticket back to the rural communities from whence they came. George Grimes argued that outport people were 'coming faster' to the city than there was 'labour to give them.'[150] This was *one* reason for the high level of relief spending in the capital. Sent back to the outports, it was argued, they would at least have their own homes and they would be in a position to provide better for themselves. This would not only lighten the state's financial burden; it would, however, ease the problems of St. John's.[151] Preaching 'the gospel of independence,' it was hoped, would encourage people to become more self-sufficient, while the cutting of relief would pressure people to move in the same direction.[152]

The Liberal government of Richard Squires, elected late in 1928 on a platform of balanced budgets and industrial development, also used the slogan that 'Dole is Degradation.' One of the new government's first acts was to establish a royal commission to investigate 'health and public charities.' Its interim report in June 1930 proposed far-reaching changes in the administration of health services and public relief, many of which became law in 1931.

Conclusion

The charity organization movement and related service groups promoted what may be called the 'voluntary ideal' when it came to dealing with social questions. It was, in essence, a middle class challenge to collectivism. Social policy had been put on the political agenda by the working class movements of the early twentieth century, which had confronted the paternalism of the dispensers of charity, and made some headway towards establishing the principle of state responsibility for income support, medical aid, and other social services. The influence of this movement reached a peak during and immediately after the Great War. Those who reacted against it in the 1920s recognized that it was politically necessary to address social issues, but they were anxious to shape the policy making process. The charity organization movement formed a powerful and articulate pressure group against government intervention in relief and in favour of much stricter policies towards the provision of poor relief.

The resistance to public relief and to indiscriminate charity was in part based on a fear of undermining working class independence and encouraging mass pauperization. It was likewise based on a desire to cut public spending. But it was also motivated by a desire on the part of charity organizers to keep the treatment of poverty under their own control. The formation of the COB in St John's was part of an attempt by the local oligarchy to re-establish control over relief and to influence substantially both policy making and administration. However, in practice the St. John's COB was never particularly successful. Charities were able to deal with poverty and unemployment only on a very limited scale. The COB proved administratively incapable of coping with the dual tasks of investigation and family case work, and its methods generated considerable hostility from people who objected to having their characters and private affairs scrutinized.

How is state policy regarding unemployment and relief to be understood? Very little is known about the thinking of policy makers in the period under consideration. The extent to which their actions were guided by theory rather than being *ad hoc* measures developed in response to particular problems must remain an open question. During the 1920s there was certainly a persistent concern with balancing budgets and with austerity. But even so the government was willing to borrow money to finance public works projects in order to prevent a major confrontation over the unemployment issue. It would seem wise to accept the suggestion that there is a 'case for emphasizing the importance of the political context for policy choices much more heavily than hitherto.'[153] Faced with external constraints which limited the possibilities for industrial expansion, the government opted for spending restraint and wage cutting. However, mounting domestic unrest could not be effectively controlled by the forces at the disposal of the government and Richard Squires found it necessary to call on the British navy for assistance. He was also reluctantly forced into expanding the police force and providing relief and work.

It was agitation and political tension which forced the Squires government to provide relief. It was always given reluctantly, and only after considerable pressure from below in a last ditch effort to forestall serious trouble. Assistance may have been provided on an unprecedented scale, but it still only scratched the surface of the problem of destitution and poverty. In 1921-22 the pattern of the government's response to the post-war economic crisis was set. When the government did respond to pressure it did so in an *ad hoc* way and on a number of fronts. Force or the threat of force was used to intimidate those pressing for assistance. A limited amount of direct relief was provided and supplies were issued to some fishermen in an attempt to allow them to engage in productive activity. But the favoured form of assistance was by means of public works and state subsidized work schemes under the control of private enterprise. Most of these work schemes proved very difficult to administer and expensive to maintain. The state lacked a body of trained and experienced officials to oversee the projects and they became noted for their laxity and wastefulness. Members of the unemployed's organization were given jobs as supervisors and foremen on the relief work projects, and although this may have helped to diffuse protest it no doubt contributed to the problem of ensuring value for money. In addition, a great deal of political influence was exercised in determining who was to be assisted.

There have been many critics of the public works program of the Squires government. For this reason it is important to place this response to the post-war crisis in context. The projects were regarded as a short-term, counter-cyclical response to unemployment. They were widely used in

Britain and elsewhere. The problems associated with them were also widely acknowledged and those faced by the Newfoundland government were no different from those faced, for example, by the British government. It was estimated by the 1933 Newfoundland Royal Commission that in 1921-22 about $2 million was spent on various forms of direct and indirect relief. Most of these schemes were developed quickly in crisis conditions at a time when there was no effective government machinery for their administration. Not surprisingly, a chaotic situation developed. Large sums of money were spent, few returns were made, and there was widespread evidence of laxity and corruption in the management of the projects and the handling of government funds.

What developed in the first quarter of the twentieth century in Newfoundland was a fairly wide-ranging, if limited, reform movement which focused its attention on medical and social problems. An early concern had been with tuberculosis and in the period after the war this expanded to take in child welfare, housing and health. A number of groups, with a high degree of overlap in membership, were established to address social issues. These included the COB, the Child Welfare Association and the Playgrounds Association, which was established by the St. John's Rotary Club, and which was also involved in social issues, having conducted a study of 'boy life' in St. John's. The object of all these efforts was, in the words of Governor Allardyce, to provide 'help and service to others.' But the movement which gave rise to these groups and, in particular the COB, had a broader and more political aim. It sought to challenge and roll back growing state involvement in the social sphere. It responded to social problems by the cheapest method available. In the final analysis this meant throwing back onto the casualties of those problems the responsibility for their solution. Some of the respectable working class were able through self-help efforts to improve their lot. But that self-help was no solution to the problems faced by vast numbers of Newfoundlanders was cruelly revealed during the early 1930s when the struggle for relief became the central feature of the country's political life.

NOTES

1   *The Liberal Press* (St. John's), 1 Nov. 1928.

2   The task of simply providing outline sketches of policy developments in most areas is only just starting. Histories like S.J.R. Noel, *Politics in Newfoundland* (Toronto 1971) and Peter Neary, *Newfoundland in the North Atlantic World, 1929-1949* (Kingston and Montreal 1988) discuss aspects of social policy and do provide some insight into the political context in which policy developed. Stuart R. Godfrey, *Human Rights and Social Policy in Newfoundland 1832-1982: Search for a Just Society* (St. John's 1985) provides a general survey of a broad range of policy developments for the period 1832-1982. Policy development in particular areas for limited periods is touched on in works such as Joyce Nevitt, *White Caps and Black Bands: Nursing in Newfoundland to 1934* (St. John's

1978). Articles such as Melvin Baker, 'The Appointment of a Permanent Medical Health Officer for St. John's, 1905,' *Newfoundland Quarterly* 14, no.2 (1983): 23-5 provide insights into some areas of policy, but there is an urgent need for further basic research. Examples of a more analytical perspective are provided by Malcolm C. Brown, 'The Public Finance of Medical and Dental Care in Newfoundland: Some Historical and Economic Considerations,' *Journal of Social Policy* 10, no.2 (1981): 209-27; Jane Lewis and Mark Shrimpton, 'Policy-making in Newfoundland during the 1940s,' *Canadian Historical Review* 65, no.2 (1984): 209-39.

3 For a general discussion of the neglect of agency in analyses of social policy development see Kirk Mann, 'The making of a claiming class: the neglect of agency in analyses of the welfare state,' *Critique of Social Policy* 5 (1986): 62-74.

4 Noel, *Politics in Newfoundland*, 77.

5 The standard source for the FPU is Ian McDonald, *"To each his own": William Coaker and the Fishermen's Protective Union* (St. John's 1987).

6 Ian McDonald, 'W.F. Coaker and the Balance of Power Strategy: The Fishermen's Protective Union in Newfoundland Politics, 1908-1925,' in James Hiller and Peter Neary (eds.), *Newfoundland in the Nineteenth and Twentieth Centuries: Essays in Interpretation* (Toronto 1980), 157.

7 Ibid., 148-80.

8 Provincial Archives of Newfoundland and Labrador (PANL), GN 2/5, file 331, McGrath and LeMessurier to Bennett, 15 Nov. 1919. All subsequent GN (Government of Newfoundland) references are to documents in this archive.

9 Robert Cuff, 'The Quill and the Hammer: The N.I.W.A. in St. John's 1917-1925,' in Melvin Baker, Robert Cuff and Bill Gillespie (eds.), *Workingmen's St. John's: Aspects of Social History in the Early 1900s* (St. John's 1982), 45-62; George H. Tucker, 'The Old N.I.W.A.,' in J.R. Smallwood (ed.), *The Book of Newfoundland* (St.John's 1937), vol. 1, 279-81; Peter S. McInnis, 'Newfoundland Labour and World War I: the emergence of the Newfoundland Industrial Workers' Association' (unpublished MA thesis, Memorial University 1987); Nancy M. Forestell, 'Women's Paid Labour in St. John's between the Two World Wars' (unpublished MA thesis, Memorial University 1987).

10 Cuff, 'The Quill and the Hammer,' 45-6.

11 Ibid., 47.

12 J.R. Smallwood, *I Chose Canada: The Memoirs of the Honourable Joseph R. 'Joey' Smallwood* (Toronto 1973), 108-09. Grimes was involved in the formation of a socialist society in St. John's in 1906. See Melvin Baker, 'George Frederick Arthur Grimes,' *Newfoundland Quarterly* 80, no. 1 (1984): 22.

13 Julia Salter Earle (1878-1945) was a suffragette and the first woman in Newfoundland to run for elected office. She achieved the latter distinction in the St. John's municipal election of 1925.

14 Tucker, 'The Old N.I.W.A.,' 279.

15 Cuff, 'The Quill and the Hammer,' 57. Whitty had earlier run as a labour candidate.

16 Ibid., 54-5.

17 Tucker, 'The Old N.I.W.A.,' 279.

18 *Evening Telegram*, 4 Jan. 1919.

19 Ibid., 9 Jan. 1919.

20   See, for example, Arthur Selwyn-Brown, 'Will the War Promote Human Retrogression?' *Newfoundland Quarterly* 20, no. 1 (1920): 11-12.

21   J.M. Winter, *The Great War and the British People* (London 1985), 300-04.

22   H.M. Mosdell, 'Retrospect and Outlook,—1914 and 1922,' *The Veteran Magazine* 2, no. 4 (1922): 43.

23   Capt. L.C. Murphy, 'The Great War Veterans' Association: A Retrospect and A Pre-View,' in Smallwood (ed.), *Book of Newfoundland*, vol. 1, 448-51.

24   C.A. Sharpe, 'The "Race of Honour": An Analysis of Enlistments and Casualties in the Armed Forces of Newfoundland: 1914-1918,' *Newfoundland Studies* 4, no. 1 (1988): 27-55.

25   See Chris Jones and Tony Novak, 'The State and Social Policy,' in Philip Corrigan (ed.), *Capitalism, State Formation and Marxist Theory* (London 1980), 146-9, for some comments on national efficiency and social policy.

26   Robert A. Brehm, 'Report of the Public Health Department for the Year 1916,' *Journal of the House of Assembly*, 1917, appendix, 523.

27   Nevitt, *White Caps*, 121-5.

28   Ibid., 122. See also, Patricia O'Brien, 'The Newfoundland Patriotic Association: the administration of the war effort, 1914-1918' (unpublished MA thesis, Memorial University 1982).

29   Nevitt, *White Caps*, 111.

30   Brehm, 'Report,' 515.

31   Ibid., 524.

32   Ibid., 510-11. Study of the diphtheria epidemic of 1916 had shown that the mortality rate for people treated in hospitals was 2.9% while it was 8.3% for those treated at home.

33   Nevitt, *White Caps*, 127-45.

34   *Evening Telegram*, 4 Jan. 1919.

35   John Anderson, 'Reconstruction Problems Suggested for Dominion of Newfoundland,' *Evening Telegram*, 3 Jan. 1919.

36   Ibid.

37   *Evening Telegram*, 14 Jan. 1919.

38   Ibid., 4 Jan. 1919.

39   Melvin Baker, 'Municipal Politics and Public Housing in St. John's, 1911-1925,' in Baker, Cuff and Gillespie (eds.), *Workingmen's St. John's*, 29-43.

40   Noel, *Politics in Newfoundland*, 151.

41   Godfrey, *Human Rights*, provides useful background on relief.

42   GN 2/5, file 458-C, Report of the Committee on Expenditure and Revenue on Poor Relief to the Colonial Secretary, Sept. 1926.

43   Ibid.

44   Ibid.

45   *Newfoundland Royal Commission 1933: Report* (London 1934), 111.

46   Ibid., 47.

47   *Evening Telegram*, 13 May 1921.

48   'Historius,' in 'Coakerism—Past and Present,' *Evening Telegram*, 26 April 1921, found the time ripe for the kind of attack on liberal-reformist politics which was to become very common in the early 1930s.

49 GN 2/5, file 399 (3), Governor Harris, 'Question of Unemployment and Distress,' Report of a Conference at Government House, 9 May 1921.

50 GN 1/3A, file 741, 1921, Governor Harris to the Colonial Secretary, 24 Sept. 1921.

51 Ibid., 'Memo on Committee on Unemployment,' Harris to Colonial Secretary, 8 Oct. 1921.

52 GN 2/5, file 411 (2), Harris to Board of Trade, 3 Nov. 1921.

53 Ibid., Harris to Colonial Secretary, 30 Nov. 1921.

54 Ibid., file 411 (2), Whitty to Squires, 28 Nov. 1921.

55 See, for example, the editorial 'G.W.V.A. Seeks Pledge from Both Political Parties at Forthcoming Elections,' *The Veteran* 3, no.7 (1923).

56 GN 1/3A, file 741, 1921, Hamilton (Private Secretary to Governor Harris) to the head of the St. Vincent de Paul Society and the president of the Dorcas Society, 20 Jan. 1922.

57 Ibid., file 190, 1922, Governor to Secretary of State for Colonial Affairs, 30 March 1922. The failure of the Committee was described as 'costly.'

58 Ibid., file 741, 1921, draft memo on costs of relief work, 22 May 1922.

59 Ibid., Deputy Colonial Secretary to Harris, 16 Jan. 1922.

60 Ibid., Governor's memo on Minutes of Council, 18 Jan. 1922.

61 Ibid., file 190, 1922, Report of F.C. Berteau, 31 Dec. 1921. No doubt it was the Auditor General's comments which stimulated Harris in early 1922 to calculate the costs and benefits of relief work.

62 Ibid., file 741, 1921, Hamilton to Butler, 22 Feb. 1922.

63 Ibid., file 190, 1922, Governor to Secretary of State for Colonial Affairs, 30 March 1922.

64 Ibid., file 741, 1921, Memo Re Governor's Public Statement, 14 April 1922

65 The use of the old railway track in St. John's had been considered for allotments.

66 GN 1/3A, file 741, 1921, Hamilton to Walsh, 1 May 1922.

67 J.R. Smallwood, *The New Newfoundland* (New York 1931), 1-4.

68 For background see, James Hiller, 'The Politics of Newsprint: the Newfoundland Pulp and Paper Industry, 1915-1939,' *Acadiensis* 19, no.2 (1990): 3-39.

69 Noel, *Politics in Newfoundland*, 77

70 The early 1920s also saw a fall in the absolute value of marine products exported. The value of marine exports rose a little in the late 1920s, but collapsed in the 1930s to levels *below* those of the first five years of the century.

71 Noel, *Politics in Newfoundland*, 159.

72 R.M. Elliott, 'Newfoundland Politics in the 1920s: The Genesis and Significance of the Hollis Walker Enquiry,' in Hiller and Neary (eds.), *Newfoundland in the Nineteenth and Twentieth Centuries*, 181-204.

73 *Journal of the House of Assembly*, 1923, appendix, 9.

74 *Evening Telegram*, 28 May 1923.

75 *Evening Telegram*, 3 Oct. 1925.

76 Late in 1923 the Bell Island mines closed and 1,100 miners were laid off (*Evening Telegram*, 30 Nov. 1923; 22 Jan. 1924). The situation in St. John's continued to be bleak. Though the labor situation in the city had improved by mid-1923 there were still many workmen unable to find employment and

an estimated 300 families 'in want of the ordinary necessities of life' in the West End. Early in 1924 relief work was again started in St. John's. Initially 100 men were employed breaking stone. Five hundred of those denied work staged a demonstration on 10 Jan. and 'quite a disturbance occurred.'

77   For the report see *Evening Telegram*, 21, 22 March 1924.

78   Noel, *Politics in Newfoundland*, 183.

79   Ibid., 179.

80   The only published account of the COB is M.F. Harrington, 'Charity Organisation Bureau,' in Smallwood (ed.), *Book of Newfoundland*, vol. 2, 93.

81   *Daily News* (St. John's), 6 Dec. 1924.

82   Ibid., 13 May 1925.

83   Paul Boyer, 'Building Character Among the Urban Poor: The Charity Organization Movement,' in Ira C. Colby (ed.), *Social Welfare Policy* (Chicago 1989), 113-34.

84   M.A. Crowther, 'Family Responsibility and State Responsibility in Britain Before the Welfare State,' *The Historical Journal* 25, no.1 (1982): 131-45. In Newfoundland the principle of family responsibility ran through all thinking about relief in the period under consideration. Both the COB and the government agreed that the principle was of central importance, for both moral and financial reasons.

85   Vic George and Paul Wilding, *Ideology and Social Welfare*, (London 1976), 30.

86   Frank D. Watson, *The Charity Organization Movement in the United States* (New York 1922), 121.

87   Kathleen D. McCarthy, *Noblesse Oblige: Charity and Cultural Philanthropy in Chicago, 1849-1929* (Chicago 1982), 122.

88   *Daily News*, 13 May 1925. Charity had a theological as well as a social significance. For many Christians there was a requirement to give without counting the cost and to give as a way of gaining grace. The giving of charity was also a social statement. The charity organizers were opposed to indiscriminate giving and were much more utilitarian in their thinking. Benefits to both donors and receivers should be maximized.

89   Ibid., 13 May 1925.

90   Boyer, 'Building Character,' 119.

91   *Daily News*, 13 May 1925.

92   Ibid., 4.

93   Ibid., 5.

94   Ibid.

95   'Busy Women: Miss Jean Crawford,' *The Premier*, March, 1929, 28 (PANL, P6/A/12-18 (various personal papers), box 1, file 4).

96   GN 2/5, file 424B, Finance Committee, GRB to Colonial Secretary, 8 Jan. 1925.

97   Ibid.

98   Ibid., Colonial Secretary to Anderson, 23 Jan. 1925.

99   Ibid., Cloud to Colonial Secretary, 29 Jan. 1925.

100   Ibid., Janet Anderson to Bennett, 1 May 1925.

101   Ibid., Assistant Deputy Colonial Secretary to Janet Anderson, 27 May 1925.

102   Ibid., Crawford to Colonial Secretary, 2 June 1925.

103   Ibid., Outerbridge to Monroe, 31 Aug. 1925.

104   Ibid., Outerbridge to Bennett, 17 Nov. 1926.

105   Ibid., Outerbridge to Bennett, 29 Nov. 1926.

106   Ibid., Brownrigg to Mews, 8 Dec. 1926.

107   *Evening Telegram*, 17 Nov. 1925.

108   Ibid., 7 Nov. 1925.

109   GN 2/5, file 424B, Outerbridge to Bennett, 17 Nov. 1925.

110   Ibid., Outerbridge to Bennett, 16 July 1927.

111   Ibid., file 435A, 'Medical Conditions, 1924-5.'

112   GN 13/1, box 357, file 29, 'Public Health Matters,' Mifflin to Minister of Justice, 31 July 1924.

113   GN 2/5, file 435A, 'Medical Conditions 1924-5,' Deputy Colonial Secretary to Brownrigg, 2 Dec. 1924.

114   Ibid.

115   Ibid., Deputy Colonial Secretary to Chisholm, 8 Dec. 1924.

116   Ibid. Notices were inserted in newspapers in late 1924. On 10 Dec. 1924 the Deputy Colonial Secretary informed the editor of the *Daily News* that he wanted the notice placed in a prominent place on the editorial page.

117   Ibid., Deputy Colonial Secretary to Brownrigg, 20 Dec. 1924.

118   Ibid., Secretary, Commission of Enquiry into Charitable Institutions to Colonial Secretary, 9 March 1925.

119   *Daily News*, 1 Dec. 1924.

120   *Evening Telegram*, 25 Feb. 1925.

121   Ibid.

122   Ibid., 8 Oct. 1925.

123   Ibid., 10 Oct. 1925.

124   GN 2/5, file 445, 1925, Deputy Colonial Secretary to O'Reilly, 28 July 1925.

125   Ibid., 1926, Rennie to Bennett, 28 April 1926.

126   Ibid., Rennie to Mews, 16 Oct. 1926.

127   Ibid., 1927, Rennie to Monroe, 2 March 1927.

128   Ibid., 1926, Rennie to Mews, 3 April 1926.

129   Ibid., 1926, Colonial Secretary to Rennie, 15 April 1926.

130   Ibid., 1927, Colonial Secretary to Rennie, 4 Oct. 1927.

131   Ibid., 1928, Rennie to Prime Minister, 30 Aug. 1928.

132   A similar pattern of erosion of state intervention occurred in Britain. See R. Lowe, 'The Erosion of State Intervention in Britain, 1917-1924,' *Economic History Review* 31, no.2 (1978): 270-86.

133   *Evening Telegram*, 17 Sept. 1923, 6.

134   Ibid., 18 Sept. 1923.

135   Ibid., 25 Sept. 1923.

136   Ibid., 13 May 1925.

137   Printed in ibid., 14 Jan. 1927.

138   Ibid.

139   The Dalzell report and the efforts of the COB and the Rotary Club stimulated the formation of a Town Planning Commission for St. John's (GN 2/5, file 504). The Commission was very much an offshoot of the COB and Jean Crawford eventually became its secretary. It seems probable that much of the

relief work in the City in the late 1920s and even early 1930s was connected with the work of the Town Planning Commission.

140   Nevitt, *White Caps*, 144-5.

141   *Daily News*, 8 Sept. 1926.

142   James Overton, 'Public relief and social unrest in Newfoundland in the 1930s: An evaluation of the ideas of Piven and Cloward,' in G.S. Kealey (ed.), *Class, Gender, and Region: Essays in Canadian Historical Sociology* (St. John's 1988), 143-69.

143   *Proceedings of the House of Assembly of Newfoundland*, 1928 (St. John's 1929), 198-205.

144   Ibid., 203.

145   Ibid., 204.

146   Ibid., 205.

147   Ibid., 199.

148   Ibid., 200.

149   Ibid., 201.

150   Ibid.

151   Ibid., 204.

152   Ibid., 202.

153   Sean Glynn and Alan Booth, 'Unemployment in Interwar Britain: A Case for Re-learning the Lessons of the 1930s?,' *The Economic History Review* 36, no. 3 (1983): 340.

The Commission of Government's Land Settlement Scheme in Newfoundland*

Gordon Handcock

D URING THE PERIOD 1934-42 the Commission of Government in Newfoundland began a programme of agricultural colonization which
involved the creation of eight settlements—Markland, Haricot,
Lourdes, Brown's Arm, Midland, Sandringham, Winterland, and Point au
Mal (figure 1).[1] In all, about 365 families were relocated into woodland areas
where it was expected they would be able to gain a livelihood fully or
partially from farming. This programme was the first of the Commission's
economic development policies designed to deal with the problems of high
unemployment, able-bodied relief and the depressed rural economy.[2]

The *Report* of the 1933 Newfoundland Royal Commission, chaired by
Lord Amulree, maintained that the cod fishery was and should remain the
mainstay of the Newfoundland economy.[3] The report recommended the
immediate institution of a scheme for the reorganization of the fishery. This
was believed essential to the country's recovery. Several British members
of the Commission of Government doubted this, and Thomas Lodge in
particular was convinced that Newfoundland was overpopulated. Lodge,
the Commissioner for Public Utilities, believed that the 'surplus' population
could not be absorbed into either the fishery or other industries, and that
technological advances would only result in more unemployment. Because
of the economic depression, emigration was thought impracticable, so
Lodge pressed for settlement on the land. Land settlement soon became his
economic panacea, and he was able to convince his British colleagues of its
promise, particularly Sir John Hope Simpson, the Commissioner for Natural Resources. Since those commissioners reluctant to endorse the scheme
lacked alternative proposals, Lodge was able to pursue the policy, and in
January 1935, following an initial experiment at Markland the previous
summer, outlined the plan 'to put our surplus population on the land.'[4] He
freely admitted that Newfoundland might not be the ideal place for agriculture, stating that anyone inclined to farming would likely choose a dozen
other countries in preference. But, he declared, 'if Newfoundlanders want
to live in Newfoundland they must in the long run get their living out of
the country.'[5]

Figure 1

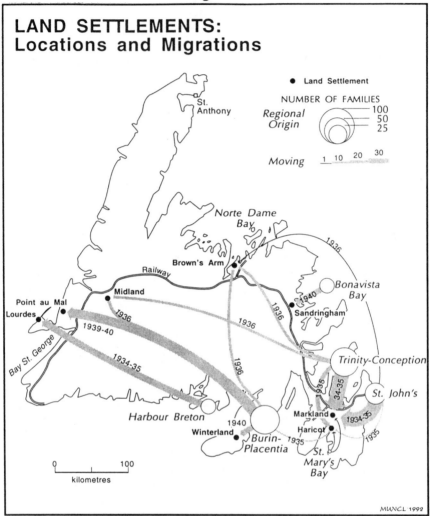

LAND SETTLEMENTS:
Locations and Migrations

The land settlement movement was not unique to Newfoundland. During the Great Depression governments in Austria, Bulgaria, Britain, the United States and Canada all sponsored various subsistence farming schemes to relieve unemployment.[6] The plan to create farm settlements in Newfoundland not only appealed to individuals such as Lodge and Hope Simpson; it also fitted in well with British colonial policy. In establishing the Colonial Development Fund in 1929, L.S. Amery had said that 'the direct settlement of men on the land...must be the foundation of any policy of economic regeneration in the Empire.'[7]

In Newfoundland, legislation to encourage land clearing and agriculture in one form or another dates back to the 1860s.[8] Agricultural projects were usually started to deal with failures in the fishery, but as soon as the fishery rebounded interest in agriculture waned. For example, Happy Adventure, Eastport, and Musgravetown were among sites settled in response to government land clearing and livestock bonuses in the late 1860s; and Blaketown, near Markland, was the product of an agricultural resettlement scheme of the 1880s. Robert Bond, premier from 1900 to 1909, had agricultural dreams,[9] and his successor, Edward Morris, allegedly promised to make the barren South Side Hills in St. John's white with sheep. But agriculture had never become an economically important factor, and in promoting his settlements, Thomas Lodge was not so much trying to introduce a new development strategy, as beginning a social experiment aimed at resolving a population problem, and at decreasing dependency on existing industries, especially the fishery.[10] He was also impressed with the rehabilitative value of work on the land following several months of experimentation at Markland in 1934. Sir John Hope Simpson caught the vision of 'a second string to their bow' and was able to obtain a loan from the Colonial Development Fund to finance the further development of Markland and the programme's expansion.

The scheme began with general hopes and expectations, but without any clear plan or agricultural expertise to direct it. Indeed, at the outset the Commission had little idea if suitable land were available, but proceeded with the scheme while searching for locations which had some agricultural potential. Following a brief trial involving the families resettled from St. John's at Markland, Lodge became optimistic that the programme could absorb some 6,000 families and that it would take only two years to complete the project. Lodge further believed that for a sum of about $800, equivalent to the cost of two years of relief, families drawn from the urban unemployed of St. John's, or from the under employed or unemployed mining and fishing population of the outports, could be transformed into self-reliant homesteaders.[11] But within two years it became obvious to all but Lodge that the cost was prohibitive, and accordingly a temporary halt was called to evaluate the programme.[12]

Lodge left Newfoundland in November 1936, and in 1937 several experts were called in to examine the settlements then in existence—Markland, Haricot, Brown's Arm, Midland and Lourdes. The most important of these experts was J.A. Hanley, a British agriculturalist, who was invited to advise on agricultural development and on how to make the land settlements self-sufficient. The government was particularly anxious to wean the 171 families in these communities from public support. Hanley visited all the settlements except Lourdes and submitted his report in December. This study was followed the next year by a more comprehensive investigation by J.H. Gorvin, a principal in the British Ministry of Agriculture and Fisheries, whose job was to advise on the broader issue of rural development. His report was published in November 1938 along with Hanley's report on agriculture and land settlement.[13]

In 1939 the government started a new phase of land settlement based upon the Gorvin and Hanley reports, and also upon detailed surveys of three particularly distressed areas—Harbour Breton to Lamaline, Lamaline to the top of Placentia Bay (including islands in the bay), and Freshwater Bay to Clode Sound in Bonavista Bay (including the islands). These surveys had been carried out in 1936 by the Department of Natural Resources in an attempt to rationalize the programme and apply it to areas of greatest need.[14] The main principles, incorporated into a three year plan, called for the enlargement of holdings in the existing settlements, the introduction of co-operative societies, the replacement of community farming by individual farms, the encouragement of home and cottage industries, and the drafting of a land development act to enable settlers to own their holdings. Gorvin proposed that the distribution of relief be related to work of a constructive and reproductive character, and that maintenance based upon community work, paid in kind, should be replaced by a system of cash bonuses for land clearing, construction, and cultivation according to an approved set of standards so that settlers could acquire equipment, livestock, seeds and fertilizers. The circulation of cash, he hoped, would help the growth of co-operatives. The three year plan also involved the establishment of a new series of small-holding land settlements. By the end of 1942 all settlement projects were finished and government management and aid were withdrawn.

As a rural development policy, the land settlement scheme failed lamentably. S.J.R. Noel claims that 'the major economic effect of land settlement...was to place a sufficient drain on the Commission's finances to render impossible any major reforms in the structure of the fishery, on which the vast majority of Newfoundlanders continued to depend for their livelihood, beyond the introduction of a regulated system of marketing.'[15] This evaluation may be somewhat overstated; nonetheless the land settlements proved a very expensive undertaking considering the results achieved. Up to 1937 over $750,000 was spent on five settlements with a total of only 171 families, or less than 3 per cent of the number that the scheme had been intended to help. It took a further six years before the development was completed, and even then, it was the general rehabilitative effects of the war effort working on the rural economy that permitted the government to end its sponsorship.

The Markland experiment

While Lodge became the main driving force behind land settlement as a government policy, the idea for the first project had come from those who became the first settlers. In the winter of 1934 William Lidstone, a St. John's ex-serviceman, applied for a land grant and financial assistance to render himself and his family, and nine of his associates and their families, financially independent. Lidstone was told that if trustees could be found to control expenditures and supervise development, the Commission of Government might go along with the scheme. Lidstone approached St. John's lawyer Fred Emerson, and he in turn persuaded Chesley A. Pippy and Sir Marmaduke Winter, both merchants, R.H.K. Cochius, a Dutch landscape engineer, and John Grieve, a medical doctor, to act as trustees. The simple basis of the initial enterprise was that the government would make available the equivalent of two years' relief to capitalize the project, and the trustees would supervise the project voluntarily until it became independent.

The central Avalon area, just south of Whitbourne, provided the setting for the first experiment. Markland, a name taken from a Viking toponym for a portion of eastern North America, was implanted to a thirty-nine square mile block of territory along the Whitbourne to Colinet Road. According to Lodge, the selection of a site involved four main considerations. It had to be far enough from St. John's to reduce the city's attraction, yet close enough to allow for convenient supervision by the trustees. It had to be built along an existing road, since a new road would make the venture too costly. Finally, it had to be near the railway to make winter visits practicable.

Ten ex-servicemen left St. John's early one Sunday morning, 30 April 1934, to travel by train to Whitbourne. Thomas Lodge was one of those who came out to wish them good luck. The settlers camped in tents and began land clearing. Within a few weeks, without mechanical aid, they had cleared half an acre. Arrangements were then made for the loan of a tractor from the Fishermen's Protective Union settlement at Port Union.[16]

The ten settlers Lodge saw leave were described by him as 'undernourished, ill-clad and with obviously lowered morale due to years of partial or complete unemployment.' When he saw them again in June he was 'profoundly impressed by the moral transformation which had taken place.' This was proof enough for him:

> So long as men could be relied upon, under the stimulus of hope or the sense of property or even merely the desire for a better standard of life, to do a good day's work, the problem of enabling them to live must be susceptible of solution...It was clear that the recovery of men of this class presented no insuperable difficulty.[17]

The Markland trustees were encouraged to expand the experiment as quickly as possible, and Lodge urged his colleagues in government to accept land settlement as the principal strategy to effect the social reconstruction and transformation of Newfoundland. He was convinced that if land settlements could be operated on co-operative principles, with non-denominational schools, they would provide model communities, the basis for the complete social reorganization of rural Newfoundland. Lodge disliked the existing denominational school system and various aspects of the Newfoundland character, especially the tendency toward independent action which he called 'rampant individualism.' He thought, as a result, that 'the problem of Newfoundland is more moral than material.' The land settlements would start the reformation.

Since supervision of the first settlers had required considerable time and attention, the Markland trustees refused to accept additional settlers unless a full-time manager was appointed. The government therefore appointed Cochius as supervisor and manager, and by the end of 1934 the Markland settlement had, in addition, seventeen paid employees—an accountant, a storekeeper, a purchasing agent, a stenographer, two teachers, a registered nurse, and ten trainees. The latter were young men recruited from Memorial University College to train as prospective managers for new land settlements. The trustees retained the services of a doctor at Whitbourne. They attempted to run the settlement on a strictly non-denominational basis but allowed free access to all churches.[18]

Between May 1934 and August 1935 some 120 families, about 600 people, moved to Markland. Slightly more than half originated from the urban poor of St. John's, the families of taxi drivers, carpenters, factory workers and labourers.[19] Another quarter were families of miners from Victoria, near Carbonear. Others came from various Conception Bay settlements, including Spaniard's Bay, Carbonear, Upper Island Cove and Harbour Grace. Six families relocated from nearby Whitbourne, and three others came from Trinity Bay. The trustees reported that their selection was based on the order of their application. To be accepted, a family had to be in receipt of able-bodied relief, and at least one adult male had to be available to work on community projects under supervision, and to undertake land clearing.[20]

The Markland project involved a number of experimental schemes and much trial and error. The trustees thought it essential to produce a good first crop, so that the settlers would be encouraged by seeing some tangible fruits from their labour. This, they thought, could be best achieved on a common field and so the first settlers were directed to clear the forest in a site by Rocky River. Communal farming would be the means to sustain the settlement, liquidate its debt, and provide families with some sustenance until they could develop and profitably operate their own homesteads. Communal farming was also tried at Haricot, Midland and Brown's Arm, but the plan was discarded in 1937 in favour of encouraging the improvement of individual homesteads, as Hanley recommended.

About two-thirds of the land in the Markland area consisted of marsh and bogland. The rest was fairly well-timbered and considered suitable for development as farmland. The land that could be improved and tilled, however, existed in pockets, and in its initial stages the development was confined to the drier land near the roadways. W.G. Ogg, director of the MacCauley Institute in Scotland, which had had some success with bogland reclamation, was invited to Markland in 1935. Following his advice settlers dug drainage ditches in a bog south of the settlement, but no attempt was made to develop it further. Settlers lacked confidence in the project, and, possibly because of the expense involved, no effort was made to carry the development beyond its initial stages.

Emerson took responsibility for education policy and decided to experiment with a curriculum combining academic and vocational subjects, based upon the models provided by folk schools in Norway and local area schools in England.[21] The children were taught to prepare their own midday meals, and were instructed in carpentry and gardening. They were also introduced to a subject known in Norway as 'Hjemstedslaere' (homestead knowledge), consisting of natural history, geography and civics. It involved the cultivation of a school garden, the care of a dairy, collecting wild flowers and studying the work adults were doing on farms. The folk school system was non-denominational, and functioned until about 1945 when it was absorbed into the regular denominational system. It turned out to be one of the most successful features of the settlement and many of the school graduates went on to successful careers.

Even with skilled and experienced farmers it would probably have been a long-term and expensive project to create a successful farming community at Markland. Apart from the harsh climatic conditions and the thin, rocky soils which generally inhibit agriculture in Newfoundland, much of the Markland area consisted of bog, marsh and water. While the better drained till hills, ridges, hummocks and knobs interspersed throughout the area were better suited for farming, steep slopes reduced considerably (by about 60 per cent) the amount of this land that could be cleared and cultivated. Although some of the area had been logged, and much of the better timber removed before 1934, Markland was still well-wooded and thus difficult to convert to a tillable condition.

At the outset, the better, more accessible, areas were set aside for communal farming and settlers were spread along woodland roads. Initially, private holdings were not formally surveyed. The manager merely marked spots for cottages to be built in areas where he judged settlers might have some suitable soils on which to create and cultivate private lots. By August 1935, 120 cottages had been built and occupied. The settlement was spread along six miles of the main road between Whitbourne to Colinet, and along a side road for two and a half miles (figure 2). Consequently, Markland was a very dispersed settlement, which presented problems for management, schooling and communication. For example, it was necessary to divide the settled area into six 'communities' to supervise community work, to build two schools, and to provide transportation for school children. Settlers were located randomly by origin, and this contributed greatly

Figure 2

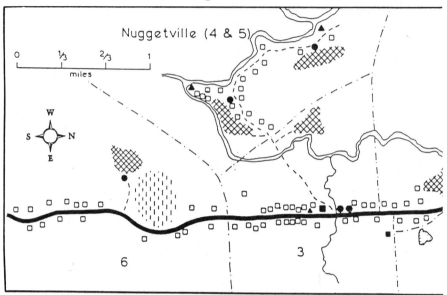

to the sense of physical and social isolation felt by many families and especially their women members. Families were not only living in a woodland wilderness, but were also separated from relatives and friends.

Settler dissatisfaction and unsuitability were such that over half of the original families left. By 1945 only 56 of the original 120 families remained. The tendency to leave was most marked among the younger and smaller-sized families from St. John's, but many from Victoria and elsewhere also went back home. Those who stayed in Markland, however, were very much a mixture in origin and religion of those who had gone there during the first year. People began leaving almost immediately. Tensions developed among the settlers as well as between management and settlers, management and government, and settlers and government. The trustees' report of 1934 acknowledged that the original settlers did not tolerate anyone who did not perform his or her share of work on community projects. Consequently one man, known to be a 'slacker' had been forced to return to St. John's. Settlers with large families tended to prefer communal work, since in return they received more favourable maintenance allowances in food and clothing from the government supply store. Others preferred to improve their individual lots, and disliked community work, especially when they found that larger families were favoured. Many also resented the labour camp atmosphere, having to work under strict direction, and the perceived (or real) denial of personal liberties by the management and trustees.

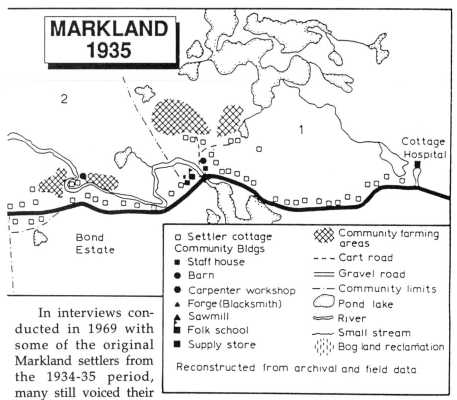

MARKLAND
1935

2

1

Cottage
Hospital

Bond
Estate

□ Settler cottage
Community Bldgs
■ Staff house
● Barn
◉ Carpenter workshop
▲ Forge (Blacksmith)
▲ Sawmill
◼ Folk school
▪ Supply store

⬚ Community farming
    areas
--- Cart road
=== Gravel road
-·- Community limits
◯ Pond lake
≈ River
~ Small stream
ᴉᴉᴉ Bog land reclamation

Reconstructed from archival and field data

In interviews conducted in 1969 with some of the original Markland settlers from the 1934-35 period, many still voiced their suspicions and dislike for the first manager, R.H.K. Cochius, whom Lodge once described as having 'a supreme artistic sense but a capacity for being incoherent in four languages.'[22] Some claimed that he violated their privacy; refused to allow visits from relatives and friends from outside the community on suspicion that they would consume food and other goods issued at government expense; denied settlers and family members the right to travel outside Markland without permission; and attempted to limit parties and socializing. It is clear that the manager did attempt to impose a strict and unwelcome discipline over many aspects of settlers' lives, and was the source of much discontent.

Another area in which Cochius was able to impose his tastes and preferences was in the siting of houses. As a landscape architect he believed that the visual impact of the community should be an important part of its design. He insisted that cottages should be highly visible and built on the crests of hills and ridges rather than in more sheltered sites, or more functionally placed on or near land to be cleared and cultivated. Clearly, Cochius had more competence as a landscape designer than as a practical agriculturalist. His effort to make Markland look aesthetically appealing made little impression on Hanley, who bluntly asserted that both Markland and Haricot suffered from a complete lack of planning in all aspects, except the schools. More importantly, Hanley reported that nobody had worked out exactly how cleared land could be made to bring in returns which would render settlers independent of government.

To the end of 1937 government expenditure in direct welfare assistance or maintenance (housing, clothing and food) accounted for three-quarters of the money invested in the land settlements.[23] Only one-quarter was spent on land clearing, farm equipment, education and administration. The private holdings Hanley observed in 1937 amounted to little more than small, scattered clearings around cottages along the roadways. The improved acreage in Markland in 1937 was 140 acres of which 60 acres were the communal lands on which settlers laboured for their maintenance and subsistence. The remaining 80 acres belonged to individual homesteads, an average of between half and three-quarters of an acre per family.

On Hanley's recommendation communal farming was abandoned in favour of individual farmsteads, and maintenance allowances were replaced in 1939 by cash bonuses for land clearing and cultivation. The precipitate decline in the number of families in Markland from 111 in 1937 to 79 in 1938 seems related to these changes. Many settlers had worked hard to improve and cultivate community farms. These were now subdivided and handed over to individuals. Larger families had come to rely on communal work for their subsistence. Now they had to start all over. Until 1940 a government supply store furnished settlers with their basic provisions in return for work on community projects. The store was then handed over to a local co-operative society, which also set up marketing agencies for eggs and vegetables. Both agencies collapsed within a year, and the co-operative society itself became bankrupt in 1943. Several settlers then opened up small general stores.

By the early 1940s the total improved area in Markland had increased to 576 acres, or about 8 acres per family. It is arguable that many Marklanders had just developed a land resource base sufficient to make a reasonable living at farming, and in spite of the marketing agency failures, had a chance for success. But in 1941 work for wages became available on the American naval base being built forty miles away at Argentia. Most of the Markland settlers took employment there, and within a year or so virtually all farming activities collapsed. The 1944 statistics record only 6 head of cattle, 12 horses and 101 poultry divided among seventy householders. The only significant item of agricultural production was 1,788 bushels of potatoes, 25 bushels per household.[24] Employment at the American base not only attracted settlers away from the land; it also provided the opportunity for the government to withdraw financial support. Only a handful of settlers have continued to use the land for subsistence or part-time farming.

Land settlement management

Initially the Markland trustees operated independently, with the government providing financial support. From early 1935 the Commissioner for Natural Resources acted as the government's settlement agent, but in September 1935 the responsibility was transferred to the Department of Public Utilities, headed by Thomas Lodge. About this time the Commissioner, together with the trustees, came to be known as the Land Settlement Board. In the cases of Markland and Haricot the trustees provided liaison between the settlers and the government. Father Michael O'Reilly, a parish priest, acted in a similar capacity between the settlers at Lourdes and the government. The managers of the other settlements dealt directly with the Land Settlement Board until it was disbanded in March 1937, and thereafter with the Department of Rural Reconstruction, which had been given total responsibility for the scheme.

For the first few years the management of Markland was confused and divided. Cochius was expected not only to supervise the development of a settlement spread out over 8.5 miles of roadway, but also to train the managerial and technical staff which would develop future settlements. At this stage Markland was frequently visited by the trustees, each of whom assumed some responsibility for directing an aspect of its development. The lines of authority were not clearly drawn either between government officials and the trustees, the trustees and the managerial staff, or the managerial staff and the technical staff. Conflicts and disputes were common. There was a much simpler managerial structure in the later settlements, where a manager was usually assisted by an assistant and a store clerk. Government employed agricultural specialists and technical personnel made periodic visits, moving from one settlement to another as required, and lent support to the management teams according to their expertise and skills. Heavy equipment operators trained at Markland were hired by the government, and made available to clear land in the other settlements. The first managers at Midland and Brown's Arm, however, had both been trained as tractor operators at Markland, and they not only managed their respective settlements but spent considerable time in land clearing.

The chief responsibility for implementing government plans rested with the young managers, most of whom had no previous experience beyond directing Marklanders to clear land. Both Hanley and Gorvin drew attention to their inexperience and lack of agricultural training. Hanley had admiration for their work, but stressed the need for more effective guidance and 'good practical agricultural knowledge.'[25] Gorvin stated that 'In no one case were these men equipped with any knowledge of the functions which they were to be called upon to perform.' He praised their high standards of education and their ability to lead men in woodland clearing, but observed that in the matter of preparing soils and cultivation 'they were almost completely ignorant.'[26] During 1939, before the government proceeded with the final phase of developing land settlements, ten managers and assistant managers associated with the first five settlements were sent to agricultural colleges in Canada. They returned in 1940 and directed the three year plan and the building of the small-holding settlements.

Agriculture had never attained a high status as an economic activity in Newfoundland, although most settlers originated from areas of agricultural importance in the southwest of England and southeast of Ireland. Many have regarded this situation as a natural consequence of, or a response to, a harsh climate and poor soils. At least one scholar has concluded that agriculture failed in Newfoundland as the result of the evils of merchant capitalism, particularly the operation of the credit, or truck, system.[27] The land settlement scheme of the Commission of Government was to some degree a chapter in a recurring dream of a Newfoundland with an agricultural interior. The dream, stated from time to time as public policy, has tended to focus upon two main principles, most recently articulated in the 1991 *Report of the Task Force on Agrifoods*—that the agricultural potential of the region was underdeveloped or undeveloped, and that agriculture offered an appropriate economic opportunity for diversification outside the fishery and other industries.[28]

The development of the minor land settlements

At the outset the land settlement scheme, as noted above, dealt only with the urban unemployed of St. John's who had been agitating for public assistance. After a few months settlers from some of the more depressed rural areas were also admitted. Settlers from Conception Bay, particularly Victoria, were mostly unemployed labourers from the iron ore mines at Bell Island. Two other distressed rural areas from which applicants appealed for aid were the islands of Placentia Bay, particularly Red Island, and the Burin Peninsula, especially the community of Lamaline. Both these areas had suffered from the 1929 tidal wave and the subsequent failure of the inshore fishery.

By the winter of 1935 Markland was filled to overflowing. The trustees had run out of accessible land, and a search was made for more. Prospective settlers were sent to clear a wooded area along the Vinland road off the Salmonier Line, north of St. Mary's Bay. As spring approached it was discovered that the area was underlain by waterlogged, gley soils, unsuitable for pasture or cultivation. Under threat that they might not be accepted into a land settlement, the men, though penniless, forced a passage by train to St. John's to protest. In response the trustees ignored an unfavourable assessment from the agricultural division of the Department of Natural Resources and selected a site for a new settlement near Haricot in St. Mary's

Bay. The land consisted of about 20 acres of alluvial flats or bottom lands at the mouth of the Haricot River, and an adjoining valley slope comprising about 400 acres. Twenty-five families were placed on narrow lots at right angles to a roadway leading down the valley slope. The alluvial land at the bottom was used for a community farm, the staff house, a supply store, a community barn and a school (figure 3).

The Haricot settlers came from fourteen settlements on the Avalon Peninsula, mainly in Conception Bay, though four families came from Winterton, Trinity Bay, and three families from St. John's. Despite the fact that St. Mary's Bay was a solidly Roman Catholic district, twenty-two of the twenty-five families belonged to four different Protestant denominations. The religious factor made for some dissatisfaction and tension. For example, when the management attempted to operate a non-denominational folk school, as at Markland, the children of the three Roman Catholic families were withdrawn and sent to the denominational school at Old Haricot. By 1941, 64 per cent of the original group had left Haricot. Six families from the local area moved in to take vacant lots, and when the government withdrew support, Haricot was left with fifteen families.

In many respects Haricot proved to have the most problems of the earlier settlements.[29] The area chosen for community farming was poorly drained and subject to flooding, while the private lots were difficult to clear and contained only small patches of cultivable land. The early managers tried to encourage livestock rearing, but the little pasture available could support only small numbers of cattle and sheep. The alluvial flats were used for producing hay early on, but later were converted to a community pasture. Had the settlers been from the St. Mary's Bay area they might have been more inclined to remain, for as soon as they were aware of job opportunities at home, the St. John's and Conception Bay families left. Ten families had gone as early as 1937. Several others later moved to Whitbourne.

First Haricot, and then Brown's Arm and Midland, were populated by families who had originally applied to go to Markland. The settlement at Lourdes on the outer Port au Port Peninsula, however, began in quite a different manner. Indeed, this development was so peculiar that some officials (including Lodge) did not consider it properly one of the land settlements.

The concept of a nucleated village as the centre of a parish in the outer Port au Port peninsula seems to have begun with a French priest, Father Pierre Adolphe Pineault, who before 1930 had started a sawmill, laid out a road system, and begun the construction of a parish house and church. The objective was to have parishoners, mostly French speaking, settle in a nucleated settlement around a central area with the church as the focal point. When Father Pineault returned to Europe never to return, his successor, Father Michael O'Reilly, took over and altered his predecessor's plans.

He became aware of Markland and the land settlement programme through a chance meeting with Hope Simpson in the early winter of 1935.[30] Shortly afterwards, the Department of Natural Resources advanced the priest financial assistance to relocate ten English speaking families from his former parish in Fortune Bay to Lourdes. Ironically though, the area into which these settlers were brought also suffered from severe poverty, and considerable tension developed between the newcomers and the existing settlers. Not only did the newcomers usurp resource areas formerly the common property of the francophones, but it was even alleged that part of the land settlement was improperly located on private property. The following year Lourdes was taken over by the government, sixteen additional families were relocated, and a land manager from among the Markland trainees was sent to supervise its growth. When he arrived, a number of houses had already been constructed, and the settlement was being built around a central area, which already contained a church, a rectory and a parish hall. The village plan was continued and completed, and Lourdes emerged as a neatly ordered community somewhat modelled after the European green village, commonly known in Germany as the Angerdorf (figure 3).

Brown's Arm and Midland were both begun in the spring of 1936. Earlier, two manager trainees from Markland had been sent, one to the Grand Falls region, the other to Corner Brook, both paper towns, to select sites for new settlements. The general rationale was that land settlements would have a fair chance to succeed if settlers could work in the pulp log industry during the winter and farm during the summer. Brown's Arm was located in a woodland area adjacent to an older settlement of the same name near Lewisporte. The Midland settlement (midway between Deer Lake and Corner Brook) was established in a heavily timbered area in the Humber Valley.[31]

As with Lourdes, the families sent to Brown's Arm and Midland were complete strangers to the regions. Similarly, just as had occurred at Markland and Haricot, no account was taken of the settlers' backgrounds, or of the cultural patterns of the new regions. Thus Brown's Arm was populated by thirteen families from seven different settlements in Conception Bay, two families each from Red Island and Argentia in Placentia Bay, a single family each from St. John's and Whitbourne, and seven families from Lamaline on the Burin Peninsula. Midland settlers had similar origins. No attempt was made to keep families of the same denomination, background or origin together. Rather, the idea that land settlement was also a social experiment, a concept espoused especially by Lodge, seems to have been carried to the extreme. Settlers from Lamaline and Red Island left home believing they were going to Markland, but on arrival at Whitbourne were directed by welfare officers and land settlement officials to travel westward by train.[32] Some were disembarked at Notre Dame Junction for

Figure 3

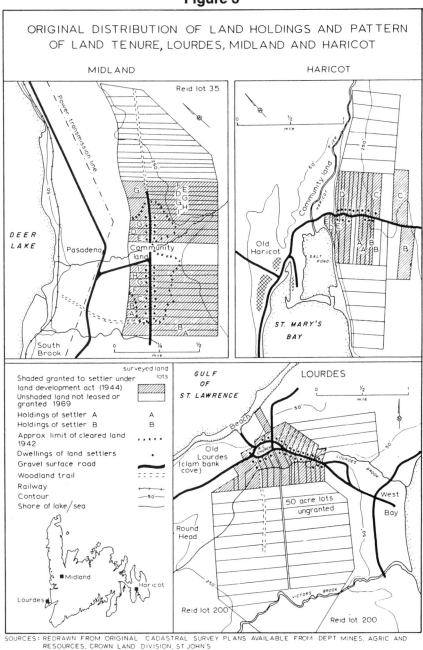

ORIGINAL DISTRIBUTION OF LAND HOLDINGS AND PATTERN
OF LAND TENURE, LOURDES, MIDLAND AND HARICOT

SOURCES: REDRAWN FROM ORIGINAL CADASTRAL SURVEY PLANS AVAILABLE FROM DEPT. MINES, AGRIC AND RESOURCES, CROWN LAND DIVISION, ST JOHN'S

Lewisporte, and from there they travelled two hours by boat to Brown's Arm; others carried on to Pasadena for Midland. *En route*, families from the same community were separated. It is difficult to judge whether the selection and assignment of settlers for Midland and Brown's Arm was a deliberate policy, or merely the result of expedient decisions coupled with bureaucratic ineptitude. In Lourdes, the settlers constituted a cohesive community of the same regional and cultural background and of the same religious denomination. As indicated, these families were invited to resettle by their former parish priest and only one family out of twenty-seven returned home, and then only temporarily. By contrast, dissatisfied with the communities and the regions in which they had been resettled, twenty-two families (88 per cent) left Brown's Arm and seven families (28 per cent) left Midland. Many of those leaving had come from large settlements on the Avalon peninsula. At Brown's Arm, in a predominatly Protestant region, all eight Roman Catholic families left. Vacant places there were mostly taken by families from nearby communities in Notre Dame Bay, while others came from settlements that had supplied some of the first settlers. When land lots and houses became vacant, relatives and friends were often informed. This was the pattern at Midland, where some abandoned lots were acquired by other families from Lamaline and Red Island. Several families who left Brown's Arm also moved to Midland, in order to be near kith and kin. The government's creation of heterogeneous settlements did little to forward the development of community life, and the settlements themselves moved naturally towards homogeneity.[33]

Housing

The first dwellings at Markland, consisting of five log cabins and five frame-houses, were built by the settlers. As the experiment expanded, outside carpenters were employed to build small framed cottages on two basic plans designed by Cochius. One was a two bedroom cottage given to settlers with three children or less. Larger families were provided with a three bedroom cottage (figure 4). These Markland cottages were later built in the other settlements. Normally five carpenters spent three days framing, roofing and clapboarding, and settlers completed the inside work with materials provided. In Lourdes the first ten houses were built with lumber cut and sawn at nearby Three Rock Cove. Five of these were two storey and styled after dwellings left behind on the south coast. While constructing their homes the settlers used the parish hall as a bunkhouse. When their families arrived the hall served for a time as a schoolroom. After the land manager arrived, houses in Lourdes were built on the Markland models.

Some early settlers at Markland and Lourdes brought household furnishings and utensils with them, but most arrived in the land settlements without any household goods and had to be provided with all the basics including stoves, beds and blankets.[34] The Markland trustees reported that many settlers had to be provided even with clothing before they could go to the settlement. The Brown's Arm and Midland settlers claimed that whatever material possessions they had previously were taken away by

Figure 4

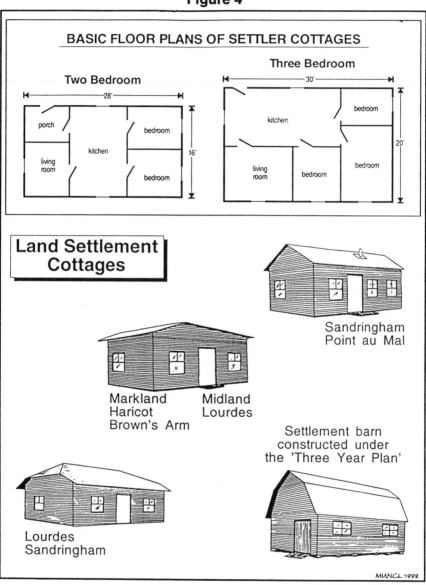

BASIC FLOOR PLANS OF SETTLER COTTAGES

Two Bedroom

Three Bedroom

Land Settlement Cottages

Sandringham
Point au Mal

Markland
Haricot
Brown's Arm

Midland
Lourdes

Settlement barn
constructed under
the 'Three Year Plan'

Lourdes
Sandringham

MUNCL 1998

relieving officers once they were accepted into the programme. Housing did not contribute significantly to the overall cost of the land settlements. The average cost of houses in the early settlements (including furnishings) ranged between $700 and $800 per family, except at Lourdes where the cost to the government was only $115 per family.

Agricultural progress and the small-holding settlements.

Until the 1945 census, statistical data on agricultural production in the land settlements are scarce, though descriptive accounts were given sporadically in annual reports.[35] In 1939, Lourdes settlers were said to be keeping a few head of livestock (mostly sheep), while Haricot settlers cultivated mainly potatoes, small amounts of turnip and cabbage, and kept a few cows, pigs, sheep, hens and ducks. Similarly, people at Brown's Arm grew mainly potatoes and turnips but had little livestock. The Midland report indicated that potatoes and turnips, which found a good market in Corner Brook, were the main crops.[36] Broadly speaking the statistical accounts of agriculture available on the land settlements from the 1945 census (giving production figures for 1944) support the general picture provided by the earlier reports. The main activity in Lourdes and Haricot was the keeping of livestock whereas Markland, Midland and Brown's Arm were mainly producing vegetables and root crops. Ironically though, by 1944 there was little farming in any of the earlier settlements. From table 1 it can be seen that only potatoes and cabbage at Midland, turnips at Brown's Arm and cattle and sheep at Lourdes were produced in quantities sufficient for what might be considered marginal commercial activity. By 1944-5 most settlers had turned away from the land to logging, carpentry, labour work and especially to jobs on the military bases.

TABLE 1
Agricultural Production in Land Settlements
Production by Crop 1944

	Potatoes (bushels)	Turnips (lbs.)	Cabbage (bushels)	Carrots (bushels)	Hay (tons)
Markland	1,788	176	-	-	95
Haricot	980	89	5,320	37	90
Lourdes	3,933	202	6,116	18	357
Midland	4,665	1,803	6,000	131	53
Brown's Arm	2,487	3,597	500	28	55
Sandringham	8,114	4,928	22,000	48	22
Winterland	2,602	3,314	27,880	61	83
Point au Mal	689	52	1,900	36	119

Numbers of Livestock Kept 1945

	Horses	Ponies	Swine	Sheep	Cattle	Poultry
Markland	10	2	1	9	6	101
Haricot	11	3	7	54	37	111
Lourdes	17	5	18	344	170	489
Midland	11	1	12	1	31	270
Brown's Arm	7	3	39	106	43	398
Sandringham	11	-	5	38	6	260
Winterland	3	19	10	95	49	259
Point au Mal	7	-	-	222	64	303

Per Capita Production, Selected Items and Leading Producers

Potatoes (bushels)	Turnips (bushels)	Cabbage (lbs.)	Hay (tons)
Sandringham 61.5	Winterland 42.0	Winterland 353.0	Winterland 1.5
Winterland 33.0	Sandringham 37.4	Sandringham 167.4	Lourdes 0.8
Brown's Arm 19.0	Brown's Arm 27.0	Midland 44.9	Point au Mal 0.7

Livestock Per Family 1945

Cattle	Horses	Sheep	Swine	Poultry
Lourdes 3.2	Winterland 1.2	Lourdes 6.4	Brown's Arm 1.3	Winterland 15.3
Winterland 2.9	Sandringham 0.5	Winterland 5.6	Winterland 0.6	Brown's Arm 13.2
Point au Mal 1.6	Midland 0.5	Point au Mal 5.6	Midland 0.5	Sandringham 10.4
	Haricot 0.5			Midland 10.4

Source: *Eleventh Census of Newfoundland and Labrador, 1945*, 2 vols. (Ottawa 1949).

To some observers Midland seemed to be the most promising of the earlier settlements. It was located on well-drained, relatively flat land in the lower Humber River valley and the soil proved to be fairly fertile. Though heavily wooded, the land was easy to clear. The 1937 report stated that the manager (also the tractor and machinery operator) was clearing a substantial strip on the side of the houses for individual lots. Meanwhile the men engaged in logging over the winter months and were paid regular wages. While it was anticipated that by the end of 1937 Midland would be independent, government maintenance and management were not withdrawn until 1941. In fact, Midland failed to fulfil expectations. By 1944 the settlement compared poorly in agricultural production against even Haricot and Brown's Arm, both of which had far less farming potential. Midland settlers clearly displayed little inclination to be farmers and drifted easily into other occupations. In 1969 approximately 4 per cent or only three out of seventy-seven men were 'farmers' compared to twenty (26 per cent) who were working in construction and seventeen (22 per cent) in services.[37] One of the three farmers was unrelated to the land settlers. He had purchased a vacant lot and developed a dairy operation, marketing his products in Corner Brook. His example, and that of several other farmers who took over abandoned lots in other land settlements, provide some evidence that the settlements could have become viable farming communities had the settlers been more prudently chosen.[38] The Midland experiment took men off the relief rolls but it failed to convert them into farmers. It merely placed them in a situation where, eventually, there were better employment opportunities.

According to Lodge, Markland suffered from being the laboratory for every experiment and for every mistake. He refused to admit that many of the same mistakes were repeated at other settlements. The 1939 three year plan did represent an attempt to correct the flaws in earlier policies. It also included Gorvin's proposal to create some twenty small-holding land settlements for fishermen at coastal localities, and four logger-farmer settlements with fifty acre lots in the interior. The coastal sites were identified from an island wide survey conducted in 1936 by district magistrates.[39] Many of the settlers came from the Harbour Breton to Placentia Bay section of the south coast, and the Freshwater Bay-Clode Sound area of Bonavista Bay, districts which had been selected for detailed surveys, also in 1936.

Three new settlements were started in 1939: Winterland, near Marystown on the Burin Peninsula; Sandringham on the Eastport Peninsula in Bonavista Bay; and Point au Mal at Port au Port Bay north of Stephenville. A small resettlement and land clearing project was also initiated at Creston, near Marystown.

The small-holding settlements were designed and developed much along the lines of Lourdes, in the hope that farming could be used to supplement income from fishing and logging. Instead of selecting only families on relief, any family having difficulty making a living was eligible. Settlers were screened for health and the ability to undertake strenuous manual labour, and in addition, there was an effort to blend the settlements into the cultural patterns of their respective regions. Both Sandringham and Winterland, for example, were founded mainly by families from neighbouring settlements. Those at Sandringham were mainly Anglican families, those at Winterland mainly United Church. Point au Mal was populated by families from the economically depressed region of central and inner Placentia Bay (figure 1), but following the Lourdes example, Roman Catholics were relocated into a Roman Catholic region. In each case there was clearly an effort to make the new settlements conform rather than conflict with established regional denominational patterns.

No sooner had the small-holding scheme begun, than it had to be cut back due to the outbreak of war. Sandringham, originally surveyed to provide five acre lots for fifty families, was reduced to twenty-five families with ten acre holdings. This was just as well, since about half of the lots originally surveyed were found to be too rocky. Land suitability was also a major limiting factor at Winterland and at Point au Mal. The Point au Mal site was underlain with shallow and ill drained soils, difficult to clear with heavy equipment, and reclaimable only for pasture and hay land. Winterland was surrounded by extensive marshlands and bogs, and the till ridge on which the main settlement was expected to develop was only large enough to provide a few arable acres for each family.

As at Lourdes, some Point au Mal settlers continued to fish, though they had poor access to Port au Port Bay because of salt water marshes and swamps. The only access, Two Guts Pond, was a shallow tidal lagoon suitable for small flat-bottomed boats. Most settlers chose to take work on the nearby United States base at Harmon Field, and few bothered to work the land after 1941. While their respective natural environments provided relatively poor prospects for farmland development, Sandringham and Winterland performed relatively well in agricultural production in 1944 (tables 1 and 2). On a comparative per capita basis, these two settlements ranked highest among the land settlements in the production of root crops—potatoes, turnips and cabbage. Lourdes, Point au Mal, Brown's Arm and Midland fared better in the production of livestock.

Table 2 provides a ranking of the leading farm communities in Newfoundland in 1944 as measured by per capita production of potatoes, turnips and cabbage. The results place Sandringham as the third largest producer of potatoes and turnips and eighth in cabbage production. Winterland ranked second as a producer of turnips, fifth in cabbage and twelfth in potatoes. Midland and Brown's Arm fell within the twelve highest producers of turnips. On a comparative basis, Sandringham and Winterland demonstrated a high degree of success in 1944, with better crop yields than many long established farm communities.

TABLE 2
Ranking of Land Settlements Among Leading Agricultural Producing Communities in Newfoundland 1944
Per Capita Production in Selected Crops

	Potatoes		Turnips		Cabbage	
Rank	Community	(bushels)	Community	(bushels)	Community	(lbs.)
1	Cartyville	72.4	Pasadena	82.0	Cartyville	1,385
2	Searston	63.6	*Winterland*	42.0	Robinsons	680
3	*Sandringham*	61.5	*Sandringham*	37.4	Searston	480
4	Robinsons	60.6	*Brown's Arm*	27.0	St. Davids	450
5	Heatherton	50.5	Cartyville	26.0	*Winterland*	353
6	Pasadena	46.6	Robinsons	18.1	McKays	320
7	Fleur de Lys	38.3	Jeffreys	14.5	Pasadena	175
8	McKays	35.9	Eastport	14.2	*Sandringham*	168
9	Jeffreys	35.6	*Midland*	13.5	Heatherton	138
10	*Midland*	34.8	Dock	13.4	Doyles	135
11	Doyles	34.0	St. Davids	12.7	Eastport	131
12	Upper Ferry	33.7	South Branch	11.5	Sandy Cove, B.B.	106
13	*Winterland*	33.0	Fleur de Lys	11.0	St. Anthony	77

Source:*Eleventh Census of Newfoundland and Labrador, 1945*, 2 vols. (Ottawa 1949).

The small-holding settlements under the three year plan were all completed according to schedule and within budget. In all, eighty-six families were involved—twenty-five in Sandringham, twenty-three in Winterland and thirty-eight in Point au Mal. By 1945 the number of families at Sandringham had remained the same, Winterland had lost six, and Point au Mal had experienced a net loss of four families.[40]

Settlement patterns and land tenure

The layout of the land settlements was essentially that of a linear (or row) village of the homestead type, with dwellings and land holdings disposed at long axes along a main roadway. But the settlements differed markedly in terms of compactness or dispersal, regularity or irregularity, the spacing of dwellings and buildings, the size and shape of land holdings and the siting of public buildings. Markland, the most irregular and dispersed settlement, was confined to a pre-existing highway and a branching woods road. No funds were allotted to construct additional roads. Consequently houses were built and clearings made only where mineral soils occurred along the roads. When the land was eventually surveyed under the Land Development Act of 1944, 100 lots were parcelled out in units ranging from one acre up to 101 acres.[41] The larger lots consisted mostly of bog, marsh and land unsuitable for clearing. The smaller lots were on the better mineral soils, some of which were subdivisions of the former communal farms. When ownership was bestowed in 1945, seventy families received holdings averaging 36.1 acres, but ranging in size from 10 acres up to 103 acres. The irregularity of the surveys and land holdings largely reflected the broken and varied physical character of the landscape.

These factors were to a lesser degree also characteristic of the other settlements. Among the earlier settlements the most regularly planned was Midland, where houses were evenly spaced along a straight road. At Lourdes, about half of the settlers had a frontage on the village green; the rest were spread along the road leading to the neighbouring settlement of West Bay (figure 3).

With the abandonment of communal farming after 1937, the three year plan aimed to provide each family with a minimum of eight acres of cleared land, and to identify additional land for expansion in the older settlements. Lots were surveyed on the boundaries of Midland, Haricot and Lourdes but remained unused. By 1941 most settlers occupied eight to ten acres of improved land and possessed a cottage, outbuildings, some livestock and farming implements. The final act of government came in 1945 when, under the Land Development Act (1944), settlers were accorded freehold title.[42]

The first generation

The success or failure of any land settlement scheme, or of an individual settlement, may be evaluated at any time from its origins to the present, though it has to be remembered that short-term failings may be followed by long-term successes, and many factors can affect different stages of development. Perhaps two of the most critical stages to examine are, first, that which immediately follows completion of the project, and second, the period following at least one generation of occupancy.

In terms of its major objective the Commission of Government's land settlement programme was a dismal failure. Only 225 families were selected for the first five settlements, though more than 2,500 applied in 1934-35 alone. In 1937 these five settlements contained only 171 families, including 55 families replacing those who had left. By this date the programme had absorbed funds that, according to original estimates, should have rehabilitated over 1,200 families. Only Lourdes and Midland had made any significant progress toward independence. To make matters worse, Newfoundland was no better off in 1937 than it had been when the

Commission of Government took office. The land settlements were now part of a major problem described by one Commissioner as 'the growing poverty in the outports.'

Little farming activity was carried on at Brown's Arm or in Midland beyond the early years. The labour force in these communities mainly relied for several decades on cutting pulp logs and subsequently on construction jobs. Only in Sandringham and Winterland was there any significant long-term agricultural development, or succession on the land after the first generation. In 1955, twelve of the original twenty-five settlers in Sandringham (48 per cent) and nine out of twenty-three in Winterland (39 per cent) classed themselves as farmers.[43] By 1969 Sandringham farmers had increased their total acreage by 42 per cent over the amount improved in 1942 and Winterland had increased by 32 per cent over the same period. While the number of farmers in these two places has continued to decline, land holdings and improvements in the two communities have increased. In 1985 each had four full-time farmers, sons of the land settlers, and a number of part-time farmers.[44]

Regional settings and recent history

Widely scattered over the island, the land settlements existed in isolation from one another, and were each influenced by their respective regional settings. Except that they were started by the government under a common plan, which involved the occasional transfer of management personnel and tradesmen from one to another, the settlements had little interaction. Indeed, most settlers were only vaguely aware of the existence of the other land settlements although most had heard of Markland—the first and most publicized of the projects. Once released from government support, the settlements were strongly influenced by the communities around them, their relative location within local settlement networks and regional economies.

Before 1935 the settlers of the outer Port au Port area lived in loose hamlets and homesteads scattered irregularly along the coastal margins. The development of Lourdes created the only centrally organized village in the area and established the settlement as the chief service centre. This centrality was controlled largely by the presence of the church, but was also promoted by the growth of the co-operative movement which became an active force in rural development. The Lourdes co-operative accepted members from the surrounding region, and branches were opened at Long Point, Black Duck Brook, Winterhouse, Three Rock Cove and Mainland. It became the main regional retail supplier, the chief handler of fish products, and a major sub-contractor for logging.

The central area of Lourdes meanwhile became the site of the main schools, the medical clinic, parish buildings, and the co-operative stores and eventually contained most of the central services for the entire outer Port au Port area. Time and a considerable amount of intermarriage between the descendants of the land settlers and the original French speaking population have helped to heal early wounds and reduce frictions between the two groups.

Whereas Lourdes developed the status of a small regional centre, the other land settlements hold low ranking in the hierarchical settlement systems of their respective regions. In recent times most have suffered the loss of schools and services through trends towards centralization. Since the 1960s most farmland at Midland has been redeveloped for suburban housing and absorbed into the nearby town of Pasadena. Some householders in Point au Mal accepted government resettlement grants during the 1960s, and relocated to Port au Port and Stephenville, leaving behind a small scattered remnant of the former land settlement. Brown's Arm has survived rather than thrived. Haricot has all but been abandoned, although a few dwellings are occupied regularly, and several others are holiday cottages. Until recently Sandringham, on the border of Terra Nova National Park, was one of the smaller communities on the Eastport Peninsula. In 1986, it was ranked third in population among seven settlements, but was one of the few communities on the peninsula to show any significant population growth in recent times. Several of the Sandringham landowners and farmers in the 1970s refused to sell their land to the National Park for the construction of a golf course. While Sandringham has become largely a community of commuters, holiday cottagers and retirees, four sons of the original settlers are still full-time farmers, and a few others engage in part-time farming. Most of their produce, mainly root crops, strawberries and tomatoes, is marketed to tourists and to local residents. Sandringham is within easy commuting range of Clarenville, Gander, Glovertown and Terra Nova National Park. This situation provides opportunities and options for services, education, training, employment and entertainment and helps to explain its recent demographic vitality. Abandoned farmland provides attractions for residential construction.

Like Sandringham, Winterland's fate has been much intertwined with development within the local region. When established, Winterland was the only inland settlement on the Burin Peninsula. Its initial isolation was largely eliminated when the main highway between Marystown and Grand Bank was upgraded and paved. Winterland currently has four full-time farmers who are descendants of the original land settlers, and a number of part-time farmers. Most of the labour force, however, commutes to work in nearby towns, especially Marystown and Burin. These towns also provide the markets for produce, especially cabbages and livestock. Some of the peatland around Winterland has been developed for pastures, hayland and root crops. In the 1960s an attempt by an Alberta rancher to establish a cattle operation in the area, with the encouragement and support of the Newfoundland government, failed lamentably. Some of the land improved for the ranch was then put to use as a regional community pasture. Some was also used to build an airfield. Winterland has been well integrated into the settlement fabric of the Burin Peninsula and a population increase of 11.6 per cent between 1981 and 1986 indicates that it has some positive attraction as a residential area.

While under the management of the trustees, Markland seems to have possessed a strong community spirit. This sense of pride and enthusiasm, however, seems to have been undermined by the failure of various projects such as the co-operative society, a furniture manufacturing scheme, and bogland reclamation. When the American base at Argentia offered wage paying jobs in 1941, the community began to fall apart. The folk schools were replaced by two denominational schools in 1945, and in later years these were closed and children were sent by bus to Whitbourne. To a large degree Markland has persisted only as a depressed rural community. A few families have gained some benefit from the land as part-time farmers. Generally, Markland consists of loose groupings of dwellings, and a scattering of homesteaders without sufficient social or economic ties to bind them into a cohesive community. Local leadership has also been lacking. The main roads were unpaved until 1991, and there is no local government. Paradoxically, the individualism that Markland, as a model community, was supposed to dispel, seems to have been one of the major deterrents to its own community development.

Conclusion

Despite the general failure of the land settlement scheme, there were modest long-term advantages to Newfoundland. Winterland and Sandringham developed as relatively successful farm communities and, at least for a generation, farming was carried on at Midland and Brown's Arm. The other settlements, however, failed as farm settlements. The Lourdes settlers cleared some land, collected their bonuses, and then went back into the fishery. Markland, Haricot and Point Au Mal settlers found work on American bases during World War II more attractive. Perhaps the most important impact on Newfoundland was that once again, if only for a few years, a government had focused attention on agriculture as an alternative to the fishery. The government also sponsored young men to attend mainland agricultural colleges and become land settlement managers. Later they were employed as agriculturalists in areas outside the land settlements. Likewise, the personnel who gained experience in land clearing using heavy equipment formed a pool of skilled labour that was later employed in base construction, in extending arable and pasture acreages in other areas, and in road construction. Perhaps most importantly, the government after World War II again offered land clearing schemes and bonuses first developed for the land settlements to all communities The acreage of productive agricultural land was thus greatly extended in areas where some commercial agricultural was already in progress. These areas included Bay St. George, the Cape Shore, the Humber Valley and Goulds-Kilbride. Additionally, a land settlement for veterans was established at Cormack which is today one of the province's main farming communities. The Lethbridge-Musgravetown area, developed in the late 1940s, has enjoyed similar success. Under the land clearing schemes of the Commission of Government more land was probably improved for farming than in all previous periods. While much of this land was subsequently abandoned, the agricultural land base of Newfoundland today is very much a legacy of the Commission era.

NOTES

*The author wishes to thank James Hiller, Peter Neary and Chesley Sanger for helpful comments on an earlier draft of this paper.

1   This paper is based largely on the author's, 'The Origin and Development of Commission of Government Land Settlements in Newfoundland 1934-1969' (unpublished MA thesis, Memorial University 1969).

2   The political and economic context of the land settlement scheme is well treated in Peter Neary, *Newfoundland in the North Atlantic World 1929-1949* (Kingston and Montreal 1988) and S.J.R. Noel, *Politics in Newfoundland* (Toronto 1971). See also Marilyn Tuck, 'The Newfoundland Ranger Force, 1935-1950' (unpublished MA thesis, Memorial University 1983).

3   United Kingdom, Parliamentary Papers, Cm. 4480, 1933, *Newfoundland Royal Commission 1933: Report.*

4   Noel, *Politics in Newfoundland,* 250-3.

5   Lodge's views on land settlements are contained in the Commission of Government files in the Provincial Archives of Newfoundland and Labrador, series GN 38. All subsequent GN (Government of Newfoundland) references are to documents in this archive. For a summary of Lodge's views see his *Dictatorship in Newfoundland* (London 1939).

6   John A. Salmond, *The Civilian Conservation Corps 1933-1942: A New Deal Case Study* (Durham, North Carolina 1967).

7   Ian M. Drummond, *British Economic Policy and the Empire* (London 1972), 41.

8   E.C. Moulton, 'The Political History of Newfoundland 1861-1869' (unpublished MA thesis, Memorial University 1960), 130-2.

9   See essay by James Hiller in this vol.

10 The general philosophy is outlined in the GN 38/S2-1-6, 'Interim Report on Markland,' Dec. 1934.

11 Ibid., Lodge, 'Memorandum on General Policy,' 25 Jan. 1935. It was estimated that 10 per cent of the total population would have to be channelled into new types of economic activity.

12 GN 38/S2-1-7, Walwyn to Secretary of State for Dominion Affairs, 31 March 1937.

13   J.A. Hanley 'Report on the Development of Agriculture in Newfoundland,'
      Dec. 1937, in J.H. Gorvin, *Papers Relating to a Long Range Reconstruction Policy
      in Newfoundland*, vol. 2 (St. John's 1938). Vol. 1 contains the 'Interim Report of
      J.H. Gorvin.' See also Gorvin, *Report on Land Settlements in Newfoundland*,
      Department of Agriculture and Rural Reconstruciton, Economic Series, No.
      1 (St. John's 1938).

14   GN 1/8/2, N.R. 86, 1934-36, Ewbank to Trentham, 20 Nov. 1936.

15   Noel, *Politics in Newfoundland*, 231-2.

16   'Interim Report on Markland,' 4.

17   Lodge, *Dictatorship*, 173, 177.

18   'Interim Report on Markland,' 14.

19   The origins of the settlers were reconstructed from field surveys, lists of
      settlers, and crown grants. See Handcock, 'The Origin and Development,'
      22-8.

20   'Interim Report on Markland,' 12-14.

21   Ibid.

22   Lodge *Dictatorship*, 172.

23   For a detailed analysis, see Handcock, 'The Origin and Development,' 15-17.
      See also GN 38/S2-1, Walwyn to Secretary of State for Dominion Affairs, 13
      Oct. 1939.

24   Data for 1944 agricultural production are given in the 1945 Newfoundland
      census.

25   Hanley, 'Report on the Development,' 48.

26   Gorvin, 'Interim Report,' 12-13.

27   Gerald M. Sider, *Culture and Class in Anthropology and History: A Newfoundland
      Illustration* (Cambridge 1986), 114-15.

28   H.W. Hulan (Chairman), *Towards the Next Century: Agriculture in Newfound-
      land and Labrador: The Report of the Task Force on Agrifoods* (St. John's 1991), 9.

29   For a fuller discussion, see Handcock, 'The Origin and Development,' 55-60,
      and Lodge, *Dictatorship*, 186-7.

30   Much of my information on the early history of Lourdes comes from personal
      correspondence with the late F.J. Warren, land manager at Lourdes, 1935-8.
      According to Warren, Father O'Reilly was returning to Newfoundland from
      Ireland by sea when he encountered Sir John Hope Simpson.

31   Lodge, *Dictatorship*, 184-6.

32   These stories were related by settlers at both Midland and Brown's Arm.

33   The details of in-migration, out-migration and replacement were recon-
      structed from field work in 1969. Original name lists and origins were
      compiled from government documents and from interviewing original set-
      tlers and their families. Crown land records provided a list of all settlers for
      1945 who received land grants.

34   'Interim Report on Markland,' 8.

35   Such reports are scattered through the files of various government depart-
      ments. See also Handcock, 'The Origin and Development,' 56-9.

36   The 1939 reports are in GN 38/S2-1-8.

37   Data from field surveys, Aug. 1969.

38   The Midland dairy farmer came from an Eastport family with a farming
      tradition. A similar case occurred at Markland, when a St. Phillip's man
      married a Markland wife, acquired land and developed a successful farm.
      Many of the World War II veterans who took land in Cormack left within a
      few years, but several very successful farms have since been developed on
      these lots.

39   Handcock, 'The Origin and Development,' 20-1. See also Gorvin, 'Interim
      Report,' Appendix IV, Table D, 56.

40   Determined from Crown land grants issued in 1945, and field survey, 1969.

41   Crown Lands Office, Howley Building, St. John's, Land Development Act
      Grants, 1944.

42   Handcock, 'The Origin and Development,' Appendix B, 'Land Development
      Act,' 340-3; Appendix C, Land Settlement Areas, 344.

43   Calculated from occupations given in Electoral Registers for 1955. Copies in
      Centre for Newfoundland Studies (CNS), Queen Elizabeth II Library, Memo-
      rial University, St. John's.

44   CNS, Electoral Registers, 1985.

'Deemed Undesirable': Newfoundland's Immigration Policy, 1900-49

Gerhard P. Bassler

The governor in commission may by Proclamation or order whenever he deems it necessary or expedient prohibit or limit in number for a stated period or permanently the landing in Newfoundland...of immigrants belonging to any nationality or race or of immigrants of any specified class or occupation, by reason of any economic, industrial or other condition temporarily existing in Newfoundland or because such immigrants are deemed unsuitable having regard to the climatic, industrial, social, educational, labour or other conditions or requirements of Newfoundland or because such immigrants are deemed undesirable owing to their peculiar customs, habits, modes of life and methods of holding property, or because of their probable inability to become readily assimilated or to assume the duties and responsibilities of Newfoundland citizenship within a reasonable time after their entry [draft immigration act, 1938].

AT FIRST GLANCE the history of immigration in Newfoundland in the first half of the twentieth century might not seem to be a field of inquiry likely to uncover much of interest. The big tides of European migrants heading for the North American mainland from the mid-nineteenth to the mid-twentieth centuries bypassed Newfoundland. Relatively few newcomers are known to have settled on the island after the arrival of the last major influx from the British Isles in the early nineteenth century. Considerable light has already been shed on the colonization of Newfoundland in the seventeenth to the early nineteenth centuries by its original English, Irish, and Scottish settlers.[1] But data about the nature and patterns of subsequent immigration are contradictory and still largely unexplored.[2] The lack of any reference to Newfoundland's immigration policy in historical and scholarly literature suggests that the country neither had nor needed such a policy. Newfoundland is known instead for its steady excess of emigration over immigration. Indeed, in its historical experience and popular mythology, twentieth-century Newfoundland has come to see itself increasingly as a country of emigration, and the incompatibility of this notion with immigration has come to be taken for granted.

In Canada, the massive post-World War II influx of continental Europeans has triggered continuing debate about the impact and merits of immigration. Sparked by Mabel F. Timlin's *Does Canada Need More People?*,[3] this debate has opened new perspectives on Canadian society, culture, and history.[4] It has also produced significant practical results by preparing the ground for official multiculturalism, a liberal approach to refugee settlement, the abolition of criteria for admission based on ethnic and racial considerations, and official apologies for wartime discrimination. So far, all this has had little effect on the analysis of Newfoundland society and history. Newfoundland historiography has focused on politics, shipping, fishing, and the search for similarities between Newfoundland's economic problems and those of the rest of Atlantic Canada.

Many of the issues explored in post-war Canadian immigration research are, however, of obvious relevance to aspects of Newfoundland history. For instance, enquiries into the experience in immigration and its multicultural dimensions illustrate the kind of challenges and adjustment problems newcomers generally face, and particularly settlers of non-British background. Similarly, an analysis of the attitudes and policies of the host society towards immigrants, in times of prosperity and depression, peace and war, reveals the kind of reception awaiting immigrants and the pattern of their assimilation into the host society. Last but not least, what were the objectives and results of Newfoundland's immigration policy? This question may be particularly relevant in twentieth-century Canada and other immigrant-receiving countries in view of the crucial role played by government policy and legislation in determining levels, structure, origins, and the ethno-cultural composition of those immigrating.

An enquiry into the relationship between Newfoundland's government policy and the negligible volume of immigration raises a host of intriguing questions. Was immigration minimal despite or because of government policy? Did policy aim at recruiting or excluding immigrants? Were Newfoundland's economic difficulties a cause, or were they also a consequence of the lack of immigration (whether government induced or not)? Did refugees seek asylum? If so, were they offered sanctuary? These and related questions must be addressed if we are to gain a more comprehensive understanding of the forces that shaped modern Newfoundland's demographic, economic, social, and cultural history.

The study of Newfoundland's pre-confederation immigration legislation and immigration policy places Newfoundland in the context of international migration and the legislative and policy responses of other countries receiving immigrants. It exposes the local elite's approach to the challenge of refugee settlement. Equally important, an analysis of policies and legislation with regard to immigration brings to light how the elite was able to direct or thwart social and economic change. Since immigration, or the lack of it, influences a wide spectrum of developments, any policy designed to regulate immigration reveals a blueprint of the kind of society envisioned by those controlling the country's destiny.

The quest for and the restriction of immigration

On 10 August 1899 the editor of the St. John's *Evening Herald* spelled out the prevailing official attitudes toward immigration, reiterating the views of a former governor, Sir John Glover (1876-81, 1883-85):

> The great disadvantage under which this country suffered was that it was so entirely undermanned. A country one sixth larger than Ireland with a population of 210,000 has a good deal of spare room. We want our solitudes filled up and our resources developed. There is ample space here for a population of five million and that number would be able to find a comfortable subsistence.

Nourished by the spectacular conquest of the American West, and the subsequent opening of western Canada, it seemed irrefutable to most members of Newfoundland's small educated and ruling elite that filling the country's open spaces with settlers meant progress and prosperity. The principal and most enthusiastic advocates of this policy came from the class of professionals, journalists, and officials based mainly in St. John's. Though they administered the colony's affairs and had a considerable influence on public policy, they ultimately depended on the patronage and acquiescence of the group of traditionally privileged fish merchants. It is said that around 1900 some fifteen firms controlled the export of fish and the consumer oriented trades and their representatives who were firmly entrenched in the Legislative Council continued to hold the reins of power. Having expanded into shipping, insurance, manufacturing and general importing, this 'fishocracy' protected its local market with high tariffs. Considering Newfoundland as their 'private trading preserve,' the merchants were interested in development, but not at any price.[5]

The faith in the benefits of a larger population was sustained by the construction of the trans-island railway and various branch lines between 1881 and 1914. The railway was 'first and foremost' to be a 'development road'[6] opening up the country to settlement in conjunction with agriculture, mining, and lumbering. In evidence given to a British royal commission in July 1914, government officials argued strongly in favour of increased immigration, although they also admitted that virtually nothing was being done to promote it.[7] And in fact, the beginning of Newfoundland's immigration policy was marked not by concrete efforts to recruit the settlers considered desirable, but by a growing fear that, instead of the coveted British, Scandinavian, or west European immigration, an uninvited influx from undesirable areas might spoil the elite's hold on the future.

The first attempt to restrict 'undesirable' immigration was made in 1904, when Newfoundland had no more than a dozen Chinese and no Japanese settlers. A bill prohibiting the entry of Chinese and Japanese passed the House of Assembly, but was defeated in the Legislative Council. The bill was inspired by a surge of anti-Asian sentiment in Canada where a 1902 royal commission had characterized Chinese and Japanese immigrants as 'obnoxious to a free community and dangerous to the state,' and where in 1903 the Chinese head tax was raised from $100 to $500.[8] Curiously, the Legislative Council debate did not touch on the presence or absence of east Asian immigrants, or on any potential economic or cultural threat they might pose to the colony. Rather, the debate centred on the concern that China might retaliate by restricting Newfoundland's and Britain's trade and access to that country.[9]

In 1906 the legislature finally passed the comprehensive legislation to restrict Chinese immigration that formed the statutory basis for systematic entry controls. Such legislation, as in Canada and the United States, was a reaction to the so-called 'new immigration' that, between the 1890s and 1914, brought to North America the largest tide of immigrants in its history. This tide did not come from traditional areas, but from 'new' ones, namely, southern and eastern Europe and Asia. Because of their cultural background and presumed transient nature, the 'new' immigrants were widely perceived to be difficult to assimilate. Thus, sweeping and discriminatory entry restrictions were introduced in Canada between 1902 and 1911, and prepared by the American Dillingham Commission in 1910.[10]

The 'new immigration' affected Newfoundland in three ways: directly, with the arrival of some 500 permanent settlers from eastern Europe, the Middle East, and China; indirectly, through the occasional stopover of steamships full of immigrants headed for the North American mainland, which resulted in and attempts by some of these immigrants to bypass Canadian and American controls; and psychologically, through the negative stereotyping of these immigrants.

Newfoundland's elite became so alarmed by the coincidence of these factors that, despite the absence of negative repercussions resulting from the new immigration, and with continued reaffirmations of the need to recruit desirable settlers, Newfoundland restricted immigration. Their small numbers notwithstanding, the arrival of these 'peculiar people'[11] was a highly visible event in a society which for generations had experienced virtually no immigration. The available evidence suggests that, in the half-century before the Great War, the newcomers from eastern Europe and Asia were the only identifiable immigrants eager to stay and settle on the island.

Official immigration statistics are scarce and incomplete. They are also unreliable, largely due to the highly transient nature of the passenger traffic moving to and through Newfoundland, and because of the virtual impossibility of registering this traffic on all ships and in all ports. For the period 1903-13, for instance, officials recorded the annual number of 'intending settlers' as between 536 and 885 among the annual average of 11,340 inward passengers (1906 when the number rose to 1,447 was an exception). But the census of residents born outside Newfoundland shows a decline from 4,008 in 1901 to 3,475 in 1911. In the latter year, the origin of all but 353 was either British (1,542), Canadian (1,304), or American (378). Many of these were transients who ultimately moved on. They were recruited to assume managerial, supervisory, clerical, teaching, ministerial, or professional positions for which local residents were apparently unavailable. The bulk of the non-Anglo-Saxon settlers, according to various sources, consisted of three main groups: Chinese, Syrians from the Ottoman empire (primarily Maronite, Christian Syrian and Druze, but also including Palestinians and Armenians), and Russian-Polish Jews.[12] The Syrians identified themselves as refugees from Turkish ethnic, economic, and political repression.[13] Similarly, the Jews were refugees from Russian anti-semitism.[14]

The newcomers did not compete with local trades or workers and, except for the apprehensions arising from imported negative stereotyping, there is no evidence that they or the immigrant traffic moving through Newfoundland to the mainland constituted an economic, medical, or social danger. The unanticipated influx indicated, however, that the colony did offer attractions and opportunities to settlers, despite the simultaneous exodus of native born to New England, Cape Breton, and beyond.[15]

In 1906 the Newfoundland government responded to the new immigration by passing 'An Act to regulate the Law with regard to Aliens' (the Aliens Act) and 'An Act respecting the Immigration of Chinese persons' (the Chinese Immigration Act). These acts ended the existing open door policy and restricted entry. Prior to 1906, only the landing of paupers, the sickly, the elderly, and the infirm was an indictable offence.[16] The Chinese Immigration Act was modelled on the Canadian Chinese Exclusion Act of 1903, and the Aliens Act on the British 'Alien's Act' of 1905. The legislation imposed a $300 per head landing fee on Chinese immigrants, and subjected all non-British aliens to medical and means tests. Aliens suffering a financial, physical, mental, or criminal debility, and 'likely' to become a charge on the public, were declared undesirable. The acts also established procedures for the identification, exclusion, and deportation of undesirables by the Customs Branch of the Department of Finance and Customs.

The 1906 legislation created the basis for a dichotomous immigration policy of soliciting British and northwest European settlers, while subjecting all other immigrants to controls that were easily expandable. Chinese immigration, for instance, was restricted, among other requirements, by the need for a permit and nominal registration, by limiting without the existence of legal authorization the local Chinese community to a maximum of 200 persons, and by totally excluding Chinese women. The Aliens Act, on the other hand, copied from its British model the principle that refugees from political or religious persecution were entitled to asylum, even if they arrived in poverty.[17]

The contradictions of the 1906 acts were evident in other ways. Entry controls were formulated by a government that contended that the lack of

immigration was hampering the colony's development. They were legis-
lated at a time of considerable prosperity, when there was a declared
shortage of labour.[18] There was no pressure to restrict immigration from
either the rural fishing population, which was in any case experiencing a
heavy drain of emigrants to the mainland, or from the urban labour movement. The St. John's Longshoremen's Protective Union endorsed the Chinese Immigration Act only after it had been introduced and debated in the
House of Assembly. Rather, entry restrictions were initiated by the class
whose equivalent in Canada and the United States traditionally promoted
the admission of cheap foreign labour.

Closing the gates to immigration, 1924-34

The established pattern of Newfoundland's immigration policy persisted
after World War I. From 1924 on, external and internal factors conspired to
stimulate an expansion of immigration controls, so that by 1932 Newfoundland's gates to immigration were virtually closed. Starting in the early 1920s
a crisis in the fishery intensified, crippled retailers and local manufacturers,
and led to widespread unemployment.[19] Beginning in 1926, a severe drop
in the world price for newsprint harmed Newfoundland's second largest
export industry and caused a decline in logging operations.[20] By 1933 the
number of destitute persons eligible for relief had climbed to 90,000, almost
one-third of the population. In contrast to 1906, there was now an obvious
socio-economic rationale to exclude immigrants. In practice, however, only
non-British 'foreigners' were excluded while immigrants from Britain,
Canada, and the USA continued to be solicited, in part because they might
possess needed skills. In 1925 lawyer Gordon Bradley pleaded with W.J.
Higgins, the Minister of Justice, to promote immigration actively:

> In the past Newfoundland seems to have held out no attractions
> sufficient to induce prospective settlers to come amongst us...The ac-
> quiring of expert mechanics is needed in Newfoundland at present and
> in view of the industrial expansion which is now and will probably be
> hereafter taking place it will be a calamity if we are not able to meet
> their demand. It is now well known to you and me that there has been
> a shortage of skilled labour...during the past year or so and this shortage
> is likely to increase rather than to lessen unless we find additional men
> somewhere.

In the spring of 1926 the management of the Newfoundland Power and
Paper Company at Corner Brook confirmed the existence of a demand for
foreign skilled labour.[21]

Government records highlight external factors as a primary cause for
tightening restrictions. Canadian and American exclusionist legislation
between 1919 and 1924 acted as a catalyst for Newfoundland immigration
policy in three ways. By excluding or deporting an increasing number of
Newfoundlanders, Canadian and American immigration controls closed

off the island's traditional safety valve for unemployment and directly affected its precarious labour market. Unable to find work upon their forced return, hundreds of Newfoundlanders became a charge on the government at a time when it could least afford to support them. In addition, the local economy lost the cash remittances—estimated at $1 million a year—these former emigrants would normally have been sending home.[22]

The new controls also prompted justifiable apprehensions that immigrants refused by Canada and the United States might be diverted to Newfoundland. These rejects, it was feared, would attempt illegal entry from Newfoundland; and if caught and deported from the mainland, Newfoundland would have to take them back. The 1926 Immigration Act, for instance, was triggered by the impending arrival of 200 Lithuanians, some of whom were quite wealthy, who allegedly intended to use Newfoundland as a stepping stone to enter the United States. As might be expected, American and particularly Canadian legislation and regulations provided an impetus and model for Newfoundland's restrictions. The acts of 1924 and 1926, the regulations of 1926, and the proclamation of 1932 are evidence of this.[23]

The 1872 Disembarkation of Paupers Act had disqualified paupers as well as criminals and the mentally ill, and had made the master of a vessel bringing such persons to the colony liable to prosecution. The 1924 amendment[24] required the act to be administered by the Department of Justice (instead of Customs), and authorized the expulsion of anyone born outside Newfoundland who might be considered 'undesirable' in the opinion of the minister. W.J. Higgins explained in 1924 that the power of expulsion would be exercised if 'there was something in [a person's] conduct or habits that would give rise to complaint against him, such as, for example, his being a labour agitator or a troublemaker in some other direction.'[25]

The people excluded or expelled under the authority of this act in the 1920s and 1930s were primarily immigrants from south and east Europe, in particular Lithuanians, Latvians, Poles, Russians, Romanians, and Italians. The most common official reasons given for expulsion were that these foreigners were undesirable, would 'likely' become a public charge, or might use Newfoundland as a stepping stone to enter Canada or the United States. In October 1927, for instance, two Italians were deported, though they had been assured prior to arrival by a British consulate and the Newfoundland high commissioner in London that they satisfied all the entry requirements; the official reason was the unproven allegation 'that if they attempt to enter the United States—as it is suspected they may do— they will probably be thrown back upon us.' Higgins argued that if the authorities chose to consider persons undesirable for reasons other than those specifically provided for in the act, the governor in council could nevertheless exclude them 'in his own unqualified discretion.'[26]

A more efficient and less costly way of dealing with unwanted foreign immigrants was by blanket exclusion according to racial, ethnic, national, and occupational criteria. This was the objective of the 1926 Immigration Act, a law designed to supplement, but not replace, the Aliens Act. The 1926 act empowered the government to prescribe, by regulation, the minimum amount of money, depending on race, occupation, or destination, that an immigrant must possess on landing. Furthermore, it authorized the government, whenever it deemed it 'necessary or expedient,' to prohibit 'the landing of immigrants belonging to any race deemed unsuited to the climate or requirements of the Colony, or immigrants of any specified class, occupation or character.' Finally, the act enabled the government to deport 'any immigrants rejected or landing without leave or landing contrary to any of the provisions of this Act.'

The administration of the 1926 act expanded the duties and responsibilities of the staff of the Customs Department, and in October 1927 the title of Chief Commissioner of Immigration was given to its deputy minister.[27] He was in charge of the required extensive screening of all immigrants at the point of entry, the temporary custody of immigrants refused permission to land, and the issuing of deportation orders compelling the ship, its owner, and its agent, to remove such immigrants at their expense. Customs officials were now able to board and inspect a ship and possessed the right of rejection in the first instance, instead of having to wait until persons were proven undesirables.[28]

Regulations issued in November 1926 required every adult immigrant to have a valid passport and $250 (dependants needed half the amount), unless the immigrant was sponsored by a first-degree relative or going to assured employment and had the means to reach it. British, Canadian, and United States citizens were exempted from these restrictions, as were the citizens of all western European and Scandinavian countries. These controls were soon considered insufficiently restrictive, especially in the light of Canadian orders in August 1930 barring the admission of labourers from central Europe and American measures of March 1931 limiting immigration from quota countries to 10 per cent of their quotas.[29] In addition, the Great Depression had hit Newfoundland severely.

In January 1932, the 1926 regulations were replaced by a proclamation (under the 1926 act) prohibiting the entry for two years of all central and east Europeans (excluding natives of countries to which Newfoundland was selling fish); persons belonging by race to any country in Asia or Africa; and all non-Newfoundlanders of the labouring classes. Even immigrants from non-prohibited countries had to satisfy the authorities that they were not likely to become public charges. As a result of the new system, steamship companies began to insist that European immigrants obtain entry permits before sailing, in order to avoid the risk of having to transport them back if they were refused on landing. In the 1930s, permits issued by the

Chief Commissioner of Immigration became a prerequisite for anyone intending to enter Newfoundland for a period of more than six weeks. The issuing of advance permits to those eligible to land became the most effective way of controlling immigration.[30]

In preparing the 1932 proclamation, which had gone through various revised drafts since August 1930, the Department of Justice ensured that the countries of origin of Newfoundland's existing non-British minorities were in the prohibited category. They were Syria, Armenia, Turkey, Egypt, Russia, Poland, and the Baltic countries. Excluded also were persons belonging by race to a prohibited country, even though they might actually be nationals of a non-prohibited country. For example, a Russian who was a German national, or a Pole who was an American national, was excluded. Immigrants were banned from Austria, Hungary, and Czechoslovakia because those countries did not import from Newfoundland, while immigrants were admissible from Germany because that country imported Newfoundland fish and iron ore.[31]

When the proclamation lapsed in January 1934, it was not renewed because the Dominions Office, fearing retaliation, objected to discrimination against specific countries or a class of countries. The appointed Commission of Government, which took office in February 1934, had no option but to comply. This change should have allowed a return to a more liberal practice based on the 1926 regulations. In reality, the immigration authorities, without fully apprising the public, continued to act in the spirit of the 1932 proclamation.

The theory and practice of unqualified exclusion, 1934-39

During 1934 and 1935 officials discussed how the severe restrictions of the 1932 proclamation might be continued, though the proclamation itself had lapsed. They had three choices. One was a quota system, but this was judged unsuitable for a country 'where immigration is infinitesimal.' Other possibilities were a general prohibition of immigration (except for special cases), or the issuing of permits by British consular officials. In the ensuing debate, British and Newfoundland officials in the departments responsible for immigration took opposing views. In particular, differences developed between the Departments of Finance (responsible for customs and immigration duties under the 1906 and 1926 acts) and Justice (responsible for the law itself, and for administering deportations under the 1924 act).

The Commissioner for Finance, E.N.R. Trentham, endorsed the argument of his adviser on customs, P.D.H. Dunn, in favour of a permit system. Prospective settlers and visitors should apply to the Board of Customs, which acted as the immigration authority, for a permit to land. The opposing view, favoured by the Commissioner for Justice, W.R. Howley, his

Secretary (i.e. deputy minister), Brian Dunfield, and the Chief Commissioner of Immigration, H.V. Hutchings, was that there should be a revised law allowing for exclusion according to specified racial and national criteria. Howley considered it 'a comparatively easy matter to make effective prohibition on such terms as will not in any way be embarrassing to international relations' and expected the Dominions Office to co-operate in drafting an appropriate proclamation.[32]

Dunfield and Hutchings, who had administered immigration and deportation before 1934, took up the defence of Newfoundland's traditional immigration policy. The 1926 act gave them the authority to declare 'undesirable' any person 'likely to become a public charge.' They could also fall back on a doctrine which the Department of Justice, in connection with the deportation of two Italian immigrants, had first communicated to the Customs Department as early as October 1927. It provided as follows:

> in the case of an immigrant who was not an undesirable person within the provision of the Acts, the Governor in Council may be the proper authority to decide on his exclusion, which the Governor in Council can do on any ground, or no ground whatever if he thought fit.[33]

Dunfield, a lawyer and economics lecturer at Memorial University College, had been Acting Deputy Minister of Justice since 1927.[34] As the government's legal expert on deportation, he was highly critical of Dunn's proposal for an 'ultra-generous' immigration policy, considering it appropriate for Britain but not for Newfoundland. In 1935 he pointed out to Sir John Hope Simpson, one of the British members of the Commission of Government, that the 1924 and 1926 acts established 'good expulsion procedure for use at any time.' The 1924 provisions for expelling undesirable aliens, he said, had been drawn up 'to exclude Communists or others of suspected undesirable activities that we could not prove, at any rate, in our Courts.'[35]

H.V. Hutchings, appointed Chief Commissioner of Immigration in 1928, also stood for continuity. Guided by the spirit of the 1932 proclamation, he refused landing permits to aliens whenever possible. His practice was challenged in 1935 and 1936 by the solicitors for two residents who applied for the admission of their fiancées from Poland and Lithuania. In each case Hutchings was advised by the Department of Justice that his refusal of landing permits was illegal, but that he had the choice between issuing new restrictive regulations prior to the arrival of the women and deporting them on arrival.[36] The records do not indicate whether the applicants were admitted.

The practices and policies of Dunfield and Hutchings reflected those of the business community as represented by the Newfoundland Board of Trade. Since Canadian immigration laws now excluded Newfoundlanders from Canada, the board was eager for the Commission to introduce new restrictive regulations, and to negotiate a reciprocal arrangement 'whereby

Newfoundlanders entering Canada may encounter equal facilities with Canadians entering this country.'[37] The Board of Trade lobby manifested distinct nativist overtones. Worried that in the absence of new controls it was 'possible for undesirable businessmen to enter the country and go into business,' the Board demanded that 'our immigration laws should be tightened very considerably indeed.' With unemployment in every area, except agriculture, a Board spokesman questioned in January 1939 whether it was 'wise for the Government to encourage immigrants, even though they be trained.'[38]

Addressing these concerns became a prime objective of L.E. Emerson, who succeeded Howley at the Department of Justice in September 1937, and also became responsible for defence in 1939. Emerson had been a cabinet member in 1924 and Minister of Justice from 1932 to 1934. Intelligent, experienced, and ambitious, Emerson quickly became a key figure on the Commission. Married into a prominent Water Street business family, and an intimate of the Roman Catholic archbishop, Emerson was highly regarded and 'well connected in the small, tightly knit elite that dominated local society.' Peter Neary has interpreted Emerson's appointment as a demonstration of British willingness and ability 'to head off establishment opposition by bringing key members of it on board.'[39] A commissioner until 1944, Emerson stood for the protection of the interests of that elite against British reforming zeal whether it came from within the Commission or from Whitehall.

The four year search for a policy solution to the unsettled issue of immigration and deportation was brought to a head by the coincidence of three developments: Germany's annexation of Austria; Britain's re-introduction, in April 1938, of visa requirements for holders of German and Austrian passports; and the receipt by the Customs Department and the local German vice-consul of a number of applications to take up permanent residence in Newfoundland from Germans and Austrians. Since it might 'not be desirable to admit' these persons, and some action was imperative, Emerson requested that the Commission agree in principle to a new act 'on Canadian lines, establishing a Newfoundland citizenship and leaving the power of deportation to be exercised departmentally, as at present, against any undesirable not a holder of such citizenship, whether technically British or alien.'[40] Emerson emphasized that Canadian law, apart from prohibiting illiterates and persons of undesirable political opinions, had a 'very broad provision against persons' who did not meet the requirements of regulations:

> The regulations may require a money qualification and prohibit or limit the number of immigrants of any nationality or race or any class or occupation or immigrants whose customs or modes of life are deemed undesirable, or who are considered not readily assimilable by Canada.

Canadian law also allowed any person, not a Canadian citizen, to be deported with his dependants, if any, upon government order. Regretting that Newfoundland law did not exclude classes of economically or racially undesirable persons, Emerson also criticized the provision of the 1906 Aliens Act 'that a political or religious refugee is not to be refused leave to land merely on the ground of the probability of his becoming a charge on the public funds.' Emerson thought this 'too liberal in present circumstances.'[41]

J.H. Penson, the Commissioner for Finance, countered Emerson's plans on the basis 'that we are bound to follow the United Kingdom and should in any case wish to do so.' Great Britain, he pointed out, was densely populated and suffering from unemployment; nevertheless, it was offering asylum as far as practicable. He wanted Newfoundland to permit the entry of a limited number of qualified immigrants who were assured employment and possessed a minimum of $250. A policy of total exclusion was harmful. 'The need of the country should override the interests of individuals,' Penson maintained:

> [W]e could well and profitably allow the settlement on the Island of well qualified professional men and other specialists. It may be too in the common interest if farmers and agriculturists of the industrious and well informed type so common on the Continent, took up permanent residence in this country.[42]

In April 1938 the Commission agreed on a compromise solution: until the passing of new legislation, Penson's proposal would be adopted. This was supposed to permit a limited immigration, controlled by the Commission's prior approval of visas granted by British consular authorities. With regard to the proposed legislation, the minutes state that 'the Commissioner for Justice will, after consultation with the Commissioner for Finance, communicate semi-officially with the Dominions Office recommending that in the treatment of British subjects and aliens, Newfoundland should follow the same practice as Canada.'[43] In a covering statement, Emerson contended that his proposed legislation 'would certainly be enacted' if self-government were restored.

When the Dominions Office, in response to a reminder from St. John's, replied six months later, it asked for more time to consider 'the rather complicated issues' raised by Emerson and suggested other interim measures, such as a permit system for aliens, or an order under the 1926 act. Although Newfoundland could not be prevented from introducing legislation similar to that passed in Canada, Emerson had raised 'a good many thorny subjects' that had troubled the Dominions Office in the past. One official, C.R. Price, believed the main difficulty with the proposed legislation was how to control the entry of political refugees without discriminatory regulations. The best solution would be a permit system for aliens. A 'less watertight solution' would be a repeal of the 1906 refugee clause, but this would perhaps 'not be politically desirable at the present time.'[44]

At the end of November 1938 Emerson made his next move. The Customs Department, he cabled London, was 'flooded with applications, mainly from Continental Jews, who desire to settle in Newfoundland,' and the permit system proposed by Whitehall would not be enough. Legislation was required. He proposed amending the 1926 act,[45] as well as issuing a proclamation to prohibit for two years the landing for residence of persons being natives of, or belonging by race to any country other than the United Kingdom, unless they had received a special permit. The legislation, he explained, would be following strictly Canadian precedents.[46]

The Dominions Office was concerned and confused about Emerson's real intentions and wanted his proposed comprehensive legislation 'on somewhat drastic lines' to be 'allowed to sleep' until it could be ascertained how the permit system was working. The main question was whether Newfoundland immigration and deportation legislation should follow the exclusionist stance adopted by the self-governing dominions, or the less restrictive approach which British colonies without self-government had taken on the advice of Whitehall. Price singled out four difficulties with Emerson's proposal. First, the Secretary of State for Dominion Affairs had to be able to defend to foreign representatives and British public opinion the effect of Newfoundland's legislation on aliens, British subjects, and alien refugees. Second, the proposed legislation, if adopted with Dominions Office assent, would be reactionary from the colonies' point of view, and might induce them to try and adopt 'dominion' legislation themselves. Third, the spectre of a future self-governing Newfoundland enacting even more drastic legislation might be forestalled by assisting in working out 'reasonable legislation on Dominion lines now.' Finally, new legislation on Canadian lines establishing Newfoundland citizenship with rules as to how it would be acquired or lost might, as in Canada, lead to wholesale deportations if, 'whether technically British or alien,' people became public charges before they became eligible for citizenship. Price realized that 'under existing legislation an expulsion order may be made on grounds *inter alia* of public charge or of mere undesirability, against any person not born in Newfoundland.' Therefore, and in view of Emerson's warning that this kind of legislation 'would certainly be enacted' if self-government were restored, Price felt the United Kingdom's only alternative was to promote the adoption of a moderate rather than an extreme course.[47]

In his official replies to St. John's the Secretary of State acknowledged with relief the Commission's decision to use a permit system to control the influx of aliens, and requested that British subjects be exempted from its requirements. Feeling 'considerable difficulty about provision for unqualified exclusion especially at the present moment when [the] refugee question is so much in the minds of governments and public,' he recommended the use of visas as a useful adjunct to the permit system in order to control both would-be settlers, and temporary visitors who presumably did not need a permit. What kind of instructions regarding visa requirements should be forwarded to British consular officers? Visas would be granted only to holders of valid passports and visitors with legitimate reasons. Non-Aryans in Germany, for example, were thus excluded from consideration because they now rarely held documents valid for return.[48]

Emerson insisted that only United Kingdom natives, not all British citizens, should be exempted from the permit requirement, but conceded that his draft proclamation was unnecessarily arbitrary and had to be modified. But no revised proclamation was forthcoming, which satisfied the Dominions Office, where Newfoundland's immigration legislation was thought to be in 'a state of considerable confusion.' A tightening of the existing permit system achieved the same effect as new restrictive laws, and from December 1938 the Commission depended on prerogative powers to exclude undesirable aliens—or 'indeed any aliens whom they did not wish to admit.'[49]

In April 1939 the chairman of the Board of Customs, G.C. Price, summarized existing procedures for the benefit of the council of the Newfoundland Board of Trade. The Board was worried that in the absence of new regulations 'pedlars, company promoters and others [could] find their way to St. John's, and in some cases subject the public to fraud, or exert other undesirable influences.' The council also wondered 'whether or not there was a system in use for the registration of alien visitors so that their whereabouts and activities can be known to the authorities.'[50] Price reassured the council that 'the Immigration Department is not only restricting the admission of aliens of the prohibited classes as commonly understood, but it is not permitting the landing in this country...of any person who proposes to engage in any trade or business which would be in competition with any established concern.' The authorities were, nevertheless, 'prepared to consider, on their merits, applications to take up permanent residence from a limited number of persons (a) of the professional classes, (b) possessing specialist qualifications, or (c) who propose to set up a new business or undertaking.' During the previous eighteen months 'only a very few permits [had] in fact been accorded' to prospective settlers and these had been 'strictly confined' to the specified classes.[51]

The council was left in little doubt that the whereabouts and activities of any aliens permitted to enter the country would be known to the authorities. All visitors had to disclose their purpose, length of stay, and the nature of their business to the police. Consuls had instructions not to issue permits or visas to 'certain nationals' without the prior concurrence of the Chief Commissioner of Immigration, who also conveyed information about the landing of any alien to the police. Price's reply to the Board of Trade was released to the local press.[52] It confirmed that access to Newfoundland for refugees from the Third Reich was entirely at the discretion of the Chief Commissioner of Immigration, who usually adhered to a policy of unqualified exclusion.

Refugees from the Third Reich as prospective settlers, 1934-41

Prior to the war, American, Canadian, and British subjects were freely allowed to enter Newfoundland as tourists for periods of up to six weeks. They did not need permits, visas, or even passports. European refugees, however, fared differently. They were refused even temporary asylum, despite proof of adequate financial resources and of guaranteed eventual entry into the United States—usually the possession of a waiting list number for an American quota visa. Governor Sir Humphrey T. Walwyn explained to the British consul general in New York that his government had been 'faced with a considerable problem in dealing with applications from persons, mainly of Jewish extraction, who desire to leave Central Europe.' Such people might not obtain a US visa, and 'difficulties regarding repatriation might conceivably arise.' Making certain they would not engage in gainful occupations might cause administrative difficulties, but, on the other hand, they might become public charges.[53]

The rise of the Third Reich had created an unprecedented mass of potential immigrants for Newfoundland in the form of refugees. In fact, the refugees pounding on Newfoundland's door from 1934 to 1941 constituted the largest group of potential immigrants for more than a century. A conservative estimate places their number at 12,000. Judged by its promotional literature, Newfoundland wanted settlers, and it offered space, a favourable climate, a low population density, undeveloped resources, and a myriad of challenges for economic development.[54] Against this background, several significant proposals for economically beneficial group settlement were advanced on behalf of refugees. The proposals took into account the country's social and economic plight and presented the Commission of Government with unique, challenging solutions in the search for economic rehabilitation, social reform, and the restoration of political sovereignty.

Apart from numerous individual petitions for sanctuary, at least eight of the proposals for refugee settlement would have provided Newfoundland with a rare windfall of middle class settlers whose professional expertise, technical skills, and resourcefulness could have been of great value. The proposals came with either firm offers or prospects of financial support by a sponsor or sponsoring agency, or assurances that the refugees would arrive with sufficient funds and would not become a financial liability. Several of the British members of the Commission of Government, as well as Dominions Office officials, recognized the contributions a select number of European refugees might make and the spectacular opportunities for stimulating social and economic development. However, unrelenting opposition from the local professional and business elite and the stubborn defence of its vested interests by the Newfoundland commissioners ensured the exclusion of all refugee applicants and the rejection of all settlement proposals.[55]

The details of the various refugee settlement proposals and development opportunities are examined elsewhere,[56] but a brief review of a few cases illustrates their nature. One proposal came in 1934 from the Jewish Colonization Association, an international agency founded in 1890 to resettle Jewish refugees from Russia. It had an excellent record of successfully resettling Jewish refugees in the Americas. After interviewing leading Newfoundland personalities in government, business, industry, and society, its Montreal representative, Simon Belkin, carefully selected forty refugee families 'who would be very useful to the country in its present predicament and who would at no time become a public charge.' This group, to be resettled at the Association's expense, included twelve doctors, two dentists, ten nurses (primarily to operate travelling clinics to outports without medical services), as well as scientists, farmers, and small manufacturers who would produce items in local demand but currently imported. The proposal, though strongly recommended by Sir John Hope Simpson, was scuttled at the insistence of the Newfoundland Medical Association. 'Is it right for 83 Newfoundland citizens to prevent thousands of other Newfoundland citizens from receiving medical care?' complained one irate resident from the outport of Burgeo.[57]

Another proposal was initiated in 1936 by local Jewish resident Frank Banikhin. In consultation with Zionist organizations, he called for the settlement 'on a considerable scale' of Jewish refugees in Labrador where they would develop the resources of its interior, especially the hydroelectric power of what is now called Churchill Falls. This proposal, too, was strongly promoted by Hope Simpson but was dropped by the Commission after his retirement. There were questions about the project's financial backing and the Crown's rights to some of the land designated for the project. But the Dominions Office did not consider these obstacles insurmountable and continued in vain to await suggestions from Newfoundland on the proposal's implementation.

In February 1939 the Commission received a submission for the settlement of 1,000 Jewish families, headed by educated farmers, engineers, and young merchants from Hungary. They did not request any financial assistance and, in fact, planned to bring some of their assets with them. The Commission rejected their petition with the argument that there was 'no prospect of room being found' on the island for such settlers.

A proposal to settle 5,000 Jewish refugees in Labrador originated in March 1939 with Henry Klapisch, a Jewish fish merchant from Seattle.

According to his plan the refugees would set up a furniture factory, a fish cannery and other industries, employing thousands of Newfoundlanders. It was to be funded by three large Jewish organizations in the United States. The project was never undertaken and the actual decisions on its fate are still unknown. At the same time, the National Coordinating Committee in New York for Aid to Refugees and Emigrants Coming from Germany, an organization working in close co-operation with the German Jewish Aid Committee in London, proposed to work out an arrangement to place in Newfoundland specially selected refugees who would be guaranteed adequate financial support by the committee. The proposal fell through because Newfoundland's Chief Commissioner of Immigration insisted on the right to judge every case on its own merits, and he was unwilling to guarantee that even such pre-selected refugees would not be barred from landing.

As late as July 1940 a community of 289 German Hutterite refugees was prepared to finance its relocation to Newfoundland with the support of North American Hutterites. The British government recommended them as an industrious community of Christian pacifists who engaged in agriculture, local industries, and education. The governor rejected their appeal with the argument that local hostility towards them would 'almost certainly be experienced here probably in marked degree.' Shortly before, the Commission of Government had expelled Newfoundland's only refugee entrepreneur. He had been admitted six months earlier. He was alleged to be a spy but had invested thousands of his own dollars in a new woodworking enterprise and had created jobs for sixty unemployed Newfoundlanders.

The reasons given for the denial of sanctuary to individuals and groups did not reflect any consistent criteria and differed from case to case. One prosperous St. John's businesswoman, a naturalized resident, was denied permission to rescue her parents and two brothers from Poland on the eve of World War II, despite five separate efforts and the engagement of the foremost St. John's law firm on her behalf. Her solicitor was prompted to decry the Commissioner's 'unfettered and discretionary power, which may be arbitrarily and secretly exercised to deal with each case as he thinks fit.'[58]

In the public debate over the admission of refugees, the overwhelming majority of the comments were opposed. Their authors for the most part were representatives of business and professional groups. Government records and the daily press do not feature any conspicuously hostile reactions from labour. Manifestations of a pervasive xenophobia towards non-British immigrants were particularly identifiable among the educated, professional, and commercial elite of St. John's. The outports did not seem to share the urban prejudices against foreign immigrants, but rather in some instances even welcomed the services that foreigners, including refugees, were willing to provide as doctors, nurses, businessmen, or sales agents (pedlars). The voice and protagonist of the urban anti-refugee and anti-foreign lobby was Newfoundland's most widely read daily newspaper, the *Evening Telegram*. Playing on the uninformed readers' instinctive suspicion of foreigners, its editorial policy seemed aimed at deflecting possible public frustration over the elite's protection of its commercial and professional interests. It propagated the message that the only acceptable settlers would have to be both productive and certain not to interfere with any sacred vested interest. In view of the control vested interests exerted over virtually every aspect of organized life, this in reality meant 'none is too many.' The same criterion was used by the Canadian immigration director, F.C. Blair, for rejecting Jewish refugees.[59]

The development possibilities associated with the refugees of the 1930s highlight the significance of immigration policy as a potential instrument for social and economic reform. At a time of severe economic depression, when the future seemed to be dictated by forces beyond local control, the government chose to reject options that might have altered the course of Newfoundland history. Refugee settlement, industrially stimulating and economically beneficial, would have been entirely within the scope of the economic recovery strategy adopted by the Commission of Government. Indeed, several British commissioners—Hope Simpson, Penson, J.H. Gorvin and Sir Wilfrid Woods—recognized in refugee settlement a unique way to move towards a self-reliant, albeit pluralistic and multicultural society, and away from those fatal dependencies long decried by local analysts as Newfoundland's seemingly inescapable destiny.

Post-war immigration policy to 1949

The direction of immigration policy in the brief interlude between the end of the war and confederation in 1949 confirms that for Newfoundland's elite, the benefits of immigration were a low priority when the price was cultural pluralism and the possible disturbance of an hitherto unchallenged control over the country's economic, social, and cultural life. Far from loosening any of the existing restrictions, the Commission of Government kept Newfoundland's gates shut tightly until 1949. The prospects for peacetime employment were not bright, the Commissioner for Finance argued in November 1945, and given the normal surplus of labour, only the immigration of specialists could be allowed. While not denying that new blood would be beneficial to the country, the only desirable settlers he could imagine were 'a number of energetic and thrifty Scottish farmers.'[60]

As late as 1948 the Commission agreed to refuse all female Chinese immigrants, to reject applications from Chinese nationals for naturalization, to prohibit Newfoundland's Chinese community from exceeding 181 members, and hence not to admit some 150 potential Chinese immigrants, although each was prepared to pay the head tax of $300. Literally until its very last month in office, the Commission enforced the exclusions provided by the 1906 Chinese Immigration Act and collected the head tax from two Chinese students who arrived in mid-March 1949. One of them applied for a refund in May 1951,[61] because on 31 March 1949 Newfoundland residents had become citizens of Canada, where the head tax had been abolished in 1923 and exclusionist legislation had been repealed in 1947.

The argument on which Newfoundland's post-World War II immigration controls were based flew in the face of wartime and early post-war economic reality. In addition to the handsome benefits accruing from the American bases, industrial production and employment remained high. In 1948 a Canadian observer rated the levels of Newfoundland's export and import trade to be the highest in the country's history.[62] These were good times in comparison with the 1930s, and prospective iron ore developments in Labrador made them appear even better. Rather than unemployment, what seemed to be looming ahead was a labour shortage necessitating the recruitment of Europeans anxious to emigrate. The *Evening Telegram* even raised the spectre of legislation that would prevent Newfoundlanders from continuing the tradition of quitting their local employment in any given industry for 'greener pastures.' It would indeed be a 'tragedy if we had too much work for the available labour and then had to import miners, foresters and others to fill the jobs,' concluded the newspaper early in 1948.[63]

The restoration of full political sovereignty was debated in Newfoundland in the late 1940s. Its proponents understood, however, that this would only be sustainable in conjunction with economic self-reliance. As perceived by the journalist Albert Perlin, the dilemma was that 'we shall have to be an importing country, for a long time, because we have not enough population to be able to produce at home most of the things we need, at prices below the cost of imported articles.'[64] The answer of Michael Harrington, another Newfoundland writer, was that controlled resource development and the 'consumer-at-home problem' required a larger population and a more dynamic society, both of which could be obtained only at the 'price' of immigration.[65]

But by 1948 a policy of strict entry controls that had helped perpetuate the island's stagnation in a world of revolutionary change was not even questioned any more. Consequently, the post-war European exodus of hundreds of thousands of displaced persons, including a high percentage of skilled specialists desperate for sanctuary anywhere, bypassed Newfoundland.[66] Amidst unprecedented postwar prosperity the Commission of Government was preoccupied with improving deportation procedures and with breathing new life 'on Dominion lines' into L.E. Emerson's highly discriminatory and exclusionist draft immigration act which the Dominions Office had aborted in 1938.[67]

Cut off from new blood—and from the new ideas, initiatives, connections, and markets that would have accompanied it—what did the future hold for an independent, self-governing Newfoundland? Few, if any, of those who regretted Newfoundland's entry into Canada appear to have asked themselves this question. The preoccupation with Newfoundland as a country of emigration was so pervasive that even for those despairing of economic, social, and cultural stagnation, the need to regenerate society never became a public issue. Swayed by the self-interest of the local elite, the Commission of Government shied away from laying the demographic foundations for an economically more viable Newfoundland. From this perspective, confederation was indeed a blessing.

To sum up, Newfoundland's twentieth-century immigration policy before and under Commission of Government was shaped by and served the interests of the merchant dominated elite. Its blueprint for the future provided for the recruitment of 'desirable' British, and possibly Scandinavian or west European settlers, to develop the country and the restriction and exclusion of all others. Newfoundland had few immigrants and remained an ethnically homogeneous society in the half-century prior to confederation, but not because the island did not appeal to prospective newcomers. Even though the twentieth century produced a steady stream of refugees looking for a haven, non-British settlers asking for asylum were excluded as undesirables. To argue that economic conditions and the emigration of Newfoundlanders precluded any prospect of immigration to the country, and to ascribe Newfoundland's present day much acclaimed 'distinct homogeneous cultural entity' solely to the English and Irish settlers of the eighteenth and nineteenth centuries, is only part of the story. It ignores the methodical, exclusionary pre-confederation policy that artificially preserved that homogeneity.

Conventional wisdom might suggest that the economic crisis and high unemployment of the 1930s dictated the closure of the country to immigrants (except United Kingdom natives). The available evidence, however, indicates that this policy deprived Newfoundland of settlers eager and qualified to contribute to its economic recovery. The pre- and post-World War II international refugee crises offered Newfoundland a chance to choose any number and type of educated and skilled settlers and, with them, open-ended possibilities of social and economic development. Because of the refugee clause in the 1906 Aliens Act, the legal framework for the acceptance of this option was already in place, and the Commission of Government's political detachment from the local electorate and mandate for reform would have enabled its implementation. But the local elite, to protect its own privileged position, successfully pressured the Commission to reject it. Newfoundland's immigration policy, instead of being a dynamic instrument of socio-economic reform and development, thus exacerbated problems whose solution have remained elusive to this day.

NOTES

1   Gillian T. Cell, *English Enterprise in Newfoundland, 1577-1660* (Toronto 1969);
     C. Grant Head, *Eighteenth Century Newfoundland: A Geographer's Perspective*,
     (Toronto 1976); John J. Mannion (ed.), *The Peopling of Newfoundland: Essays in
     Historical Geography* (St. John's 1977); and 'Old World Antecedents, New
     World Adaptations: Inistioge (Co. Kilkenny) Immigrants in Newfoundland,'
     Newfoundland Studies 5, no.2 (1989): 103-75; Gordon Handcock, *So longe as
     there comes noe women: Origins of English Settlement in Newfoundland* (St. John's
     1989); Margaret Bennett, *The Last Stronghold: Scottish Gaelic Traditions in
     Newfoundland* (St. John's 1989). There is also an extensive popular literature
     on the topic.

2   Among inquiries touching on the subject are Alison Kahn, *Listen While I Tell
     You: A Story of the Jews of St. John's, Newfoundland* (St. John's 1988); William G.
     Reeves, '"Our Yankee Cousins": Modernization and the Newfoundland-
     American Relationship, 1898-1910,'(unpublished PH D thesis, University of
     Maine 1987); Michael Staveley, 'Population Dynamics in Newfoundland: The
     Regional Patterns,' in Mannion (ed.), *The Peopling of Newfoundland*, 49-76;
     Patricia A. Thornton, 'Newfoundland's Frontier Demographic Experience:
     The World We Have Not Lost,' *Newfoundland Studies 1*, no.2 (1985): 141-62.
     For the post-confederation period see Lisa Gilad, *The Northern Route: An
     Ethnography of Refugee Experiences* (St. John's 1990), and Gerhard P. Bassler,
     'Central Europeans in Post-Confederation St. John's, Newfoundland: Immi-
     gration and Adjustment,' *Canadian Ethnic Studies 18*, no.3 (1986): 37-46.

3   Toronto 1951.

4   Publications reflecting this debate include David C. Corbett, *Canada's Immi-
     gration Policy* (Toronto 1957); Freda Hawkins *Canada and Immigration: Public
     Policy and Public Concern* (Montreal and London 1972); Harold Troper, *Only
     Farmers Need Apply: Official Canadian Government Encouragement of Immigra-
     tion from the United States, 1896-1911* (Toronto 1972); Howard Palmer (ed.),
     Immigration and the Rise of Multiculturalism (Toronto 1975), and *Patterns of
     Prejudice: A History of Nativism in Alberta* (Toronto 1982); Alan Green, *Immi-
     gration and the Postwar Canadian Economy* (Toronto 1976); Gerald E. Dirks,
     Canada's Refugee Policy: Indifference or Opportunism? (Montreal and London
     1977); Irving Abella and Harold Troper, *None is Too Many: Canada and the Jews
     of Europe, 1933-1948* (Toronto 1983); Reg Whitaker, *The Secret History of
     Canadian Immigration* (Toronto 1987); Barbara Roberts, *Whence They Came:
     Deportation from Canada 1900-1935* (Ottawa 1988); Charles M. Beach and Alan
     G. Green (eds.), *Policy Forum on the Role of Immigration in Canada's Future*
     (Kingston 1989). See also the 14 vols. of the series *Generations: A History of
     Canada's Peoples* (Toronto 1976-88).

5   Ian McDonald, *"To Each His Own": William Coaker and the Fishermen's Protec-
     tive Union in Newfoundland Politics, 1908-1925* (St. John's 1987), 12, 18-19; S.J.R.
     Noel, *Politics in Newfoundland* (Toronto 1971), 17-25; Kenneth Kerr, 'A Social
     Analysis of the Members of the Newfoundland House of Assembly, Executive
     Council, and Legislative Council for the Period 1855-1914' (unpublished MA
     thesis, Memorial University 1973).

6   James Hiller, 'The Railway and Local Politics in Newfoundland, 1870-1901,'
        in James Hiller and Peter Neary (eds.), *Newfoundland in the Nineteenth and
        Twentieth Centuries: Essays in Interpretation* (Toronto 1980), 123.

7   United Kingdom, *Royal Commission on the Natural Resources, Trade and Legis-
        lation of Certain Portions of His Majesty's Dominions: Minutes of Evidence Taken
        in Newfoundland in 1914,* Cd. 7898, 1915.

8   Jin Tan and Patricia E. Roy, *The Chinese in Canada* (Ottawa 1985), 8.

9   Robert G. Hong, 'To Take Action Without Delay: Newfoundland's Chinese
        Immigration Act of 1906' (unpublished BA honours essay, Memorial Univer-
        sity 1987), 1-4.

10   See Maldwyn Allen Jones, *American Immigration* (Chicago 1960), 177ff, 247ff;
        Government of Canada, Department of Citizenship and Immigration, *Evolu-
        tion of the Immigration Act* (Ottawa 1962), 5-9.

11   *Evening Herald* (St. John's), 4 March 1899.

12   No reliable figures are available. The 1911 census breaks the national origin
        of the 353 non-natives into 109 French, 44 Turkish, 39 Norwegian, 30 German,
        26 Chinese, 25 Russian, 4 Spanish, 3 Dutch, 2 Danish, 1 Italian. This is
        inconsistent with a 1914 police count of adult alien males, which includes 77
        Turkish, 44 Chinese, and 42 Russian Jews (Provincial Archives of Newfound-
        land and Labrador (PANL), GN 1/1/7, 1914). All subsequent GN (Govern-
        ment of Newfoundland) references are to documents in this archive.

13   *Evening Herald,* 9, 11 May 1906; *Daily News* (St. John's), 10 May 1906.

14   Kahn, *Listen While I Tell You.*

15   The chain migration of Newfoundlanders to the mainland was neither unique
        nor is it solely attributable to the alleged reduced absorptive capacity of the
        economy. Reeves ('Yankee Cousins,' 449-502) observes that the exodus was
        fuelled by all kinds of reasons and touched all classes of society. David
        Alexander argued that a disproportionate number of the better educated left
        the country ('Literacy and Economic Development in Nineteenth Century
        Newfoundland,' *Acadiensis 10,* no.1 (1980): 3-34) and Patricia Thornton noted
        that outmigration originated neither from the most overpopulated, nor from
        the traditional inshore fishing areas ('The Problem of Out-Migration from
        Atlantic Canada, 1871-1921: A New Look,' *Acadiensis 15,* no.1 (1985): 12, 24,
        29).

16   Entitled since 1892 'Of the Disembarking of Paupers,' the act was first pub-
        lished in the *Consolidated Statutes of Newfoundland 1872* (St. John's 1874), 511,
        under the title 'Of Mendicant and Infirm Immigrants.' A similar statute was
        enacted in Canada in 1869. On this point I am grateful for the assistance of
        Joan Ritcey, Centre for Newfoundland Studies, Queen Elizabeth II Library,
        Memorial University, St. John's, and Norma Jean Richards, Legislative Li-
        brary, St. John's.

17   In legally entrenching a refugee's right to sanctuary, the United Kingdom and
        Newfoundland—as far as can be ascertained the only countries enacting such
        a right of asylum at that time—were half a century ahead of its universal
        adoption by the United Nations. See Michael R. Marrus, *The Unwanted:
        European Refugees in the Twentieth Century* (Oxford 1985), 37ff. The right to
        asylum was formally confirmed in the 1951 United Nations Convention on
        Refugees (see Louise W. Holborn, *Refugees, a Problem of Our Time: The Work of*

the *UN High Commissioner for Refugees, 1951-1972* (Metuchen, New Jersey, 1975), 17).

18 See *Royal Commission*, 2-10.

19 Noel, *Politics in Newfoundland*, 151ff., 186ff.; McDonald, *"To Each His Own,"* 106ff., 145.

20 J.D. Sutherland, 'A Social History of Pulpwood Logging in Newfoundland during the Great Depression' (unpublished MA thesis, Memorial University 1988), 78.

21 *Evening Telegram* (St. John's), 30 March 1926; GN 13/2/A, box 227, 'Immigration (1921-1926).'

22 Peter Neary, 'Canadian Immigration Policy and the Newfoundlanders, 1912-1939,' *Acadiensis 11*, no. 2 (1982): 69-83; Robert H. Tait, *Newfoundland: A Summary of the History and Development of Britain's Oldest Colony from 1497 to 1939* (New York 1939), 36.

23 GN 13/2/A, box 227, files 'Immigration (1921-1926)' and 'Re: Immigration'; GN 1/3/A, 1907, no. 101; GN 2/5, file 525F.

24 Officially entitled the 'Act to amend Chapter 73 of the Consolidated Statutes (Third Series) Entitled "Of the Disembarkation of Paupers."'

25 GN 13/2/A, box 227, file 'Immigration (1921-1926).'

26 Ibid., files 'Immigration' and 'Immigration (1921-1926).'

27 Ibid., file 'Immigration (1921-1926)'.

28 *Proceedings of the House of Assembly*, 1926, 651, 747-50.

29 *Daily News*, 22 Aug. 1930; *Evening Telegram*, 5 March 1931.

30 GN 13/2/A, box 227, file 'Immigration.'

31 Ibid., file 'Re: Immigration,' Deputy Minister of Justice (Acting) to Deputy Colonial Secretary, 8 Oct. 1930, and Deputy Minister of Justice (Acting) to Secretary of State, 15 Dec. 1931.

32 Ibid., Howley to Trentham, 14 Nov. 1934.

33 Ibid., file 'Immigration.'

34 *Evening Telegram*, 2 Nov. 1939.

35 GN 13/2/A, box 227, memo to Hope Simpson, 1 April 1935. In early 1937 Dunfield became Commissioner L.E. Emerson's right-hand man in the Department of Justice. He was appointed a judge of the Supreme Court in Nov. 1939.

36 GN 13/2/A, box 227, file 'Re: Immigration.'

37 PANL, P8/B/11 (Newfoundland Board of Trade papers), box 30, file 7 and box 32, file 38.

38 Ibid., box 36, file 35.

39 Peter Neary, *Newfoundland in the North Atlantic World, 1929-1949* (Kingston and Montreal 1988), 45, 66, 354.

40 GN 38/S4-1-5, J.24-'38, conf. memo by Emerson, 'Immigration and Deportation,' 11 April 1938.

41 Ibid.

42 GN 13/2/A, box 336, memo submitted by the Commissioner for Finance, 12 April 1938.

43 GN 38/S1-1-2, minute of meeting of 13 April 1938.

44　Public Record Office, Kew, DO 35/720/M651/2. All subsequent DO (Dominions Office) references are to documents in this archive. Transcripts of crown copyright records in the Public Record Office appear by permission of the controller of H.M. Stationery Office.

45　The proposed substitution of section 12 (b) of the 1926 act is quoted at the beginning of this essay (GN 13/2/A, box 336, file 'Admission of European Immigrants to Nfld, 1939, Retain').

46　See GN 1/3/A, 1934, no. 316, 'Immigration into Nfld.'

47　DO 35/720/M651/5, 'Newfoundland Immigration Regulations.'

48　GN 1/3/A, 1939, no. 316, and 1938, nos. 11-302A. According to a German decree of 7 Oct. 1938, all German passports belonging to Jews of German nationality who resided in the British Empire became invalid. Holders of such passports were required to hand in their passports to the local German passport authority in the district where they were staying. Failure to comply with this decree within a specified time was declared a punishable offence in Germany.

49　DO 35/720/M651/5, 'Newfoundland Immigration Regulations.'

50　P8/B/11, box 36, file 35, Secretary (Renouf) to Penson, 22 April 1939.

51　Ibid., Price to Renouf, 29 April 1939.

52　*Evening Telegram*, 6 May 1939; *Observer's Weekly* (St. John's), 9 May 1939.

53　GN 1/3/A, 1939, file 9/39, Governor to British Consul General, 17 Aug. 1939.

54　These are some of the recurring themes featured in the guidebooks prepared for prospective (British and American) settlers and tourists from 1907 to 1949. See D.W. Prowse, *The Newfoundland Guide Book* (London, 1907, 1911) and Karl Baedeker, *The Dominion of Canada with Newfoundland and an Excursion to Alaska: Handbook for Travellers* (Leipzig 1907). Baedeker's section on Newfoundland was written by the Rev. Dr. Moses Harvey for the 1894 edition. See also H.M. Mosdell (comp.), *Newfoundland: Its Manifold Attractions for the Capitalist, the Settler and the Tourist* (St. John's, 1920) and the essay by Gerald L. Pocius in this vol.

55　See Gerhard P. Bassler, 'Newfoundland and Refugees from the Third Reich, 1934-1941,' *Newfoundland Studies* 3. no. 1 (1987): 37-70; 'Attempts to Settle Jewish Refugees in Newfoundland and Labrador, 1934-1939,' *Simon Wiesenthal Center Annual 5* (1988): 121-44.

56　See Gerhard P. Bassler, *Sanctuary Denied: Refugees from the Third Reich and Newfoundland Immigration Policy, 1906-1949* (St. John's 1992).

57　*Observer's Weekly*, 11 Aug. 1934.

58　See Bassler, 'Attempts to Settle Jewish Refugees,' 136.

59　The details are in Bassler, *Sanctuary Denied*.

60　GN 38/S7-1-3, file 1, Ira Wild memorandum, 17 May 1945.

61　It could not be ascertained whether he received it (see GN 2/5, file 926; GN 13/2/A, box 345, files 47 and 48).

62　*Evening Telegram*, 27 and 28 Feb. 1948.

63　Ibid., 16 Jan. 1948.

64　*Daily News*, 'The Wayfarer,' 14 Feb. 1944.

65　Ibid., 'What Price Immigration,' 16 Feb. 1944.

66   See Dirks, 122-75; Milda Danys, *DP Lithuanian Immigration to Canada After the Second World War* (Toronto 1986); Gerhard P. Bassler, 'Canadian Postwar Immigration Policy and the Admission of German Enemy Aliens, 1945-50,' *Yearbook of German-American Studies* 22 (1987): 183-97.

67   On 17 May 1945 the Commissioner for Finance, Ira Wild, submitted to his colleagues a memorandum on immigration policy which ended with a proposal 'to remind the Dominions Office that we still await their further advice as we should like to proceed with the drafting of the legislation [agreed in 1938] as soon as an opportunity occurs' (GN 38/S7-1-3, file 1).

'A Mortgaged Property': the Impact of the United States on Newfoundland, 1940-49*

Peter Neary

IN 1921, A CENSUS YEAR, Newfoundland (including Labrador) had a population of 263,000 and was a self-governing dominion in the British Empire.[1] Economically, this small country lived off a few export industries, principally fishing, pulp and paper manufacturing and mining. At the same time almost the whole of Newfoundland's banking business was in the hands of Canadian institutions. The country's public debt in 1921-22 was \$49,033,035.[2] Interest payments on this were made semi-annually out of public revenues most of which came from customs' receipts. Newfoundland lived by trade and the government paid its creditors out of income derived from trade.

All of this made the country highly sensitive to world market forces and when the Great Depression struck, Newfoundland was quickly overwhelmed financially. Government revenues fell and the cost of able-bodied relief rose dramatically while interest payments were unchanged. This created a stark choice between paying the foreign creditors or supporting the local poor. By 1931-32 interest payments consumed fully 59.7 per cent of government revenue.[3] Through a series of increasingly desperate financial expedients, the country stumbled from interest payment to interest payment until in the autumn of 1932 a newly elected conservative government contemplated a unilateral rescheduling of the public debt. The United Kingdom took strong exception to this whereupon Newfoundland backed off. At the end of 1932 the United Kingdom and Canada assisted Newfoundland to meet her interest payments. But this assistance was given on condition that Newfoundland agree to the appointment by London of a royal commission, to include nominees from all three countries, to enquire into and make recommendations about her future.

British policy at this stage was to prevent a default, but to do so by acting jointly with Canada. This approach accorded with a longstanding British objective, namely, the eventual union of Newfoundland with Canada. In July 1933, however, while the commission of enquiry was going about its work, Canada refused any more financial assistance to Newfoundland. One key Canadian minister summed up the view in Ottawa at this time when he declared himself 'against Confederation as the Newf[ound-lande]rs would really in effect become another Ireland - not in the racial sense, but a nuisance and always grumbling and wanting something.'[4] The Canadian abandonment of Newfoundland left the British to carry on alone. This they undertook to do but at a high political price: Newfoundland's self-government would have to be suspended in favour of administration by a British appointed Commission of Government which would be responsible to the United Kingdom Parliament through the Secretary State for Dominion Affairs. Newfoundland agreed to this and appropriate legislation was then passed in London. This provided for Newfoundland to get self-government back when she was self-supporting and on a request from her people; but no definition of self-supporting was given and no procedure was specified whereby a request could be made. These, it would turn out, were critical omissions. The Commission of Government assumed office in February 1934. It consisted of a governor and six commissioners, three 'drawn from Newfoundland and three from the United Kingdom.'[5] The British, of course, appointed all these officials and, counting the governor, their nationals could outvote their Newfoundland colleagues four to three.

The record of the Commission of Government in the 1930s was mixed. London paid annual grants-in-aid to St. John's and some important reforms were carried out in Newfoundland. But towards the end of the decade the so called Roosevelt Recession, which affected the global economy, hit the country hard and in the spring of 1939 there were more people on relief than there had been in the spring of 1934. At this stage the British had good reason to believe that their hold on Newfoundland was shaky. Accordingly, they approved plans for an expensive and politically tricky overhaul of the country's whole rural and fishing economy. By definition this would pit Whitehall and the Commission of Government against powerful local vested interests.

As it happened, the outbreak of war in September 1939 made the carrying out of these plans unnecessary. Because of her constitution, Newfoundland, unlike Canada, was automatically covered by the United Kingdom's declaration of war. At first the Commission of Government, in the interest of the war effort, planned to cut back expenditures but it was soon taking in and spending money in unprecedented amounts. This was the result of Newfoundland's strategic location in an age of air and submarine warfare, an advantage that quickly touched off an investment boom in the country. In the dark days of 1933 Canada had been able to walk away from Newfoundland's troubles but she now saw that militarily her destiny and Newfoundland's were inextricably linked.[6] In the late 1930s, the British and Newfoundland governments, to facilitate an experiment in transatlantic air service, had built a large airport at Gander and a seaplane base at Botwood. The Commission's answer to the expensive and administratively complex defence problem posed by these facilities was to recommend to London that they be turned over to Canadian operation and control for the duration of the war. The British at first resisted this idea but in the sombre month of June 1940 gave way on the issue. Having assumed this first obligation in Newfoundland, Ottawa proceeded to undertake many others. In time Canada built air bases at Torbay, near St. John's, and at Goose Bay in Labrador, whose boundary with neighbouring Quebec had been defined in 1927. Canada also ran on behalf of the Admiralty a naval base at St. John's that was vital to the Allied effort in the Battle of the Atlantic.

The United States burst militarily on the Newfoundland scene with the destroyers for bases agreement of September 1940. This agreement was embodied in an exchange of letters between the United Kingdom ambassador in Washington, the Marquess of Lothian, and Secretary of State Cordell Hull. *Inter alia* the United Kingdom promised the United States in the agreement the lease of base sites in Newfoundland for ninety-nine years 'freely and without consideration.'[7] For its part the United States undertook to pay whatever compensation was mutually agreed upon between the two countries to private owners who had to give up property through expropriation or who suffered damages in connection with the establishment of the bases.

Soon after the Lothian-Hull letters Newfoundland was visited by the commission established by President Roosevelt to choose base sites. The commission was headed by Admiral John W. Greenslade and Brigadier General J.L. Devers. Sites were decided upon in Newfoundland in the St. John's, Argentia-Marquise and Stephenville areas. At St. John's and Marquise, army bases, named respectively Fort Pepperrell and Fort McAndrew, were built. At Stephenville an airfield was constructed and at Argentia a large naval and air base was built. In February 1941 after the United States had picked out the properties it wanted in the various British western hemisphere territories covered by the September agreement, an Anglo-American conference met in London to work out the full details of the bases accord. Prior to this, because of the war situation, Newfoundland had agreed to allow construction to begin and people to be moved, a hard matter in the middle of a local winter. This was done without any agreed formula for compensating the owners of private property affected by the base construction. Nevertheless, in February 1941 Newfoundland established a board of arbitration to adjudicate claims.

Newfoundland was represented at the London conference by Commissioners L.E. Emerson and J.H. Penson, the first a native son and the second British. With lend-lease being negotiated in the background, the United States was able to drive a hard bargain in these talks and the two Newfoundland negotiators were shocked by the concessions made to the Americans. In effect the bases were made extensions of the American homeland itself. A particular concern of the Newfoundland representatives was the sweeping legal jurisdiction given the United States. This included the right to try a British subject who was accused of committing a military offence in a leased area and was arrested there.[8]

So sweeping were the rights given the Americans that the Commission of Government feared trouble over them, despite the war emergency. In fact, the 27 March 1941 Anglo-American leased bases agreement was accepted in Newfoundland without serious incident and was a public relations triumph for the government. On their way back from London Emerson and Penson went to Washington where they were given assurances by the State Department, later made public in Newfoundland. These were that the legal jurisdiction the United States had obtained in the agreement would be treated as a reserve power and that at the appropriate time the United States would 'consider sympathetically the commercial relations between the two countries with a view to the development of mutual trade.'[9]

In 1942 about 20,000 Newfoundlanders were at work on base construction, American and Canadian, which, along with recruitment for overseas service, had wiped out unemployment in the country. So well off was the Commission of Government indeed that it was now making interest free loans of Canadian dollars to the United Kingdom, which had paid out its last grant-in-aid in 1939-40. Providentially, the Cinderella of the Empire, as Newfoundland had been called, had been fitted with her glass slipper. In May 1942, the Kentucky native George D. Hopper, who the previous June had been named United States Consul General in St. John's, reported to Washington a 'state of mind' among many Newfoundlanders which indicated 'complacency and indifference as to the war effort.'[10] As evidence of this, he forwarded an editorial from the *Trade Review*, a publication of the Newfoundland Board of Trade. This asked the question 'Is there a war on?,' a query justified as follows: 'Business is not "as usual" but very much better than usual. Shopping crowds positively throng the streets in fine weather. Covetous renters are charging abnormal rentals to families of servicemen of one or other of the United Nations. There appears to be no diminution of social life or amusement.'[11] Hopper was dismayed by what he perceived to be the 'tendency of many Newfoundlanders to lag behind' his own countrymen 'in willingness to undergo personal sacrifice of long enjoyed privileges,' but then he had not been in Newfoundland during the 1930s.[12] If he had been, the indulgence he claimed to see about him would have been more understandable. Collectively, Newfoundlanders had been let out of the poor-house, and if they paused to enjoy the view, this was understandable. Perhaps Governor Sir Humphrey T. Walwyn came closer to the mark when he wrote in August 1943 that Newfoundlanders were 'dazzled by American dollars, hygiene and efficiency.'[13]

With a few hitches, relations between United States and local officials were from the beginning of the bases era generally very good in Newfoundland. In June 1941 the arrangement between the United States and the

United Kingdom for compensating owners of private property was finally completed. This sanctioned the recommendations of the arbitration board Newfoundland had established but provided that if the United States disputed the findings of the board in a particular case the matter would 'be settled under arrangements to be determined and agreed by the United States Government and His Majesty's Government.'[14] The last phrase was important because until Newfoundland resumed self-government the United Kingdom was deemed responsible by the United States for carrying out the provisions of the leased bases agreement.

In August 1942 the Newfoundland government submitted to the American authorities an accounting of the amounts it had paid out to date to cover claims decided on by the board of arbitration. This submission was disputed by the United States on the grounds that the board had taken 'disturbance' into account in rendering its decisions, a factor that did not apply in similar circumstances in the United States.[15] Washington also challenged the amounts submitted by Newfoundland for lawyers fees (calculated according to Newfoundland custom as part of each award), while denying any responsibility for the expenses of the board itself. According to the State Department it was not the size of the Newfoundland bill that was in question as much as what might happen if Congress were asked to meet charges that did not accord with United States practice in similar claims. Ultimately, a sticky negotiation was ended when the British offered to assume responsibility for all compensation payments under the leased bases agreement. This offer—the *Times* of London called it 'Lend-Lease in reverse'[16]—was readily accepted by the United States, whereupon the understanding arrived at between the two countries was made public on 9 August 1943. The advantages of this outcome were various. From the Newfoundland point of view the settlement ensured payment in full. At the same time the arrangement relieved the United States Administration of the task of seeking an appropriation from Congress that might have proved embarrassing. Lastly, for the United Kingdom, the cost involved could be seen as a charge against good public relations in the United States and in simplified dealings over a complex and touchy subject with a variety of junior governments. By a single act, a host of conflicting interests had been reconciled.

Another delicate issue posed by the base building boom was what should be paid the Newfoundlanders who went to work for United States and Canadian employers. The basic position of the Commission of Government on this issue was set forth in a January 1941 memorandum which argued for an informal arrangement with foreign defence contractors in the country to stay within established local wage rates. The basic need of the country, it was argued, was for more employment rather than employment at higher rates. The effect of higher rates brought on by 'transient conditions' would be to reduce government employment, threaten established enterprise, 'accentuate the tendency for the fishing industry to be manned by those too unenterprising to escape from it altogther or to react to modern requirements,' and to make Newfoundland less attractive for investment in new industries.[17] Hence the need for Newfoundland employers, including the government itself, to set the rates for the foreign employers rather than the reverse. Holding the line would also head off 'the growth of mushroom Trade Unions' for which the existing situation in the country provided 'a golden opportunity.' On balance, therefore, the 'wisest course' for the Government would be 'to refuse point blank' to reveal on the grounds of confidentiality, anything about its discussions with the visiting employers on the subject of wage rates, and to leave its own rates where they were.

As might be expected, some of the Newfoundlanders who went to work on the American bases saw things in a different light, though there was not much they could do about the informal understanding that existed between their employers and their government. What Newfoundlanders, either individually or collectively, could expect from the Americans in bargaining was made plain in March 1941 by Lt. Col. Philip G. Bruton, the district engineer in charge of army construction in the country. The governing principle of American policy on wages, he explained, was to match local rates. All Newfoundland would be treated as one wage area. Accordingly, any trade union which sought wage increases for local employees would have to produce a signed contract with a Newfoundland employer showing that a higher rate was being paid elsewhere in the country than that offered by the United States for the work in question. The matter would be then taken up with Washington. Within the existing framework, however, local base workers could increase their wages by showing adaptability and thereby improving their job classifications.

In April 1941 a group of labour leaders pressed the Newfoundland government to increase the wages paid common labourers in the construction industry generally. This appeal was received poorly, and the recommendation of Sir Wilfrid Woods, the septuagenarian British Commissioner whose portfolio covered labour matters, was that the government should respond with a twofold policy. In the case of its own jobs it should simply wait any strikers out, but where the bases were concerned it would have to be ready to protect men willing to work at going rates from union intimidation. While the Commission contemplated these heroics, the Newfoundland workers on the leased bases who might be affected by them were having to make other kinds of adjustments. For example, they had to work alongside Americans who could buy duty-free cigarettes at 7 cents a pack, and to learn to drive on the bases on the right hand side of the road. This was the opposite of the system in force elsewhere in Newfoundland, which kept with British practice of driving on the left. At the base gate, entering

Newfoundland drivers switched from left to right, a circumstance that made plain just how much parts of their country had been taken over.

As the construction of the bases ended and the relations in Newfoundland between the military and civilians settled into well established routines, the opinions of the United States officials towards Newfoundlanders were both critical and complimentary. Basically the Americans believed that Newfoundlanders were conservative and backward but on the whole trainable and deserving. A major irritant to the Americans while they were getting established—and this echoed Canadian views—was a supposed lack of application on the part of Newfoundland workers. In December 1941, after hearing complaints through Emerson about living conditions for local men employed at Argentia, Hopper sent the Commissioner a testy rejoinder. The commander at Argentia, he told Emerson, had reported 'a steady turn over in Newfoundland personnel caused by dissatisfied workmen...not accustomed to working through out the day at the speed set by their foremen.'[18] 'The natural habits' of these employees, the Consul General continued, 'accumulated through years of slow motion at their usual jobs at their outports and other places,' made it difficult for them to meet the precise production requirements of their American foremen. Complaints about the quality of the meals being served at Argentia were attributed by Hopper to the fact that many Newfoundlanders working there were 'not accustomed to the variety of the food served as directed by the management in accordance with well-known principles of providing a properly balanced diet for men engaged in that kind of work.' This inexperience led 'quite a few' of the workmen in question to want a daily diet of 'fish and potatoes' instead of the variety normally served. Nevertheless, most local employees at the base 'seemed to enjoy the food and often returned for a third helping.'

In January 1942, Hopper reported to the State Department that Newfoundlanders who had earlier been inclined to ask why the Americans were in such a hurry when they had '99 years to finish the job' were beginning to wake up to the realities of the war.[19] In the labouring population, however, the tradition of 'hibernating during the long winter months' lived on. Thus, despite appeals to their patriotism, many local employees at the bases had quit work before Christmas and gone home on 'extended holidays.' In one two-week period at Argentia only ten per cent of 3,800 Newfoundland labourers employed had continued to work. Moreover, many of the absentees had departed with the intention of not returning before spring, their purpose, according to Hopper, being to 'loaf at home' until they ran out of money. Not surprisingly, Hopper also recommended against hiring Newfoundlanders for work in labour starved industries in the United States itself but this advice was not heeded and by 1945 more than 1,900 contract workers had been thus recruited.

The censorious Hopper likewise frowned on marriages between American servicemen and Newfoundland women, which began in St. John's while the United States forces were still under canvas. In May 1942, he told the State Department that 'at least ninety per cent' of the marriages in question were being 'contracted by enlisted men or noncommissioned officers, or defence base workers below the position of foremen, with waitresses, housemaids, clerks and unemployed Newfoundland girls.'[20] The Consul General's explanation for this phenomenon was decidedly unsentimental: 'The American men,' he wrote, 'are rendered more susceptible by changed surroundings and absence from home ties, also by the feeling of prosperity resulting from regular pay checks, regardless of their previous financial situation. On the other hand the Newfoundland girls are influenced, in some instances at least, merely by a desire to immigrate to the United States to enjoy the better living conditions they believe to exist there.' In fact, however, a Newfoundland woman who married an American man had to go through normal immigration procedures to enter the United States and, having married an alien, lost her right to a Newfoundland passport. In October 1943, the situation facing marriage minded United States-Newfoundland couples was further complicated by an order of the United States army commander in the country. Citing military necessity, he decreed that, under pain of punishment, no member of the Newfoundland Base Command could marry without the approval of the unit's commanding general. The order further stipulated in advance of such requests that permission would not be given for marriages between base personnel and aliens. Hopper welcomed this change and told the State Department that an earlier increase in the allowances paid to the dependents of American servicemen had led to an upswing in the number of marriages in Newfoundland between base personnel and local women. The 'types of girls,' he now asserted, who married enlisted personnel in Newfoundland, were 'far from desirable.'[21]

Harsh as such private sentiments undoubtedly were, they did not endanger the public dealings of the two countries. In comparison to the Canadian forces in the country, the Americans were given high marks by Newfoundland officialdom, a view which might have been helped by the lavish American entertainment of local higher-ups. As Governor Walwyn wrote in March 1944, 'the behaviour of the Americans, except in isolated incidents in the early days, has been infinitely better than that of the Canadians, and is so to-day.'[22] In a similar vein the governor reported in October 1945 that 'the conduct of the United States forces outside the bases and in relation to Newfoundland citizens' had, generally speaking, 'been exceedingly good.'[23] They had been 'distinctly better behaved in the mass than their Canadian friends and than the gangs of civilian toughs who were often at the bottom of international street fights for which the visitors were too readily blamed.' Moreover, the Americans had done and would continue to do 'much towards the modernization of Newfoundland building, architecture, communication systems and the art of better and more comfortable living generally.'

Needless to say the extent of this United States influence was not lost on Ottawa, which by one Canadian reckoning was out-spent militarily three to one by Washington during the war. Nor was the contrast between the rights given the United States and those granted to Canada. In the leased bases agreement of 1941 the United States carved out extensive extraterritorial rights on the island for ninety-nine years. These rights went far beyond anything ever conceded to Canada. Ottawa's best deal was in the 1944 lease for ninety-nine years of the property on which Goose Bay air base stood, but this required a long and bruising negotiation. Moreover, it stirred deep resentment in Newfoundland, where nationalist sentiment was now on the rise, without going as far as the 1941 Anglo-American agreement. What explains the disparity between United States and Canadian rights? The answer is that in the critical 1940-41 period Canada was in the war and could be counted on for support while the United States had to be won over. In other words, in the complex process of give and take which went on behind the scenes over Newfoundland, the United States and Canada were in fundamentally different positions *vis-à-vis* the United Kingdom, to whom belonged the final word as she controlled the Commission of Government. Willy-nilly, Canada was caught up in a competition with the United States in Newfoundland during the war but much depended on the British as to where this would lead.

What was at stake was well understood in London, where it was decided early on in the war that the economic and social changes now occurring in Newfoundland would make constitutional change there imperative. Deputy Prime Minister Clement Attlee visited Newfoundland in September 1942 and thereafter despatched a parliamentary mission to the country. With its findings in hand, the British government announced in December 1943 that 'as soon as practicable' after the war in Europe had ended, it would provide Newfoundlanders with 'machinery...to express their considered views as to the form of Government they desire, having regard to the financial and economic conditions prevailing at the time.'[24] With this announcement the British effectively pre-empted any attack on the commission system with the argument that change was coming anyway and that in the meantime everyone should concentrate on winning the war.

Central to British thinking about the future of Newfoundland was the belief that the present prosperity was transitory and that difficult economic times lay ahead. Based on this logic London first envisaged the return of responsible government to Newfoundland but with safeguards to prevent another financial crisis provided in advance. There would be a British funded development plan and a tight rein on the ability of an independent Newfoundland government to borrow. In time, however, the British came round to the view that they could not afford the reconstruction plan suggested for Newfoundland. Accordingly, they turned with renewed interest to the idea of confederation, which they believed the events of the war had at last made possible. In September 1945 P.A. Clutterbuck of the Dominions Office, a key British official, was sent to Ottawa to discuss the future of Newfoundland. His message was simple: the United Kingdom could not continue to support Newfoundland and if Canada did not want a closer Newfoundland-United States relationship than now existed, she had better do something about it. The result of Clutterbuck's mission was an understanding between London and Ottawa that they would henceforth promote confederation with Canada for Newfoundland. Both sides believed that there had to be no public suggestion of Anglo-Canadian co-operation if confederation were to come about. Rather, the initiative must be seen to come from Newfoundlanders themselves.

Having thus succeeded with the Canadians, the British announced in December 1945 that a National Convention would be established in Newfoundland with its members elected from geographical consitituencies to *advise* the United Kingdom on the choices to be put before the people in a referendum on Newfoundland's constitutional future. Cleverly, the British did not say whether the advice of the National Convention would be accepted or not. This left to themselves the final say over what would appear on the referendum ballot. The National Convention, which was elected in 1946 in the first country-wide vote held since 1932, turned out to be a windy and turbulent body. A delegation it sent to London to investigate possible forms of future association with the United Kingdom was given a polite but icy reception. By contrast, the work of a delegation sent to Ottawa led to the submission to the Convention by the government of Canada of draft terms of union between the two countries. Several attempts were made in the Convention to send a delegation to Washington but the Commission of Government would not permit this. Reciprocity with the United States was an old Newfoundland ambition but it was a cause that had failed in the past and could not succeed now. A frequent refrain in the Convention picked up on an old Newfoundland sense of betrayal. The Commission of Government, it was claimed, had made bad deals for Newfoundland and these would have to be reopened if the country were to get its just deserts. In sum, Newfoundland had not been adequately compensated for what it had given up during the war and for the rights that other countries still enjoyed on her soil.

At the close of deliberations the National Convention recommended to the United Kingdom government that the referendum feature two choices: 'Responsible Government as it existed prior to 1934' and 'Commission of Government.' This, of course, was not what the British wanted and therefore they exercised the power they had kept in reserve. Newfoundlanders, it was announced in St. John's on 11 March 1948, would have three choices, namely, 'Commission of Government for a period of five years'; 'Confederation with Canada'; and 'Responsible Government as it existed in 1933.' By careful planning the British had got confederation before the Newfoundland people, but in the end it was the latter who would decide whether they wanted it or not. In another shrewd move, however, the British ruled that the choice to be followed would have to command majority support. Accordingly, a second vote would have to be held if the first one, scheduled for 3 June 1948, did not produce a majority result. The second vote would be between the two leading choices on the first.

The United States attitude towards current political developments in Newfoundland was made clear in November 1946 when Raymond Gushue, the Commission of Government's top fisheries official, visited the State Department and was given an earful by his American hosts. A State Department memorandum noted that Newfoundlanders both within and without the National Convention were busy persuading themselves that Newfoundland was 'owed a *quid pro quo* for the bases, preferably in the form of a substantial concession to their fishing interests.'[25] It was, they held, 'the *moral* obligation of the U.S. to give them some return!' In truth, however, there was 'no reason, moral or otherwise,' why the United States should give a *quid pro quo*, and there was 'no chance in the world' of the Newfoundlanders 'getting anything' in return for the bases. This particular analysis acidly concluded that in fact Newfoundland's war effort had 'contained a larger element of *get* than *give*.' Gushue was told by John Hickerson, the main American official involved, that a 'political union between the United States and Newfoundland' would not be desirable.[26] Nor would Congress be likely to approve a 'unanimous application in that sense' from the National Convention.

In March 1948 the situation facing the State Department in Newfoundland took on a different complexion when Chesley Crosbie, a leading St. John's businessman who had served in the National Convention, announced the launching of the Party for Economic Union with the United States, with himself as president. Since its objective was not specifically included on the ballot, Crosbie's party campaigned for responsible government as a first step in the direction it favoured. The Economic Union party enjoyed strong journalistic support from the recently established St. John's *Sunday Herald*, an American style tabloid.

Yet if ever there was a suitor whose attentions were unwanted, it was Crosbie's party. The last thing the United States wanted to have in Newfoundland was a government, however nominally well disposed, that might be tempted to reopen a one-sided deal considered to have been forced on the country by a sell-out government, in this case the 1941 bases deal. Washington had what it wanted in Newfoundland and not unnaturally wanted to keep it. As one American official once succinctly and memorably wrote, Newfoundland was 'a mortgaged property.'[27] In these circumstances the United States had no reason to go counter to the wishes of the United Kingdom and Canada so far as the constitutional future of Newfoundland was concerned. On the contrary, they had every reason, as a guarantee of their own position, to go along with what was the decided policy of those countries towards Newfoundland. If through force of circumstance the United Kingdom had to give up its role in Newfoundland, then Canada from Washington's point of view promised to be a reliable alternative partner. It was better to deal with a government in Ottawa whose interests in relation to the United States were multifarious and continental in scope than with an independent government in St. John's driven by an *idée fixe*.

In March 1948, in keeping with all this, the State Department's Division of British Commonwealth Affairs gave all officers in Canada and Newfoundland the following summary of where the United States stood on the Newfoundland constitutional question: 'There appears to be increasing agitation in Newfoundland for union with the United States. There is, however, no expectation that the people will be given a chance to vote on this alternative. The position of the Department on this question is that there has been no official approach whatever from the United Kingdom or the Government of Newfoundland, that the matter is one of internal concern in Newfoundland, and that this Government has no views and no comment.'[28] This hands-off approach was also evident when the Newfoundland government approached the Consulate General in St. John's to allow polling booths for the 3 June referendum to be set up on United States bases in the country. When the Consulate expressed the wish that this not be done, Newfoundland dropped the issue.

American officials also ignored the information given them by supporters of responsible government and economic union that Joseph R. Smallwood, the leader of the confederation forces, had been 'communist trained in New York' and allegedly had been associated years before with Leon Trotsky.[29] For his part Smallwood made much of a memorandum prepared by Manley O. Hudson, a legal scholar at Harvard University. This did not rule economic union out theoretically but severely questioned its practicality. As part of its campaign, the *Sunday Herald* individually contacted all the members of the United States Senate to find out how many would be willing to meet with a Newfoundland delegation to discuss economic union, should this cause succeed with the electorate. To 14 May seventy replies were in hand, which the Consulate General in St. John's analyzed as follows: 'unreservedly favourable,' twenty-nine; 'favourable' but wanting the approach to be made through the State Department, ten; 'conditionally favourable,' nine; unwilling 'for various reasons,' nine; 'no opinion owing to illness or absence,' thirteen.[30] On 11 May the *Herald* wrote to those Senators who had responded favourably to its initial appeal, asking them to get in touch with the paper before accepting at face value any request for a retraction they might receive from the confederation side, which was now portrayed as an 'anti-American minority party spreading class hatred.'[31]

Subsequently, the owner of the paper attempted to have broadcast a recording of a statement favourable to his cause written by Senator C. Wayland Brooks, an Illinois Republican, but not read by the senator himself. On receipt of a public complaint, however, the Commission of Government banned the broadcast of the recording over the facilities of the Broadcasting Corporation of Newfoundland. This was done on the grounds that the stations of the publicly owned system should not be available for persons outside Newfoundland to comment of the constitutional issue now before the country. Earlier Chesley Crosbie had told an official of the United States Consulate in St. John's 'confidentially and categorically' that should his party come to power it would not attempt to renegotiate the bases agreement.[32] But this, of course, was merely the word of one individual and in any case his was only one of two organizations campaigning in favour of responsible government. Significantly, the Responsible Government League went through the campaign still committed to the policy of using Article XXVIII of the 1941 agreement to obtain economic concessions from the United States in return for the 'free gift' that country had been given in Newfoundland.[33] Under this article the signatories to the agreement had undertaken 'to give sympathetic consideration' to representations from the other, looking towards the modification of the document 'in the light of experience' and on a mutually acceptable basis.[34]

At the end of the day, the outcome in Newfoundland satisfied the goals of the British, Canadian and United States policy makers. In the first referendum responsible government led with 69,400 votes. Confederation was a reasonably close second at 64,066 and commission of government a distant third at 22,311. A second referendum was then held on 22 July. This time 78,323 voted for confederation and 71,334 for responsible government. Next final terms of union were negotiated between Newfoundland and Canada. These were signed on 11 December 1948, whereupon Newfoundland became a province of Canada immediately before the expiration of 31 March 1949. Canada had rounded off her territory; the United Kingdom had been relieved of an unwanted burden and had achieved an old objective; and the United States had acquired a new but reliable guarantor of her essential rights in the region. The marriage of convenience of Newfoundland and Canada was not made in the U.S.A. but Uncle Sam certainly helped to force the issue.

NOTES

*This paper introduces and summarizes one of the main themes of my *Newfoundland in the North Atlantic World, 1929-1949* (Kingston and Montreal, 1988). Readers are referred to that vol. for a more detailed account of the events under review. The paper was prepared for the 1987 annual meeting of the American Historical Association, Washington, D.C., and is published here with the permission of McGill-Queen's University Press.

1   The 1921 census showed a population of 259,259 on the island of Newfound-land and a population of 3,774 in Labrador. See United Kingdom, Parliamen-tary Papers, Cmd. 4480, 1933, *Newfoundland Royal Commission 1933: Report*, Appendix A, 234.

2   Ibid., 47.

3   Calculated from ibid., 57, 63. Revenue in 1931-2 was $7,931,047 while interest on the public debt was $4,731,571.

4   Quoted in Neary, *Newfoundland in the North Atlantic World*, 20.

5   United Kingdom, *The Public General Acts*, 1933-4 (London [1934]), 9.

6   For Canadian policy towards Newfoundland see David MacKenzie, *Inside the Atlantic Triangle: Canada and the Entrance of Newfoundland into Confederation 1939-1949* (Toronto 1986).

7   United Kingdom, Parliamentary Papers, Cmd. 6224, 1940, *Exchange of Notes regarding United States Destroyers and Naval and Air Facilities for the United States in British Transatlantic Territories*, Lothian to Hull, 2 Sept. 1940. For this agreement and its impact see also Richard Straus, 'The Diplomatic Negotia-tions Leading to the Establishment of American Bases in Newfoundland, June 1940-April 1941' (unpublished MA thesis, Memorial University 1972) and Ian M. Stewart, 'The "Revolution of 1940" in Newfoundland' (unpublished MA thesis, Memorial University 1974).

8   The Americans could also try 'a member of the United States forces or any other foreigner who...committed an offence of a military nature (including sabotage and espionage) either within or without a leased area' and 'a foreigner who committed any other offence in a leased area.' The quotations are from a summary of the American right to arrest and try given in Public Record Office (PRO), Kew, DO 114/111, 3. All subsequent DO (Dominions Office) references are to documents in this archive. Transcripts of crown copyright records in the PRO appear by permission of the controller of H.M. Stationery Office.

9   Provincial Archives of Newfoundland and Labrador, GN 38/S4-2-5, file 2, 'Discussions in Washington April 7th to 12th, 1941,' memo by J.H. Penson, 25 April 1941. All subsequent GN (Government of Newfoundland) references are to documents in this archive.

10   National Archives and Records Administration (NARA), Washington, D.C., RG 59 (Dept. of State, General Records), 843.00/128, report by Hopper on 'Political Developments During the Month of April, 1942,' 20 May 1942, 4. All subsequent RG (Record Group) references are to documents in this archive.

11   Enclosure in ibid.

12   RG 59, 843.00/128, report by Hopper on 'Political Developments During the Month of April, 1942,' 20 May 1942, 5.

13   DO 35/1141/N402/11, Walwyn to Machtig, 31 Aug. 1943.

14   GN 38/S4-2-3, file 15, Butler to Dunn, 20 May 1941.

15　RG 84 (Dept. of State, Records of the Foreign Service Posts), Records of the Consulate General, St. John's, 1943, vol. 13, memo of conversation, 15 Jan. 1943.

16　*Times* (London), 10 Aug. 1943.

17　GN 38/S4-2-5, file 2, memo by Woods, 17 Jan. 1941.

18　RG 84, Records of the Consulate General, St. John's, 1941, vol. 1, Hopper to Emerson, 19 Dec. 1941.

19　Ibid., 1941, vol. 6, Hopper to Secretary of State, 15 Jan. 1942.

20　Ibid., 1942, vol. 11, Hopper to Secretary of State, 27 May 1942.

21　RG 59, 811.22/386, Hopper to Secretary of State, 21 April 1944.

22　DO 35/1376, Walwyn to Machtig, 4 March 1944.

23　DO 114/111, 46-9, despatch from GN, 15 Oct. 1945.

24　United Kingdom, *Parliamentary Debates* (Commons), 5th ser., vol. 395, 1943-4, cols. 599-600.

25　RG 59, FW 843.628/10-2146, memo by Parsons to Hickerson, 8 Nov. 1946.

26　Ibid., memo by Hickerson to Parsons, 14 Nov. 1946.

27　Ibid., 843.7962/11-1048, memo by Snow to Hickerson and Wailes, 10 Nov. 1948.

28　RG 84, Records of the Consulate General, St. John's, 1948, 800 file, circular newsletter no. 2 from Division of British Commonwealth Affairs, Department of State, 15 March 1948.

29　Ibid., memo by Abbott, 14 Jan.1948, encl. in Abbott to Secretary of State, 16 Jan.1948; FW 843.00/5-1948, memo by Foster, 24 May 1948.

30　RG 59, 843.00/5-1448, Abbott to Secretary of State, 14 May 1948.

31　Ibid.

32　RG 84, Records of the Consulate General, St. John's, 1948, 800 file, Abbott to Secretary of State, 27 May 1948.

33　Ibid., Abbott to Secretary of State, 28 May 1948. The history of the Responsible Government League is explored in Jeff A. Webb, 'The Responsible Government League and the Confederation Campaigns of 1948,' *Newfoundland Studies* 5, no.2 (1989): 203-20.

34　For this article see United Kingdom, Parliamentary Papers, Cmd. 6259, 1941, *Agreement between the Governments of the United Kingdom and the United States of America relating to the Bases Leased to the United States of America (and exchange of notes) together with Protocol between the Governments of the United Kingdom, Canada and the United States of America concerning the Defence of Newfoundland: London, March 27, 1941.*

How Newfoundland Veterans became Canadian Veterans: a Study in Bureaucracy and Benefit

Peter Neary

O N THE EVENING OF 14 March 1945 Albert Walsh, the Commissioner for Home Affairs and Education in the British appointed Commission of Government, which had been administering Newfoundland since 1934, gave a radio address over stations VONF and VOCM, St. John's.[1] It was a well-established practice for the members of the Commission of Government to explain basic policy on the radio and Walsh's subject on this occasion was a matter of especially pressing concern. This was the plan of the government for re-establishing in civilian life the many Newfoundlanders who had volunteered for service in the world war which had now been in progress since 1939.

Newfoundland's contibution to the war effort had been diverse. In the 1914-18 war the country had raised and sent overseas a regiment of infantry.[2] The Newfoundland Regiment suffered great losses at Beaumont Hamel on 1 July 1916, the opening day of the Battle of the Somme. In 1917, in recognition of its valour and accomplishments, the unit was given the honour of being named the Royal Newfoundland Regiment. The cost of maintaining the regiment had been heavy for a small country and the debt caused by the war was one of the principal reasons for the financial crisis that beset Newfoundland in the 1930s and which led to the suspension of self-government and the establishment of the Commission of Government. Moreover, conscription to keep up the flow of recruits overseas had been introduced in 1917 in the face of considerable popular resistance. Many other Newfoundlanders had served in the Great War in the Royal Navy and indeed members of the Royal Naval Reserve had been the first local men to go overseas. Newfoundland had also sent overseas a uniformed forestry corps and a small number of nurses. When the Second World War began, the Commission of Government decided on quite a different course of action.[3] No units were raised for overseas service and conscription was eschewed throughout the war. Newfoundlanders were encouraged to enlist in the British forces and the Royal Navy, Royal Artillery and Royal Air

Force all recruited in the country. Initially artillery recruits went into the 57th (Newfoundland) Heavy Regiment, Royal Artillery. From November, 1941, however, there were two distinctly Newfoundland Regiments—the 59th (Newfoundland) Heavy Regiment, Royal Artillery, and the 166th (Newfoundland) Field Regiment, Royal Artillery, which superseded the 57th. Thereafter the 166th served in North Africa and Italy and the 59th in Northwest Europe, after the D-Day landings. In the same spirit the 125th (Fighter) Squadron of the Royal Air Force was given a Newfoundland designation.

In October 1939 the Commission created a militia, known from March 1940 as the Newfoundland Regiment, for home defence. In May 1942 Newfoundland gave permission to the Royal Canadian Air Force to recruit in Newfoundland for its Women's Division and thereafter other branches of the Canadian forces were also allowed to recruit in the country.[4] Newfoundland was said to be the only other country from which Canada thus recruited directly during the war.[5] Newfoundlanders also volunteered to serve as merchant seaman while others were recruited by the Department of Defence of the Commission of Government to go overseas to work on rescue tugs. Finally, a large contingent of Newfoundland men went to the United Kingdom as members of the Newfoundland Forestry Unit (NFU).[6] This unit was formed by the Commission of Government at British request in the autumn of 1939 and by the end of 1942 3,597 loggers had joined its ranks.[7] The unit was commanded by Captain Jack Turner, a veteran of the Royal Newfoundland Regiment who at the time of his appointment was Chief Forestry Officer in the Department of Natural Resources. The Newfoundland foresters were employed, mainly in Scotland, cutting timber that was urgently needed for the war effort. The first draft of the unit, 300 men, left Newfoundland in December 1939 and by February 1940 there were apparently 2,100 Newfoundland foresters overseas.[8]

According to a 1948 Government of Canada report, the number of Newfoundlanders who had enlisted in the British, Canadian and Newfoundland forces to 30 June 1945 was as follows: Royal Navy (including Rescue Tug Service), 3,419; Royal Artillery, 2,343; Royal Air Force, 713; Canadian forces, 1,752; Newfoundland Regiment, 860.[9] The figures for the British forces included 787 men who had originally joined the Newfoundland Regiment but later transferred to overseas units. These figures also included 533 members of the NFU who, on the termination of their engagement with the foresters, had joined the British armed forces. Of these 267 had gone into the Royal Navy, 219 into the Royal Air Force and 47 into the Royal Artillery. The total given for the Canadian forces did not distinguish between men and women but in fact, to 30 September 1945, 524 Newfoundland women had enlisted in those forces as follows: Women's Royal Canadian Naval Service, 74; Canadian Women's Army Corps, 190; and Royal Canadian Air Force (Women's Division), 160. In all more than 12,000

Newfoundlanders left the country in connection with the war effort. Clearly, the Commission of Government faced a big task to re-absorb into society the many thousands who would be coming home when peace was restored.

After World War I returning Newfoundland members of the armed forces had been assisted in their readjustment to civilian life by the 'Civil Re-Establishment Committee.' Chaired by Justice J.M. Kent, this committee had included a medical officer, Major W.H.Parsons, and a vocational officer, the prominent educator Dr. W.W. Blackall, who also served as secretary.[10] Newfoundland had also devised a pension scheme for disabled veterans who were not eligible for imperial benefits. This was administered by a Board of Pension Commissioners for Newfoundland.[11] To keep alive the memory of wartime sacrifice and to define and advance their interests, Newfoundland veterans, like their Canadian counterparts, looked principally to the Great War Veterans' Association (GWVA).[12] Founded in Winnipeg in 1917, the GWVA was launched in Newfoundland at a meeting in St. John's on 20 August 1918.[13] The founding president was Harold Mitchell of the Royal Newfoundland Regiment, a veteran of the Gallipoli campaign who had been invalided home.[14] The new organization carried on from and absorbed an association of returned soldiers and rejected volunteers. The objectives of the Newfoundland GWVA as set forth in its 1918 constitution and by-laws were those of its sister Canadian organization.[15] The official name of the organization formed in St. John's was 'The Great War Veterans' Association of Newfoundland.' In 1948 it was reported that the Newfoundland GWVA, which had membership in the British Empire Service League, had twenty-seven branches and 3,000 members.[16] In the interwar years the GWVA was one of the country's best organized and most powerful lobbbies. It was a prop for and a stay to authority but a claimant whose brief, writ in blood, always had a special edge. The approach of the organization was 'to conduct negotiations with Government in a friendly atmosphere' and to present 'the viewpoint of servicemen by reasoned discussion' but to do so 'with the firm conviction of right and justice.'[17] In the deep public financial crisis triggered in Newfoundland by the Great Depression, the GWVA supported the change to Commission of Government.[18] Organized veterans looked to the new administration, which had the British Treasury behind it, for a better deal. New pension legislation was in fact passed in 1935.[19] The GWVA was also active in giving help to needy veterans and their families through the relief committees of its various branches. When the war brought unprecedented prosperity to Newfoundland, thanks mainly to Canadian and United States base construction, the GWVA campaigned hard for improved pension benefits for the veterans of World War I. It also sought to make a place within its ranks for a new generation of veterans.

The interests of veterans were also fostered by the Newfoundland Patriotic Association, a voluntary organization formed in 1940 by members of the St. John's business and social elite. In a radio adddress on the need for such an association, the organization's honourary secretary, John G. Higgins, a lawyer and another veteran of the Royal Newfoundland Regiment, condemned the way the country had neglected those Newfoundlanders who had served in the Great War:

> If the history of the aftermath of the last war is inquired into it will be seen that few, if any, of the good positions were given to returned men, though there were men available to fill them. It cannot be said that ex-servicemen came back and demanded the country. Far from it. After doing their duty they settled down quietly to face the future. They were a very conservative body of men who did not stint themselves in public services or in their desire to care for their less favoured comrades. The taint of bolshevism was not in their blood and their hearts were not hardened.[20]

But for the GWVA, 'there would have been little organized effort to help those who broke under the strain of service.' This time the country had to do better and one of the purposes of the Patriotic Association was to ensure it. Those who served their country must be given 'a helping hand' on their return and veterans who needed 'encouragement and support' must not find themselves lacking them.

The Commission of Government listened attentively to the GWVA and the Newfoundland Patriotic Association and dealt with immediate needs while attempting to devise a master plan for the post-war period. Work on this was carried on by a committee on demobilization, civil re-establishment and post-war planning which had an advisory committee attached to it. This consisted mainly of businessmen and professionals but included some labour representatives.[21] Walsh's address to the country on 14 March 1944 was the culmination of the Commission's long-range planning for veterans.

The scheme of benefits detailed by him went far beyond what Newfoundland had previously attempted and reflected both the prosperity of the times and the belief, held everywhere in the Anglo-American world, that the war was being fought not just to defeat Hitler but also to usher in a better world. War would not be followed by depression but by a golden age of fairness and plenty. This would be underwritten by the state and made possible by planning. What the Commission of Government proposed, Walsh explained, owed much to the plans which had been developed in Canada but took account of Newfoundland's special circumstances, that is to say the country's 'general economy' and its 'financial ability.'[22] In devising its programme the government had been guided by three principles, as follows:

(1) A discharged man should have the opportunity of improving his educational and technical competence with due regard to his abilities and the probability of employment.

(2) A discharged man should be encouraged to engage in the country's basic industries.

(3) The transition from war service to civil life should be made as easy as possible without financial embarrassment.[23]

To give substance to these principles the government would offer 'maintenance allowances, educational benefits, vocational guidance and training, agricultural courses, assistance for fishermen, assistance for certain small individual enterprises, unemployment benefits, free medical treatment and employment preference.'[24] These benefits would be in addition to the deferred pay, clothing, transportation, discharge furlough, supplementary pension (for United Kingdom pensioners), and employment assistance benefits which had been announced in November 1943. The maintenance allowance would be paid to a veteran taking advantage of one of the opportunities on offer that did not produce immediate earnings, say further education. The allowance would be paid on a sliding scale and would take account of marital status and, in the case of married men, their dependents. The allowance would be paid for a fixed number of months according to the requirements of the particular training or other opportunity being pursued. In the case of unemployment, the allowance would be paid for one year.

The new benefits announced by Walsh would apply to servicemen discharged after 1 April 1945 who had served either in the Newfoundland Regiment (the home defence force) or in the armed forces of the United Kingdom. In the case of men who had previously been honourably discharged from the eligible forces, the government would consider on an individual basis what further assistance was appropriate. Walsh's presentation, phrased in the crisp and careful official prose of the Commission, put a brave face on what the government intended. Newfoundland was keeping faith with those who had served the cause of freedom. In truth, however, the government intended also to keep costs and eligibility within strict bounds and initially it planned to exclude foresters and merchant seamen altogether. The Commission's position on the foresters was that they had 'been in civilian employment in comparative safety' and that many of them had accumulated 'considerable savings.'[25] They neither needed nor deserved any special assistance but could return to their usual employment. Those who had volunteered as merchant seamen could likewise be passed over. While it was true that they 'had incurred great risk,' they had also received 'high wages.' Most had been seamen before the war and they could continue in their usual line of work. In practice about 150 merchant seamen and members of the Rescue Tug Service were given limited assistance under the Newfoundland re-establishment programme. Eligible merchant seamen were those recruited in Newfoundland by or on behalf of the British Ministry of War Transport and who had 'signed agreements to undertake service in war zones for the duration of the war.'[26] By contrast the only concession made to ex-members of the NFU was to allow them to participate in a land settlement scheme at Cormack if there were insufficient veteran applicants.[27] Not surprisingly, the whole letter of the law approach of the government sowed the seeds of much future discontent and public controversy. In varying degrees, foresters, merchant seamen and rescue tug men were left feeling cheated.

Following from Walsh's speech the Division of Civil Re-establishment, the administrative unit of government responsible for the civil re-establishment programme and which had offices on the second floor of the King George V Institute, Water Street East, issued two booklets to explain the Commission of Government's plans. The first was entitled *When You Come Home* and the second *Now That You Are Home*.[28]

The official in charge of the Division of Civil Re-establishment was J.A. Cochrane, a former principal of Prince of Wales College, St. John's, who had served as president of the Newfoundland Teachers' Association from 1931 to 1938.[29] His efforts and those of the Commission generally produced mixed reviews from returning servicemen, who had recourse to the ever watchful GWVA, to the Newfoundland Patriotic Association and to a Citizens' Rehabilitation Committee.[30] Kicking and complaining has a long history among men who have laid down arms and have had to adjust back to civil society and the constraints of domesticity. Newfoundland's World War II veterans, however, had specific grievances besides the normal post-war letdown. In May and June 1946, Captain G. Campbell (Cam) Eaton, who had served in the British forces and been awarded the Military Cross, published a series of articles in a new St. John's newspaper, the *Sunday Herald*,[31] that were highly critical of the treatment being given ex-servicemen. His purpose, he explained in the first issue of the paper, was to 'put before the general public the difficulties our ex-servicemen are having in readjusting themselves and their impressions of this country after years abroad.'[32] Ex-servicemen, he asserted, felt badly let down and had a particular cause of complaint in the lamentably inadequate job the government was doing in vocational education:

> The return to "Civvie Street" has been very different than was expected by a great majority...They were given the impression while in Italy, Germany, England and many other parts of the world that it would be smooth running as soon as they were discharged. Unfortunately such has not been the case. The Government has let them down badly to begin with in vocational training. True the vocational training centre is now open and there are some one hundred and fifty men undergoing training but this should have begun over a year ago. What is to happen to the remainder of the applicants? They may be waiting for as long as three years before they can even begin a course. This is an appalling state of affairs to say the least. Thoughtful and practical consideration by the Commission of Government should be given to the extension of the training facilities and put into effect as soon as humanly possible. It is an item which cannot wait. Every month wasted by these applicants will have a demoralising effect on them and eventually if present

conditions continue they will be of no use to their communities or themselves.

In another of the articles Captain Eaton noted that there were more than 700 veterans drawing the unemployment benefit. They were men who had 'given the best years of their lives in the service of their country' and they deserved better.[33] The government and people had to act quickly to give the veteran a better deal before a 'serious problem' developed. The government should immediately call a meeting of representatives of the Newfoundland Board of Trade and of labour leaders to find a way out of the unemployment dilemma. Earlier on the Board of Trade had adopted the slogan 'They were behind the guns then—are you behind them now?' This was a question, Eaton concluded, which every Newfoundland community might now do well to ponder.

Just how close Captain Eaton was to the mark was shown on 28 June 1946 when veterans attending the ex-servicemen's school at Fort William, St. John's, staged a protest meeting attended by W.R. Dawe and Major F.W. Marshall, respectively President and 1st Vice-President of the Dominion Command of the GWVA.[34] The immediate cause of the protest was the publication of a memorandum by the government limiting educational and vocational training to twelve months. This document, it was charged, put so many conditions in the rehabilitation scheme veterans had been promised as to put them at an 'extreme disadvantage.'[35] The information booklets the government had issued 'contained a lot of fancy clauses' but the reality now facing veterans seeking retraining and further education under the Commission's rules belied the promises which had been made.[36] The St. John's *Evening Telegram* supported the protesters and called on the government 'to give the greatest encouragement' to ex-servicemen who honestly desired to better themselves educationally. There must be an immediate end to 'bumbledom.'[37] The Commission responded with a more liberal plan for education and unemployment benefits.[38] By September 1948 some 4,903 veterans had received assistance under the Newfoundland re-establishment scheme at a cost to the Commission of more than $2,506,000.[39] As in so many other policy areas in the immediate post-war period, Newfoundland's appointed government showed itself adept at steering its way around the shoals of confrontation. Nevertheless its relations with its veteran clients evidently remained uneasy.

As the re-establishment programme unfolded, moreover, those relations were overshadowed by a larger question about the future. This was the effect that constitutional change for their country would have on their status and benefits. Soon after the Second World War began, the British concluded that the prosperity the conflict was bringing to Newfoundland made constitutional change imperative.[40] It could be delayed on the grounds that the war must be won first and that victory took precedence over everything else, but once the fighting ended in Europe, the United

Kingdom must be ready with a plan of action for Newfoundland. In keeping with this approach, the British government publicly committed itself in December 1943 to provide Newfoundlanders at the end of the war in Europe with machinery whereby they could decide their own constitutional future. During 1944 British policy makers concluded that the only practical future for Newfoundland was to join the Canadian confederation and in 1945 they were able to make an agreement with Canada to work together behind the scenes to promote this objective. Then, in December 1945, the British announced that a National Convention would be elected in Newfoundland to advise them about choices to be put before the people in a referendum on their constitutional future. The National Convention was duly elected in the summer of 1946 and began meeting in September of that year. The subject of confederation with Canada was soon introduced into its proceedings and made a focus of attention in the country mainly through the efforts of the highly energetic member for Bonavista Centre, Joseph R. Smallwood. Every Newfoundlander had a big stake in this debate but veterans had particular concerns. For them the possibility of union with Canada posed obvious and immediate questions. In the event of union would they be eligible equally with other Canadian veterans for the Dominion's benefits? What were those benefits? And would they be better off as Canadians or as Newfoundlanders? If Canada were generous, the veterans' vote in Newfoundland might count at the ballot box in favour of confederation. Conversely, Ottawa had to think carefully about establishing precedents in negotiations with Newfoundland that might lead to unwanted expenditures elsewhere in the country.

As might be expected, political developments in Newfoundland were followed closely within the Department of Veterans Affairs (DVA) in Ottawa. Though its officers had only a rudimentary knowledge of Newfoundland, there had been important contacts over the years between Newfoundland and Canadian officials concerning veterans' questions. In 1918 an agreement was reached between the Board of Pension Commissioners for Canada and the Newfoundland Board of Pensions whereby in the case of Canadians living in Newfoundland, the latter agency would conduct investigations on behalf of the former.[41] The Canadian board likewise agreed to pay pensions and provide medical treatment to those pensioners of the Newfoundland board who were resident in Canada.[42] According to the instruction on it issued by E.R. Scammell, Assistant Deputy Minister of the Department of Soldiers Re-establishment, the Newfoundlanders were to be paid and treated 'as though they were ex-members of the Canadian Forces.'[43] For his part W.W. Blackall of Newfoundland's Civil Re-establishment Committee had sought and been given advice by Ottawa on vocational matters.[44]

The recruitment of Newfoundlanders into the Canadian forces during the Second World War brought more business. In August 1943, Air Vice

Marshall Sully brought to the attention of Walter Woods, the Associate Deputy Minister for Rehabilitation in the Department of Pensions and National Health, a difficult situation that had arisen over Newfoundland women serving in the Canadian forces.[45] Woods' department was responsible for the care of women discharged from the forces because of pregnancy. In general, Sully noted, the arrangements for pregnant ex-servicewomen were 'working satisfactorily' but if a Newfoundlander became pregnant, she would have to be discharged in Canada and remain there in order to avail herself of Canadian medical and rehabilitation benefits. Complicating this was the fact that many of the Newfoundlanders in the Royal Canadian Air Force (Women's Division) had been posted back to their own country. If a pregnant Newfoundland servicewoman were discharged in Canada, she would find herself without legal residence in the country and could be deported by the immigration authorities. In addition Canadian welfare agencies were reluctant to make arrangements for a child who would have no legal status in the country. Conversely a discharged Newfoundland woman who sought to go home with a child ran the risk of trouble with the Newfoundland authorities on the grounds that the child was an alien and therefore inadmissible to the country. Sully also complained that the rehabilitation benefits currently available to ex-service personnel could only be taken in Canada. On discharge, therefore, Newfoundlanders, women and men, would have to stay in the country to take advantage of their rights as veterans. The Air Vice Marshall recommended that consideration be given to removing the restrictions that tied rehabilitation benefits to Canadian residence. And he made a special plea to Woods to do something about the bureaucratic tangle in which Newfoundland women found themselves when discharged because of pregnancy. In response to this and other appeals, improvements were made over time in the rights Newfoundland veterans of the Canadian armed forces who went home following discharge had to Ottawa's benefits.[46] In the case of the Newfoundland women singled out by Air Vice Marshall Sully, arrangements were eventually proposed whereby the Department of Pensions and National Health would cover expenses in Newfoundland for pre-natal domiciliary care, confinement and post-natal care as required. Nevertheless Newfoundland veterans of the Canadian forces remained at a disadvantage in the immediate post-war period in comparison to veterans of the Canadian forces who were residents of Canada.

The benefits available by 1945 to Canada's World War II veterans had been worked out through a long process of planning and executive and legislative action. A key event was the issuance on 1 October 1941 of order in council PC 7633.[47] Known as the Post-Discharge Re-establishment Order, this provided benefits for veterans who were unemployed, who were pursuing vocational training or higher education, who were incapacitated, or who were awaiting returns from private enterprise. The order also provided that, subject to certain conditions, service in the armed forces could be counted as insurable employment under the Unemployment Insurance Act of 1940. Fullfilling the promise of PC 7633 was a major objective in wartime Ottawa and when the time came for full-scale demobilization Canada had ready a scheme of veterans' benefits that was both comprehensive and readily available. To facilitate the administration of this scheme the Department of Pensions and National Health was broken up in 1944 into two new Departments, Veterans Affairs and National Health and Welfare. The first Minister of Veterans Affairs was Ian Mackenzie, the former Minister of Pensions and National Health. The first Deputy Minister was Walter Woods, who moved with Mackenzie from the latter's old department. Woods (originally Sainsbury-Woods) had come to Canada from England in 1905 at the age of twenty-one.[48] He had first worked in the country on an Ontario farm and he had gone overseas in 1914 with the First Canadian Contingent. He was an indefatigable and imaginative public servant in the tradition of the mandarinate dubbed by J.L. Granatstein 'the Ottawa Men.' Woods was a driving force behind and one of the principal architects of Canada's 'Veterans Charter.' This was the name eventually used to describe the country's programme of veterans' benefits. In 1947, in the midst of the big post-war adjustment, the phrase was used as the title of a government of Canada publication that brought together in one volume all the acts that parliament had passed to assist veterans.[49] This publication also included a comparison of the benefits being provided to assist in the rehabilitation of the veterans of World War II in the United Kingdom, the United States, Australia, New Zealand, South Africa and Canada. The message of this section was that Canada's veterans' benefits were second to none and in truth the Canadian arrangements were a model of their kind.

What the government planned for them was explained to members of the Canadian forces in the publication *Back to Civil Life*. In the main, men and women were equally eligible for the benefits of the Veterans Charter, though a married woman whose husband was 'capable of maintaining her either wholly or mainly and under obligation to do so' did not qualify for the out of work benefit.[50] It was also the case that the rate for out of work benefit paid to a former member of any of the women's units formed in the Canadian armed forces during the war could not exceed her rate of pay on discharge.[51] Yet another disadvantage for women was that, given the preponderence of males in the armed forces, the programmes of the Charter were designed primarily with them in mind. Equality in law for many benefits did not therefore produce equality of condition. Nevertheless the benefits given Canada's nearly 50,000 World War II women veterans marked a notable change in how women were treated in Canadian society. The basic philosophy behind the Veterans Charter was to promote personal independence and enterprise by giving veterans 'OPPORTUNITY WITH SECURITY.'[52]

On leaving the forces, an honourably discharged member, male or female, was entitled to a clothing allowance of $100 and could keep one uniform and personal items.[53] Those with six months service were entitled to a cash rehabilitation grant. This was equal to thirty days pay and full allowances plus whatever pay and allowances was due in lieu of unexpended leave. Honourably discharged members of the forces were also provided with free transportation to their place of enlistment in Canada or to any other destination in the country that could be reached without additional cost. Meals and sleeping facilities were provided *en route* as required. Under the terms of the War Service Grants Act of 1944 all volunteers who were honourably discharged and those honourably discharged conscripts who had served overseas (including the Aleutian Islands) were eligible for a gratuity. This was in two parts. The basic gratuity was calculated on the basis of thirty day periods of service either in the Western Hemisphere or overseas. For each of the former a payment of $7.50 was made and for each of the latter a payment of $15. A supplementary gratuity gave seven days pay and allowances, at the rate in effect at the time of discharge, for each six months service overseas, with a proportionately lower payment being made for a period of less than six months. The whole gratuity was paid in monthly instalments upon discharge. These were limited to the amount of thirty days pay and allowances at the time of discharge. To 31 March 1951 the Government of Canada had paid out $469,065,790.34 in war service gratuities, $47,158,730.02 to navy veterans, $219,125,150.24 to army veterans and $102,781,210.08 to air force veterans. Some 961,975 men and women had qualified for this benefit and the average payment per person had been $488.[54]

Looking to the longer term, the Veterans Charter offered a choice of benefits. A veteran, male or female, could take a re-establishment credit; acquire property under the terms of the Veterans' Land Act of 1942; start a business or get launched in a professional career using the assistance provided for in the Veterans' Business and Professional Loans Act of 1946; or take vocational training or go to university under the terms of the Veterans Rehabilitation Act of 1945. The re-establishment credit had the most takers by far. This benefit also derived from the War Service Grants Act of 1944. It was applicable to those who qualified for the gratuity and was equal in amount to the basic gratuity. It could be applied for within ten years of discharge and could be used for a variety of housing, household furnishing, work-related and business purposes. It could also be used to purchase government annuities or the insurance available to veterans under the Veterans Insurance Act of 1944. To 31 March 1951, $267,794,786.47 was paid out by the government of Canada in re-establishment credits. Individual applications paid to that date in all categories of support numbered 1,827,298 and the average liability of the government with respect to persons eligible for the benefit amounted to $384.61.[55]

While they were making a fresh start in life, duly qualified Canadian veterans enjoyed the protection of various medical, unemployment (with the limitations for women noted above) and 'awaiting returns' benefits. For three months after discharge veterans were also entitled to reinstatement in jobs they had held for at least three months prior to enlistment. They were furthermore given preference for jobs on offer through the National Employment Service and in the civil service. The civil service preference accorded them had originally been introduced for World War I veterans and has recently been described as 'the longest and most powerful affirmative action program ever applied in the federal service, as well as being the least controversial.'[56] Subject to a means test and to various service and age restrictions, a veteran might also qualify for a living allowance in later years under the War Veterans' Allowance Act. This was also payable to a veteran who at any time in life became totally incapacitated. This allowance was commonly called a 'burnt out' allowance or pension. The act had been passed in 1930 and was administered by the War Veterans' Allowance Board. Pensions for the dependents of those killed in the two world wars and for disabled veterans and their dependents were administered by the Canadian Pension Commission. This commission had been established in 1927 and was the successor administrative unit to the Board of Pension Commissioners for Canada. In 1941 the Pension Act was overhauled to take account of the requirements of World War II. Canadian veterans also qualified for various medical benefits which were administered under the terms of DVA's treatment regulations. Disabled pensioners received lifetime free treatment for their disabilities. On discharge a veteran needing treatment would receive this free for one year at full pay and allowances. Able-bodied veterans who could not provide for themselves were also eligible for free medical treatment for twelve months following discharge. By the same token all veterans were eligible for free dental care on discharge provided application was made within ninety days. Canadian merchant seamen who had served the war effort fell into a separate but related category.[57] Beginning in 1941 they had become eligible for a war risk bonus and beginning in 1944 for a war service bonus. In 1945 a special bonus, payable on discharge and given for service in dangerous waters, was added to these. Following discharge merchant seamen were eligible for a number of benefits including reinstatement in previous employment and free medical treatment according to the pensionable or non-pensionable status of the individual concerned. A pensionable merchant seaman who, owing to disability, could not continue his normal line of work was eligible for vocational training and for the benefits of the Veterans' Land Act. Those merchant seamen who had received the war service bonus or the special bonus were also eligible for veterans' insurance. Merchant seamen were also eligible for training grants from the Department of Transport and when awarded these came under the provisions governing technical and vocational training of the Post-Discharge Re-establishment Order. In 1948, subject to various disability criteria, the vocational training and training allowances authorized by the Veterans Rehabilitation Act of 1945 were extended to merchant seamen under the age of thirty who had received or were eligible to receive the war servive bonus or the special bonus. In sum, though merchant seamen were not considered 'veterans' in Canada, they enjoyed some of the benefits of veterans. In 1946, moreover, the Civilian War Pensions and Allowances Act, which was administered by the Canadian Pension Commission, conferred rights on merchant seamen and a number of other civilian groups with special claims for recognition of service to the war effort. In the same year three other civilian groups—'Special Operators,' overseas 'Supervisors,' and members of the Corps of (Civilian) Canadian Fire Fighters—were also given benefit rights by separate acts of Parliament.[58]

Newfoundland veterans of the Canadian forces who returned home on discharge received the normal clothing allowance and rehabilitation grant and were eligible for the gratuities provided for in the War Service Grants Act.[59] These were paid directly to the veteran irrespective of where he or she lived. On the other hand, Newfoundland residents could only obtain the re-establishment credit provided for in the same act to purchase veterans' insurance. This was because the re-establishment credit was intended for re-establishment in Canada. By virtue of the Veterans Rehabilitation Act, Newfoundland residents could 'attend educational institutions in Newfoundland under the same financial benefits as Canadian ex-service personnel received in Canada.' If a veteran resident in Newfoundland wanted to attend an educational institution in Canada, he or she was eligible for the same financial benefit as a Canadian resident but no travelling expenses were paid. Veterans resident in Newfoundland might also attend vocational training institutions in Canada, again with the same benefit that Canadian residents received. In this case a veteran would have his or her fare paid from the port of entry into Canada to the location of the school. Veterans resident in Newfoundland were also eligible for treatment of any condition which had been ruled by the Canadian Pension Commission as a pensionable disability and for any condition existing at discharge requiring 'active remedial treatment' and for which application had been made to DVA within thirty days of that event. What Newfoundland residents were losing out on, apart from the full use of the re-establishment credit scheme, were Canadian out of work benefits, temporary incapacity benefits, awaiting returns benefits and the benefits available under the Veterans' Land Act. This added up to a very substantial loss of entitlement indeed. The prevailing policy of DVA with respect to Canadian veterans resident in Newfoundland was that they were 'entitled to exactly the same benefits as any other veterans of the Canadian armed forces who...[did] not reside in Canada'—no more and no less.[60] The fact that Canada had been allowed to recruit directly in Newfoundland did not affect the situation. It would be impossible to extend the full benefit package to residents of Newfoundland without making similar provision for veterans resident in other countries and such a general extension of benefits would not be 'advisable.'[61] Yet another wrinkle in all this was that Newfoundland men who had served in the Canadian armed forces were eligible for some benefits under the Newfoundland re-establishment scheme not covered by their Canadian entitlement. In practice some seventy-four were assisted by the Commission of Government.[62] In contrast, women who had served in the Canadian forces were ineligible for any benefits under the Commission of Government's programme.[63] Clearly whatever attractions confederation might have had for Newfoundland veterans at large, it offered certain benefit to veterans of the Canadian armed forces living in Newfoundland. If union were to take place, residence requirements limiting their access to those benefits still in effect in Canada would automatically disappear. In July 1945 the Royal Canadian Navy's Director of Rehabilitation had observed that the Newfoundlanders who had joined the Canadian forces had done so believing that they were enlisting 'under the same conditions and subject to the same benefits as Canadians.'[64] In practice, this expectation had not been realized, despite the unique recruiting arrangement between the two countries. Union with Canada held the promise, at least as far as Ottawa's continuing benefits were concerned, of redress. There is, of course, no way of knowing the opinions of these veterans or of veterans in general on the constitutional future of Newfoundland but for the residents of the country who had served in Canada's armed forces, confederation most likely had a special appeal.

In addition to administering benefits to eligible residents of Newfoundland, DVA had another substantial item of Newfoundland business after the war. This was to assist the Commission of Government in carrying out its own re-establishment programme. As Walsh noted in his seminal 1944 radio address, Newfoundland had looked to Canada as a model while drawing up its own plan for veterans and in keeping with this outlook the key Newfoundland officials concerned with the administration of the Commision of Government's scheme visited Ottawa. In October 1944, M.G. Chambers, who would take charge of re-establishment administration following J.A. Cochrane's death in August 1947, went to the Canadian capital to attend a course for personnel counsellors offered by the Department of National Defence for Air.[65] The next September J.S. Macdonald, the Canadian High Commissioner in St. John's, reported that he had been asked by J.A. Cochrane if places could be found in Canada's vocational training centres for a limited number of Newfoundland applicants.[66] Macdonald himself was sympathetic to this request and reported that while Newfoundlanders were now arriving home in large numbers the Commission of Government was not very well equipped to provide vocational courses. In fact to meet the need the Newfoundland authorities had to secure buildings and equipment still being used by the Canadian army. Macdonald saw in Cochrane's request an excellent opportunity 'to carry on the close co-operation that had existed between the two countries during the war' and 'to lay a foundation for closer and more cordial relations' in the future.[67] While admitting that Canadian vocational centres were crowded, he nevertheless pressed for the admission of some Newfoundlanders. His advice was taken and the terms on which Newfoundland trainees could come to Canada were spelled out in an order in council (PC 7032) issued on 23 November 1945.[68] The Minister of Veterans Affairs was authorized to act as agent of the government of Newfoundland in placing veterans in Canadian schools and other institutions, provided priority was given to the needs of Canadians. No administrative charge was to be levied against Newfoundland for the service thus provided but the minister was enjoined to get "appropriate assurances" from St. John's concerning the costs of the training to be provided. The minister was also required to supervise Newfoundland trainees while they were in Canada and to arrange for their return home once they had finished their courses. J.A. Cochrane visited Ottawa in January 1946 to work out the details of this scheme and on his return to St. John's publicly thanked the Canadian authorities for their co-operation.[69] In November 1946, when he reported to the Newfoundland people in a radio address on the first twenty months of the civil re-restablishment scheme, Cochrane noted that there were currenly 130 men in Canada taking training under the auspices of the Newfoundland government.[70] Courses being taken in Canada included most of the subjects available at Newfoundland's own vocational institute but veterans were also studying welding, radio operating and technology, and were taking farm and commerical training. For DVA the training agreement with Newfoundland gave a foretaste of the much larger role it would soon come to play there.

The formal involvement of the department with issues arising out of the constitutional future of Newfoundland began in July 1946 when it received a twofold request from the Under-Secreatry of State for External Affairs. In view of the interest in confederation that was developing in Newfoundland, he explained, the government might 'some months hence' be faced with the question whether it was 'prepared to admit Newfoundland, and if so, on what terms.'[71] To prepare for this eventuality an interdepartmental committee had been formed under the chairmanship of R.A. MacKay of External Affairs. This committee was compiling information and wanted an estimate from DVA of the cost of extending its services to Newfoundland. The committee also wished to know 'of any special problems union might raise' for the department. The estimate forthcoming was for an annual cost, low in the event, of $1,704,000.[72] This was based on two assumptions: that there had been 9,100 enlistees from Newfoundland in the armed forces of the United Kingdom and Canada (members of the NFU and merchant marine were purposely excluded); and that 'the immediate post-war rehabilitation period' would be over 'if, as and when union with Newfoundland became a matter of direct concern to the Canadian Government.' The Department saw no 'special problem' in extending its administration to Newfoundland.

The distinction thus made between 'the immediate post-war rehabilitation period' and the longer term was crucial to subsequent negotiations over veterans' questions between Canada and Newfoundland. In February 1947 the National Convention adopted an omnibus resolution that led eventually to the despatch of delegations of enquiry first to London and then to Ottawa.[73] The Ottawa delegation was in the Canadian capital from 24 June to 30 September. During its visit its discussions covered the whole range of issues which confederation posed. A smaller group from the main Canada-Newfoundland negotiating team looked at the problems of veterans. This sub-group was chaired by Mitchell Sharp of the Department of Finance.[74] Discussions took place in September and the discussants had before them a 'Comparison of Benefits for Ex-Service Personnel Canada and Newfoundland' prepared by E.J. Rider, a research adviser at DVA.[75] The practical result of the talks was an understanding which was incorporated into a document prepared by the government of Canada detailing 'proposed arrangements' for the union of the two countries 'should the people of Newfoundland desire to enter into Confederation.'[76] This document, dated 29 October 1947, was submitted by Ottawa, through the governor of Newfoundland, to the National Convention, after the return of the delegation to St. John's. The subject of 'War Service Benefits' was covered in Annex I.[77] Part A of this Annex dealt with war veterans and Part B with merchant seamen. By the terms of Part A Canada proposed to extend to Newfoundland veterans a variety of benefits 'on the same basis as if these Newfoundland veterans had served in His Majesty's Canadian forces.' Newfoundland veterans of the two World Wars would be eligible for Canadian disability and dependents' pensions. Canada would assume Newfoundland's pension liability (which included some merchant marine pensioners), would supplement disability and dependents' pensions paid by the United Kingdom or Allied governments to Newfoundlanders up to Canadian rates, and would pay pensions for disabilities pensionable under Canadian but not British law.[78] Newfoundland veterans would also be eligible for the War Veterans' Allowance and for the free hospitalization and treatment made available to Canadian veterans. Newfoundland veterans of World War II would be eligible for benefits under the Veterans' Land Act; for contributions to the National Unemployment Insurance Fund; for veterans' business and professional loans; for veterans' insurance; and for vocational and educational training. In the case of the latter Canada would 'assume from the date of union, the cost of vocational and educational training of Newfoundland veterans on the same basis as if these veterans had served in His Majesty Canadian forces.'

The benefits proposed for merchant seamen were categorized under 'War Benefits' and 'General Benefits.' By the former, Canada would extend disability and dependents' pensions to Newfoundland merchant seamen who had served during World War II on Canadian, British or Allied ships 'employed in service essential to the prosecution of the war.' These would be paid if a disability 'occurred as a result of enemy action or counteraction, including extraordinary marine hazards occasioned by the war.' A Newfoundland seaman in receipt of a disability pension from the United Kingdom or an Allied nation would be entitled 'during residence in Canada' to have his pension raised to the Canadian scale. Disability pensioners would likewise be entitled to free hospitalization and treatment, and would qualify for vocational training and for the benefits of the Veterans' Land Act and the Veterans Insurance Act. Newfoundland seamen who had served during World War II on Canadian ships and who were eligible for the special bonus would qualify for unemployment insurance contributions, vocational training and veterans' insurance 'on the same basis that they were made available to Canadian merchant seamen.'

No overall philosophy of integration of veterans' benefits was spelled out in the proposed terms of union. E.J. Rider's 'general impression' of the 1947 talks, however, was 'that only benefits of a continuing nature would be considered since items such as "Out-of-work" allowances would not be effective by the time of possible confederation due to time limits.'[79] It was further understood, again according to Rider, that Ottawa's liability for the vocational and educational benefits offered, which had strict post-discharge deadlines under Canadian law, would extend only to Newfoundlanders in training at the time of union. Conversely, even though Canada's re-establishment credit scheme had an application deadline of ten years from discharge and would likely still be in effect at union, the only reference to this important benefit in the offer made to Newfoundland was a note to the effect that at union Newfoundlanders who had served in the Canadian armed forces would become fully eligible for it.[80] This proved highly controversial and indeed agreement between the two countries came to hinge on the eligibility of Newfoundland World War II veterans in general for the re-establishment credit on the same basis that it was available to Canadians. The re-establishment credit scheme had no Newfoundland equivalent, though on discharge members of both the Newfoundland Regiment and the British forces were eligible for gratuities. For the Newfoundland Regiment the terms and amount of the gratuity, together with pension rights, were fixed in regulations published by the Commission of Government in 1944.[81] Newfoundland veterans of the British forces collected their gratuities from the United Kingdom government but these were far below Canadian rates.[82] Would Canadian rates now apply? And would the Canadian re-establishment credit scheme, which was tied to eligibility for gratuities, be extended to Newfoundland veterans? Qualifying for re-establishment credits would amount to a windfall gain for Newfoundland veterans. Not surprisingly, therefore, it was the addition of this benefit to what Ottawa had already offered that spokesmen for Newfoundland veterans identified as the *sine qua non* of equality between them and Canadian veterans.

The stage was set by events in Newfoundland during the summer of 1948 for the resolution of this and the many other complex issues which union posed.[83] In January 1948 the National Convention completed its work and recommended to the British government that in the referendum to follow, the electorate be offered a choice between 'Responsible Government as it existed prior to 1934' and 'Commission of Government.' The British, who had kept to themselves the final wording of the ballot, then announced in March that there would be three choices: 'Commission of Government for a period of five years'; 'Confederation with Canada'; and 'Responsible Government as it existed in 1933.' They now also ruled that the choice to be followed would need majority support. If a first referendum failed to produce this, there would be a second referendum which would offer a choice between the two options leading in the first vote. A second ballot was in fact needed and this was held on 22 July when 'Confederation with Canada' outpolled 'Responsible Government as it existed in 1933' by 78,233 to 71,334. The Commission of Government then appointed a delegation, chaired by Albert Walsh, to go to Ottawa to negotiate final terms of union. The Newfoundland delegation began talks in the Canadian capital on 6 October.

It was with confederation soon to become a reality that the GWVA held its 1948 annual conference at Grand Falls from 13 to 16 September. A resolution was passed at this gathering which addressed the complaint that the organization was 'not represented in any way' on the delegation the government was despatching to Ottawa.[84] To remedy this situation a committee was appointed to study the implications of confederation for Newfoundland veterans and to meet with and make recommendations to the delegation. If the committee found that it would be beneficial to name an adviser to the delegation, this should also be done. The members named to the committee thus formed and instructed were F.W. Marshall (President), Cam Eaton (Vice-President), W.R. Martin (Secretary) and F.G. Harnett. Marshall and Martin were veterans of World War I and Eaton and Harnett of World War II. Marshall was also president of the Responsible Government League which had campaigned for 'Responsible Government as it existed in 1933' and which was now manoeuvering to challenge the legality of the whole constitutional process the United Kingdom government had followed. When the GWVA's committee met with the delegation headed by Walsh before the latter group left for Canada, it was agreed that should the veterans' organization send representatives to Ottawa, meetings could be arranged with the Newfoundland negotiators. On the other hand, the members of the delegation apparently resisted the idea of giving the GWVA a direct role in the pending talks on the grounds that this would open the door for numerous other groups to claim the same standing. After the delegation began its work in Ottawa, however, it requested the assistance of the GWVA, whereupon W.R. Martin and Cam Eaton went there.[85] They were then present at the bargaining table when the final deal on veterans' benefits for Newfoundlanders was struck.

On the Canadian side, in preparation for the final round of talks, Milton Gregg, the Minister for Veterans Affairs, called for consideration of the anomaly in the 1947 offer to Newfoundland over gratuities and re-establishment credits. The omission of these benefits did not accord with the principle of 'making available to Newfoundland veterans the benefits still available to Canadian veterans.'[86] The truth was, Gregg acknowledged, that if Newfoundland veterans of World War II were not given these benefits, they would not be treated on the same basis as if they had served in the Canadain armed forces. Subsequently, it was estimated by DVA that the cost of giving eligible Newfoundlanders the gratuity at Canadian rates and the re-establishment credits would be $10,400,780.16.[87]

On 14 October, with the issue raised by Gregg still open, the Newfoundland delegation submitted to the Canadian cabinet committee on Newfoundland a lengthy memorandum on 'problems connected with union.'[88] This was in fifty one parts and had six appendices. Part XII dealt with 'Benefits to Newfoundland Veterans of World War II.'[89] In accordance with the established procedure in the overall negotiations, this item was next referred for study to a sub-committee to be convened by the Minister of Veterans Affairs. The first meeting of this sub-committee was held on 19 October.[90] Present from Newfoundland were five members of the delegation, including Albert Walsh; J.G. Channing, who was secretary of the delegation; with W.R. Martin and Cam Eaton of the GWVA. In addition to Milton Gregg the Canadian members were E.B. Armstrong of the Department of Finance; six senior DVA officials including Deputy Minister Walter Woods; and J.C.G. Herwig, the General Secretary of the Canadian Legion who had attended the GWVA's 1948 convention in Grand Falls.[91] Three sub-committees of the main veterans' affairs sub-committee were formed to report on pensions, free hospitalization and treatment, and the administration of the Veterans' Land Act in Newfoundland. The work of these sub-groups proceeded smoothly and non-controversial reports from all three were received on 25 October at the second meeting of the main sub-committee.[92] It was at this session that the issue of the gratuity and the re-establishment credits was joined. The request for their inclusion was made by Cam Eaton and in reply Milton Gregg, who along with Woods and Herwig stood high in the estimation of the Newfoundlanders, asked for a brief from the GWVA representatives. This was duly submitted and made the case to the Canadian authorities, by now familiar to them, that if the

War Service Grants Act was not extended in its entirety to the new province, the Newfoundland veteran would "not be treated on the same basis as if he were a veteran of His Majesty's Canadian forces."[93] No recommendation was made on the submission of the GWVA but in the final report of the sub-committee, which was adopted on 27 October, it was agreed that the minister would take the matter up with the government. Gregg likewise agreed to discuss with his colleagues the status of the 'Awaiting Returns' benefits available to various categories of Canadian veterans.[94] The GWVA representatives had argued that these should also be extended to Newfoundlanders.

Within DVA there were two opinions on the issue of gratuities and re-establishment credits. In a memorandum dated 13 October, G.H. Parliament, the Director General of Rehabilitation, argued that the war service gratuity had been paid 'to recompense Canadians who served in the Forces for service rendered to Canada.'[95] Therefore it would not 'seem logical to extend the same benefit to Newfoundlanders who were not able to render such service.' In the view of this official the Newfoundland side might have 'a good point' about the re-establishment credits but the fact that this benefit was linked in amount to the value of the Canadian gratuity would make its administration difficult. The gratuity paid to members of the British forces, Parliament noted, was small compared to what Canadian ex-service personnel had received. A contrary view of the whole issue, however, was taken in a memorandum prepared for use by the minister in his discussions with the Newfoundland delegation. The conclusion here was 'that some concession' would have to be made to the Newfoundland view of gratutiies and re-establishment credits if 'good relations' were to be maintained.[96]

When the sub-committee report was submitted, it was this conciliatory view that prevailed at cabinet level. Thus Canada proposed and Newfoundland agreed that while the gratuity scheme should not be extended to Newfoundland veterans, re-establishment credits and awaiting returns allowances should be.[97] The cost of extending re-establishment credits on this basis had been estimated by DVA at $4,000,000.[98] The agreement thus made was next incorporated into the final terms of union which were signed at an elaborate ceremony in the Senate chamber on 11 December. Why the Canadian government was willing to accommodate Newfoundland veterans to such an extent can only be speculated upon but several factors may have influenced the situation. The Newfoundland veterans had made it to the bargaining table and denying them in face to face negotiations would have been tricky. Moreover, Milton Gregg, who had served in the two world wars and had won the Victoria Cross in the first, exhibited a fellow-feeling for the Newfoundland veterans that encouraged a generous approach. He wanted to do the honourable thing and with wartime secrifice still a recent memory his attitude would have been difficult to counter, especially in good times. It was also the case, of course, that the re-establishment credits scheme was still in effect in Canada and that the cost of extending it to Newfoundland veterans would be but a tiny fraction of Canada's total bill for the benefit. Yet another factor may have been the closeness of the vote in Newfoundland in the second referendum. This overshadowed the whole of the negotiations between the two countries and underlined for the Canadian authorities just how important it was to make a good start in Newfoundland. Leaving Newfoundland veterans feeling disgruntled would certainly not have accorded with that approach. Veterans' benefits were covered in term 38, which revised the offer made by Canada in 1947 so as to take account of the outcome of the 1948 negotiations.[99] In final form, the agreement made with respect to the payment of the pivotal re-establishment credits was as follows: 'a re-establishment credit will be made available to Newfoundland veterans who served in the Second World War equal to the re-establishment credit that might have been made available to them under the War Service Grants Act, 1944, if their service in the Second World War had been service in the Canadian forces, less the amount of any pecuniary benefits of the same nature granted or paid by the Government of any country other than Canada.' In the final terms of union the benefits to be extended to Newfoundland merchant seamen were covered in a separate section, number 42.[100] This varied the wording of the section on merchant seamen in the 1947 offer but was substantially the same. In February 1949 the Parliament of Canada passed the Statute Law Amendment (Newfoundland) Act which altered existing Canadian law to take account of Newfoundland's pending entry into confederation.[101]

On their return to St. John's W.R. Martin and Cam Eaton submitted a report to the executive of the GWVA on what had been accomplished in Ottawa.[102] This summarized events since the 1948 general meeting of the organization and offered a detailed explanation of term 38 of the terms of union. The tone of the report was of a good job well done and certainly Eaton and Martin had reason to be pleased with what had been achieved in Ottawa. By September 1949 payments to Newfoundland veterans under the re-establishment credit scheme reached $500,000. This event was duly celebrated in a ceremony at DVA's offices, which were located at Buckmaster's Field in St. John's.[103] Among those present for the occasion was Joseph R. Smallwood, now premier of the Province of Newfoundland. By 31 March 1951, 10,750 Newfoundland veterans had received re-establishment credits worth $1,827,627.[104] Of this amount 60% had been spent on furniture. Nor was this all. Canadians who had been conscripted into the armed forces under the terms of the National Resources Mobilization Act of 1940 and who had served only in the Western Hemisphere were ineligible for gratuities and re-establishment credits. By contrast, Newfoundlanders who had served at home with the Newfoundland Regiment during the war were ruled eligible for the re-establishment credits on the grounds that they had enlisted without territorial limitation.[105] Years later Cam Eaton recalled that at one memorable moment in the bargaining that had gone on in Ottawa in 1948 over this particular benefit, Phil Gruchy of the Newfoundland delegation had said: 'Mr. Minister, if we are coming into Confederation we are coming right into your living room, we ain't staying on your back stoop.'[106] In truth, for those Newfoundlanders who enjoyed the status of veteran, this objective was achieved by the terms of union. The GWVA representatives had not obtained retroactive supplementation of gratuities to Canadian rates and had not been able to turn the training clock back to 1945 but they had obtained satisfaction on every other issue of importance to them. According to one contemporary observer, when Smallwood had learned what Newfoundlanders would qualify for under the Veterans' Land Act alone, he had whistled and said, 'Heck if I had known about this before, I could have swung Confederation without half the trouble.'[107] This spoke for itself about the quality of the bargain that had been struck for veterans in Newfoundland. It also showed just how much Smallwood had to learn about Canada and just how much he had been flying by the seat of his pants in the referenda campaigns.

While the terms of union were being hammered out in the autumn of 1948, DVA was simultaneously laying the groundwork for its subsequent administration in Newfoundland. The key official in this regard was Paul B. Cross, the Regional Administrator for the Maritime Provinces. In January 1948 he had produced a preliminary report on the organizational requirements of the department in Newfoundland.[108] He concluded that the department should lay plans to duplicate the sort of organization it had in the Quebec City area and that eventually the entire staff should consist of Newfoundlanders. In May Cross produced a much more detailed report, this time an appreciation of conditions in Newfoundland as they affected the rehabilitation of veterans.[109] Next, in August, he set out the terms of reference for a departmental committee on Newfoundland, which he subsequently chaired.[110] The purpose of this committee was to make detailed proposals to the deputy minister concerning the setting up of a district organization in Newfoundland. The first meeting of the committee was held on 1 September and it met thereafter as required.[111] In the same month Cross and E.A. Fergusson, the superintendent of Cornwallis Hospital for veterans in Nova Scotia, went to Newfoundland, the latter to make a survey for the department of treatment services. Fergusson had been posted to Newfoundland during the war for two years and already had a good knowledge of the medical situation there.[112] His report, a most useful source for the social history of Newfoundland in the period, had appended to it the following: information, under several headings, about every hospital, of which there were 30; a list of all drug stores, of which there were 23 in St. John's and 17 elsewhere; lists of all doctors (St. John's, 47; elsewhere, 60), consultants (St. John's, 21; elsewhere, 6) and dentists (St. John's, 9; elsewhere, 6); and a table showing the number of graduate nurses at work (305) and where they were employed.[113] The list of doctors gave the name and place of graduation of each practitioner and the list of consultants the address of each. In October a sub-committee of the department's Newfoundland committee was formed to deal with the especially thorny problem of setting up a central registry of veterans. The information for it was scattered in the files of a variety of administrative units in Newfoundland and the United Kingdom.[114] In November 1948 two members of the sub-committee, E.C. Forrest, Chief Administrative Officer (Treatment) and C.C.P. Graham of the Canadian Pension Commission went to St. John's to survey the records there.[115] On the basis of their report procedures were then worked out for compiling a central registry in Newfoundland.[116]

In January 1949, with the approval of the Interdepartmental Committee on Newfoundland, which was directing the flow of officials to St. John's, a party of four DVA officials visited the Newfoundland capital on business connected with the pending administrative changeover.[117] They were O.C. Elliott, who was to be the first District Administrator; E.A. Fergusson, who was to be District Medical Officer; C.H. Scott, who was to supervise the work of the Veterans' Land Act; and F.G. Hewett, who was to preside over the creation of the central registry. In March the department began distributing to Newfoundland veterans, initially through the branches of the GWVA, a booklet entitled *Canada's Veterans' Charter: how it applies in the Province of Newfoundland.*[118] By the appointed moment of union, that is to say "immediately before the expiration of the thirty-first day of March, 1949,"[119] the Department was ready to carry out its responsibilities in Newfoundland. On 2 April Elliott reported from St. John's that the first day of business had 'passed uneventfully.'[120] Eighty-six veterans had been seen, ten for treatment, nine for pensions, twenty-four for re-establishment credits, and twenty-six for war veterans allowance. Seventeen others had made general enquiries.

Much had been acomplished both politically and administratively and DVA and its clients in Newfoundland had reason to be pleased with the results. There were other Newfoundlanders, however, for whom the outcome of the 1948 negotiations was a disappointment. For merchant seamen the effect of the terms of union was mixed. While it was true that they would enjoy greater benefits as Canadians, it was also the case that they, along with merchant seamen everywhere else in Canada, did not enjoy the status of veteran with all the benefits which that status conferred. Two other groups of Newfoundlanders, moreover, had been totally ignored in the terms of union. They were the members of the NFU and the group of men who had worked overseas on rescue tugs. The tugmen had been recruited by the Newfoundland Department of Defence and had been posted initially to Royal Naval training centres at Lowestoft, Campbellton and other places for special training.[121] The fact that Newfoundlanders had been singled out for this mission was a tribute to 'their long recognized seamanship as small boatmen.'[122] During the course of the war the duties of the tugmen had included picking up survivors, towing bombed out vessels and moving floating docks from port to port. They had also been involved in the Normandy landings and had helped lay the pipeline across the English channel. They had done arduous and dangerous work in small vessels and in 'extremely cramped quarters.'[123] The ships they had served on were commissioned and they were subject to naval discipline under the terms of an agreement each man was required to sign. Obviously there was much to be said in their favour because of their singular contribution to the war effort. Paul Cross argued in 1949 that they were 'morally' entitled to veterans' benefits but they were nonetheless ruled out.[124] This was done on the grounds that the section of their agreement subjecting them to naval discipline implied that they were not naval personnel but 'civilians subject to naval discipline in certain circumstances.'[125]

The argument used to deny veterans' benefits to the ex-members of the NFU was different but no less decisive. On 1 October 1944 the foresters had formed the Newfoundland Overseas Foresters Association (NOFA). Its constitution and by-laws were included in *Timber!!*, a publication printed in the United Kingdom at war's end that celebrated the history and achievements of the unit.[126] The first president of the association was Jack Turner, now Lt.-Colonel, the commander of the unit. In the autumn of 1948 he went to Ottawa to be on hand during the negotiation of the final terms of union and to look out for the interest of the Department of Natural Resources. Unfortunately, he died in his sleep at the Lord Elgin Hotel on the night of 26 September, soon after arriving in Canada.[127] This left the foresters without a spokesman to attempt to do for them the job that Martin and Eaton would so ably do on behalf of the GWVA. Of course, it cannot be proved that Turner's presence would have produced a different result, but the record of the GWVA participants clearly supports the view that there was a decided advantage in being represented directly in Ottawa.

The position of DVA on the foresters was spelled out in detail soon after confederation in a letter from Milton Gregg to Smallwood.[128] Gregg's letter was written in response to representations made by W.J. Keough, the Newfoundland Minister of Natural Resources, to J.A. MacIsaac, the department's District Pension Advocate in St. John's. Specifically, Keough had called for extending to former members of the NFU the benefits of the Civilian War Pensions and Allowances Act. Gregg categorically denied that ex-NFU personnel qualified under the act:

> I have looked into this matter and find that during the recruitment of this Unit, the Newfoundland government acted solely as agent for the United Kingdom authorities, that they were recruited for the purposes of cutting pit props or timber in the United Kingdom, and that they were enrolled purely as workmen at a given rate of wages, plus board, lodging, bedding, tools, medical services, etc. Provision was made if they were hurt they were to be returned home without charge. This Unit

was not recognized as members of the forces either by the British government or the Newfoundland Commission government. It appears that their work was normal labour somewhat far removed from hazardous areas.

Gregg reminded Smallwood that in the negotiations leading up to union the status of the NFU had been considered but it had been concluded to the satisfaction of all concerned 'that there was no enabling Canadian authority by which they could become eligible for benefits.'

DVA stood firm again later on in 1949 when a former member of the NFU, now resident in London, Ontario, made application to the London district office for contribution towards unemployment insurance in respect of service in the armed forces after 30 June 1941.[129] In response to his application a further review of the foresters' status was undertaken in the department and on the basis of this a circular letter was sent on 14 December to heads of branches, chiefs of divisions, district administrators, pension medical examiners and all others concerned.[130] The letter dealt definitively with both the NFU and the Rescue Tug Service. According to this instruction, members of the NFU had not been recognized as members of the forces by either the British or Newfoundland governments and were not therefore eligible for veterans' benefits. In the case of the Rescue Tug Service, employment was not equivalent to service with the armed forces either. Therefore neither was considered eligible for benefits as veterans. In 1952, however, DVA notified its offices of a decision of the Canadian Pension Commission whereby ex-members of the Rescue Tug Service were eligible for consideration under the terms of the Civilian War Pensions and Allowances Act.[131]

Meanwhile on 21 June 1950 the issue of the foresters entered a new phase when Walter Woods and Paul Cross met in St. John's with members of the executive of NOFA and Isaac Mercer and Frank O'Dea of the St. John's law firm of Mercer, Mifflin and O'Dea, the association's solicitors.[132] The meeting was held at the home of Isaac Mercer and the Newfoundlanders pressed in particular for two benefits: recognition of the foresters as veterans for purposes of preference in employment under the National Employment Service and recognition of them under the Civilian War Pensions and Allowances Act.[133] Mercer handed Woods a file and this was next circulated for consideration by the deputy minister to key officials in his department.

The Newfoundland submission received a stern response indeed from J.L. Melville, the Chairman of the Canadian Pension Commission.[134] There was no doubt, he wrote, that NFU personnel had played 'a very great part in the war effort' and had worked far from home. But it was also the case that they had been 'far removed from the air attacks of the enemy.' Even in Mercer's own file the men were clearly described as 'civilians.' Their situation had been thoroughly discussed during the 1947 negotiations with the delegation sent to Ottawa by the National Convention and again in the 1948 negotiations that produced the terms of union. In the latter negotiations, Melville recalled, 'it was made quite clear we had no Canadian authority, nor was it considered the circumstances of their occupation were such as to warrant special consideration.' Newfoundland had accepted no libility for the foresters before 1 April 1949 and Canada therefore had no liability from that date. The terms of employment which the foresters had signed had made plain that in the event of illness or accident, the provisions of the United Kingdom's Workmen's Compensation Act would in general apply. Melville was equally discouraging in relation to the Civilian War Pensions and Allowances Act. There was 'no group within the Civilian Act' or any provision there which would allow consideration for ex-NFU members. It had to be remembered that a number of Canadians had been employed outside the country during the war, especially in the United Kingdom, but they had not been members of the forces and there was no enabling legislation which provided special consideration for them. It was true that the Newfoundlanders had worked alongside Canadian foresters whose members were eligible for benefits but the difference was that the Canadians were veterans of the forces. 'To sum up the situation,' Melville concluded, 'the claim is not a new one. It was brought to the attention of the Committee when the "Terms of Union" were being considered and, there being no provision in the Statute Law Amendment (Newfoundland) Act, the Commission cannot deal with any claims either under the Pension Act or the Civilian War Pensions and Allowances Act.'

When Woods contacted the Newfoundland Provincial Command of the Canadian Legion, which had by now absorbed the GWVA, he received a mixed reply.[135] Woods told the Legion that granting the veterans' preference in employment to the foresters would mean 'a considerable dilution' of the body of Newfoundlanders eligible for this advantage. It was also the case that veterans' preference had not been given to Canadian merchant seamen or to civilian overseas fire-fighters. The Newfoundland Legion endorsed these views in a telegram sent over the signature of W.R. Martin.[136] Ex-members of the NFU, he reported, were not eligible for membership in the Legion and the provincial organization was therefore reluctant to express an opinion on the matters raised by Woods. But the prevailing 'thought' of the Newfoundland Legion was that preference in employment would give the foresters an unjustified advantage over merchant seamen, civilian fire-fighters and veterans without service overseas. On the other hand, the claim of the foresters for recognition of pension rights was thought to be 'a fair request.'

With this reply and J.L. Melville's analysis in hand, E.L.M. Burns, who had now succeeded Woods as deputy minister, advised Gregg against entertaining the requests of the Newfoundland foresters.[137] His advice was taken and Gregg duly informed Premier Smallwood in letters dated 20 and 25 July 1950 of the department's decision and of the reasons for it.[138] Isaac Mercer heard the bad news directly from Burns a few days later.[139]

If the foresters were disappointed, they were not deterred. Mercer soon countered with a letter to Burns in which he reported that the executive members of NOFA were 'very saddened and even bitter' about the department's decision.[140] That decision, the lawyer asserted, was based 'on the same old and equally weak arguments.' The claim that Canada had only taken over such liabilities as Newfoundland had at union was but 'a broad general point' that needed qualification. It failed to take account of the fact that 'it took a few years after the war before the members of the Unit could recollect themselves in Newfoundland and get properly organized to go after the Government.' Had Newfoundland's union with Canada been delayed for a year, there could be no doubt 'but that the Newfoundland Government would have recognized their responsibility and duty to these deserving men.' 'Just because we had a government not responsible to the people and the Unit had not the time to press their claim on such a government,' Mercer asserted, 'is considered to be a very weak argument and one that the Government of Canada should not be taking advantage of now.'

The argument about the members of the NFU having come under the jurisdiction of the United Kingdom's Workmen's Compensation Act was likewise weak. This failed to take account of the fact that 'everything ended when the employment of these men in Scotland was terminated.' The DVA position failed to acknowledge the fact that no compensation had been paid 'for any permanent injuries or any illness' arising out of the foresters' employment. The workmen's compensation clause in the agreement individual foresters had signed was 'absolutely useless to them' and it made no sense for the government to use it as an argument to deny them hospital and medical benefits now. Nor was it surprising to find that the Civilian War Pensions and Allowances Act did not specifically mention the NFU. Why should it when the act in question had been passed before Newfoundland became part of Canada? It was, however, the case that 'more and more groups' were gradually being covered by the legislation. The argument that Canadian foresters were in uniform and Newfoundland foresters were not should simply be dropped. The Newfoundland foresters were 'not claiming to be put on a par with uniformed men' but were seeking to come under the terms of an act to compensate civilians. Was the government, Mercer asked in conclusion, willing to amend that act to bring its benefits to his clients?

Mercer's letter was routed to J.E. Melville and given a pro forma reply whereupon the issue of the foresters went off DVA's policy agenda until 1958 when W.J Browne, the Solicitor General in the Diefenbaker government and Newfoundland's first Progressive Conservative representative in the federal cabinet, reopened it.[141] Browne set out the case for the foresters once more in two letters to A.J. Brooks, Diefenbaker's first Minister of Veterans Affairs; but he was unable to move the department from its established position.[142] It was essential, Brooks told him, to maintain the principle of a line between those who had served in the armed forces and those who had not. It was true that two small civilian groups—Auxiliary Service Supervisors and Special Operators—had been deemed 'to be veterans' for purposes of the Veterans Charter, but their circumstances were exceptional. The Auxiliary Service Supervisors had 'served with the troops in forward areas' and the Special Operators, fifty-seven men, had 'carried out highly hazardous work in enemy territory during hostilities.' With these exceptions parliament had 'not seen fit to extend veterans benefits to civilians who [had] made valuable contributions to the war effort.' It was, however, the case that 'a modified form of benefit' had been given 'to such as the Corps of (Civilian) Canadian Fire Fighters for service in the United Kingdom.' But they were different because they had been 'called upon to face hazards that were not faced by the civilian population.'

In 1960 Brooks gave a reply along the same lines to Hazen Argue, a Co-operative Commonwealth Federation member of the House of Commons, when Argue approached him about a brief he had received from NOFA.[143] This brief was printed and was signed on behalf of the association by Thomas Curran (President), C.R. Baggs (Secretary) and Isaac Mercer (Solicitor).[144] It was presented to the House of Commons Standing Committee on Veterans Affairs on 31 March 1960 by Curran and Baggs.[145] The brief gave the fullest statement to date of the foresters' case. It began with nine 'whereas' clauses and then moved on to a statement of 'facts and information' which was presented in question and answer form. The brief concluded with the arguments as to why the claims of the association were fair and just. Much was made in this brief of the fact that large numbers of foresters had become members of the 3rd Inverness (Nfld.) Battalion of the United Kingdom Home Guard and had been awarded the Defence of Britain Medal. This unit was said to be the only battalion of the Home Guard to be formed 'by Overseas men.' Above and beyond the benefits that members of the NFU as a whole might legitimately claim, the men who had joined the Home Guard arguably had a special claim. This was to be treated equally to former members of the World War II Canadian Forestry Corps, who were fully eligible under the Veterans Charter. It was wrong that Canadians and Newfoundlanders who had done the same work overseas should be treated differently simply because one group was in uniform and the other was not. It was also wrong that, on the same basis, Newfoundland foresters who had gone overseas in World War I qualified as veterans and those who had gone overseas in World War II did not. All three groups—the Newfoundland foresters of World War I, the Canadian foresters of World War II and members of the NFU—should be treated equally. Yet another telling comparison was with members of the Newfoundland Regiment of World War II. They had not gone overseas at all, yet were completely covered by the Veterans Charter because of having been in uniform. All this was made worse by the fact that the reason the first contingent of foresters had not been in uniform was that they were needed so 'badly and fast.' It had been 'much less expensive for the Government to send them in their own civilian clothes' and the men had been able to 'work with greater ease and more comfort in these clothes than in uniforms.' The first Newfoundland foresters were in the United Kingdom by February 1940 whereas the first Canadian foresters did not arrive until later in the year. Everything considered, the brief ventured, ex-members of the NFU 'should be treated the same way as':

(a) Ex-service men in so far as jobs and Government sponsored rehabilitation schemes are concerned, and/or

(b) Canadian civilians who served overseas in hazardous occupations as far as the benefits of the Canadian Civilian War Pensions and Allowances Act is concerned. This may apply to members of the Unit who did not join the Home Guard in Scotland and/or

(c) The members of the Canadian Forestry Corps. This may apply to members of the Unit who joined the Home Guard units, and/or

(d) Persons recruited in Canada by United Kingdom Authorities for special duties in War Areas as set forth in "The Special Operators War Service Benefits Act." This should apply to all member of the Newfoundland Overseas Forestry Unit.

Following the submission of the brief there was a further organizational drive among ex-members of the unit in which the labour leader Esau Thoms played a prominent part.[146] This produced vocal and new lobbying groups in St. John's and St. Mary's. In July 1960, during discussion of the estimates of DVA, the brief of the foresters was endorsed on the floor of the House of Commons by several Newfoundland members of parliament.[147] Then, in October Tom Curran pressed A.J. Brooks for action in a letter that itemized various recent developments that were favourable to the association's cause.[148] In 1958, Curran noted, the executive council of the Newfoundland Provincial Command of the Canadian Legion had gone on record as 'favouring the efforts' of NOFA to obtain recognition from the federal government. Moreover, in 1960 the Legion had gone a step further when at its convention in Windsor, Ontario, the Dominion Command had adopted a resolution which made those members of the NFU who had been awarded the Defence of Britain Medal eligible to join the organization. It was also notable that all Newfoundland members of parliament, both government and opposition, had publicly supported 'getting the Newfoundland Forestry members included under the Veterans Acts on the same level as the Canadian Forestry Corps of World War I and II and the Newfoundland Forestry Corps of World War I.' For his part Premier Smallwood had gone on record that if at the time of the negotiation of the terms of union he had known 'the full facts about the enlistment, works and activities of the Newfoundland Forestry Unit...he would have put forward a much stronger plea for their inclusion in veterans benefits.' Noting that the minister, in answer to questions in the House of Commons, had said that the case of the NFU would be reviewed as part of a pending general review of veterans' legislation, Curran sought assurance that the promised review was indeed taking place and that there was 'some likelihood' that the men he spoke for would 'be included under the various Benefit Acts, on the same par as the Canadian Forestry Corps.'

Curran heard back only that the promised review was in progress but in truth a breakthrough of sorts for NOFA was in the making.[149] Thus in October 1961 when Gordon Churchill, who had succeeded Brooks as Minister, reported to cabinet on the review that had been undertaken, he recommended that the Civilian War Pensions and Allowances Act be amended.[150] The change proposed would 'permit the award of allowances, during indigency, to surviving former and certain dependents of deceased members' of eight civilian groups that had 'made outstanding voluntary contributions to the war effort during World War I or World War II.' Included in these groups were members of either the Canadian merchant marine or the merchant services of Allied countries and the members of the NFU. The benefit would apply to those who had served in Britain and to widows and orphans of deceased members, provided, in both cases, that an individual member had contracted to serve in the unit for the duration of the war or had joined the Home Guard. On this basis, Churchill reported to cabinet, there were currently about sixty eligible claimants and the annual cost to the government of the benefit proposed would be about $60,000. The changes advocated by Churchill were duly incorporated into a bill which received assent on 23 February 1962.[151]

NOFA had finally got its foot in the benefit door but, considering how few ex-NFU members would be eligible for the new benefit and the amount the government would be called upon to spend annually, it had hardly done more than that. Not surprisingly, the association was soon lobbying for more, that is to say for easier eligibility for the new benefit. His associates, Curran told W.J. Browne in April 1962, were 'very dissatisfied' in particular with two features of the amendment which had been made.[152] The first related to the 'service requirement' governing eligibility under the new legislation. The six months overseas requirement was satisfactory but the requirement of 'engagement to serve for the Duration' of the war was not only unfair but discriminatory. The first drafts of men to go overseas—the 2,100 who were in the United Kingdom by February 1940—had signed up for six months service. Before the period covered by their initial service agreements had elapsed, the Dominions Office, backed by the Commission of Government, had started a campaign to get members to re-engage for a further term. They had been offered a choice of twelve months, two years or for the duration of the war while new recruits to the unit were now all being signed on signed on for the duration. Most of those already overseas when the choice of terms was offered had chosen the twelve month option and had continued to renew on this basis throughout the war, some until July 1946. The result was that some men who had gone overseas in 1941 'as duration men' but who had in fact stayed for only six months were now eligible for benefit while the 'great number' who had stayed overseas on the basis of successive limited term contracts were not. It was 'the opinion of every member' of the Forestry Unit, Curran reported, that the service requirement for eligibility 'should be changed and changed immediately.' The word 'duration' should be dropped from the legislation and eligibility for benefit should be 'six months service overseas' combined with 're-engagement to remain in the Forestry Unit for a further period.' Unfortunately, the service records of the unit, which were now held by the provincial Department of Mines and Resources, did not include any re-engagement forms signed by ex-members in the United Kingdom but this should not be allowed to stand in the way of the proposed change. In the case of those with service numbers to 2,100, who had initially signed six month contracts, proof of re-engagement could be deduced from the date on an individual's discharge papers. This was possible because no member of the unit whose contract expired had been allowed to remain overseas unless he had signed on again. For ex-members of the unit with service numbers above 2,100 the issue of re-engagement did not apply because they had all signed 'duration contracts.'

Curran's second complaint about the amendment made to the Civilian War Pensions and Allowances Act was that it provided nothing for members of the unit who had 'suffered disability during their overseas service' whereas the members of the other civilian groups mentioned in the act were covered in this regard. In short, only some former members of the NFU had become eligible for benefits and only then for 'Burnt out Allowances.' The additional benefits available to other civilian groups under the act had been omitted entirely.

DVA readily conceded Curran's point about the eligibility problems faced by members of the unit who had signed successive limited term contracts rather than a duration contract.[153] Thus it was noted by the officials concerned that the War Veterans' Allowance Board, which was responsible for administering the act, was already taking as *de facto* proof of a duration contract the fact of discharge after VE Day (8 May 1945). From the foresters' point of view, of course, this administrative concession, though welcome, was only as good as far as it went and in truth that was not very far. Accordingly, the protests from Newfoundland continued. In August 1962 Augustus Greene, the chairman of the foresters' organization at Placentia, told the Newfoundland members of parliament that what had been done in 1961 was not enough and that what he and his associates wanted was to be treated equally with Canadian foresters, that is to say as veterans.[154] Greene told Prime Minster Pearson the same thing only to receive yet another re-statement of the DVA position.[155] The members of the Newfoundland Forestry Corps of World War I and of the Canadian Forestry Corps of World War II had formed part of the armed forces and had been 'subject to military discipline in all respects.' By contrast, members of the NFU had 'served as civilians under contracts willingly entered into with specified rates of pay, length of service etc.' To be a veteran one had to be 'a former member of H.M. Armed Forces' and the former members of the NFU did not fall into that category. In 1963, by virtue of the same logic, the then Minister of Veterans Affairs, Roger Teillet, explained to Richard Cashin, the Liberal member of parliament for St. John's West, that former members of the NFU were not eligible for any benefits under the Veterans' Land Act.[156]

The stalemate thus reached between DVA and the Newfoundland foresters and their political supporters continued into 1965. In that year, however, there was a sign of change when, in response to a letter from C.W. Carter, the Liberal member for Burin-Burgeo and a longstanding and tireless ally of NOFA, Teillet undertook to study the situation of foresters receiving disability pensions with a view to bringing those pensions up to Canadian rates.[157] Then, in 1967, after further discussions between the Newfoundland members of parliment and DVA, in which J.W. Pickersgill played a prominent part, the 1962 benefits were extended to all former members of the NFU who had served overseas for more than six months and to members who had been repatriated on medical grounds while they were serving.[158] The estimated annual cost of the additional coverage was $287,000.[159] By this change the department conceded something to Newfoundland opinion while maintaining the crucial distinction between 'veteran' and 'civilian.' In November 1966 Teillet reminded J.W. Pickersgill that the Government 'would be in a pretty untenable position if it were to grant the Newfoundland foresters benefits significantly in excess of those available to certain other groups who had meritorious war service in a civilian capacity.'[160] 'I am thinking particularly,' he further cautioned, 'of the large numbers of merchant seamen who, during the war years pursued a much more hazardous occupation than the Newfoundlamnd foresters, virtually all of whom operated in the forest lands of Scotland.' Clearly, further progress for the Newfoundlanders would depend on an enhanced status for all the civilian groups who could claim benefit on the basis of special service to the war effort. In 1979 former members of the Rescue Tug Service were reclassified as veterans but this goal continued to elude ex-members of the NFU who remained under the terms of the Civilian War Pensions and Allowances Act.

In recent times it has become fashionable in Newfoundland to criticize the whole bargain that was struck with Canada in 1948. In the process those who led the campaign for 'Responsible Government as it existed in 1933' have found a new constituency, especially among commentators anxious to make their mark by challenging established views, whatever the evidence and logic behind them. All of this reflects a provincialist tide which has been running strong in the province since the early 1970s and which, ironically, is itself evidence of the success of confederation. As Newfoundlanders went up the scale of development as Canadians, a new middle class emerged among them. It was members of this group in particular that found fault with confederation as it existed and sought, if not outright independence, to shift the balance of power between Ottawa and St. John's in favour of the latter.[161] As in so many other parts of the country, Ottawa laid the basis during the 1950s, 1960s and 1970s for decentralization through its social security and equalization payments and its promotion of regional economic expansion. To a generation of Newfoundlanders who looked to an oil rich future, Ottawa often appeared to be an obstacle to progress, and this attitude was easily extrapolated to past events.

For those Newfoundlanders who enjoyed the status of veteran, however, there can be little doubt that confederation was a decided boon. Thanks to the skilful lobbying of the GWVA, Newfoundland veterans entered confederation on a footing of equality with Canadian veterans. Union with Canada, moreover, gave them a benefit package that went far beyond anything that the Commission of Govermnment had ever envisaged and in all likelihood anything that an independent Newfoundland government could have provided. Individual Newfoundland veterans might have complaints after 1949 but collectively Newfoundland's ex-servicemen and women were equal to their counterparts everywhere else in the country. Former members of the merchant marine were likewise much better off as Canadians, though they and their comrades elsewhere in Canada were still denied all the benefits available to veterans.

The omission in the terms of union of any reference to the former members of the NFU raises different issues. The foresters may well have paid dearly for not having had a spokesman in Ottawa in 1948 but even if Jack Turner had lived to influence the negotiation of the final terms of union there is good reason to believe that he would have faced an uphill fight. Albert Walsh after all was a member, perhaps the key member, of the government of Newfoundland and it was that government which had denied the foresters any benefits in the first place. Assuming Canada would henceforth pay the bills, he might have had a change of heart but this can only be speculated upon and in any case did not need Turner's presence. At the same time it must be said that the 1948 negotiations represented a unique opportunity for the foresters to press their case. Their best argument was probably their claim to be treated equally with members of the Canadian Forestry Corps. It was true that they had done much the same work as this unit and that a good many of them had gone overseas long before the first Canadians had set sail. Perhaps the one chance they had to capitalize on all this was in the negotiations leading to the terms of union; once Newfoundland became part of Canada their cause would inevitably get mixed up with the claims of other civilian groups. For DVA the necessity to maintain a clear distinction between 'veteran' and 'civilian' was fundamental and to single out the Newfoundland foresters for inclusion in the veterans' group would have been to risk trouble elsewhere in the country. If the change of status had been made in the terms of union, the department might have had a credible line of defence in the argument that the adjustment thus made was exceptional, that is to say part of a larger agreement between two countries and therefore a matter separate from Canadian policy and law. But this course was never contemplated because there was no disagreement between the Canadian and Newfoundland negotiators in 1948 as to how the foresters should be regarded.

In the last analysis perhaps the experience of the Newfoundland foresters can best be related to a larger theme in the history of veterans' affairs and of the welfare state more generally. In their pioneering study, *Winning the Second Battle: Canadian veterans and the return to civilian life, 1915-1930*, Desmond Morton and Glenn Wright contend that veterans were pathfinders for the welfare state.[162] Their sense of entitlement, so the argument goes, prefigured a general sense of entitlement. This makes sense. Yet it must also be remembered that veterans' benefits as they evolved in western democratic countries promoted a vision of the welfare state that was hierarchical and competitive. Arguably it was this vision that typified the whole of the welfare state as it developed in Canada in the 1940s and 1950s. The underlying purpose was not to produce a society of equals but to promote individualism, sustain the market economy and preserve the values of a society dominated by small property holders in the face of growing interdependency and revolutionary technological change. Welfare state measures did this through timely infusions of capital and by allowing individuals progressively to transfer to the state liabilities—the mounting costs of sickness, old age, education etc.—which limited or even threatened their enjoyment of private property, including provision for and expectation of inheritance. In sum, the essential purpose of the Canadian welfare state as it unfolded in this period was conservative rather than collectivist. Hence the incremental, programme approach and the heavy emphasis on status and on criteria for eligibility. Benefits derived not from citizenship but from particular need, service or qualification and were decided upon through an ever more complex bureaucracy. The many distinctions fostered by war only reinforced the individualist and bureaucratic thrust of the emerging welfare state. It is in this context that the Veterans Charter and its goal of 'OPPORTUNITY WITH SECURITY' must be seen. Concomitant with that goal, which tells us much about Canada then and now, went the elaborate pecking order of benefits from which the Newfoundland foresters found themselves so unhappily excluded for so long.

NOTES

*I acknowledge with thanks the astute literary advice of A.P. Bates of London, Ontario, and the expert help of G. Campbell Eaton, O.C., M.C., C.D. LL.D. of St. John's, Newfoundland. I am grateful to Judith A. Murnaghan, Joyce Gaudet and Ken Hawkes of Veterans Affairs Canada, Charlottetown, Prince Edward Island; Alan Setterington and Timothy Vanderveen of Veterans Affairs Canada, London, Ontario; and J.R. Walsh of Veterans Affairs Canada, St. John's, Newfoundland, for facilitating my research for this paper.

1   *Evening Telegram* (St. John's), 15 March 1945.

2   For Newfoundland's role in the Great War see G.W.L. Nicholson, *The Fighting Newfoundlander* (Government of Newfoundland 1964); S.J.R. Noel, *Politics in Newfoundland* (Toronto 1971); Patricia O'Brien, 'The Newfoundland Patriotic Association: the administration of the war effort, 1914-1918,' (unpublished MA thesis, Memorial University 1981); and J.R. Smallwood (ed.), *The Book of Newfoundland* (St. John's 1937), vol. 1, 353-451.

3   For Newfoundland's role in World War II see National Archives of Canada, RG 24 (Records of the Dept. of National Defence), vol. 10995, file 290-NFD-013-(D1), A.M. Fraser, 'History of the Participation by Newfoundland in World War II'; Peter Neary, *Newfoundland in the North Atlantic World, 1929-1949* (Kingston and Montreal 1988); and G.W.L. Nicholson, *More Fighting Newfoundlanders: A History of Newfoundland's Fighting Forces in the Second World War* (Government of Newfoundland and Labrador 1969).

4   See Paul Bridle (ed.), *Documents on Relations between Canada and Newfoundland*, vol. 1, 1935-49 (Ottawa 1974), 839-51.

5   Records of the Dept. of Veterans Affairs (DVA), Daniel J. MacDonald Building, Charlottetown, Prince Edward Island, file SECTY-6517-45/V2, 'Acts: Union of Newfoundland,' vol. 1, McDonald to Chant, 30 July 1945.

6   This was the official name. The unit is, however, commonly referred to as 'the Newfoundland Overseas Forestry Unit' or, sometimes, 'the Newfoundland (Overseas) Forestry Unit.' The rationale for these variations is self-evident.

7   Neary, *Newfoundland in the North Atlantic World*, 118.

8   Ibid and DVA, file SECTY-7143-01, 'Civilians: Newfoundland Overseas Forestry Unit,' Curran to Browne, 17 April 1962.

9   SECTY-6517-45/V2, vol. 1, Cross to Deputy Minister, 29 Sept. 1948. Fraser, 'History,' gives the same totals to 30 Sept. for the Royal Navy, Royal Artillery and Royal Air Force (430-6). See also statistics in the *Evening Telegram*, 3 Nov. 1945. In 1987 J.R. Walsh, Sub Regional Director (Nfld.), Veterans Affairs Canada, provided the author with World War II recruitment figures for Newfoundland as follows: Royal Artillery, 2,390; Royal Navy, 3,232; Royal Air Force, 734; Newfoundland Regiment, 1,668; Newfoundland Forestry Unit, 3,596. These figures were obtained from nominal rolls in his office. Other sources yield slight variations on all these numbers. A DVA memo dated 18 Sept. 1945 categorized enlistments from Newfoundland in the Canadian forces to 31 March 1945 as follows: Navy—396 men, 86 women; Army—369 men, 226 women; Air Force—394 men, 294 women. These figures gave totals

of 1,159 men, 606 women and 1,765 overall (SECTY-6517-45/V2, vol. 1, memo to Director of Training, 18 Sept. 1945. See also note 116 below.

10   See DVA, file 34-NF, 'District Administration, NF[Newfoundland]-District, St. John's,' vol. 2, Blackall to Barron, 30 Dec. 1919.

11   See *Acts of the General Assembly of Newfoundland*, 1919 (St. John's 1919), 95.

12   Smallwood (ed.), *The Book of Newfoundland*, 448-51.

13   See *Evening Telegram*, 20 Aug. 1918, and *Daily News* (St. John's), 20 Aug. 1918.

14   Robert H. Cuff, Melvin Baker and Robert D.W. Pitt (eds.), *Dictionary of Newfoundland and Labrador Biography* (St. John's 1990), 225.

15   *The Great War Veterans' Association of Newfoundland Constitution and By-Laws, 1918.* This item was published by the Association. There is a copy in the Centre for Newfoundland Studies, Queen Elizabeth II Library, Memorial University, St, John's.

16   34-NF, vol. 3, Cross to Deputy Minister, 29 Sept. 1948.

17   Centre for Newfoundland Studies Archives (CNS(A)), Queen Elizabeth II Library, Memorial University, St. John's, John G. Higgins Collection, COLL-087, 4.04.003, GWVA, *A message to the men who have served in the present war* (St. John's 1945).

18   Neary, *Newfoundland in the North Atlantic World*, 37.

19   *Acts of the Honourable Commission of Government of Newfoundland 1935* (St. John's 1935), 75-106.

20   CNS(A), COLL-087, 4.05.001, typescript of radio address, 'The Necessity for the Newfoundland Patriotic Association.'

21   Neary, *Newfoundland in the North Atlantic World*, 196.

22   *Evening Telegram*, 15 March 1945.

23   Ibid.

24   Ibid.

25   Neary, *Newfoundland in the North Atlantic World*, 242.

26   *Now That You Are Home* (St. John's 1946), 37. See also 34-NF, vol. 3, report by M.G. Chambers, 1 Jan. 1948; SECTY-6517-45/V2, vol. 1, Cross to Deputy Minister, 29 Sept. 1948, 3.

27   Tom Curran, *They Also Served: the Newfoundland Overseas Forestry Unit 1939-1946* (St. John's 1987), 95-6.

28   See *Evening Telegram*, 29 June 1946. I am grateful to J.R. Walsh for a copy of *Now That You Are Home.*

29   For his career see Cuff, Baker and Pitt (eds.), *Dictionary of Newfoundland and Labrador Biography*, 62.

30   The monthly report for July 1946 of the Citizens' Rehabilitation Committee is in CNS(A), COLL-087, 4.04.004. See also *Evening Telegram*, 26 Jan. 1946.

31   For Eaton's career see Cuff, Baker and Pitt (eds.), *Dictionary of Newfoundland and Labrador Biography*, 97.

32   *Sunday Herald* (St. John's), 12 May 1946.

33   Ibid., 19 May 1946.

34   *Evening Telegram*, 29 June 1946. For the general approach of the GWVA see also ibid., 1 Dec. 1945. For the GWVA executive at the time see ibid., 22 Sept. 1945.

35   Ibid., 29 June 1946.

36   Ibid.

37   Ibid., 2 July 1946.

38   Ibid., 27 July 1946.

39   See SECTY-6517-42/V2, vol. 1, Cross to Deputy Minister, 29 Sept. 1948. This source summarized the assistance given as follows:

TOTAL NUMBER	BENEFIT	TOTAL $ COST TO GOV'T
1,000	Fisheries	664,000.00
350	Small Enterprises	175,000.00
2,500	Awaiting Returns & Unemployment	1,500,000.00
600	Education (University, High School and Agriculture)	51,000.00
600	Vocational Training	46,000.00
2,000	Medical Treatment	55,000.00
150	Miscellaneous	15,000.00
300	Land Settlement and Fur Farming	(no figure available)
7,500	*TOTAL*	$2,506,000.00 plus

The discrepancy between the 4,903 given in the text for number assisted and the 7,500 given here arises out of the fact that many veterans qualified for more than one benefit. The 7,500 number is also given in 34-NF, vol. 3, report by M.G. Chambers, 1 Jan. 1948. In this report 'numbers availing of assistance' are accounted for under eleven headings: Education; Vocational Training; Fishery Assistance; Agriculture, Land Development, and Fur Farming; Small Individual Enterprises; Assistance to Apprentices; Provision of Tools; Free Medical Treatment; Unemployment Benefit; and Merchant Navy and Rescue Tug Service.

40   For a detailed account of British policy towards Newfoundland during and after the war see Neary, *Newfoundland in the North Atlantic World.*

41   34-NF, vol. 1, Secretary, Board of Pension Commissioners for Canada, to McGrath, 15 June 1919.

42   Ibid., Scammell to Assistant Directors, Department of Soldiers Civil Re-establishment, 15 March 1919.

43   Ibid.

44   Ibid., Blackall to Segsworth, 5, 7 Oct. 1918; Segsworth (unsigned) to Blackall, 15 Oct. 1918.

45   SECTY-6517-45/V2, vol. 1, Sully to Woods, 12 Aug. 1943.

46   DVA, box 564, file 543/03-4, vol. 13, Robertson to High Commissioner, 10 July 1944.

47   For this Order and the amendments made to it see Walter S. Woods, *Rehabili-tation (A Combined Operation)* (Ottawa 1953), 465-76.

48   See clipping in DVA, file 32-3-2, vol. 2 from the *Standard*, Montreal, 4 Nov. 1944.

49   *The Veterans Charter: Acts of the Canadian Parliament to Assist Veterans* (Ottawa 1947).

50   Woods, *Rehabilitation*, 469, 481.

51   Ibid.

52   Ibid., 16.

53   Except as noted, this account is based on ibid, 23-30.

54   Ibid., 64, 69.

55   Ibid., 70-1. By category, payments had been made as follows: home-owning under the National Housing Act, 6,460; home-owning not under the National Housing Act, 76,694; home repair and modernization, 113,252; home—discharge of indebtedness, 11,236; home—purchase of furniture and equipment, 1,344,293; business—working capital for, 114,761; business—purchase of tools, etc., 126,050; business—purchase of, 7,802; insurance premiums, 20,344; educational—purchase of books and equipment, 6,340; clothing, 66. An individual veteran could, of course, obtain assistance under more than one category up to the limit of his or her entitlement.

56   Nicole Morgan, *The Equality Game: Women in the Federal Public Service (1908-1987)* (Ottawa, 1988), 6.

57   This account is based on Woods, *Rehabilitation*, 228-35.

58   A 'special operator' was 'a person certified by the Under-Secretary of State for External Affairs as having been enrolled in Canada by United Kingdom authorities for special duty in war areas outside the Western Hemisphere...and who, at the time of such enrolment, was resident in Canada' (*Veterans Charter*, 209). A 'supervisor' was 'a duly selected and approved representative of (i) Canadian Legion War Services Inc., (ii) The National Council of the Young Men's Christian Associations of Canada, (iii) Knights of Columbus Canadian Army Huts, or (iv) Salvation Army Canadian War Services, who was attached to and served with the naval, military or air forces of Canada outside the Western Hemisphere' (ibid, 217).

59   SECTY-6517-45/V2, vol. 1, Woods to Under-Secretary of State for External Affairs, 16 May 1946.

60   Ibid.

61   Ibid.

62   DVA, file 67-28, 'Re-Establishment Credits: Newfoundland,' Hogan to Director General, Veterans' Welfare Services, 4 April 1949.

63   SECTY-6517-45/V2, vol. 1, Cole to Russell, 17 July 1945. H.W. Cole was Staff Officer Rehabilitation with the Royal Canadian Navy in St. John's. He summed up the eligibility situation at the time as follows: 'You are already familiar with the fact that Newfoundlanders who return to this country from Canadian services automatically exempt themselves from the Canadian benefits with the exception of the Gratuity, Rehabilitation Grant and University and Vocational Training. On the other hand they do become eligible for Newfoundland benefits such as Farming and Fishery assistance, out of work benefits while awaiting returns from Private Enterprise, one year's medical

attention and allowances while incapacitated, all of which appear to be based on the Canadian plan. It is unfortunate though that the Newfoundland scheme does not include women in any instances. It is argued here that the Canadian Government opened recruiting offices in this Country and thus responsibility lies with them. On the other hand it is impossible that Canada could extend to women any of the benefits I have listed with the exception of the year's medical treatment and allowances.'

64 Ibid., McDonald to Chant, 30 July 1948.

65 Ibid., Macdonald to Secretary of State for External Affairs, 19 Oct. 1944. For Cochrane's death see *Evening Telegram*, 9 Aug. 1947.

66 DVA, file 66-67-2, 'Training: Newfoundland, Newfoundlanders in the Imperial Forces,' Macdonald to Secretary of State for External Affairs, 11 Sept. 1945.

67 Ibid.

68 There is a copy in ibid.

69 Ibid., Acting High Commissioner, St. John's, to Secretary of State for External Affairs, 3 Jan. 1946.

70 Ibid., encl. in Macdonald to Acting Secretary of State for External Affairs, 29 Nov. 1946.

71 SECTY-6157-45/V2, vol. 1, Robertson to Deputy Minister, 16 July 1946.

72 Ibid., Woods to Under-Secretary of State for External Affairs, 31 July 1946.

73 For these events in the National Convention see Neary, *Newfoundland in the North Atlantic World*, 295-8.

74 SECTY-6157-45/V2, vol. 1, Rider to Burns, 23 Sept. 1948.

75 This document is attached to ibid.

76 *Proposed arrangements for the entry of Newfoundland into Confederation* (Ottawa 1948).

77 Ibid., 11-12.

78 Under the Commission of Government's 1935 pension legislation, pensions were decided upon by War Pensions Commissioners. Pensions were administered through the Department of Public Health and Welfare. In 1947 the War Pensions Officer was C.C. Oke, who was assisted by a seven member staff (34-NF, vol. 3, 'War Pensions staff with brief details of duties'). There was also a Pensions Medical Board. This consisted of a Chairman and Examiner, who was employed part-time and an assistant doctor, who was paid per case (ibid). Newfoundland's pension liability in Oct. 1948 consisted of 1,130 World War I pensioners and 710 World War II pensioners for a total of 1,840 (SECTY-6517-45/V2, vol. 1, Cross to Melville, 20 Oct. 1948).

79 SECTY-6517-45/V2, vol. 1, Rider to Burns, 23 Sept. 1948.

80 *Proposed arrangements for the entry of Newfoundland into Confederation*, 11.

81 Government of Newfoundland, *The Newfoundland Regiment (Pensions and Gratuities) Regulations, 1944* (St. John's 1944).

82 Effective 1 Jan. 1942 the United Kingdom had provided a 'Post War Credit' of sixpence per day for other ranks in its armed forces. From the same date the Commission of Government had provided 'Deferred Pay' of 30 cents per day for Newfoundlanders, officers and men, serving with the British forces. These payments were separate from gratuities (SECTY-6517-45/V2, vol. 1, Cross to Deputy Minister, 1 Oct. 1948).

83   For these events see Neary, *Newfoundland in the North Atlantic World*, 313-24.

84   CNS(A), COLL-087, 4.04.006, 'Report of the Great War Veterans' Association delegation to Ottawa,' encl. in Martin to Editor, *Newfoundlander*, 17 Jan. 1948.

85   I am grateful to Cam Eaton for this information and for letting me read a diary he kept in Ottawa.

86   SECTY-6157-45/V2, vol. 1, Gregg to Pearson, 15 Dec. 1948.

87   Ibid., Parliament to Woods, 4 Oct. 1948. This allowed for the deducation of the gratuity paid by the British Government (ibid., 'Memorandum for use by the Minister in discussing Proposal No. 12 of the memorandum submitted by the Newfoundland Delegation, October 1948.' The estimated cost of extending Re-establishment Credits to Newfoundland veterans based on the gratuity they had received from the British Government was $397,000.

88   Paul Bridle (ed.), *Documents on Relations between Canada and Newfoundland*, vol. 2, pt. 2 (Ottawa 1984), 1122.

89   Ibid., 1126.

90   The minutes of the meeting are in SECTY-6517-45/V2, vol. 1.

91   Herwig afterwards told Louis St. Laurent that he had explained to his 'Newfoundland Comrades that the Legion's policy would be to have Newfoundland veterans, when they became Canadians, treated in the same way as their Canadian comrades under our pension and rehabilitation legislation' (ibid., Herwig to St. Laurent, n.d.). There is a copy of St. Laurent's reply, dated 25 Sept. 1948, in the same file.

92   The minutes of this meeting are also in SECTY-6517-45/V2, vol. 1.

93   Ibid., 'Memorandum re War Service Gratuities and Rehabilitation Credits from the Great War Veterans' Association Newfoundland.'

94   The minutes of the 27 Oct. meeting and the report of the sub-committee are also in SECTY-6517-45/V2, vol. 1.

95   Ibid., Parliament to Deputy Minister, 13 Oct. 1948.

96   Ibid., 'Memorandum for use by the Minister in discussing Proposal No. 12 of the memorandum submitted by the Newfoundland Delegation, October 1948.'

97   Bridle (ed.) *Documents*, vol. 2, pt. 1, 1183. In his 1953 book *Rehabilitation* Woods gave this explanation of the arrangements made for Newfoundland veterans: 'Some of the Rehabilitation benefits which were provided under the Veterans Charter were designed for the period immediately after discharge from the Service. These provided cut-off dates which had expired at the date of Union. Those benefits were not made available to the Newfoundland veteran—just as they were no longer available to the veterans from the other nine Provinces.

       Not all Rehabilitation benefits provide a cut-off date but the period for which some of these benefits were intended had long been passed before Union took place and they were therefore not deemed payable to Newfoundland veterans. Cases in point were the Rehabilitation Grant comprising the equivalent of 30 days' pay and allowances and the War Service Gratuity. These benefits provided under The War Service Grants Act were payable immediately upon discharge. No time limit was provided in the Act but they were obviously designed to take care of the veterans immediate post discharge needs. As Newfoundland did not enter Confederation until almost four years after the end of the War in Europe it was considered that the period for which these benefits were granted had passed. In any event Newfoundland veterans upon discharge had been granted by their country what was considered to be appropriate benefits of this nature.

Likewise in the matter of training, Canada's Veterans Rehabilitation Act provided that those wishing to take vocational training must apply for the same within twelve months of the date of their discharge, and in the case of university training the applicant must commence his training within fifteen months of the date of discharge. Exceptions were made with respect to those taking treatment and in cases where the training facilities were not available and so forth, but it will be seen that with few exceptions on the date of Union this legislation had become outlawed by time in the case of Canadian veterans and of course could not be reopened in the case of Newfoundland veterans.

Nevertheless when Union took place there were 62 Newfoundland veterans still taking training, 60 of whom were in universities. Canada of course at the time of Union took those over until their rights under The Veterans Rehabilitation Act were exhausted.

Legislation that was still open at the time of Union to Canadian veterans and consequently became available to Newfoundland veterans comprised such important measures as the Pension Act, the Veterans' Land Act, Re-establishment Credits under the War Service Grants Act, the Veterans Insurance Act and the War Veterans' Allowance Act, the Treatment Regulations, etc.' (248-9).

98   SECTY-6517-45/V2, vol. 1, 'Memorandum for use by the Minister in discussing Proposal No. 12 of the memorandum submitted by the Newfoundland Delegation, October 1948.'

99   Bridle (ed.), *Documents*, vol. 2, pt. 1, 1255-6.

100   Ibid., 1257.

101   *Acts of the Parliament of the Dominion of Canada*, 1949, Part I, Public General Acts (Ottawa 1949), 37-58.

102   CNS(A), COLL-087, 4.04.006, 'Report of Great War Veterans' Association Delegation to Ottawa,' encl. in Martin to Editor, *Newfoundlander*, 17 Jan. 1948.

103   *Evening Telegram*, 10 Sept., 1949. See 34-NF, vol. 5, Woods to Gregg, 21 Sept. 1949.

104   Woods, *Rehabilitation*, 250.

105   67-28, Gunn to Woods, 2 April 1949.

106   Unpublished speech by Cam Eaton to St. John's Rotary Club. I am grateful to Mr. Eaton for allowing me to copy this item.

107   *Daily News*, 15 Jan. 1949.

108   SECTY-6517-45/V2, vol. 1, Paul B. Cross, 'An Appreciation of Conditions in Newfoundland as they affect veterans' rehabilitation,' 14 May 1948, 1.

109   Ibid.

110   Ibid., Cross to Assistant Deputy Minister, 27 Aug. 1948.

111   The minutes of the first meeting are also in SECTY-6517-45/V2, vol. 1.

112   Ibid., Warner to Deputy Minister, 26 Aug. 1948.

113   Ibid., Fergusson to Director General of Treatment Services, 30 Sept. 1948, encl. in Farmer to Deputy Minister, 7 Oct. 1948.

114   34-NF, vol. 4, DVA committee on Newfoundland, minutes of second meeting, 29 Oct. 1948, 2-3.

115   SECTY-6517-45/V2, vol. 2, Cross to Chambers, 3 Nov. 1948.

116   34-NF, vol. 4, Elliott to Hewitt, 11 Dec. 1948 and attachment. On 25 June 1949
      Baxter Peckham, Chief, Central Registry, NF District, reported from St. John's
      that 'enlistments from Newfoundland in both World Wars taken from official
      records' were as follows: World War I—Royal Newfoundland Regiment,
      6,264; Royal Naval Reserve, 2,053; Forestry Corps, 500; Nursing Service, 43;
      Canadian and other forces, 3,000; enlisted in United Kingdom, 62; World War
      II—Royal Navy, 3,230; Royal Artillery, 2,390; Royal Air Force, 734; New-
      foundland Regiment, 1,668 (transfers from this Unit, 1,000); Tug Service, 201;
      other units other than Canadians, 52; served with Canadians, 1,700. These
      figures gave a total for World War I of 11,922, a total for World War II of 8,975
      and an overall total of 20,897. Of these 'approximately 2,500' were said to be
      'active Pensioners' (ibid., vol. 5, report by Baxter Peckham, 'Monthly Work-
      load—Central Registry,' 25 June 1949).

117   Ibid., vol. 4, Cross to Howes, 20 Dec. 1948.

118   I am grateful to J.R. Walsh for a copy of this booklet.

119   Bridle (ed.), *Documents*, vol. 2, pt. 2, 1259.

120   SECTY-6517-45/V2, vol. 2, tel., Elliott to Cross, 2 April 1949.

121   DVA, file SECTY-7142-01, 'Civilians: Newfoundland Rescue Tug Service,'
      Anderson to Lapointe, 16 Nov. 1953.

122   Ibid.

123   Ibid.

124   Cross commented as follows: 'such people in my opinion morally should be
      entitled because of the fact that whereas they were not on Naval pay, they
      were definitely under Naval discipline, served in Naval uniform and were
      required to serve anywhere during the period of their engagement, which
      varied under three sections of the plan; namely, so long as their ship was
      under Naval commission, or for one year, or for the duration of hostilities.
      Men serving under this Royal Navy plan actually served in most cases in the
      most vulnerable ships afloat, namely, Armed Merchant Cruisers. Those who
      served with the Rescue Tug Service were also in an extremely hazardous
      occupation, namely, that of towing in disabled merchant ships, in most cases
      unprotected, after the ship had been torpedoed or otherwise damaged' (34-
      NF, Cross to Dixon, 25 May 1949).

125   SECTY-7142-01, Drury to Deputy Minister, 20 Dec. 1953 and unsigned copy
      of letter to T.D. Anderson, 29 Dec. 1953.

126   There is a copy of this in SECTY-7143-01. Tom Curran's 1987 book *They Also
      Served* updated *Tumber!!.*

127   *Evening Telegram*, 28 Sept. 1948.

128   SECTY-7143-01, Gregg to Smallwood, 3 June 1949.

129   Ibid., Denovan to District Administrator, DVA, St. John's, 29 Aug. 1949.

130   Ibid., Circular Letter 1949-80.

131   SECTY-7142-01, Circular Letter 1952-5.

132   SECTY-6517-45/V2, vol. 1, Cross to Deputy Minister, 27 June 1950; Woods to
      Parliament, 28 June 1950.

133   SECTY-7143-01, Cross to Deputy Minister, 27 June 1950.

134   Ibid., Melville to Deputy Minister, 30 June 1950.

135   Ibid., Woods to Anderson, 3 July 1950.

136   Ibid., Martin to Kines, copy of tel., n.d.

137   Ibid., Burns to Gregg, 19 July 1950.

138   Ibid., Gregg to Smallwood, 20, 25 July 1950.

139   Ibid., Burns to Mercer, 4 Aug. 1950.

140   Ibid., Mercer to DVA (attention E.L.M. Burns), 21 Aug. 1950.

141   Ibid., Burns to Mercer, 6 Sept. 1950; Melville to Mercer, 30 Sept. 1950.

142   Ibid., Brooks to Browne, 6 June 1958.

143   Ibid., Brooks to Argue, 5 Feb. 1960.

144   For the brief see House of Commons, Standing Committee on Veterans Affairs, *Minutes of Proceedings and Evidence*, 24th Parliament, 3-4th Sessions, 1960-61, 91-8.

145   See ibid., 89-117.

146   *Evening Telegram*, 1, 4 April 1960.

147   House of Commons, *Debates*, 1960, vol. 6, 6761, 6765, 6768-9.

148   SECTY-7143-01, Curran to Minister of Veterans Affairs, 1 Oct. 1960.

149   Ibid., Churchill to Curran, 24 Nov. 1960.

150   DVA, file 6555-60-6/1, 'War Veterans Allowance/Civilian War Allowances— Amendments (Cojoined) 1961-1967,' memo to Cabinet by Gordon Churchill, 27 Oct. 1961.

151   *Acts of the Parliament of Canada*, 1962, pt. I, Public General Acts (Ottawa 1962), 31-7.

152   SECTY-7143-01, Curran to Browne, 17 April 1962.

153   Ibid., Christian to Copp, 18 May 1962.

154   Ibid., Greene to Carter, Batten, Granger, Pickersgill, Tucker, McGrath, Cashin, 16 Aug. 1962.

155   Ibid., Churchill to Greene, 9 Nov. 1962.

156   Ibid., Teillet to Cashin, 27 Nov. 1963.

157   Ibid., Teillet to Cashin, 11 Jan. 1965.

158   *Acts of the Parliament of Canada*, 1967-8 (Ottawa 1968), 113.

159   6555-60-6/1, memo for the cabinet by Teillet, 3 May 1967.

160   SECTY-7143-01, Teillet to Pickersgill, 30 Nov. 1966.

161   The best account of these developments is James Overton, 'Towards a Critical Analysis of Neo-Nationalism in Newfoundland' in Robert J. Brym and R. James Sacouman (eds.), *Underdevelopment and Social Movements in Atlantic Canada* (Toronto 1979), 214-49.

162   See, for example, xi, 130, 177, 223-5.

The Problem of Newfoundland: the Fisheries and Newfoundland's Integration into Canada, 1948-57

Raymond Blake

L IFE FOR THOSE WHO LABOURED in poverty and deprivation in the isolated outports and bays of Newfoundland in 1949 had changed little since their ancestors first arrived from the British Isles to catch, salt, and dry codfish. From its inception, the traditional inshore fishery had had unpredictable markets, low productivity, low prices, and low returns, and provided a bare subsistence living for thousands of fishermen and their families. When Ottawa began to share responsibility for the Newfoundland fishery, the average per capita income in the new province was $475, which was 49.5 per cent of the Canadian average, and considerably less than the Maritime average of $689. With incomes ranging between $200 and $400, the fishermen of Newfoundland were considerably worse off.[1] Many Newfoundlanders realized after their country joined Canada that they were now part of a nation whose standard of living rivalled that of the United States. Most Canadian communities had their own teachers, doctors and clergy. This was normal as were electricity and water and sewage facilities; but these were the exception in most of Newfoundland's scattered and isolated settlements. Newfoundlanders were no longer content to live in poverty and under primitive and wretched conditions. In examining fishery policy after confederation, therefore, it must be remembered that this involved more than the catching, curing, processing and marketing of fish; it involved changing a whole way of life, and if the people wanted a dramatic improvement in their standard of living, then the fishery had to change dramatically.

The task ahead for Ottawa and St. John's after 1949 was more than merely developing the fishery. If they had been concerned only with economics, it might have been possible to provide strong support to a threatened industry. The fresh frozen fishery was seen as the hope of the future and Ottawa and St. John's sought to direct production in that direction and away from dependence on the salt cod fishery which still relied on methods used in the explorer John Cabot's time. Several commissions and investigations confirmed that changes were necessary. If the governments had pursued the policies recommended by these enquiries, they would have created a small corps of fishermen concentrated in a smaller number of communities engaged in both the salt and fresh frozen fisheries from modern boats and trawlers with greatly increased capacity. In the case of saltfish, the curing would have been done by mechanical dryers, or at centralized drying flakes or wharves. But governments had to consider more than the bottom line on a balance sheet. It had become clear to Ottawa by 1954 that there was no other work for the thousands of fishermen that might be displaced. From that point on, Ottawa realized that there was little hope for rationalizing the fishery. The best that it could hope to achieve was a small measure of centralization, and an improved standard of living for fishermen through various income support programmes. This eventually became Ottawa's objective. Premier Joseph R. Smallwood originally hoped that the new industries he was promoting would absorb any labour displaced from the fishery. When he had accepted the failure of this part of his plan for economic development, he turned his fury on the federal government, blaming it for the destruction of the fishery. But Smallwood must share the blame, for he had little interest in fishery reform. On the other hand, Ottawa recognized the severe problems the fishery had, but it saw modernization with a reduction in the number of fishermen as the only solution. It did not seek alternatives when it realized this could not work. Nor did the provincial government push for alternatives. Political considerations in the Maritime Provinces also hampered Ottawa in its approach to solving the problem. It could not be seen there as favouring Newfoundland. Consequently, with Smallwood's acquiescence, Ottawa merely propped up the industry and allowed it to stagger along, going from crisis to crisis.

I

Before union there had been considerable talk about reforming the Newfoundland fishery, but few changes had been made. When the Newfoundland Royal Commission of 1933 recommended the surrender of responsible government, it tied economic recovery and the restoration of democracy to a reformed and improved fishery.[2] A decade later, P.D.H. Dunn, Commissioner for Natural Resources in the Commission of Government, argued that the salt cod fishery alone could not provide fishermen with a reasonable standard of living. In his view production per man had to be increased in a fresh and frozen fishery geared to American markets.[3] Raymond Gushue, chairman of the Newfoundland Fisheries Board (NFB), saw a similar future for the Newfoundland fishery.[4] Moreover, the fisheries committee of the National Convention reported in October 1946, that it too saw a new course for the fishery. It predicted that the markets for saltfish would decline as living standards improved and refrigeration became more widespread. The future lay in the American market, and the government, whatever form it might take, must continue to encourage greater development of the fresh frozen industry.[5] Yet for all this, the transition from salt to fresh and frozen production, which was already well underway in New England and Nova Scotia, made before 1949 only minor gains in Newfoundland,[6] as most fishermen continued to rely on the production of saltfish.

The Commission of Government had recognized many of the problems confronting the fishery. In fact, during its life (1934-49) it proposed many of the policies adopted after union. But it followed a conservative approach, linking improvements in the fishery to the improved marketing of salt cod, and ignored the low productivity of individual fishermen, which was the most serious problem. A commission of enquiry appointed in 1935 concluded 'that if market prospects and returns were improved, then the incentives for increased investment and innovative technology and production would exist.'[7] The Commission of Government based its fishery policy on this principle. In 1936 it created the NFB[8] and charged it with regulating most aspects of the fishery from production to distribution. The NFB, to rationalize the marketing system, subsequently formed the Newfoundland Associated Fish Exporters Limited (NAFEL), and gave it exclusive jurisdiction over the export of salt cod.[9] In 1944 the Commission of Government finally launched a policy of financial support to fish merchants to encourage the development of fish filleting and refrigeration plants, and the purchase of deepsea trawlers.[10]

Such a policy ignored the problems confronting the vast majority of fishermen. Neither the Commission's new nor its earlier plans were directed towards improving the productivity of individual fishermen. In a shrewd observation made in 1951, the Newfoundland born H.B. Mayo, an Oxford graduate, wrote as follows:

> it is remarkable how little attention has been given to this fundamental problem [low productivity among individual fishermen]: official inquiries have ignored it or, having dimly perceived it, have shied away from the unpleasant implications and have concentrated instead on subsidiary issues such as [the] credit system, or the local control of marketing.[11]

Although fish prices were buoyed by a heightened demand for foodstuffs during the Second World War, Newfoundland had not emerged from this prosperous period with more efficient fishing methods. Saltfish merchants and the government continued to ignore the fact that the existing practices of fishermen would not raise individual productivity and so lead to a better standard of living. Both naively believed that if saltfish exporters were assured adequate markets, fishermen would reap the benefits through increased investment, innovative technology, and higher prices. History had clearly shown otherwise. The fishery had been unable to provide an acceptable living for fishermen even during so-called normal years when the industry was unhampered by low prices, currency problems, or a shortage of fish. 'What is often overlooked,' Mayo argued in 1951, 'is that public relief for the fishermen, and relief disguised as public works, have always been marked recurring features of the island's finances.'[12]

II

When the 1948 Newfoundland delegation travelled to Ottawa to negotiate the final terms of union with Canada, the fishery was naturally a major priority because of its economic importance to the prospective province. The delegation showed little concern, however, with fishery development and the role the federal government should play in it. Instead, the focus was on the marketing of salt cod. This stemmed, in part, from the pressure exerted on the delegation by a clique from the St. John's upper class involved primarily in the export of saltfish.[13] The delegation was told repeatedly that Newfoundland must retain access to European markets, despite the shortage of hard currency there, in order to prevent the impoverishment of thousands of fishermen. During the negotiations the Newfoundlanders argued that if their fish were shut out of Europe, markets would have to be found in the Western Hemisphere at the expense of the fishing industry in Canada.[14]

Since the onset of exchange difficulties in Europe after the Second World War, the Newfoundland government had arranged with Whitehall to have sterling earned from European fish sales applied against the Newfoundland sterling debt. Exporters then received payment from the Newfoundland government out of its accumulated dollar surplus.[15] Ottawa quickly realized that if it did not continue the arrangement, Newfoundland might face a severe economic slump in the wake of union. London agreed, and the Canadian government used sterling received from European purchases of fish to redeem the Newfoundland sterling debt that it inherited at union.[16]

The NFB and NAFEL met with less enthusiasm in Ottawa. Both were threatened by union, and Vincent C. MacDonald of the Dalhousie University Law School had prepared NAFEL for the worst. 'The whole matter of the trade in salt fish as between Newfoundland and any other Province or country,' he wrote in a legal opinion rendered at NAFEL's request, 'will come under the exclusive jurisdiction of the Parliament of Canada.'[17] Those who supported NAFEL immediately rushed to its defence. F.A.J. Laws, manager of NAFEL, complained to Governor Sir Gordon Macdonald that the saltfish trade was not represented on the delegation. He claimed that NAFEL had gradually cultivated a marketing system 'considered to give the best results to our exporters and fishermen under existing world conditions.' His predictions for the industry without NAFEL were dire. Any tampering with the marketing mechanisms was tantamount to disaster for the fisheries of both Canada and Newfoundland, he warned. Raymond Gushue appeared before the delegation to support Laws' claims. Norway,

Iceland, and the Faroe Islands, the major competitors, had exporting agencies, and all of the consuming nations co-ordinated their buying. It made little sense, then, for Newfoundland exporters to operate individually and hope to achieve maximum returns for their products.[18] The Newfoundland Board of Trade and the Salt Codfish Association echoed these sentiments.[19]

Canadian officials disagreed. NAFEL competed with saltfish exporters in the Maritime Provinces, and it had allegedly dumped saltfish in traditional Canadian markets. It was termed, 'with some justice, a Fascist monopoly,' Mitchell Sharp, the Director of the Economic Policy Division at the Department of Finance, pointed out. He noted, however, that NAFEL had had a successful career, in part because of a general wartime rise in fish prices, but prices in Canada had risen as much without an equivalent of NAFEL as they had in Newfoundland.[20] Fishermen in Newfoundland had received lower prices than their Canadian counterparts, but the NFB was identified with the return of high prices and strong markets and was synonymous with prosperity. If the NFB and NAFEL were dismantled at union, Canada would be seen as the culprit if for whatever reason the price of fish fell. That was no way to start confederation.

Canadian negotiators were worried about the political repercussions if NAFEL were allowed to continue. They feared that the Maritimes might demand similar boards to protect themselves. Moreover, Ottawa's bargainers did not want to create the impression that they were conceding the delegation's every demand.[21] Nevertheless, despite strong lobbying by Maritime politicians and cabinet ministers, the cabinet reluctantly agreed to keep the agencies for a transitional period of five years after it had realized that the delegation might balk at union without them. NAFEL was given control over both the interprovincial and export trade of Newfoundland saltfish. Ottawa insisted, however, on having greater control over NAFEL if it happened to act against the interests of the federal government. Canadian officials insisted that the NFB would have to be a federal agency under the authority of a federal minister because several of its powers, such as control over exporters, were not subject to any form of regulation in Newfoundland law.[22] Donald Jamieson, who covered the negotiations for one of the St. John's daily papers, considered the decision on NAFEL to be a Newfoundland victory. 'It is one of the biggest surprises to come out of the negotiations,' he reported.[23] After union, sea fisheries fell under federal jurisdiction, and Newfoundland's became a separate division within the Department of Fisheries. Ottawa assumed responsibility for the general administration of Newfoundland's fisheries and her bait service. Many of Newfoundland's fishing laws remained, but were administered for Canada by the NFB until a thorough study of the effect of Canadian laws on the fishery had been completed. The federal government could, with the consent of Newfoundland during the first five years of union, repeal or alter any of the fishery laws inherited from the new province.[24] The staff of the

NFB was absorbed into the federal Department of Fisheries, and Gushue was appointed Chief Supervisor and Inspector of the newly-created Newfoundland division. Gushue had become familiar with Canadian fishery policy and Canadian officials while chairman of the NFB after 1936 and while chairman of the fishery products committee of the International Combined Food Board during the Second World War. Consequently, his appointment facilitated integration as he became responsible for all federal fisheries matters in the new province. L.S. Bradbury, former secretary of the NFB, was appointed director of the Newfoundland fisheries division at Ottawa, to look after Newfoundland's affairs.[25] The Canadian Fisheries Act, though not proclaimed in Newfoundland until 1 May 1958,[26] finally brought under one statute the administration in Canada of all fisheries.

III

Ottawa wasted little time after union in announcing a five year programme to develop Canada's east coast fisheries. On 5 May 1949, R.W. Mayhew, Minister of Fisheries, announced that the time had arrived to recognize the fishery as an important national enterprise. He promised that the government would direct its efforts towards fundamental remedial action to improve the quality of the product and the catching methods, to maintain and expand export trade, and to increase domestic consumption.[27] Unlike agriculture, he conceded, little encouragement had been given to the fisheries. The programme he envisaged was the first of its kind for the fishery in Canada and focused on the fishermen. 'Notwithstanding ready access to the resources, which are the world's greatest,' Mayhew said, 'the industry has been unable to provide a dependable livelihood for the people directly employed by it.' While this may have been rhetoric for the upcoming election, the expected demand for price support[28] to supplement the traditionally low incomes in the backward Newfoundland fishing industry provided much of the impetus for Ottawa's initiatives. An emphasis on saltfish destined for the southern European markets, where living standards and purchasing power were both low, held little hope for developing backward areas and improving living conditions. The industry had to be weaned from lower grade products to ones of higher quality, such as fresh and frozen fish that could be marketed in North America.[29] Mayhew realized, though, that the saltfish industry would remain crucial to Newfoundland, and he hoped that improved fishing methods would increase individual productivity and raise incomes.[30]

Premier Joseph R. Smallwood realized, too, that the salt fishery had failed to provide a decent living for most fishermen. In fact, many fishermen had left their boats as other jobs opened up. During the Second World War, when other work and more secure and higher incomes were available at the American and Canadian military bases, the number of fishermen declined by one-third.[31] Smallwood feared a massive exodus as confederation opened new opportunities. He promised fishermen that union would breathe new life into the fisheries. 'It is time,' he said during the May 1949 provincial election, 'for our fishermen to get their share of the good things of life, and it is our policy to bring this about without delay.'[32] This would be best achieved, he thought, by greater production of frozen fillets for the American and Canadian mainland using modern deepsea draggers.[33] Consequently, the provincial government expanded the scope of the policy introduced earlier by the Commission of Government whereby capital was advanced as loans and guarantees for the development of fish filleting and refrigeration plants and the purchase of trawlers.[34] Though Ottawa shared Smallwood's aims, it rejected his policy of financial support for the processing companies, claiming this might lead to over expansion and interfere with plans to centralize the industry.

The serious difficulties encountered in marketing salt cod in the first years after confederation served to reinforce the need for radical change. The prosperity brought by war disappeared as the fishing fleets of competitor nations re-emerged in a reconstructed Europe.[35] Also, despite the postwar hope for freer multilateral trade, import restrictions by some European countries and bilateral trading arrangements within the sterling bloc aggravated the situation. Tenders issued by Greece, for instance, stipulated that the fish sellers had to be members of the European Payment Union to revitalize intra European trade. Governments were very reluctant to use dollar reserves for saltfish, when there was urgent need for raw materials and machine tools. Monetary exchange problems, too, made the task of marketing Newfoundland fish more difficult. The devaluation of most European currencies in September 1949 made Newfoundland fish more expensive than Icelandic and Faroese fish, and added to Newfoundland's problem as Greece and other European nations turned to cheaper supplies. European competitors not only squeezed much of the Newfoundland fish out of Europe but also competed successfully with Newfoundland in the Western Hemisphere.[36] By 1955 Newfoundland's saltfish exports to Europe were down 75 per cent from 1947-48.

Throughout this period, Newfoundland looked to Ottawa for a solution. The shortage of dollars in Europe seriously threatened the precarious existence of the Newfoundland fishermen and only the intervention of the federal government averted a disaster. Between 1950 and 1955, to aid the slumping saltfish industry, Ottawa spent more than $3 million in direct price support and several millions more in fish purchases for United Nations relief.[37] Newfoundland's representative in the federal cabinet, Gordon Bradley, acknowledged Ottawa's assistance when he said that 'We [Newfoundland] faced disaster, and, had we been dependent entirely upon our own resources, would have been confronted with one of the most serious problems in the history of the industry.'[38]

For many fishermen, confederation arrived just in time. Ottawa had pressed London to continue the sterling convertibility arrangement into 1951 in order to clear the way for sales to Europe. Mayhew continued to help to overcome the marketing difficulties abroad, and to encourage the expansion of the domestic market. In fact, the Canadian government arranged for the sale of about $4 million worth of Newfoundland fish to Europe. This was about 40 per cent of the province's 1951 production.[39] The situation was helped when Brazil agreed to purchase $1.75 million of the 1951 and 1952 production as part of a barter deal for pulp.[40] Nevertheless, the marketing crisis continued for several years after union, and the federal government had to bail out the industry by purchasing much of the surplus between 1949 and 1954. Ottawa became involved only because the problem was unique, and because the new province was economically so far behind the rest of Canada. Yet the federal government never lost sight of the fact that the fishery had to change.[41] Mayhew had maintained throughout the crisis that it was imperative that government action did not prevent converting production from salt to fresh frozen cod, for in this lay the long-term solution to the problem of the Newfoundland fisheries.[42] When Norman Robertson, the clerk of the Privy Council and secretary to the cabinet, visited Newfoundland in 1950, he found that both the provincial government and the fishing industry also recognized the necessity of a shift from dried salt cod to fresh and frozen fish. This change might take more than a decade to complete. In the meantime, Ottawa had to improve the conditions in the fishing industry for the individual fisherman and his family.[43] Throughout the marketing crisis, Ottawa expressed disappointment over the 'quality' of the argument presented by the saltfish industry in Newfoundland. It was consumed with the issue of markets, and paid scant attention to long-range solutions to persistent problems.[44] W.C. MacKenzie of the Markets and Economics Branch of the Department of Fisheries later remarked that fishermen, exporters and the public of Newfoundland were so concerned with fish prices that this issue tended to divert attention from the real problem of its fishing industry. This was the low productivity of individual fishermen.[45] Ottawa wanted to make this the focus of fishery reforms.

IV

Persistent market difficulties only served to strengthen the need for change even though both governments had recognized much earlier the necessity for major surgery. On 27 January 1951 Smallwood and Mayhew announced the formation of a joint Fisheries Development Committee to draw up a programme for developing the inshore and offshore fisheries. This would have to be 'capable of implementation by both the Federal and Provincial Governments and those engaged in the fishing industry.' It would also have to outline 'the respective responsibilities of each, and their agreed shares in carrying out the programme.' The committee included representatives from both levels of government, fishermen, and industry and was chaired by Sir Albert Walsh, the Chief Justice of Newfoundland and former chairman of the delegation to negotiate the terms of union.[46]

Smallwood believed that the committee's recommendations should constitute a programme of development for the fishery. What he did not know, however, was that Ottawa had already formulated its policy, and it was at variance with his. He saw an important role for government through cash incentives and loan guarantees. On the other hand, Ottawa believed that the 'development of [fishery] resources should be left to...individuals and associations of individuals acting as private citizens,' with government performing a very limited role which would not encroach on private enterprise. Government should assume responsibility for the major part of investigative and experimental undertakings, if they contributed to an improvement in national enterprise. In other words, government should only provide 'an environment in which private initiative and capital...[could] venture and flourish through Governmental assistance.' Private enterprise, of course, should provide the capital necessary for the exploitation of the resources uncovered or expanded through federal programmes. However, if private industry refused to become involved, 'the use of public money to exploit a resource, when such exploitation leads to social betterment, seem[ed] quite justifiable. This [was] especially so where an operation of this kind [was] necessary to overcome general inertia and the reluctance of private capital to pioneer in an area or community.' Because government was using public funds on which there were many demands, it was 'mandatory' that government investment 'be based upon careful and objective economic analysis' because the ultimate goal was to lure private capital. Of course, if the results of government policies were not encouraging, private capital would steer away. 'Development can only be regarded as successful,' Ottawa maintained, 'if it attracts to itself investment capital from the citizens who are participating. Unwise projects carried out under the aegis of governments would only prejudice the whole fishery development scheme. Unsound works bring in their train loss of confidence, unscrupulous dealings and finally public scorn.'[47]

Ottawa's primary objective was to improve the standard of living of the people involved in the fishery. Yet it realized that 'there [was] little hope for that part of an industry [salt cod production], which use[d] methods of operation in vogue two centuries ago, to provide a satisfactory living for its dependents or to remain in existence for very long, except by the benevolence of governments.'[48] This was not Ottawa's policy. Prime Minister Louis St. Laurent's approach to the role of government in the national economy has been described elsewhere as 'minimalist,' and he was not about to make an exception for the Newfoundland fishery.[49] With such a policy, Ottawa had effectively closed the door on what Smallwood hoped to achieve through the Walsh committee even before it had begun its investigation.

Like two ships passing in the night, Ottawa and Newfoundland were on separate courses and very unlikely to meet.

V

On 15 April 1953, the report of the Newfoundland Fisheries Development Committee was tabled in the House of Commons. The Walsh report painted a depressing portrait of the Newfoundland fishery. The industry was characterized by extreme inefficiency, with meager capital investment, averaging about $500 per man. Fishermen were restricted to the near inshore waters where the season was generally short and the run of fish sporadic; and so their productivity was low. The necessity of being close to the resource had drawn the fishermen to remote, isolated headlands and islands where living conditions were generally poor. In addition to being isolated, many lacked the amenities of civilized life. The typical family income averaged less than $1,500 annually of which only about half was derived from fishing.[50] The Walsh report also pointed out the changes sweeping the province:

> The general social improvement which has been taking place in the Province for some years is resulting in the liberation of women from the hard and unsuitable work of fish-making and allowing them to devote their time to their household duties and to live in an atmosphere of human dignity as wives and mothers. It is also resulting in the liberation of children to pursue their education and receiving [sic] a formation preparing them properly for a career to which they should have equal opportunity with all other children. The Committee considers that in a programme of development of the fisheries, child and female labour should find no place, except in the case of young women who will be employed at suitable work in plants and senior school children who will undoubtedly continue to help in fish curing during the summer vacation.[51]

The typical family enterprise whereby the men caught the fish and the women and children dried them on the flakes was a relic of the past and in the 1950s peculiar to Newfoundland. The committee found a universal desire among fishermen to dispose of their fish fresh and get rid of the difficult, time-consuming, and tedious work of curing their catch.[52]

This was, in large part, a consequence of the changes evident across Newfoundland, changes that had their roots in the period of prosperity during the war.[53] 'With a suddenness that is startling,' Newfoundland Minister of Finance, Gregory Power, said in his budget speech of April 1953, 'our people in all sections of the Province seem to have awakened to a keen realization of the many ways in which Newfoundland had been lagging behind in the march of progress for most of the present century.' Power also noted that the old-time complacency and contentment of Newfoundlanders had weakened, while 'their wants had expanded enormously.' 'A deep-seated desire for progress and improvement, sleeping through the decades,' seemed 'suddenly to have come to life.' There was a strong desire to bridge the gap with the rest of North America. Power saw the awakening in the 'sudden clamorous demand for new roads, and for improvement of old roads...It explains the all but irresistible demand for new hospitals, hospital boats, air ambulances, and other modern health services...[and] the swelling demand for more and better schools.'[54] Each week in the House of Assembly, petitions from all across the province were presented to the government demanding roads to end isolation, to provide better health and educational services and, in general, to improve the standard of living.[55] There was a new consciousness in the Newfoundland people, reflected in a 'new and urgent demand for progress, [an] insatiable impatience manifest in almost every nook and corner of the Province.' 'It is a most gratifying development,' Power concluded, 'and it must lead inevitably to great changes and improvement in our Newfoundland life.'[56]

The fishing industry had already started to show signs of change. The bank or deepsea fishery,[57] once an integral part of the salt fishery, had practically disappeared in little more than a decade as vessels started to supply the fresh fish industry.[58] In 1937, banking schooners had produced over 250,000 quintals of fish for salting, but production dropped to 120,000 in 1949 and to only 5,000 quintals in 1951. The decrease in the number of vessels was equally sharp, from eighty-eight in 1949 to only two in 1951. Fresh fishing generally resulted in higher and quicker returns, and the banker crews found employment on local trawlers or in the Nova Scotia fishery. A similar trend was discernible in the Labrador fishery, but there it was due primarily to the uncertainties of the market for the Labrador cure. Only 30 schooners or 'floaters' operated 'on the Labrador' in 1951, compared with 65 in 1950 and 144 in 1949. The decline continued into 1952.[59] Gordon Bradley thought that the greatest change in the industry was the growing reluctance of fishermen to continue in the ways of their ancestors. 'It is a definite fact,' he wrote to Hazen A. Russell of Job Brothers, a major fish company, 'that the great bulk of Bonavista fishermen have no desire whatever to salt fish nowadays. They want to sell it green [fresh]. It has taken them some time to realize that the time and labour expended by them upon the fish after it is brought to land gives them far less in the way of return than that time would afford them if they spent it in catching.'[60] His outlook was stark: 'unless we can evolve better methods of both catching and curing, the day is not far distant when the Newfoundland salt codfish industry will be a thing of the past, for the simple reason that the young men of today will not tolerate the standards of life of...[their] forefathers. This is increasingly apparent since confederation...opened up the growing opportunities of this vast and ever-expanding nation of ours to the youth of our province.'[61] Bradley also believed that the catching and curing of the fish must be separated, with the latter looking to skilled and scientific management to produce a standard product of high quality.

W.J. Keough, Newfoundland's Minister of Fisheries and Co-operatives, noted similar changes in early 1952. 'Many fishermen who produce light-salted or shore fish,' he said, 'have declared that they will not make [dry] fish any more. And I suppose all fishermen wish to sell their catches green from the boat.' He also noted that it was difficult for fishermen to make a decent living at light salted or shore fish, but if the fish were cured at central shore stations, the cost of labour and investment would push the price of a quintal of fish up by $2. What this also meant, he said, was that 'the fishermen, who have not considered their labour as wages to be charged against the fish but rather as a service inseparable from the function of catching fish, have been subsidizing every cod's tail of light salted fish sold in export markets.'[62] Given all this, it is not surprising that the swing away from the traditional shore cure towards mass-produced fillets continued throughout most of the 1950s.[63]

The Walsh committee reached a similar conclusion. If the fishery failed to provide an income and working conditions as attractive as those in other occupations, fishermen would continue to leave the industry. Despite the preoccupation with fish prices in Newfoundland, an increase in the price, it warned, would have only a slight effect on family income because productivity was so low. Walsh said that individual productivity had to be increased to avoid a mass exodus of fishermen and to raise their income. Moreover, they had to be provided with a standard of living and amenities and services regarded as normal for rural areas. Walsh wrote that as far as development was concerned 'the most important feature of the programme is centralization of the industry by [the] establishment of plants capable of diversified production and economic operation. Most of the other features are auxiliary to this but necessary for success.' In order to create a productive inshore fishery, radical changes were necessary indeed.[64]

The recommendations contained in the Walsh report were focussed on the northeast coast of the island where the industry was particularly depressed. On the ice free south coast filleting and freezing were already developing satisfactorily. But the northern regions, ice bound for several months each year, had not benefited from the new technology. They had continued to rely on saltfish processing, though diversification was certainly encouraged. If private enterprise failed to take the initiative, Walsh recommended that government should become involved, either to provide loans or to finance projects completely. What the Walsh recommendations implied, James Sinclair, Mayhew's successor as federal Minister of Fisheries, later reported to the cabinet, was the 'concentration of the fishing fleets around such plants, in order to ensure stability of supply.' It followed that modernization involved 'withdrawal from the widely-scattered "outports" and centralization of the fishing industry at a comparatively small number of locations.'[65]

The federal government did not decide quickly on the recommendations in the Walsh report though it agreed with its analysis of the Newfoundland fishery. During the summer of 1953, in usual governmental fashion, St. Laurent appointed an interdepartmental committee of senior officials to review the report and to submit a proposal to the cabinet; but before any decision was made parliament was dissolved and an election called. Smallwood threw himself into the federal campaign. 'It is of life and death importance to all our fishermen for the Liberal Government in Ottawa to be put back in power,' he told the fishermen: 'A vote for the seven Liberal candidates in this election is a vote for your Newfoundland Government, a vote for vast and wonderful development of our fisheries, a vote for making our fishermen prosperous.'[66] Perhaps Smallwood hoped that a good showing by Newfoundland Liberals would make the prime minister more amenable to the Walsh recommendations, but above all he was concerned to secure the election of J.W. Pickersgill, the former secretary of the cabinet, who had agreed to run in Bonavista-Twillingate, a Liberal stronghold. The Liberals did in fact win all seven seats, but Smallwood failed to convince Ottawa that his approach was the right one. But in Pickersgill, who became Newfoundland's representative in the cabinet, Smallwood and his fishermen supporters had found an important ally in Ottawa.[67]

Before the cabinet made up its mind on Walsh's recommendations, another group of senior bureaucrats went to Newfoundland to examine the situation at firsthand. Neither this group nor the earlier one saw any need for a radical departure from Ottawa's policy on fishery development. Ottawa believed in an integrated, all encompassing approach to developing the fishery that would involve both levels of government and private enterprise. Following a thorough survey of potential sites, Ottawa wanted to select (as the report had recommended) several locations for development. Various federal departments were to provide the necessary marine works, navigational aids, and marine radio-telephone service. Power, water supply, and other municipal services would be furnished by the provincial government. The two governments would co-operate and share the cost of building vessels, training of personnel, and housing. In other words, government would create the infrastructure. Once the services were provided, private enterprise, perhaps with the help of the Industrial Development Bank, would then take over and make the projects viable.[68] Ottawa refused, however, to become involved in undertakings in Newfoundland that it did not support elsewhere in Canada. And so the interdepartmental committee recommended against federal assistance to build highways and docks, as such federal encroachments would establish an undesirable precedent. In keeping with government policy, the committee warned against providing assistance to private enterprise beyond what was available through the normal operations of the Industrial Development Bank. There should be no special legislation for Newfoundland to rehabilitate its fishery, except perhaps to provide saltfish warehouses and holding stores at winter shipping ports.[69] Moreover, the productivity of individual fishermen could only be raised by a substantial reduction in the number of fishermen. This was a sensitive issue in Newfoundland and one the bureaucrats warned against emphasizing publicly. The government also had to be careful that the large number of fishermen who had left their boats for higher wages on new construction sites or at other jobs in the province would not rush back to the fisheries in the expectation that the Walsh report would create new opportunities.[70] Ottawa feared that the centralization of the industry would be seriously impeded if the province were to rehabilitate some communities without considering their long-term potentials.[71]

This approach was too slow for the provincial government. When the Walsh committee submitted an interim report in mid-1952, Ottawa made clear to Smallwood its plans for the fishery. Above all, there would be no financial aid to private industry. This prompted an outburst from Smallwood in the House of Assembly. He charged that the greatest disappointment of union had been the fisheries: 'Ottawa seems to have virtually no realistic understanding or appreciation of the almost incalculable importance of fisheries in the economy of Newfoundland, and the economy of Canada...Union with Canada must always be something less than a success so long as the Government of Canada fails to do for the fisheries a fair fraction of what has been done for other primary industries and is being done.'[72] For his part W.J. Keough believed that in the matter of saltfish production it was naive for Ottawa to think that any of the existing fishing companies in Newfoundland would invest in the development of plants to process the product. 'Unless the Government of Canada was prepared to reach agreement in respect of capital aid for development in the salt fish industry,' he argued, 'two years would have been wasted awaiting the final report and recommendations of the Fisheries Development Committee.'[73]

Ottawa remained firm. Its goal was to improve the standard of living for fishermen and, in co-operation with the provincial government, it started a number of projects, all of them experimental and recommended by the Walsh report, which were designed to overcome some basic problems faced by outport fishermen. The purpose was to increase the productivity of fishermen by separating the catching and curing processes. The projects to achieve this were undertaken at Quirpon and Seldom Come By. The nature of the experiment was to abandon the system of individual production in favour of a small saltfish plant in each community with centralized flakes. The plants would buy the fish green directly from the fishermen, thus giving them more time to fish.[74] The federal government hoped to achieve its second objective of more consistent quality by providing small groups of fishermen with adequate and sanitary curing facilities, a development that foreshadowed the introduction of community stages.[75]

Mayhew and St. Laurent liked these projects because they promised to help fishermen to help themselves while improving the amenities available to them.[76]

Because the future development of the saltfish industry depended on the successful introduction of a low cost dryer that would mechanize and standardize production, an experiment along these lines was undertaken at Valleyfield-Badger's Quay. The plan was for lightly salted or semi-dried fish to be taken from the surrounding area to the experimental plant. A similar large-scale community project, with a saltfish plant and plans for the eventual production of fresh frozen fish and fish meal, was also approved for La Scie. By leading the way in mechanization, Ottawa hoped to demonstrate the viability of the saltfish industry. Other experiments were aimed at developing better fishing craft and catching gear. In the same spirit, and with a view to promoting greater concentration of population, a systematic search was undertaken for new fishing grounds. By all these means Ottawa and St. John's hoped together to provide some of the amenities of life which were lacking in the isolated outports but taken for granted elsewhere in the country. The federal government believed that if the fishery could be improved through technological innovation, private investment would follow. Both governments accepted that the centralization of the population was the only way that services could be extended to the remote areas of the province so as to overcome the curse of isolation. It was also agreed that improvement would mean a substantial reduction in the number of fishermen.[77]

In 1954 $2.3 million was allocated by Ottawa for the projects.[78] The provincial allocation was $1.1 million. The Canadian government had clearly understood the problem as presented in the Walsh report. Yet Ottawa was timid. This was evident in its refusal to follow the recommendation in the report to stimulate the industry by an infusion of capital to private enterprise or for projects of the provincial government.[79] But Ottawa's hope to stimulate investment by creating an infrastructure rather than through capital assistance to private enterprise was wishful thinking.[80] It resisted 'considerable pressure' from Smallwood to finance existing industries and become involved in various processing operations. Mayhew had told the prime minister in 1952 that such activities would lead Ottawa 'away from [its] real responsibility in that Province. We think that our responsibility is very clearly defined, and we are prepared to recognize our responsibility and take action as quickly as possible.' Mayhew did not want to establish a precedent for federal intrusion into the fishery, and he realized, moreover, that if Ottawa assisted the Newfoundland fishing industry, it would be doing so 'at the expense of a neighboring [Nova Scotia] industry which was doing everything on its own.'[81] He realized too that Maritime producers would be extremely critical of the government's intervention. In sum, political considerations were put ahead of the needs of the

Newfoundland fishery. The easy way out was for the federal government to fall back on capitalist ideology and persevere in the attitude that publicly sponsored enterprise was to be avoided.[82] By following this course, however, Ottawa failed to acknowledge the gravity of the problems that plagued the Newfoundland fishery. In truth, it could have silenced potential critics by making the case that the Newfoundland fishing industry was backward compared to that of the Maritimes and by insisting that any special assistance given was of a temporary nature.

In the first decade of union it was the provincial government that took the initiative in providing financial assistance to the industry. Throughout that period, it gave the fishing industry more than $13 million in loans and working capital. Most of this went to the fresh frozen business. In introducing the legislation to establish the Newfoundland Fisheries Authority, Smallwood advanced this justification for the action being taken: 'The only reason the Government of Newfoundland has had to lend money or guarantee loans for development is because capital, for investment in the fisheries or new industries for that matter, has not been available in Newfoundland or on the Mainland of Canada or in the United States.' The task of the new Authority, the Premier explained, was to carry out those recommendations of the Walsh report which fell within provincial jurisdication. According to Smallwood, confederation had given Newfoundland entrepreneurs greater opportunity for profit in the sale of consumer items. This in turn had discouraged the long-term investment of venture capital and especially in the fishery. Several of the major fishing companies were either shifting their operations to the fresh and frozen sectors, or getting out of the industry altogether. Bowring Brothers, one of the most powerful and largest firms in the saltfish trade, had decided by August 1950 that greater prosperity beckoned in the retail trade. One of the larger exporters engaged in the Labrador fishery, James Baird Limited, quit the fishery in 1952 and, by 1957, ten companies had withdrawn from the saltfish trade. Smallwood later charged that it was the merchants, not the governments, that had lost interest in the fishery.[83]

Even with his promise of generous financial assistance, Smallwood had failed to attract private enterprise to the saltfish business, but he remained convinced that government must continue to lead if the fishing industry as a whole was to remain viable. While Ottawa hoped for a better day through experiment, Smallwood thought the way forward was to throw money at the industry to enable it to move quickly to producing fresh and frozen fish. 'We have refused no firm that was willing to expand and was able to meet our terms,' he told the legislature, 'and this policy we shall continue to practice.' 'We have gone further,' he continued, 'for we have approached firms and urged them to expand and offered to assist them to finance the suggested expansion, provided they were willing to meet our financial terms...In short, by the end of the present calendar year [1951] our policy will have resulted in the filleting and freezing of a quantity of codfish that would, if salted and dried, amount to about 100,000 quintals, that would have to find markets in competition with the bulk of our codfish production.'[84] Though his policy eventually led to an over capacity in the frozen sector,[85] its short-term effect was rapid growth and substantially improved incomes in a number of fishing settlements. Moreover, in acting as he did, Smallwood was in step with the position Ottawa itself had advocated immediately after union. This was that if private enterprise did not initiate development, then government must act to show what could be done. The Walsh report also favoured this plan of attack.[86] Nevertheless, the federal authorities were not impressed with what Smallwood was attempting. Ottawa's reluctance stemmed in part from Newfoundland's seeming recklessness.[87] Gushue had cautioned Mayhew shortly after the Walsh committee was formed that 'the Federal Government must avoid the head-long approach from which the Provincial Government finds it difficult to escape, and indeed, to which it is virtually committed.'[88] 'Such guarantees,' Stewart Bates, the Deputy Minister of Fisheries, told Gushue, 'are a little like the signing of personal notes—something you do in the expectation you will never be called on to make them good. Such guarantees moreover, are apt to be subjected to strong political pressures, to be ad hoc in their application, and to induce hasty consideration of projects.'[89]

Perhaps it was Gordon Bradley more than anyone who helped sour Ottawa on the Walsh recommendation for public funds and steer it clear of Smallwood. Many in Ottawa were already beginning to question the premier's development scheme.[90] Bradley had reservations about Smallwood's ability to govern effectively. 'There was not one single man in the whole outfit with any actual administrative experience, not even Joey himself,' he wrote a friend by way of assessment of the provincial government formed in 1949. 'That in itself was a unique situation.' The only thing, Bradley concluded, that could prevent chaos with Smallwood as provincial leader was an extraordinary run of good luck.[91] When the Walsh committee was appointed, Bradley held out little hope for it. The problem of the Newfoundland fishery, he suggested, was not one for the lawyers, merchants, civil servants, and fishermen, who made up the committee. It was a problem for scientists and engineers to be solved 'in the laboratory...not in the committee room.' Bradley feared that the action recommended by the committee would be dictated by the provincial government, and that Smallwood would simply throw money at the fishery, as a measure of relief, without any regard to a long-term solution.[92] 'A perusal of this interim report,' he wrote to Hazen A. Russell, one of the committee members, 'made it quite clear that it was, in fact, founded upon the policy of getting industries going by Government financing and, in this instance, at any rate, with little regard to the possibilities of success and none to the improvement of curing methods.' Bradley thought that the committee was being run by Clive

Planta, Newfoundland's impulsive Deputy Minister of Fisheries, and that its approach was in keeping with the province's general economic policy, that is to say to plunge in, usually with generous financial aid, but without adequate knowledge or experience.[93] The schemes for economic develop- ment which were being floated in Newfoundland, he lamented, made no sense except in 'the desire of some industrialists to sneak across the Atlantic so as to provide a nest-egg for themselves if they have to fly...in the event of a Russian advance.' Smallwood and his Director-General of Economic Development, the Latvian economist Alfred Valdmanis, were building 'castles in the air.'[94]

Ottawa's confidence in Smallwood's administrative ability was also shaken in the early years of union when the premier landed himself in hot water on several occasions. Federal officials and politicians became skepti- cal about working with him, save at arm's length. It was believed in Ottawa that he had abused both the old age pension agreement and the unemploy- ment assistance program.[95] Yet another mark against him was that before the Newfoundland Hotel had been transferred to Canadian National Rail- ways under the terms of union, he had sold to a local car dealership a parcel of land belonging to the hotel. Bradley, who gave the prime minister formal notice of Newfoundland's wish to transfer the hotel to Canadian National, hastily rebuked Smallwood for what he had done. Legal questions aside, he wrote, the whole episode would 'leave the Provincial Government with a reputation for very sharp practices'; a price of even $40,000[96] was 'a poor substitute for the loss of confidence' which would result from the sale. When confidence was 'destroyed,' Bradley pronounced, co-operation be- came 'very difficult.'[97]

Bradley warned Smallwood that he must avoid incidents that would impair good relations between the province and Ottawa.[98] Smallwood paid him no heed. In early 1951, he announced an investigation into the price paid for the 1950 catch[99] after the federal government had already an- nounced plans to conduct a similar investigation. To make matters worse, he appointed a federal official on loan from the Dominion Bureau of Statistics to duplicate the work of federal officials. Bradley was exasperated: 'Why on earth,' he asked, 'do you embark upon projects of this kind where the Federal government is involved without first giving me any information whatever about the matter?' 'As it now stands,' he continued, 'I can only try and straighten up an awkward situation which you yourself have created...I have told you time and again that is one of your great failings. You go ahead and on your own, make decisions and proceed to implement them without consulting others who have a stake in the matter and who can perhaps give you some sound advice.'[100] Bradley despaired when he concluded that Smallwood had not changed during his first three years in office.[101] Nor was he alone in thinking that Smallwood was unreliable. Officials such as Mitchell Sharp and R.B. Bryce recall having reservations about Smallwood's schemes for economic development, and they both claim that their views were shared by many others in the bureaucracy.[102] With such thinking in official Ottawa it is little wonder that the federal government was reluctant to follow the path, already well-worn by Smallwood, of aiding private industry. Not surprisingly, Ottawa continued the established federal role of fostering a proper environment for industry. Within that environment investors would have to fend for themselves.

This prevailing view of Smallwood undoubtedly played a role in Ottawa's rejection of Walsh's recommendation to establish a joint federal-provincial organization to administer a programme for development. Walsh thought that a joint body might temper Smallwood's recklessness. But instead of trying to exert some measure of control, Ottawa pursued its own course, and though the two did co-operate on several experimental projects, Smallwood continued on his own. W.C. MacKenzie, who spent two years in Newfoundland as the representative of the Department of Fisheries on the Walsh committee, saw as a grave mistake Ottawa's failure to appoint a co-ordinator for the Newfoundland fishery development. He feared that the provincial government, in its impatience for quick results, would ignore the recommendations on adult education and a grassroots organization to lay a foundation for fishery co-operatives, and instead opt to create such organizations from the top down. But he also realized that Ottawa was constrained by Nova Scotia which saw the Walsh report as a threat to its own fishing industry. In fact Nova Scotia's position was based on a misconception, as the programme of modernization suggested for Newfoundland involved contraction as well as expansion.[103]

After Ottawa introduced its programme, Clive Planta told Smallwood that 'we actually gained more than we came prepared to accept as reasonable for immediate commencement, with a view to completion in 1954.' The federal government, he acknowledged, was hampered in its policy towards the Newfoundland saltfish industry by political considerations in Nova Scotia and by possible American retaliation against other Canadian fish products. The government had decided to purchase saltfish for overseas relief efforts rather than to initiate direct price support fearing countermeasures by Washington.[104] Certainly this was the approach of James Sinclair when he came to the fisheries portfolio in October 1952. 'If the government,' the Department of Fisheries warned, backed 'fish prices then the U.S. would have a strong case against Canadian fish entering the American market and tariff concessions would be dropped in favour of a high levy.'[105] Moreover, if support were given to Newfoundland, it would weaken the market generally and prompt protests from Nova Scotia.[106] These were not minor concerns. Planta believed that Newfoundland would gain more within the normal services and functions of the federal government than through special consideration. The latter, he noted, would depend on the willingness of the government to take a political risk, and if public debate ensued, which was quite possible, Newfoundland could not hope to win.[107]

In the end Smallwood was also conciliatory. On 1 October 1953, he stated publicly that 'the Government of Canada see clearly...that Newfoundland's action in entering the family of Canadian Provinces can have full success for Newfoundland only if our fisheries are fully developed...This is the real meaning of the decision that has now been reached between Ottawa and St. John's.'[108]

VI

In 1954, following these events, Smallwood sanctioned the absorption of NAFEL by the federal Department of Trade and Commerce. Neither St. John's nor Ottawa particularly liked the saltfish marketing agency instituted by the Commission of Government. Both governments disapproved of a marketing method which left all the risks to the fishermen, though much of the antagonism towards NAFEL can be traced to the marketing crisis from 1949 to 1953 that wreaked havoc on the industry. Ottawa felt that NAFEL had buried its head in the sand, and that its primary interest was to get cheap fish from the fishermen to maintain a strong competitive position in the markets.[109] Later, Stewart Bates charged that although NAFEL was a monopoly created by government and enjoyed all the advantages of being a monopoly, it refused to accept the associated responsibilities. 'It had,' he charged, 'shown no concern with development of the salt fish industry' but had been 'satisfied with the status quo.' The deputy minister was right. NAFEL had been content to rake in the profits during the Second World War without any concern for the long-term viability of the industry. In the marketing crisis after union it called on Ottawa to bail it out and threatened to cease outfitting fishermen if Ottawa did not guarantee it a market. It had not assumed full responsibility when things went wrong in 1949-50, Bates reminded the minister, and instead had stopped buying from the fishermen and had called upon the Prices Support Board to step in and take over the product.[110]

Major changes were made to NAFEL in 1953 and again in 1954. The barrier to interprovincial trade was removed to silence the critics of the agency in Nova Scotia, while restrictions were added to regulate the purchase of salt bulk[111] for use in Nova Scotia's mechanical dryers. To do otherwise might have courted chaos, as fishermen might have put up too much salt bulk, hoping to dispose of it on the mainland.[112] Moreover, federal officials were concerned that NAFEL had become too reliant on government to support the price to fishermen. They also wanted more direct supervision. When Ottawa assumed control, smaller firms were allowed to join NAFEL, and as a further indication of Ottawa's interest in them, fishermen were represented on the board of directors for the first time. Furthermore, merchants selling through NAFEL had to undertake at the beginning of the season to pay, subject to government approval, a minimum price to fishermen, and to agree to a system of profit sharing from any increase in the general price over the minimum set.[113] The Minister of Trade and Commerce, C.D. Howe, warned NAFEL that it must 'do everything possible to facilitate such negotiations and...co-operate in ensuring the successful operation of any agreements...reached.'[114]

Smallwood's expectation about the transfer of responsibility for Newfoundland's saltfish export trade to the Department of Trade and Commerce was typically expansionist.[115] He had often praised Howe whose experience with the Canadian Wheat Board was legendary and had much impressed him. Pickersgill believed that Howe's personal interest was the 'best thing that had happened to the Newfoundland fisheries for a very long time,' and he told the premier that Newfoundland's interests would be best served if Howe and his officials were given a chance to make things work.[116] Howe also reminded Smallwood that since Ottawa had assumed sole responsibility for export marketing, it would no longer be appropriate for the province to participate in discussions about NAFEL and fish prices. Smallwood agreed. Newfoundland's best contribution, he told Howe, would be 'to refrain from becoming involved.'[117] Thus, Smallwood gave Howe a free hand in marketing Newfoundland salt cod, and Ottawa consolidated its control over the marketing process. Within three months, Canada completed trade agreements with Italy, Spain and Greece that reopened Newfoundland's traditional saltfish markets.[118]

VII

Protecting traditional markets, however, was not enough. The industry could only survive if it provided an acceptable standard of living. This obviously had not happened in the first years of union, and by 1955 over 10,000 men had left the fishery. Some 17,000 remained. It must have seemed to Ottawa that there was little hope for stability in the salt fishery: only during wartime had there been buoyant markets and relative prosperity. In the first five years of union, Ottawa had spent nearly $4 million on price support alone. This had been designed only for emergency circumstances, not as a substitute for sound production and marketing practices. Mayhew said in 1950 that there was in price support 'an inherent danger that it may be used to subsidize inefficiency and to perpetuate rather than solve the basic problem...[It] will not be used as a means of relieving the merchandizing branches of the industry when they find themselves with a carry over at the end of the marketing season, nor will it be used in low income areas where the low incomes are the result of causes other than a sharp decline in price.'[119] By 1955, Ottawa was doing precisely that. Price support was rarely required in mainland Canada, except for Saguenay County in Quebec where conditions paralleled those of Newfoundland. Moreover, Newfoundland fish competed with Quebec and Nova Scotia fish, and any measure of price support for Newfoundland weakened the competitive position of mainland fish.[120]

Newfoundland quickly lost faith in Ottawa's commitment to the fishery. Political constraints and criticism from Nova Scotia, Clive Planta claimed, prevented the federal government from assuming leadership in developing the fisheries. Ottawa, he believed, felt that modernization meant concentrating on several communities and allowing the rest to die so that eventually the saltfish industry would become a shadow of the fresh frozen industry.[121] By July 1955, Smallwood had apparently adopted a similar attitude, though he might have been playing to a national audience when he lambasted Ottawa for its failure in the Newfoundland fishery; he had a penchant for the dramatic and he rarely missed an opportunity to berate 'Uncle Ottawa' on the national stage for not doing enough for Newfoundland. Before the Dominion-Provincial conference of that summer, Beland Honderich, editor in chief of the *Toronto Star* asked him for his opinion on what Canada had done to assist Newfoundland. In a reply that perhaps gave Honderich more than he had bargained for, Smallwood delivered a scathing indictment of Canadian policy:

> I am ashamed and angry to say it, but the altogether stupid, bungling, inadequate effort of Great Canada to assist the Atlantic fishing industry (which is potentially almost as valuable in dollars and cents and much more valuable in numbers of families that can be supported than the oil industry of Alberta) is a reproach to a great and progressive country. The whole policy of the Department of Fisheries of Canada, insofar as there appears to be a policy for Newfoundland, is to drive the fishermen away from fishing. The present Minister of Fisheries told one very prominent Newfoundlander that it wouldn't matter if the Newfoundland fishermen had to leave the fisheries, because they could always find work in some other part of Canada.[122]

Smallwood had placed great hope on the Walsh committee, and he no doubt felt that Ottawa had not done its share. Yet one must question his own commitment to the fishery, especially the salt fishery. He makes little mention of it in his memoirs. And, after all, Smallwood had initiated in 1953 a plan to resettle fishermen from their isolated communities. His government's support for the industry was mainly financial aid to the producers of frozen fillets, not to the saltfish industry. When in October 1955 he appeared in St. John's before the Royal Commission on Canada's Economic Prospects, chaired by Walter Gordon, Smallwood barely mentioned the fishery. On the other hand, he rambled on for quite some time about how Newfoundland's bogs could be turned into wonderful cattle grazing areas and how federal investment could turn the province into cattle country, complete with rodeos and its own stampede. Only in the 1960s did Smallwood turn to the inshore fishermen.[123] By then it was far too late.

About 500 fishing communities depended on the salt fishery and many of them were concentrated along the northeast coast of Newfoundland.

Ottawa could not ignore them. The experimental projects for centralization and community rehabilitation were limited to a dozen communities. About 90,000-100,000 people in scattered fishing villages were left to continue as before, and await the results. Many of the problems persisted in spite of the Walsh report and increased spending by the government on the fishery. According to Frederick W. Rowe over $100 million was spent directly and another $200 million indirectly.[124] At the end of the first decade of union, incomes were still far below the national average, and no great strides had been made to provide services to the outports. A working party, appointed by the federal and provincial governments to review the fishery and evaluate the changes that had occurred between 1953 and 1958, concluded that 90 per cent of the fishermen had 'hardly been touched by the development programme as implemented to date and their average gross income from the cod fishery remains at from $500 to $700 for the annual period of the fishery.' Although the number of fishermen continued to decline, the working party suggested, that it must be further reduced. The Walsh committee, of course, had suggested this five years before. More than 5,000 had left between 1953 and 1958, but overall production had been maintained largely because of the shift to long liners and company owned trawlers. For the majority of the fishermen who remained, there had been little increase in productivity. Walsh's main recommendation, therefore, had gone largely unfulfilled.[125]

Nor had the community development projects turned out as the government had hoped. They had become much larger and more expensive than had been originally anticipated but the community interest and co-operation needed to make them successful had not materialized. And it was in these experiments that Ottawa had placed its hope for a rehabilitated fishery. Quirpon, Seldom Come By and Merasheen were to demonstrate that fishermen's incomes could be improved by increased productivity and a better quality of salt cod. Quality improved, but as the Newfoundland Fisheries Development Authority lamented in 1960, with few exceptions 'the fishermen have not taken advantage of [the] opportunity to increase their earnings by extending their fishing activities at the beginning and end of each season.' This seems to suggest that some of the persistent problems can be attributed to the fishermen themselves.[126] Although this may be putting the blame on the individual fishermen, it does seem that too many of them failed to increase their annual catches.[127] The main benefit, therefore, was freedom from the task of making or curing saltfish.[128]

In the first decade of union the problem of Newfoundland was the 10,000-12,000 workers who continued in the salt fishery just as their forefathers had done. They could not develop and maintain even the most simple institutions and services. The objective of both governments continued to be the elimination of the small, remote settlements in favour of selected 'growth areas' where modern communities might develop acceptable standards of living. To carry out such a policy was necessarily a gradual process, and though it was executed with some success during the 1960s and early 1970s, the federal government sought a new strategy for the transition period.

From at least 1955, Ottawa politicians and bureaucrats realized there was no easy solution to the persistent low incomes of the fishermen in Newfoundland. Consequently, they came to see the fishery in Newfoundland as a problem in social welfare as much as one in economics. J.N. Lewis of the federal Department of Fisheries noted that Ottawa's policy was 'to administer palliatives based solely on humanitarian consideration.' In 1956 James Sinclair wrote his provincial counterpart, John T. Cheeseman, that a programme for salt assistance met two of Ottawa's objectives: it was generally free of serious criticism from the Maritimes, and it put money directly into the hands of the fishermen. Sinclair agreed that the programme did not address the basic problems of the salt fishery, but it would increase the incomes of individual fishermen.[129] While price support, salt rebate assistance, unemployment insurance, and later local construction programmes related to the fishery contributed to the financial improvement of many fishermen and their families, they might also have put a brake upon the natural forces that might have solved, however harshly, the problem represented by the shore fishermen of Newfoundland.[130] As Lewis observed, the placebo that the government prescribed would 'prolong the transition period and stretch out the years during which these people...[would] continue to represent a problem that...[would] tax the resources of the province and invite crisis after crisis for [the] Department [of Fisheries].' The federal department lamented that each fishermen who was encouraged to remain in the inshore fishery was a potential problem in the future.[131]

Lewis could not have been more accurate even with a crystal ball. Since the Walsh report, the fisheries have been enveloped in crisis after crisis. In almost every case, the solution put forth has been similar to that recommended in the early 1950s by the Walsh committee and Ottawa.[132] Yet this is not to suggest that changes did not occur. The fresh frozen sector grew rapidly, perhaps too rapidly. Capacity exceeded demand in the late 1950s and the federal plans for exploratory fishing, improved gear and boats, and mechanical drying facilities certainly paid off. On the other hand, centralization did not pay the dividends hoped for by planners. Despite the criticisms of the programme, it did have the effect of bringing many Newfoundlanders into the twentieth century.

The federal government is generally blamed for not doing enough to rehabilitate the fishery.[133] But Ottawa's task in 1949 was more than rehabilitation. The fishery in Newfoundland had been largely ignored for centuries, and while Ottawa must share responsibility for what happened after 1949, especially in managing the fish stocks and for much of the over fishing by foreign ships, it cannot be blamed for the problems it inherited at union.

Premier Smallwood was correct when he said in 1951 that 'what we have to overcome today is the accumulated neglect and short-sightedness of the past half-century in our fisheries.' The years of neglect prior to 1949 could not be remedied easily or quickly. Although a strategy for development was devised, the federal government refused to venture outside normal government services to rehabilitate the industry. Nor was it able to administer the medicine that might have put the fishery on the road to recovery. It lacked the political will to implement the Walsh recommendations, and it was limited in its actions by political considerations in the Maritime Provinces. Moreover, Smallwood showed little interest in the fisheries until the early 1960s when he realized the futility of his other development schemes. The structural problems cut so deeply that a massive infusion of funds was required and not the timid approach finally adopted by the federal government. If Ottawa had followed the Walsh report and accepted the views expressed by its own Department of Fisheries and by St. John's, the fishery would have been concentrated in several areas around the province which would have meant relocating people and taking many fishermen out of the industry. There is no evidence that Ottawa sought other plans to reform the fishery. Massive unemployment would inevitably have resulted if a large number of fishermen had been forced out of the industry to create an elite body of fishermen to operate modern and efficient boats to supply the needs of mechanized salt and fresh fish processors. Other opportunities for working did not exist in Newfoundland. In other words, the federal government was hampered by the same humanitarian and social concerns that it hoped to rectify. The number of fishermen had to be drastically reduced if the fishery was to be improved and this would create the additional problem of massive unemployment.[134] Ottawa came to realize also that fishing in Newfoundland was more than a means of livelihood. It was a way of life that could not be changed overnight.[135] In the end, the federal policy amounted to little more than a subsidy to increase the incomes of fishermen. This was a far cry from what was needed.

The Canadian approach to the fishery demonstrates clearly that while Newfoundland made major gains in social welfare after confederation, the new province received little assistance in developing its economy. Ottawa avoided bold economic action in Newfoundland. And even if the federal government had possessed the political will to invest vast quantities of public money into the fishery, it is quite conceivable that the outcome in Newfoundland would not have been very much different and the frozen fish trade would still have largely supplanted the traditional saltfish industry. The fate of the inshore salt fishery, carried out as it was at the time of union, was already sealed and, *ipso facto*, it would have declined in the social reformation of the 1950s. Perhaps the best Ottawa could do was to treat the symptoms and ignore the cause of the ailment. In practice, that is precisely what it did.

NOTES

1   Statistics for the fisheries are not easy to find. Here, I have relied on the Government of Canada, Dept. of Fisheries, *Annual Reports;* Government of Canada, Dept. of Fisheries, *Trade News*, 1, no. 10 (1949); *Historical Statistics of Newfoundland* (St. John's 1970); and Atlantic Provinces Economic Council, *Atlantic Provinces Statistical Review* (Halifax 1970).

2   United Kingdom, Parliamentary Papers, Cmd. 4480, 1933, *Newfoundland Royal Commission 1933: Report.*

3   Centre for Newfoundland Studies (CNS), Queen Elizabeth II Library, Memorial University, St. John's, P.D.H. Dunn, 'Fisheries Re-Organization in Newfoundland,' radio address, 21 Jan. 1944.

4   See Newfoundland Fisheries Board *Report of the Fisheries Post-War Planning Committee,* (St. John's, 1944).

5   Dept. of History, Memorial University, St. John's, James Hiller and Michael Harrington (eds.), 'Report of the Fisheries Committee of the National Convention,' unpublished proceedings and reports of the National Convention, 1990.

6   See Harold Innis, *The Cod Fisheries: The History of an International Economy* (Toronto 1954), especially 418-43.

7   See Government of Newfoundland, *Report of the Commission of Enquiry Investigating the Seafisheries of Newfoundland other than the Sealfishery* (St. John's 1937).

8   See David Alexander, *The Decay of Trade: An Economic History of the Newfoundland Saltfish Trade, 1935-1965* (St. John's 1977) and Peter Neary, *Newfoundland in the North Atlantic World, 1929-1949* (Kingston and Montreal 1988).

9   See Alexander, *The Decay of Trade.* For fishery policy under the Commission of Government, see Neary, *Newfoundland in the North Atlantic World* and Peter R. Sinclair, *State Intervention and the Newfoundland Fisheries: Essays on Fisheries Policy and Social Structure* (Aldershot 1987), 22-35.

10 For an alternate view see Alexander, *The Decay of Trade,* 16. He argued that low productivity of fishermen 'was a response to inadequate markets and few employment opportunities. If market development had been more satisfactory, there would have been an expansion of productive investment from private rather than public sources, generating higher labour and capital productivity and higher incomes, without any real or disguised reduction in the size of the fishing labour force.' When the export value of fish nearly tripled between 1939 and 1948, however, there was no appreciable increase in capital in the producing sector.

11 H.B. Mayo, 'The Economic Problems of the Newfoundland Fisheries,' *Canadian Journal of Economic and Political Science* 17, no.4 (1951): 488-90.

12 See ibid., 482-93.

13 See Provincial Archives of Newfoundland and Labrador (PANL), P4/36 (Sir Albert Walsh papers), box 2, 'Submissions by various organizations and institutions to the Newfoundland delegation, July-Sept. 1948.'

14 Ibid., box 1, file 5, 'Memorandum Submitted by Newfoundland delegation to Ottawa,' Oct. 1948, 5-6. By 1948, most of the Canadian saltfish was marketed in the Caribbean and South America.

15   Paul Bridle (ed.), *Documents on Relations Between Canada and Newfoundland*, vol. 2, pt. 2 (Ottawa 1984), 1106-10.

16   National Archives of Canada (NAC), RG 23 (Records of the Dept. of Fisheries and Oceans), vol. 1739, file 794-7-4 [1], Clutterbuck to Clark, 30 Nov. 1948.

17   PANL, GN 10, box 2, file 20, Laws to Macdonald, 2 Aug. 1948; and NAFEL 'Memorandum on Salt Fish Marketing for Consideration of Newfoundland Delegation to Ottawa,' 21 Sept. 1948. All subsequent GN (Government of Newfoundland) references are to documents in this archive.

18   Ibid., box 2, file 20, 'Notes prepared by the Newfoundland Fisheries Board [Raymond Gushue] for Consideration in Discussions of Fishery Matters between Canada and Newfoundland, Memorandum No. 1,' 1 Sept. 1948.

19   Ibid., Newfoundland Board of Trade to Walsh, 13 Aug. and 17 Sept. 1948. See also P4/36, especially boxes 3 and 4.

20   RG 23, vol. 1132, file 721-54-4 [8], 'Memorandum to the Cabinet on Points Likely to be raised by Newfoundland Delegation,' 25 Sept. 1948; Bridle, *Documents*, 1066-71.

21   RG 23, vol. 1132, file 721-54-4 [8], 'Memorandum to the Cabinet on Points Likely to be raised by Newfoundland Delegation,' 25 Sept. 1948.

22   Bridle, *Documents*, 1171-2, 1195.

23   *Daily News* (St. John's), 1 Dec. 1948.

24   Government of Canada, Dept. of External Affairs, *Reports and Documents Relating to the Negotiations for the Union of Newfoundland with Canada* (Ottawa 1949), 18-19. Eleven fisheries items were included in 'Statements on Questions Raised by the Newfoundland Delegation,' including reference to market representatives of NAFEL and the Newfoundland Bait Service (see 36-8).

25   GN 31, file 830, vol. 2, Bates to Gushue, 2 April 1949. See also RG 23, vol. 63, file 710-202-3, pt. 1, 'Minutes of Meeting of the Newfoundland Fisheries Board,' 11 April 1949; *Evening Telegram* (St. John's), 2 June 1949; *Reports and Documents Relating to the Negotiations for the Union of Newfoundland with Canada*.

26   *Trade News* 10, no. 11 (1958). The Fisheries Act was a comprehensive document that outlined the powers of the minister and fishery officers. It provided for the conservation and protection of various species of fish and gave authority for fisheries regulations. It also dealt with the pollution and obstruction of streams, and the licensing of vessels and fishermen.

27   NAC, RG 2 (Records of the Privy Council Office), vol. 125, file D-14, 'Dept of Fisheries, 1949,' 'Memorandum to Cabinet on Fisheries Development,' by R.W. Mayhew, 12 Oct. 1949; RG 23, vol. 541, file 711-25-36 [2], 'Statement to the House of Commons' by Mayhew, 6 Dec. 1949.

28   The Price Support Board was established in July 1947 under the direction of the Minister of Fisheries. It was part of Ottawa's plan to promote orderly adjustment in the fishery from wartime to peacetime conditions and to ensure an adequate return from the fishery compared with other occupations. The Board was authorized to purchase fish or to pay fishermen the difference between a price set by the Board and that which the industry paid them (see Dominion Bureau of Statistics, *The Canada Year Book 1950* (Ottawa 1950), 493-4).

29   GN 34, file 11/4, vol. 2; RG 23, vol. 541, 711-25-36 (1), 'Background Notes to
     Minister of Fisheries' Statement on Developmental Programme,' 6 May 1949,
     and 'Memorandum as to a Programme for the Development of the Fisheries,'
     May 1949.

30   RG 23, vol. 125, file D-14, 'Memo to Cabinet on Fisheries Development' by
     Mayhew, 12 Oct. 1949; vol. 541, file 711-25-36 [2], 'Statement to House of
     Commons on Government Programme for Fisheries Development' by May-
     hew, 6 Dec. 1949.

31   See Sinclair, *State Intervention*. The number of fishermen declined from 25,220
     in 1939 to 17,645 in 1942 but rose again to 28,000 by 1948.

32   Centre for Newfoundland Studies Archives, Queen Elizabeth II Library,
     Memorial University, St. John's, J.R. Smallwood Collection, COLL-75,
     3.06.042.

33   GN 34, file 96/1, 'Federal Government Assistance to the Fishing Industry in
     Various Provinces,' memo unsigned and undated; COLL-75, 3.12.046, Small-
     wood to Dunstan, 26 July 1951.

34   In *Newfoundland in the North Atlantic World*, 357, Neary suggests that the
     mould for the development of the fishery was cast in the early 1940s.

35   PANL, P8/B/11 (Records of the Newfoundland Board of Trade), box 51, file
     4, Newfoundland Fisheries Board, 'Review of the Newfoundland Fisheries
     for 1949,' 15 Dec. 1949.

36   GN 1, file 140/39, Gushue to Bates, 25 June 1949. See also Sinclair, *State
     Intervention*, 42-4.

37   See Government of Canada, Dept. of Fisheries, *Annual Reports* of the Fisheries
     Prices Support Board, 1949-55. For a fuller discussion of the problems with
     the marketing of salt cod after 1949 see Raymond Blake, 'The Making of a
     Province: The Integration of Newfoundland into Confederation, 1948-57'
     (unpublished PH D thesis, York University 1991).

38   F.G. Bradley papers (in possession of family), 'Radio Broadcasts, 1949-53,' 27
     Oct. 1951.

39   RG 23, vol. 1740, file 794-7-4 [5], Mayhew, 'Statement in House of Commons,'
     17 May 1951; Abbott to Clutterbuck, 4 May 1951. See also RG 2, vol. 195, file
     T-50-9, vol. 1, 'Cabinet Memorandum Prepared by R.W. Mayhew on Price
     Support Policy for Fisheries - 1951 Production Season,' 14 May 1951.

40   RG 23, vol. 1740, file 794-7-4 [7], Secretary of the Inter-departmental Fisheries
     Trade Committee to Lewis, 4 Jan. 1952; COLL-75, 3.12.073, Smallwood to
     Grouchy, 23 June 1951; to Bowater's Newfoundland Ltd., 23 June 1951; to
     Howe, 16 July 1951; NAC, MG 26 L (Louis St. Laurent papers), vol. 225, file
     F-11, 'Summary on Canadian Fisheries Markets,' n.d.

41   RG 23, vol. 1740, file 794-7-4 [2], Bates, 'Minute for File: Re: Newfoundland
     Salt Fish Situation,' 22 April 1950; RG 2, vol. 195, file T-50-9, vol. 1., Bates to
     Robertson, 26 April 1950. Also included was a statement dealing with the
     saltfish situation in Newfoundland, and Canada's desire to adopt a long-term
     strategy for the industry.

42   RG 2, vol. 1654, file 20-191, pt. 1, Cabinet Conclusions, 18 April 1950; RG 23,
     vol. 1740, file 794-7-4 [2], 'Minute for file,' 22 April 1950.

43   RG 2, vol. 195, T-50-9, vol. 1, Bates to Robertson, 20 March 1950; RG 23, vol.
     1740, file 794-7-4 [2], Robertson to Mayhew, 3 April 1950.

44 *Evening Telegram*, 6 May 1950; RG 2, vol. 195, file T-50-9, vol. 1, James to Robertson, 29 May 1950.

45 NAC, MG 32 B34 (J.W. Pickersgill papers), Newfoundland Series, box 2, file N1-29, W.C. MacKenzie, 'Fish Marketing Part 1, Memorandum on Newfoundland Fisheries,' 14 July 1953.

46 RG 23, vol. 1748, file 784-17-1 [1], 'Joint Announcement by Premier J.R. Smallwood and Honourable R.W. Mayhew, Re: Fisheries Development in Newfoundland,' 27 Jan. 1951; GN 81, file 27/1, 'Fishery Conference,' Scott to Keough, 10 July 1950.

47 GN 34, file 27/1, 'Fishery Conference,' 'A Development Program for the Fisheries of the Atlantic Coast Provinces,' memo attached to Bates to Scott, 7 June 1950.

48 Ibid.

49 See Robert Bothwell, Ian Drummond, and John English, *Canada Since 1945: Power, Politics, and Provincialism* (Toronto 1989), 165. For a different view, see Ernest R. Forbes, 'Consolidating Disparity: The Maritimes and the Industrialization of Canada During the Second World War,' *Acadiensis* 15, no. 2 (1986): 3-27.

50 MG 32 B34, Newfoundland Series, box 2, file N1-28, 'Memorandum of Inter-Departmental Committee, Re Walsh Report of Newfoundland Development,' 9 May 1951.

51 Report of the Newfoundland Fisheries Development Committee, St. John's, 1953, 102. This was commonly referred to as the Walsh report.

52 GN 34, file 8/45/9, 'Proposals by C. Planta and C.M. Lane for Alternate Market Set-up to NAFEL,' Nov. 1952. See also Innis, *The Cod Fisheries* and the Walsh report, 13.

53 On this point, see S.J.R. Noel, *Politics in Newfoundland* (Toronto 1971), 262-4.

54 Province of Newfoundland, *Budget Speech*, delivered by Gregory J. Power, 29 April 1953. In 1951, the growing independence of fishermen was discernible but Raymond Gushue described it as a 'we won't fish unless...attitude.' He blamed the change on the 'vote-catching propaganda of the past several years,' particularly on Smallwood whom he regarded as a propagandist by nature (RG 23, vol. 1748, file 794-17-1 [1], Gushue to Mayhew, 14 May 1951).

55 See *Evening Telegram*, 10 Aug., 15 Oct. 1949, 28 Feb. 1950, 1 May 1951. The *Evening Telegram* reported on 10 Aug. 1949 that 'daily in the House of Assembly the electorate in Newfoundland are voicing their demands for roads.' That day alone, one member presented petitions from five communities.

56 Province of Newfoundland, *Budget Speech*, 29 April 1953; RG 23, vol. 1748, file 794-17-1 [1], Gushue to Mayhew, 14 May 1951. See also J.R. Smallwood, *I Chose Canada: The Memoirs of the Honourable Joseph R. 'Joey' Smallwood* (Toronto 1973), 370-2.

57 The bank fishery was carried on in large vessels or schooners. Each vessel carried a number of dories, small flat-bottom boats, which fished near the schooner (see Raoul Andersen, 'Usufruct and Contradiction: Territorial Custom and Abuse in Newfoundland's Banks Schooner and Dory Fishery,' *MAST: Maritime Anthropological Studies* 1, no. 2 (1988): 81-102).

58   The fresh frozen industry in Newfoundland received an impetus from the demand for food during the Second World War. See J.R. Smallwood (ed.), *Encyclopedia of Newfoundland and Labrador*, vol. 2 (St. John's 1984), 159-60 and R.A. MacKay (ed.), *Newfoundland: Economic, Diplomatic, and Strategic Studies* (Toronto 1946), 92-6.

59   Raymond Gushue, 'Newfoundland Fisheries in 1951,' in *Newfoundland Journal of Commerce* 19, no. 1 (1952): 55; Government of Canada, Dept. of Fisheries, *Annual Reports*, 1950-1 and 1951-2.

60   Bradley papers, 'Hazen Russell Correspondence, 1949-52,' Bradley to Russell, 14 Sept. 1951.

61   Ibid., 'Radio Broadcasts 1949-53,' 'Radio Broadcast,' 27 Oct. 1951.

62   RG 23, vol. 1749, file 794-17-1, [3], 'Speech made by William Keough over Radio Station CJON,' 12 Jan. 1952. Keough also said that 'this would seem to shed some light on why salt fish export merchants have never built up central splitting, salting and curing stations to make light-salted or shore fish.'

63   CNS, J.W. Pickersgill, *Report from Parliament Hill*, 23 Jan. 1954.

64   Walsh report, various references.

65   MG 32 B34, Newfoundland Series, box 2, file N1-28, 'Fisheries Development, Memorandum of Inter-Departmental Committee, Re Walsh Report on Newfoundland Development,' 9 May 1953.

66   COLL-75, 7.02.006, 'Radio Broadcast' by Smallwood, 16 July 1953. On the relationship between Pickersgill and Smallwood, see Smallwood, *I Chose Canada*; Richard Gwyn, *Smallwood: The Unlikely Revolutionary*, rev. ed. (Toronto 1972); and J.W. Pickersgill, *My Years With Louis St. Laurent: A Political Memoir* (Toronto 1975).

67   Pickersgill was largely responsible for changes in the Unemployment Insurance Act that allowed fishermen to receive benefits in 1957 (see his *My Years With Louis St. Laurent*, 227-9).

68   MG 32 B34, Newfoundland Series, box 2, file N1-28, 'Fisheries Development, Memorandum of Inter-Departmental Committee, Re Walsh Report on Newfoundland Development,' 9 May 1953.

69   RG 23, vol. 1749, file 794-17-1 [6], 'Memorandum to Cabinet by Robert H. Winter, Re: Report of the Newfoundland Fisheries Development Committee,' 15 May 1953.

70   Ibid., vol. 1750, file 794-17-1 [7], 'Memorandum to Cabinet, Re: Newfoundland Fisheries Development,' 8 Sept. 1953. This was the report of the party of senior officials.

71   COLL-75, 3.12.040, Smallwood to Monroe, 25 March 1953.

72   Ibid., 7.02.005, speech file, 1952.

73   GN 23, file 11/4/5, 'Notes on Discussion between Sinclair, Keough and Bates, Memorandum to Executive Council, Subject: Submission of Memorandum Received from Fisheries Development Committee,' 17 Dec. 1952.

74   RG 23, vol. 1750, file 794-17-1 [8], 'Memorandum on Newfoundland Fisheries Development Programme,' n.d. but obviously late Dec. 1953.

75   RG 2, vol. 237, file T-50-11-N, Mayhew to St. Laurent, 29 May 1952.

76   Ibid., Cabinet Conclusions, 8 May 1952.

77   Ibid., vol. 237, file T-50-11-N, Mayhew, 'Memorandum to Cabinet Re: Newfoundland Fisheries Development,' 7 May 1952; Bradley papers, 'Newfound-

land Fisheries Development Committee, Consideration of Proposals of New-foundland.'

78 RG 23, vol. 1750, file 794-17-1 [8], 'Memorandum on Newfoundland Fisheries Development Programme.'

79 See Walsh report, 116-21.

80 GN 34, file 11/4/5, 'Notes on Discussion between Sinclair, Keough and Bates, Memorandum to Executive Council, Subject: Submission of Memorandum Received from Fisheries Development Committee,' 17 Dec. 1952.

81 RG 2, vol. 237, file T-50-11-N, Mayhew to St. Laurent, 29 May 1952.

82 MG 32 B34, Newfoundland Series, box 2, file N1-28, 'Fisheries Development, Memorandum of Inter-Departmental Committee, Re Walsh Report on New-foundland Development,' 9 May 1953.

83 Alexander, *The Decay of Trade*, 139-40, and J.R. Smallwood, *The Time Has Come to Tell* (St. John's 1980), 72-3. See also Vince Walsh, 'Stagnant Capital and Mobile People,' in Rex Clark (ed.), *Contrary Winds: Essays on Newfoundland Society in Crisis* (St. John's 1986), 21-3.

84 Province of Newfoundland, *Budget Speech*, 9 May 1951.

85 See Government of Canada, Dept. of Fisheries, *Annual Reports*, 1956-60.

86 COLL-75, 3.12.023, Smallwood speech, 'Fisheries Development Authority Legislation,' 1953. In his 1954 *Budget Speech*, Gregory J. Power, Minister of Finance, said that during 1953 the plant to which the government had loaned $7 million employed 3,000 workers and paid $6.25 million in wages.

87 For Smallwood's industrial development policy see Gwyn, *Smallwood*; Harold Horwood *Joey* (Toronto 1989); Gerhard Bassler, 'Develop or Perish: Jospeh R. Smallwood and Newfoundland's Quest for German Industry, 1949-53,' *Acadiensis* 15, no. 2 (1986): 93-119.

88 RG 23, vol. 1748, file 794-17-1 [17], Gushue to Mayhew, 5 May 1951.

89 Ibid., file 794-17-1 [1], Bates to Gushue, 3 July 1951.

90 On the relationship between Smallwood and Bradley see James Hiller, 'The Career of F. Gordon Bradley,' *Newfoundland Studies* 4, no. 2 (1988): 163-80.

91 Bradley papers, 'George Sellars, Correspondence 1952-53,' Bradley to Sellars, 3 April 1952. After all, Bradley wrote, 'Smallwood himself was a man of no experience. He had been a doctrinaire socialist with a hobby for publicity and a desire to get into public life' (Bradley to Sellars, 11 Feb. 1952).

92 COLL-75, 3.10.024, Bradley to Smallwood, 7 Oct. 1949.

93 Bradley papers, 'Hazen Russell (Job Brothers & Company Ltd.) Correspon-dence,' Bradley to Russell, 8 May 1952. W.C. MacKenzie who served for a time as Ottawa's representative on the committee denies that Planta had such control (interview with MacKenzie, Feb. 1990).

94 Ibid., 'George Sellars, Correspondence 1952-53,' Bradley to Sellars, 11 Feb. 1952. On the career of Valdmanis, see Gwyn, *Smallwood*, 140-69 and Horwood, *Joey*, 170.

95 See Blake, 'The Making of a Province,' ch. 3.

96 Bradley later said that the property was valued at $200,000 within a few months.

97 COLL-75, 3.10.024, Bradley to Smallwood, 7 Oct. 1949.

98 Ibid., Bradley to Smallwood, 29 March 1950.

99 Because Ottawa had control over support payments for a sudden drop in prices, there was little Smallwood could do to correct the situation without the aid of the federal government. His rationale for the inquiry can be found in a letter to Bradley in early 1951: 'Our fishermen generally are in a poor mood. They feel, or had begun to feel, that the Liberal Party and Governments had abandoned them to the tender mercies of the merchants. Our appointment of Clive Planta as Deputy Minister of Fisheries, the joint appointment of the new Fisheries Development Committee, the fisheries price investigation by the Federal Government and the fish prices and fish profits investigation by the Provincial Government, together with this drive initiated by us to organize the fishermen—all these should go far to show the fishermen that they have not become the "forgotten men" of liberalism' (ibid., Smallwood to Bradley, 24 Feb. 1951).

100 Ibid., Bradley to Smallwood, 20 Feb. 1951.

101 Bradley papers, 'George Sellars, Correspondence 1952-53,' Bradley to Sellars, 13 March 1952.

102 Interviews with R.B. Bryce, 14 Feb. 1990, and Mitchell Sharp, 12 Feb. 1990.

103 MG 32 B34, Newfoundland Series, box 2, file N1-29, Clark, to Maloney, 15 July 1953. MacKenzie's memorandum was also included.

104 Ibid., file N1-29, Bates to Pickersgill, 7 Oct. 1953.

105 Ibid., file N1-28, Granger to Pickersgill, 16 Sept. 1953, and McArthur to Lane, 21 Oct. 1953. See also RG 2, Cabinet Conclusions, 12 June 1953. St. Laurent wrote President Dwight Eisenhower expressing his disappointment about threats of American countervailing duties on Canadian groundfish and oats. For a discussion of US demands for higher tariffs against Canadian fish, see Margaret E. Dewar, *Industry in Trouble: The Federal Government and the New England Fisheries* (Philadelphia 1983), especially 43-76.

106 MG 32 B34, Newfoundland Series, box 2, file N1-28, Granger to Pickersgill, 16 Sept. 1953; McArthur to Lane, 21 Oct. 1953.

107 COLL-75, 3.12.011, Planta to Smallwood, 28, 29 Sept. 1953.

108 Ibid., Smallwood press release, 1 Oct. 1953.

109 RG 23, vol. 1740, file 794-7-4 [7], McArthur to Bates, 27 Feb. 1952.

110 Ibid., vol. 1133, file 721-54-16 [1], Bates, 'Memorandum, Re: NAFEL,' 26 March 1953.

111 Salt bulk is heavily salted fish that has not been dried. During the 1940s several Nova Scotia firms had installed mechanical dryers, but as fishermen started to sell their catch fresh, the source of supply for the dryers was cut off. Then, Nova Scotia looked to Newfoundland for its supplies of salted fish.

112 RG 23, vol. 1133, file 721-54-16 [1], Sinclair to Crosbie, 27 March 1953.

113 GN 34, file 8/45/7, 'Discussions in Ottawa, 5 March 1954, to Decide Alternative System of Marketing Salt Codfish, News Release, Department of Fisheries,' 22 March 1954.

114 RG 23, vol. 1133, file 721-54-16 [3], Howe to Crosbie, 11 May 1954.

115 J.W. Pickersgill maintains that Ottawa did this to placate Smallwood who, Pickersgill says, could not agree with James Sinclair on anything (interview with J.W. Pickersgill, 11 Feb. 1989).

116 MG 32, B34, Newfoundland Series, box 7, file N1-161-1, Pickersgill to Smallwood, 3 April 1954.

117 COLL-75, file 3.10.028, Howe to Smallwood, 7 April 1954; Smallwood to Howe, 20 April 1954.

118 Alexander claims that the Department of Trade and Commerce was interested in helping NAFEL, but it was inexperienced in the overseas saltfish trade (see *The Decay of Trade*, 132).

119 RG 2, vol. 195, file T-50-9, vol. 1 (Trade, Commerce, Industry), 'Draft Statement for the Minister of Fisheries,' June 1950.

120 Ibid., Cabinet Conclusion, 12 May 1955.

121 COLL-75, 3.12.002, Plant to Smallwood, 21 April, 3 July 1954.

122 Ibid., 3.06.016, Smallwood to Honderich, 5 July 1955.

123 Government of Canada, Royal Commission on Canada's Economic Prospects, 'Hearings,' St. John's, 18 Oct. 1955, 50-60; Alexander, *The Decay of Trade*, 159-60.

124 Frederick W. Rowe, *The Smallwood Era* (Toronto 1985), 42.

125 RG 23, vol. 1750, file 794-17-1 [1], 'Report of the Working Party on Newfoundland Fisheries Development,' 7 Jan. 1958.

126 A similar work ethic was discernible in the forest industry. When H.M.S. Lewin, the manager of the Bowater's pulp and paper mill in Corner Brook, appeared before the Gordon Commission he complained that the average man came to work for not more than 50 days at a time. As soon as he had earned enough money to keep him going for a while, he left only to return when it ran out (Royal Commission on Canada's Economic Prospects, 'Hearings,' St. John's, 18 Oct. 1955).

127 Shortly before his early death, David Alexander had turned to the subject of illiteracy in the Newfoundland workforce and the relationship between educational levels and economic development. Though his conclusion was tentative, he wrote that 'it is difficult to see how the country could rise to meet its opportunities and challenges when its educated population was so small...It is difficult to believe that this deficiency did not impose heavy costs upon the country in limiting its capacity to adapt, innovate, and face the external world with pride and self-confidence' (David Alexander, *Atlantic Canada and Confederation: Essays in Canadian Political Economy*, Eric Sager et al., comps. (Toronto 1983) 136-7. Even today Newfoundland would benefit from a programme of adult education.

128 Government of Newfoundland, Newfoundland Fisheries Development Authority, *Annual Report* (St. John's 1960).

129 Maritime History Archive, Memorial University, St. John's, John T. Cheeseman Collection, 31-D-4-33, Sinclair to Cheeseman, 15 March 1956.

130 RG 20 (Records of the Dept. of Trade and Commerce), vol. 1962, file 20-191-4, pt. 1, J.N. Lewis, 'Memorandum on Newfoundland and the Salted Fish Industry,' 26 June 1958.

131 Ibid.

132 See *Globe and Mail* (Toronto), 9 Nov. 1990. The Federal Fisheries Minister, Bernard Valcourt, announced a $10 million aid package for fishermen. The money was designed for community development projects that would allow fishermen to qualify for unemployment insurance benefits.

133 See Alexander, *The Decay of Trade*, 1-19, 158-65.

134   It is worth pointing out that between 1951 and 1961 the number of loggers in Newfoundland decreased by nearly 40 per cent, but individual productivity increased over 30 per cent. Between 1954 and 1963 the number of inshore fishermen increased by 25 per cent but their share of landed fish dropped from 78 to 75 per cent (see R.I. McAllister (ed.), *Newfoundland and Labrador: The First Fifteen Years of Confederation* (St. John's 1964), 99-101, 123-5).

135   See A. Paul Pross and Susan McCorquodale, *Economic Resurgence and The Constitutional Agenda: The Case of the East Coast Fisheries* (Kingston 1987), 20-1.

The Interplay of Private and Public Enterprise in the Production of Electricity on the Island of Newfoundland, 1883-1966

Melvin Baker

ECONOMIC DEVELOPMENT IN twentieth-century Newfoundland has been wedded to efforts at harnessing the island's water-power resources. In his 1931 book *The New Newfoundland* Joseph R. Smallwood, a future premier of Newfoundland, confidently predicted that 'the future possibilities of hydro-electric development in Newfoundland' were 'great.' Newfoundland, he wrote, was 'out for industrialization' and wouldn't be happy until she got it.[1] Water-power resources, the St. John's *Evening Telegram* commented in 1930, must be developed by capitalists with government driving 'a hard bargain, such a bargain as we would insist upon if a rich gold field were the subject of negotiations.'[2] The notion of hydroelectric development as an economic panacea for the island of Newfoundland (Labrador is a separate story and will not be dealt with here) is perhaps best exemplified in the journalistic and political career of Smallwood. He was born in 1900 and became one of Newfoundland's most colourful and controversial public figures.[3] During the 1949 provincial election campaign, in the early days of a premiership that would last until 1972, Smallwood promised voters that his government, if successful at the polls, would push forward the development of water-power resources. He explained his purpose as follows:

> cheap power is the foundation of industry. Grand Falls and Corner Brook would never have amounted to anything without lots of cheap power. Newfoundland has been blessed with great water-power. Most of it is running to waste. The Liberal Party will develop it...[There] will be...lots of cheap power for Newfoundland's present and new industries to-be, and to light homes and provide power throughout the country. This plentiful supply of cheap electric power is a basic condition in the development of this country. We can never grow industrially without it.[4]

Before this time hydroelectric development in Newfoundland had been carried out exclusively by private companies and had two distinct categories of enterprise. First, there were small hydro projects; these dated from 1900 and were found close to large communities on the Avalon, Bonavista and Burin Peninsulas. The generating capacity of the small projects was usually between 3,000 and 5,000 horsepower of installed capacity. Then there were the large-scale hydro developments, situated in the central and western sections of the island, and built in the early twentieth century to serve the specific industrial needs of pulp and paper mills at Grand Falls and Corner Brook. All these systems, large and small, were far from one other, and when Newfoundland became a province of Canada in 1949, there was as yet no island wide transmission system. The absence of such a system had been a serious impediment to the industrial and social development of Newfoundland in the first half of the twentieth century and one of the principal challenges facing the Smallwood government was to overcome this obstacle to progress.

Smallwood and his ministers also faced another problem which had long bedevilled the private utilities in Newfoundland: this was how to get power into the many small communities scattered around the coastline of the island. In keeping with the needs of its fishing economy, Newfoundland's pattern of settlement had resulted in a widely dispersed population. Thus, outports had been established in the remotest harbours and on the most distant reaches of peninsulas and headlands jutting far into the Atlantic. Geography had always presented a formidable obstacle to the provision of services in Newfoundland and the provision of electricity was no exception. When Newfoundland joined Canada only 50.4 per cent of households had electrical service. After 1949, the people of the new Canadian province expected their government to provide that service as soon as possible. For Smallwood this meant a judicious balancing of private and public elements. In order to complete the system public enterprise would build upon what private enterprise had already achieved.

Private power development in Newfoundland before 1949

Electrical power was introduced into Newfoundland in 1883 when St. John's businessman Moses Monroe installed a small electric plant in a cordage factory he had recently constructed on the outskirts of the capital.[5] Two years later Monroe brought the boon of electricity to St. John's by starting a small station using imported coal to generate electricity. The power thus generated was used to light the city's streets, major public buildings and a limited number of private houses. Electricity was first produced from water-power in 1898 when the St. John's firm of Harvey and Company started Newfoundland's first pulp mill at Black River, Placentia Bay. This mill, however, closed after a few years apparently because of water shortage. In 1900 the Reid Newfoundland Company began an electric street car service in St. John' using power generated at a hydroelectric station at Petty Harbour, a small fishing community eight miles south of St. John's. This station had a capacity of 1,868 horsepower and also provided power to other Reid enterprises: these included the St. John's dry dock and various machine shops associated with the Reid Newfoundland Company's operation of the Newfoundland railway. By 1920, despite improvements to increase its generating capacity, the Petty Harbour plant could not meet the growing power demands of city industry. Nor was Reid Newfoundland financially able to develop additional water-power sites. Finally, in 1923 the Reid family sold the railway to the government and the city electrical and street car operations to Royal Securities Corporation of Montreal. The latter company was controlled by the financier Isaak Killam.

In 1924 Killam and Royal Securities reorganized the St. John's utility as the Newfoundland Light and Power Company Limited (NLP). This enterprise in turn depended for managerial and engineering expertise on Montreal Engineering Company, a management and consulting firm also owned by Royal Securities. After 1926 NLP became part of International Power Company, a holding company Killam formed in that year to manage his non-Canadian utilities. Killam's primary interest in Newfoundland was to sell power to the large iron ore mines on Bell Island, which had been opened in the mid-1890s by Nova Scotia businessmen. The iron ore mines quickly became the utility's major industrial customer. Between 1924 and 1939 NLP made substantial improvements to the Petty Harbour station and constructed a new power station at Pierre's Brook (eighteen miles south of Petty Harbour) to meet the increased power requirements of both the iron ore mines and of the St. John's area in general. During World War II several new hydro stations were constructed south of Petty Harbour to keep up with the demand created by the building of Canadian and American military bases in the St. John's area. In 1948 NLP gave up the street car services, having arranged with the St. John's Municipal Council for a Canadian transportation company to operate a bus service on city streets, where the street cars had previously had a monopoly.[6]

In 1949 Killam divested himself of exclusive ownership of NLP. In that year the company's outstanding 24,000 shares of common stock, valued at $100 per share, were converted to 12,000 shares of preferred stock, valued at $100 per share, and 120,000 shares of common stock, valued at $10 per share. By July 1949 there were 1,600 shareholders of common stock. Killam remained a company director until his death in 1955 by virtue of his continuing financial interest in Royal Securities, now a minority shareholder in the Newfoundland utility.[7]

NLP was not the only power utility to be established on the Avalon Peninsula in the first half of the century. In 1902 businessmen in the Conception Bay towns of Carbonear, Harbour Grace and Heart's Content formed the United Towns Electrical Company (from 1921 the United Towns Electric Company) to provide domestic lighting and industrial power to their towns. By 1919 United Towns Electrical served an area with a total population of approximately 30,000 residents. It supplied power to more than twenty factories employing over 500 men and women in industries as diverse as barrel making, shipbuilding, butterine manufacturing, and the production of woollen goods and boots and shoes. Many of these factories existed simply because of the power available from United Towns Electrical. The driving entrepreneurial forces behind the company in 1919 were John Joseph Murphy, aged seventy, and his twenty-eight year old son, Robert. In 1876 John Murphy had founded one of Newfoundland's first lumbering operations, which he sold in 1904 to a business consortium consisting of Harry Crowe (a Nova Scotia timber speculator), William D. Reid (of Reid Newfoundland) and Henry Whitney (an American capitalist with utility and mineral interests in Nova Scotia). Murphy invested part of the money from the sale in an electrical utility at Sydney Mines, Cape Breton, and part of it in United Towns Electrical. In 1904 he was its largest shareholder. Murphy was the company's majority shareholder by 1914 and in 1915 he took over control of its management when he was appointed president and his son managing director. In 1919 they also established the Avalon Telephone Company to provide an improved telephone service in the area of St. John's. In the same year they purchased the St. John's assets of the Anglo-American Telegraph Company which operated a separate telephone service in the city.

The Murphys had expansionary plans for United Towns Electric and over the next decade added generating capacity to service more rural areas. They also considered entering the St. John's market to compete with Reid Newfoundland, but with the sale of the latter company's utility in 1924, United Towns Electric agreed to sell surplus power to NLP. The company's philosophy of growth, as Robert Murphy told another local businessman J.P. Powell in 1927, was 'not so much for the immediate returns which are hardly adequate to justify...expansion but to be prepared to meet demands for power supply' from new industrial developments.[8]

In 1929 United Towns Electric expanded service to the Burin Peninsula and in the early 1930s it was able to provide power to a fluorspar mine, recently opened at St. Lawrence by American financial interests. Two years later the Murphy enterprise purchased another small utility, Wabana Light and Power Company, which provided electricity to residents of Bell Island living outside the service area of the mining company. The latter company was now generating electricity of its own both for industrial and domestic use. In 1931 Wabana Light and Power provided service to over 300 customers with power purchased from the iron ore mining company.[9] In 1931 United Towns took over the Public Service Electric Company, which had been supplying power since 1919 to Heart's Content, Trinity Bay, and to the

Conception Bay centres of Carbonear and Harbour Grace. This company's power came from a 2,000 horsepower hydroelectric plant at Heart's Content. The company had never paid a dividend but had competed for customers with United Towns in the three towns it served.[10] In the 1940s United Towns expanded service to the west coast, through a subsidiary, West Coast Power, which sold power to Harmon Field, the American military base at Stephenville, and in the town of Port aux Basques. Power for Stephenville was generated at a nearby 3,850 horsepower hydroelectric station; in Port aux Basques West Coast Power installed several diesel units.

After United Towns, the next largest electrical utility formed before 1949 was the Union Electric Light and Power Company established in 1916 on the Bonavista Peninsula by William F. Coaker, the president of the Fishermen's Protective Union (FPU). Its purpose was to provide power to the model town the FPU had established at Port Union. A small, 400 horsepower, hydroelectric station was put in service in 1918 and subsequently provided power to several nearby communities. In 1945 the company increased its generating capacity by installing a 150 horsepower diesel caterpillar unit at its Port Union plant. This was to provide standby service in the event of a water shortage and to guarantee a twenty-four hour power supply to the large privately owned fish plant at Bonavista. Since Union Electric did not have sufficient funds for the diesel unit, the company's general manager, Aaron Bailey, and several associates guaranteed a bank loan of $15,000.[11]

In the early 1950s the utility had approximately 1,300 customers and an installed generating capacity of 1,250 horsepower. By contrast, NLP, the largest utility on the island had an installed capacity in 1949 of 21,350 horsepower.[12] This came from four plants.[13] In 1950, United Towns Electric, the next largest utility, had an installed capacity of 16,710 horsepower and eight small plants.

Until the 1960s a high percentage of Newfoundland's installed generating capacity was used by the two large pulp and paper mills located at Grand Falls and Corner Brook. The first, constructed by the Anglo-Newfoundland Development Company (AND), opened at Grand Falls in 1909. In 1914 the hydroelectric station at Grand Falls which provided power to this mill had a generating capacity of 25,000 horsepower. In 1916 AND purchased the paper mill and power station at nearby Bishop's Falls from the Albert E. Reed Company of Great Britain. The Reed power station at Bishop's Falls had been opened in 1911 with a generating capacity of 14,000 horsepower. Over the years AND increased this capacity so that by 1966 it was 21,900 horsepower; by the same year capacity at Grand Falls itself had been increased to 43,500 horsepower.[14] The AND company supplied domestic power to the four communities where it was the major employer: Grand Falls, Windsor, Bishop's Falls and Botwood.

The power station for the Corner Brook paper mill was located at Deer Lake, thirty-five miles to the north and went into service in 1925 with a generating capacity of 112,000 horsepower. It supplied domestic power to both Deer Lake and Corner Brook townsite, the planned settlement for the company's staff. In 1926 residents living outside the townsite formed the Bay of Islands Light and Power Company to supply power, purchased from the Deer Lake station, to those communities surrounding the townsite that did not have service.[15] The hydroelectric developments at Grand Falls, Bishop's Falls, and Deer Lake were for the exclusive use of the two paper companies and generally speaking no surplus electricity was made available for other industrial use.[16]

In search of the New Newfoundland, 1949-53

In the area of energy policy, Smallwood's ambition as premier was to break out of existing supply constraints, to promote new industrial development and simultaneously to bring electricity to remote parts of the province. Nor was the crusade for more electricity entirely his own; confederation triggered a revolution of rising expectations in Newfoundland and in 1957 Smallwood himself observed that the people were 'up in arms demanding hydro-electric development.'[17] In 1949 Smallwood told voters that he intended to establish a public utility commission along the lines of Ontario Hydro and to this end he was negotiating with Dr. Thomas Hogg who had been chairman of the huge Ontario enterprise from 1937 to 1947. The proposed Newfoundland commission, Smallwood announced, would control the generation and distribution of electricity in the province. The commission would issue its own bonds on the strength of the sale of the power it would develop.[18] For his part, although willing to provide advice, Thomas Hogg was not interested in becoming chief executive officer of the body Smallwood had in mind. In the event, Smallwood moved slowly, telling Hogg in 1952 that he had set his 'heart on getting you to organize and become head of a commission here.'[19] Smallwood did, however, quickly follow through on one election promise he made in his 1949 campaign. Once the election was over, the private utilities operating in the province were quickly brought under the regulatory control of a Board of Commissioners of Public Utilities. Henceforth rate increases would require the approval of this body.[20]

While thus regulating established investor owned utilities, Smallwood also looked to private capital to continue the development of water-power resources. His government advertised and promoted widely the province's hydroelectric potential and had its natural resources assessed by various experts. In 1949 Smallwood commissioned studies of several of the island's larger rivers by Power Corporation of Canada[21] and had its findings in hand when he called a surprise election in 1951. The surveys that had been done, Smallwood proclaimed on the hustings, showed that in the Bay d'Espoir area 'huge amounts of electric power' could 'be produced [at] very reason-able cost.'[22] He made similar claims for other regions of the island.

At this juncture Smallwood was pinning his industrial hopes on his recently acquired Director-General of Economic Development, Alfred Valdmanis, whom he had hired on the recommendation of federal officials. An energetic individual, Valdmanis had served as Minister of Finance, Trade and Commerce for the independent republic of Latvia. From October 1939 to June 1940 he had been in charge of his country's public electrification commission. Valdmanis had emigrated to Canada in 1948. He believed that the key to progress for Newfoundland lay in attracting German capital and expertise to the province. In practice, much of his effort came to focus on the development of the water-power potential in the region of the south-west coast.[23]

On Valdmanis' recommendation Smallwood turned down a 1950 re-quest from United Towns Electric for government backing of a $1 million bond issue to be used to develop a 5,000 horsepower site on the Burin Peninsula. The company's case was that frequent power shortages were hindering the operation both of fish plants on the peninsula and the fluorspar mine at St. Lawrence. Moreover, there could be no further indus-trial expansion in the area until more power became available.[24] For his part, Valdmanis recommended that the government concentrate its efforts on the interest being shown by European investors in the construction of a pulp and paper mill at Bay d'Espoir.[25] In September 1952 Smallwood heard from some of the Europeans his government was courting that a $25 million power station could be developed on the Grand Le Pierre River with a generating capacity of about 100,000 horsepower. This in turn would lead to the development of an aluminum industry and the construction of transmission lines to the Burin, Avalon and Bonavista Peninsulas.[26]

In following the advice of Valdmanis, Smallwood put aside a proposal by NLP for developing Bay d'Espoir power. In mid-August 1952 the company's general manager, Herbert Forbes-Roberts, discussed this matter with Smallwood who was about to leave for Europe to seek foreign inves-tors. The premier told Forbes-Roberts about the aluminum plant scheme and expressed the preference that NLP rather than government should provide the necessary power. Smallwood offered to pursue the matter further upon his return but this contact led nowhere. Earlier Forbes-Roberts had complained about the difficulty of pinning down exactly what the province's power requirements would be. The plans were 'extremely vague and hush hush.'[27]

In August 1952 Smallwood, his Attorney-General, Leslie Curtis, and Valdmanis travelled to London and appeared before the Fleet Street press to announce that Newfoundland was open to development by British investors. Next, following talks with British Prime Minister Sir Winston Churchill and financier Edmund de Rothschild, Smallwood managed to patch together a consortium of business interests consisting of N.M. Roth-schild and Sons, English Electric Company, Bowater Paper Corporation, AND, Rio-Tinto Zinc Corporation Ltd., Anglo-American Corporation of South Africa, and Frobisher Limited. This consortium formed the British Newfoundland Corporation (Brinco),[28] which in 1953 received from the province extensive land and water-power rights including the right to develop the Bay d'Espoir area. In effect Brinco was given all the important water power rights that remained in public hands. Smallwood envisioned Brinco as the ideal partner in his plan to industrialize the province. Brinco subsequently carried out feasibility studies of possible hydroelectric devel-opment sites, including Bay d'Espoir, while Smallwood continued his search, without great success, for the industry to use the power he hoped would be produced.[29]

Rural electrification and private power in the early 1950s

While Smallwood promoted his various power development schemes in the early 1950s, the private utilities were busy carrying out plans of their own. Between 1948 and 1953 NLP built several new power stations on the southern shore of the Avalon Peninsula to meet anticipated demand in the St. John's area. In early 1953 the utility considered developing a site on Piper's Hole River, 115 miles from St. John's. The proposed development would be at the point where the river flows into Placentia Bay, at the juncture of the Avalon and Burin Peninsulas. As envisaged, the $16 million development would generate 30,000 horsepower and approximately dou-ble the company's generating capacity. It was, however, abandoned in September 1953 when company engineering studies indicated that there was less power potential than had originally been thought and that the development cost would be higher than first estimated.[30] Instead, the company decided to meet further load demand in the St. John's area by constructing a steam plant with a capacity of 13,300 horsepower. This was put in service in 1956 in the capital city.[31] Outside the Avalon Peninsula the company embarked on its own rural electrification programme to bring service to areas where it was practical and economical to do so. On the west coast, NLP purchased in 1951 the electrical distribution system previously operated in Corner Brook by Bowater's Newfoundland Pulp and Paper Mills Ltd. Then, in 1954 it started a rural service in the Corner Brook area, bringing 106 new customers on line. Over the next ten years the company greatly expanded this service. In 1956 it moved into the Grand Falls area, taking over the distribution system previously owned and operated by the AND. Both paper companies now preferred to concentrate on paper mak-ing and leave the distribution of electricity to a utility company. Since AND wanted all the power it could generate for its own mill, NLP's expansion in the Grand Falls area necessitated the construction of a new power plant. In the event, a 7,500 horsepower hydro station was built at Rattling Brook, about twenty miles from Grand Falls. In 1958 this new station enabled service to be extended forty miles eastward to Gander which hitherto had depended upon a limited supply of diesel generated power provided by the federal Department of Transport, the operator of the international airport there. Power was now also brought to several other small communities along the line to Gander.

In May 1954 ownership of United Towns Electric was transferred to the Power Corporation of Canada and the investment house of W. C. Pitfield Limited, both Montreal based enterprises. This change brought with it new capital investment and improvements and additions to service in the Conception and Trinity Bay areas, including the construction of a 5,000 horsepower hydroelectric station at New Chelsea, Trinity Bay.

For its size Union Electric also had ambitious plans in this period and set out to electrify the whole of the Bonavista Peninsula, from Clarenville at one end to Bonavista at the other, a distance of about fifty miles. In 1952 Union Electric paid $40,000 for the Clarenville Light and Power Company, a small electrical utility that operated in Clarenville and several nearby communities. The Clarenville company sold out to Union Electric because it was financially unable to undertake the capital expenditures required of it by the Board of Commissioners of Public Utilities to improve and extend electrical service in its operating area.[32] In 1956, with government assistance through the backing of a $1 million company bond issue, Union Electric put in service at Lockston a 2,000 horsepower hydroelectric station. This gave a more reliable supply and allowed the company to reach its objective of providing improved electrical service from Clarenville to Bonavista. In the Catalina-Bonavista area Aaron Bailey was able to interest Fishery Products Limited, one of the province's leading frozen fish companies, to build a processing plant at Port Union by promising cheap hydroelectric power.[33] The alternative source of power for the area was by the installation of expensive diesel power units, which the provincial government was prepared to support on the recommendation in 1953 of a joint federal-provincial committee on the fisheries headed by Chief Justice Sir Albert Walsh. Walsh had called on the government to help install small diesel units in fish plants in communities that could not easily be reached by lines from hydroelectric stations.[34] In the Catalina-Bonavista area the expansion achieved by Union Electric made this unnecessary.

In the 1950s also several remote communities set out to develop their own electricity supply. Lewisporte, on the island's northeast coast, for example, hired a hydro consultant in 1954 to examine whether the Eel Brook and the nearby Rattling Brook could be developed with help from the provincial government. The consultant, George Desbarats, proposed a 7,500 horsepower station that would provide electricity for both Lewisporte and Gander Airport. Lewisporte town council subsequently secured a lease to the water-power rights of the Rattling Brook area from Reid Newfoundland but in June 1955 its plans fell through when it was denied the necessary government funding.[35] Between 1953 and 1958, the rural district council of Badger's Quay-Valleyfield-Pool's Island, Bonavista Bay, also considered a scheme of hydroelectric development, the objective here being to supply communities on the northeast coast from Greenspond to Lumsden. Desbarats surveyed the area and determined that several small sites were indeed available for development. But as with Lewisporte, the local authority was denied financial support.[36]

Establishment of the Newfoundland Power Commission, 1954

Smallwood correctly understood that the only way possible for government to extend electrical service to the island's outports was by a large hydroelectric development such as that proposed for Bay d'Espoir. Rural electrification, moreover, was a matter in which he took 'a very close and intimate interest' and he resented any suggestions, public or private, that he had to be 'pushed or hustled' on the issue. As he wrote to one Gambo resident in March 1954, 'I am the one who is doing the pushing. And I am the one who knows all the facts of the case.'[37]

The 'facts of the case' were brought into sharp focus in February 1953 when Smallwood, who was also Minister of Economic Development, received a telegram from Angus L. Macdonald, the premier of Nova Scotia. It requested information on Newfoundland's rural electrification programme and arose out of a nationwide enquiry conducted by Macdonald into the subject of providing power to rural Canadians. Smallwood replied that Newfoundland had no programme of financial assistance and sent Oliver Vardy, director of the tourist division of the Department of Economic Development, to Halifax to examine the information being collected by the Nova Scotia government.[38] In May 1953 Vardy, a close adviser and friend of Smallwood, informed him that no extensive rural electrification programme for Newfoundland was possible without a transmission network connecting all the province's towns to the sources of electricity. In Vardy's view the government had two possible courses of action. It could undertake power development projects itself in areas to be serviced, or it could concentrate efforts on areas which already had transmission networks available, but which had not been serviced by the private utility companies because it was uneconomical to do so. With respect to the second alternative, Vardy noted that in Nova Scotia the provincial government, through the Nova Scotia Power Commission, subsidized the private utilities to provide electrical service. The subsidy was based on the number of customers per mile in a given area. From 1937 to 1952 Nova Scotia had spent $2,248,555.29 on this approach to rural electrification, but the 'scheme had failed completely in its original aim to bring economic development to the rural areas.'[39] Officials at the Nova Scotia Power Commission advised Vardy that if the Newfoundland government was not prepared to have public ownership of power plants, then the province should at least establish a public body to co-ordinate all efforts at power development in the province. This would avoid any possible duplication of costs and services. Vardy's own assessment of the Newfoundland situation was as follows:

> any program of rural electrification based upon the Nova Scotia program would be an expensive one for Newfoundland. Most of Nova Scotia's capital expenditures were made prior to the present increase in costs of labour and material. Because of the remoteness of certain areas and the limited customer potential the provision of power is likely to be a costly undertaking. On the other hand, the situation is not hopeless and an energetic program of investigation might disclose many unanticipated advantages.[40]

For the moment, however, Smallwood pinned his hopes on Brinco. During legislative debate in April 1953 on the bill to give Brinco its land and water-power rights, Smallwood gave this optimistic forecast of what might be expected in Newfoundland of the English Electric Company, one of Brinco's founding companies:

> They have their various hydro-electric commissions, in Nova Scotia, in New Brunswick, in Quebec, Ontario and other Provinces of Canada and in place of a Newfoundland Hydro-Electric Commission providing rural electrification to our remote farm areas and to our logging settlements we will benefit by the coming of the English Electric company to this Province...My own personal ambition is that English Electric will come here to the Island and will establish a great transmission network to bring electric light to the tens of thousands and hundreds of thousands of those of our people scattered about the Island providing rural electrification to our remote farm areas and to our fishing settlements. That is my hope—that of course I cannot guarantee, I can only hope.[41]

His hope was misplaced, for in February 1954 Brinco general manager Bill Southam wrote him that the company would not yet be ready to undertake any hydroelectric development until more engineering and financial studies were completed.[42] In the end, Brinco offered no solution to the problem at hand; it turned out to be primarily interested in large scale power projects in Labrador, and at Bay d'Espoir. Projects under 10,000 horsepower,[43] which is what a rural programme needed, were of no interest to the corporation.

Brinco's lack of interest brought United Towns and Union Electric back into play as agencies for the rural electrical revolution Smallwood was attempting to promote. But before offering either company financial assistance, he approached Ontario Hydro, in mid-1953, for engineering consultants to examine the financial operations of the Newfoundland utilities. Gordon Kribs and Richard Thomas Jeffery were sent from Ontario Hydro to undertake this work. Kribs' study of the United Towns distribution system clearly highlighted the problem of providing power in isolated rural areas. Of United Towns' operations on the Burin Peninsula, for instance, Kribs wrote that 'it must be remembered that the Company is supplying an extended rural system, consisting of small communities and sparsely set-tled areas separated by considerable distances. The hamlets themselves are usually spread out at considerable length, around the end of bays or along the seashore, the ground conditions being either rocky or barren, which all makes for a difficult and expensive region to serve. In such an area it is impossible for an electric utility to give the same service as in a city like St. John's, where the customers are closely grouped and concentrated in a comparatively small area.'[44] The reports he and Jeffery submitted recom-mended provincial generation and distribution of electricity. If the province was not prepared to take this course of action, Jeffery suggested the creation of a public body to co-ordinate the activities of the existing private utilities and to encourage them in an active rural electrification programme. This body would provide the expert engineering advice government needed to make rational decisions about present and future power needs.[45]

Smallwood also had the benefit of a more detailed study on rural electrification in various provinces of Canada that Oliver Vardy completed in late 1953. Reviewing the main points of his May 1953 report to the premier, Vardy told Smallwood that the cost of providing electricity to all, or almost all, of the island's outports, about 26,000 homes, would be approximately $20 million. The province had three options. The first was to encourage the establishment of one large private utility company to purchase the two small companies presently serving rural areas. The new and larger company would then have responsibility for rural extensions. The second option was for the government to set up a public power commission which would generate its own power and distribute and sell it to rural customers. But this approach would have the disadvantage of creating a large and expensive technical and administrative bureaucracy to carry out work which could more economically be done by the existing private utilities. The third option was for the government to create a 'control or advisory board.' This was what Vardy recommended.[46]

Smallwood accepted his advice and legislation to give effect to the recommendation was introduced into the House of Assembly in 1954. Armed with his various reports, Smallwood explained the government's purpose as follows: 'we are not so sure that it is a hydro-electric commission we want...as they do in the other Provinces of Canada. But we are quite sure that we have to do something to take control and take the right to regulate hydro-electric matters.'[47] The proposed commission would be essentially an advisory and investigative body. It would have authority to investigate new sources of electrical energy, examine all electrical development pro-posals submitted to the government, and contract to supply electricity to any part of Newfoundland. With government approval the Commission could construct and operate its own power plants.[48] In practice the commission did not begin operations until 1956 because the individual Smallwood had in mind for the chairmanship, George Desbarats, was not available until then owing to previous consulting commitments to Union Electric.[49]

A one man power commission, 1956-68

It was typical of Smallwood to announce a forthcoming major economic initiative with a personal publicity extravaganza. With a provincial election pending, he grabbed centre stage in late 1955 with his rural electrification plans. In a television interview on 22 December he told Don Jamieson of CJON, St. John's, that 1956 would see major progress in rural electrification. He also announced that George Desbarats had been appointed chairman of the Power Commission and would be taking up his duties early in the new year.[50] In February 1956 the government announced that it would be spending a considerable sum to help the utility companies provide electricity in areas where, for financial reasons, it was not available.[51] In the same month, in response to one community's petition for electricity, Smallwood stated that Desbarats would be drawing up a list of places requiring the government's immediate attention. This would be preliminary to funds being voted for rural electrification at the next session of the legislature.[52] Smallwood assured voters that substantial efforts at rural electrification would soon begin and that the needs of ten or twelve communities pressing for electrical service would soon be addressed.[53]

Desbarats assumed his duties as commission chairman on 1 March 1956. An Ottawa native and a graduate in electrical engineering from McGill University, he had served during World War II as an officer in the Royal Canadian Navy and had been stationed for one year in St. John's. He returned to Newfoundland in 1947 to conduct a water-power survey of Newfoundland and Labrador for the Commission of Government.[54] In the early 1950s Desbarats operated consulting and construction businesses at Mount Pearl. His clients included the Newfoundland government, the local utilities, and various municipalities. Accordingly, he brought to the chairmanship of the Power Commission a wealth of knowledge of the local business scene.

In August 1956 Desbarats presented the premier with a detailed programme of action for the Power Commission. Part of his work involved examining how electricity could be provided to communities not within easy reach of the distribution systems of the existing utilities. Desbarats proposed the immediate construction by the Power Commission of small hydroelectric stations with installed capacity of about 1,000 horsepower to serve ten rural communities. While the plants were being built, the Commission would study possibilities in five other areas. Meanwhile, negotiations were in progress with the private utilities to expand capacity in their service areas.[55] Desbarats and Smallwood differed as to the role the Power

Commission should play in the generation and distribution of electricity. Desbarats preferred an active role and, as early as 1950, had urged Smallwood to create a public hydroelectric commission.[56] Smallwood, with an eye to Brinco's power plans for Labrador and Bay d'Espoir, resisted this approach despite occasional public musings to the contrary. Even after the formation of the Power Commission, Smallwood did not want it directly involved in providing electricity to communities. Rather his approach as late as 1956 was to subsidize the private utilities to provide service extensions. Only as a last resort was he willing to give the Power Commission authority to generate and distribute electricity.[57] Politically, he preferred that the utilities and not the government be responsible for imposing and collecting electricity rates.

Desbarats wanted the government to allow the Power Commission to develop and operate small hydroelectric systems. Where small-scale hydroelectric development was not possible, he favoured the installation of diesel electric units to be owned and operated by the Power Commission.[58] When a community requested electrical service, Smallwood would send Desbarats to investigate and survey its requirements.[59] Between 1956 and 1958 Desbarats visited many communities to examine how electricity could be provided to them. In this role—he was the Commission's only professional staff member—Desbarats served the government's purpose by reassuring residents that the coming of electricity to their communities was imminent.

Rural electrification programme, 1958

During the campaign leading up to the federal election of 10 June 1957 the Progressive Conservative party, led by John Diefenbaker, promised to lend money at low interest rates to the governments of the Maritime Provinces to build thermal generating stations and extend transmission lines into areas without electricity. In late 1957, with Diefenbaker in office at the head of a minority government, Ottawa offered the same assistance to Newfoundland, thereby making it possible for the province to borrow money on behalf of the Power Commission for rural electrification purposes. In November 1957 Smallwood requested from Brinco and the Newfoundland utility companies their views on rural electrification. The matter was also discussed at a meeting on 29 November 1957, between Smallwood, Gordon Pushie (Director-General of Economic Development) and Claude Howse of Brinco. Smallwood now stated that Newfoundland had no intention of getting 'involved in the retail distribution of electricity.' Instead, the Government would 'supply blocks of power to private groups' at rates that would 'warrant distribution by these groups on a commercial basis.' Smallwood also told Howse that the province was considering asking Brinco to relinquish some of its existing water-power rights on the island to a publicly owned hydro commission, which would then develop its own hydroelectric power. Brinco's future hydro plans were also examined at this meeting. The corporation, it turned out, was currently revising engineering studies on the Bay d'Espoir region in preparation for construction once demand reached 70,000 horsepower of electricity, the minimum power requirement for the development to go ahead.[60]

In January 1958 Pushie met in Montreal with Denis Stairs and Vivian Ainsworth of NLP and Bill Southam and Claude Howse of Brinco. Stairs, a highly regarded hydro engineer, was president of NLP and vice-president of Montreal Engineering.[61] The participants at the January meeting discussed a memo, dated 17 December that Stairs had prepared on rural electrification for the Newfoundland government in response to Small-wood's request for the views of the private utility companies on the matter. Stairs proposed that the government assist the utilities to provide service extensions to outports that could be reached from existing electric systems. In his view the Prince Edward Island model of rural electrification could be adopted in Newfoundland. In that province the government had signed an agreement in 1954 with the privately owned Maritime Electric Company, whereby the building of uneconomical lines in rural areas would be subsidized. Maritime Electric had formerly been controlled by Izaak Killam and used the same engineering consulting company as did NLP, namely, Montreal Engineering. In January 1958 Ainsworth gave Pushie a copy of Stairs' proposals which was subsequently handed to Smallwood.

The Atlantic Provinces Power Development Act which received assent in January 1958 provided for federal assistance to any of the four Atlantic provinces for the construction of thermal generating stations and for the building of transmission lines to areas without electricity. The assistance, however, was only available for publicly owned thermal power projects. This, of course, posed a considerable problem for Newfoundland where the generation of electricity remained in private hands. Smallwood attempted, unsuccessfully, to persuade the Diefenbaker government to change the assistance programme to include small scale hydroelectric developments, which Desbarats' work had shown would best meet the needs of Newfoundland's small and isolated outports. The Newfoundland premier also wanted the legislation changed to assist the province to erect distribution lines. Because many outports were located far from existing transmission lines, it was more appropriate in Newfoundland's case that federal assistance include the construction of both transmission and distribution lines. On the Avalon Peninsula it was physically possible to build distribution lines to outports within the existing framework of support, but outside the Avalon geography made this financially prohibitive.[62] Newfoundland was served exclusively by private electrical utilities and in an August 1958 letter Smallwood explained to Diefenbaker that the takeover of these companies, was 'beyond the financial resources' of the Province.[63]

Smallwood next launched his own rural electrification scheme. On 15 March 1958, in the midst of another federal election campaign, he an-

nounced, in a province wide radio broadcast, a rural electrification programme that would cost about $5 million over several years. It was, he said,
a programme the province would pay for itself. Should the existing federal
scheme be changed or improved, Newfoundland could make application
to it and be spared some part of the expense to which it was now committing
itself.[64] The provincial programme would result in the construction of 800
miles of new transmission line. Electricity for the 5,000 additional households to be helped under the programme would be distributed by the
private utility companies. The Power Commission would pay the utility
companies to construct transmission lines and then enter into contracts with
them to maintain the new lines. The utility companies would sell the power
to rural customers whose rates would be subsidized by government. The
government through the Power Commission would decide when and
where extensions would be made. Where it was not practical to build a line
to provide power from a central station of one of the utilities, the government would assist municipalities to purchase diesel electric plants. The
government also planned to provide electricity to the Labrador town of
Happy Valley, which had been the subject of one of Desbarats' feasibility
studies.[65]

In September 1958 Smallwood announced the details of the rural
electrification contracts the province would sign with the three private
utility companies[66] and the appointment of John Ryan to succeed Desbarats
as chairman of the Power Commission. Desbarats' reason for leaving the
job was to devote more time to his construction and consulting businesses.[67]
His thirty-three year old successor, John Ryan, who took office on 1 November, was an experienced thermal engineer and came from Montreal Engineering.[68] His work experience included the supervision of the construction
of a steam plant for NLP at St. John's. Ryan was assisted at the Power
Commission by Ernie Dickinson, who was appointed chief engineer. Dickinson was also a former employee of Montreal Engineering and since 1946
had been Chief Engineer for United Towns Electric. He was well-experi-
enced in rural electrification through his work in Western Canada before
1939.[69] Over the next few years more appointments were made to the
permanent staff of the Power Commission until by 31 March 1961 it had
twelve members.[70]

Between 1958 and 1964 the Power Commission's main concern was to
bring electricity to rural residents where it was financially feasible and
practicable to do so. At times, however, immediate political considerations
could alter its priorities. Ryan, for example, planned to bring power to
Trepassey in 1964 but Smallwood intervened and a diesel plant was
installed there in 1959.[71]

By 1964 the Power Commission's record stood at 9,966 new customers
served, 611 miles of new transmission lines built, and 14 diesel plants
installed.[72] In some instances, new lines were constructed by the utility

companies and in others by the Power Commission itself using seasonally hired construction staff. Where a diesel plant had to be installed, the Power Commission paid the capital cost and local residents the maintenance cost through rates levied by the local council. By 31 March 1964 the province had spent over $4 million on capital works in its rural electrification programme. After 1963 the province benefited greatly from a federal programme of assistance to towns with diesel generated power.

Despite the considerable investment made during the 1950s in the production of electrical energy in Newfoundland, the province did not have enough power in the mid 1960s to permit new industrial growth. Indeed, some existing industries were having to curtail production because of power shortages. In these circumstances the Smallwood government had to choose between the old approach of combining small scale hydroelectric developments with thermal plants or push forward the development of Bay d'Espoir where low cost power could be generated. Something would also have to be done about connecting the various unconnected power systems of the province; if one area were short of water, there was still no way of feeding power into it from another area which had an abundant water supply. The Corner Brook-Deer Lake area, moreover, operated on a fifty-cycle frequency as did the paper mill at Grand Falls while the rest of Newfoundland used the standard North American sixty-cycle frequency. Developing Bay d'Espoir would not only provide the island with a large new source of energy, but would facilitate an integrated provincial grid system and augment the province's rural electrification efforts. It would also enable Smallwood to fulfil a longstanding election promise of the early 1960s: lower electricity rates for domestic consumers.

In 1963, after the Liberals had regained power in Ottawa under the leadership of Lester Pearson, the federal government through the Atlantic Development Board made $20 million available for the development in Bay d'Espoir. The grant, however, was conditional on the work being carried out by a public body, a condition that excluded Brinco. The province subsequently reacquired the water-power rights in the area given to the corporation and gave the Power Commission responsibility for the Bay d'Espoir development. The project, which was eventually completed in 1970, cost about $150 million and brought on stream an initial supply of 300,000 horsepower in 1967.[73] Bay d'Espoir power led to the creation of a trans-island transmission grid by the Power Commission and made practicable the huge industrial projects which Smallwood had long sought. In 1968, for instance, a $40 million phosphorous complex built by British capitalists went into production at Long Harbour and in 1973 an oil refinery promoted by the American businessman John Shaheen began production at Come by Chance, Placentia Bay.

As for the three private utilities, the enhanced role of the Power Commission after 1965, the development of Bay d'Espoir, the increasing need for an integrated provincial grid system, and political pressure from the provincial government for a uniform electrical rate for customers across the province, all pointed in one direction—amalgamation. Fear of a government takeover also favoured this. In truth, after 1963 Smallwood embarked on his own particular version of public power. This had no counterpart in any other province. Thus, in December 1963 he explained to general manager Vivian Ainsworth that while he did not intend the government to buy out the private utility companies, he believed that it should take over the generation of electricity and possibly the construction of transmission lines so as 'to deliver power at a uniform price to the companies for resale at uniform rates.'[74]

For several years prior to this NLP and United Towns had discussed a merger of their operations in the St. John's urban area. As the city of St. John's expanded into newly built suburban areas, NLP's own expanding distribution system eventually met that of United Towns. In 1963 it was agreed by the two companies that a 'single large power system' would deliver power 'at the least possible cost' and that money and effort were being wasted by 'the separate ownership of...transmission lines and substations around St. John's.'[75] Merger negotiations between the two companies collapsed, however, when agreement could not be reached on a fair share exchange in an amalgamated company.

In 1965 Union Electric's Aaron Bailey entered the sporadic merger talks between NLP and United Towns. His advice to the two companies was frank and direct. He later recalled that he told Denis Stairs that 'unless we get together, the government is not going to be satisfied to have us operate and have... different rates around the island, because politically they can't have it.'[76] A political confidant of Smallwood, Bailey kept the premier informed of the progress of the negotiations of the three companies. Smallwood approved of amalgamation in principle, but nevertheless referred the proposed merger to the Power Commission for its consideration after the companies finally reached agreement in June 1966. In July the Power Commission recommended that the province acquire the common and preferred shares, estimated to be worth $32 million, of the amalgamating companies. Smallwood ignored this advice which ran counter to his own instincts and in September 1966 the three private utilities merged into a new company, Newfoundland Light & Power Company.[77]

All of this agreed with Smallwood's strategy for economic development in the first fifteen years of Newfoundland's participation in confederation. This strategy emphasized large-scale hydroelectric development paid for by private enterprise. As Smallwood explained in his 1973 memoirs, *I Chose Canada*:

> I worried about the danger of losing our population and I knew, even before Confederation Day [March 31, 1949] that I had to inspire the Newfoundland people with new faith in their prospects...We had to

develop our resources...The price of failure would be disaster, and so
our slogan had to be 'Develop or Perish.'[78]

In 1964, with the financial assistance of the federal government, Smallwood
took a big step in a new direction when he made the Power Commission
responsible for developing Bay d'Espoir and for all future new generation
of electricity on the island. Once it got started on the Bay d'Espoir scheme,
the Power Commission quickly blossomed into a sizable crown corporation and the central player in the province's energy field. In the process it
also became an important instrument of economic growth and development for the province, the Newfoundland equivalent of the other provin-
cially owned utilities that loom so large on the Canadian economic
landscape.

Conclusion

Before 1960 many rural areas of Newfoundland sought electricity not only
for domestic use but also as a means to promote new industry. Speaking to
the St. John's Rotary club in 1930, Robert Murphy of the United Towns
Electric Company declared that where power went, industry followed.
'Modern methods of preserving, curing or packing our staple products,' he
said, 'can be introduced and new avenues of wealth opened up.'[79] Unfortunately for Newfoundland, until the late 1960s most of the island's largest
sources of hydroelectric power were located far from its many small fishing
communities. This made industrial diversification difficult at best. In particular, the shift towards frozen fish production in the fishing industry was
slowed by the lack of abundant and cheap sources of power that only
hydroelectricity could provide. Before confederation the electricity generated on the Avalon Peninsula from water-power was required for the iron
ore mining industry at Bell Island and for domestic and commercial use in
the city of St. John's. Some progress was made in frozen fish production but
the saltfish business, which relied on the sun for drying, remained strong.
In the 1950s the Smallwood government sought to break out of this pattern
through financial support to private companies to install diesel generators
in their plants where the more economical electricity generated by water-
power was not available. This allowed the frozen fish business to grow
rapidly, and hastened the decline of the saltfish industry. This trend was
magnified in the 1960s both by a large infusion of federal funds as part of
a federal-provincial resettlement programme and by the development of
the water-power resources of Bay d'Espoir.

Water-power development in Newfoundland has always involved
large capital outlays and this in turn has always meant external financial
support. For the hydroelectricity projects associated with the construction
of pulp and paper mills at Grand Falls and Corner Brook, the capital
required came from the United Kingdom. For the island's other hydroelec-

tricity projects, apart from those of the United Towns Electric Company and the Union Electric Company, capital was provided by Montreal financial interests associated either with the Reid Newfoundland Company or, later on, with Izaak Killam's Royal Securities Corporation. Thus, despite its geographical proximity to and social and economic ties with the Canadian Maritime Provinces, Newfoundland has had greater ties financially in the twentieth century to Montreal. It has indeed in large measure been part of that city's economic domain. What Newfoundland perhaps had most in common with the Canadian Maritimes before 1949 was subordination to Montreal business—whether through banks, insurance companies, or venture capital to develop water-power resources.

After 1949 the provincial government perforce had to become a big player in the electricity field. The interplay of private and public interests has produced a unique outcome in the province. On the island of Newfoundland today approximately 90 per cent of all electricity is produced by a crown corporation but consumers get 85 per cent of their power from a private company. This is a situation not found in any other province in Canada. In the production and distribution of electricity, as in so much else, Newfoundland remains distinctive. Truly, history and geography have combined to make this so.

NOTES

1   J.R. Smallwood, *The New Newfoundland* (New York 1931), 94, 224.

2   *Evening Telegram* (St. John's), 17 Dec. 1930.

3   For Smallwood's career see Richard Gwyn, *Smallwood: The Unlikely Revolutionary*, rev. ed. (Toronto 1972); Frederick W. Rowe, *The Smallwood Era* (Toronto 1985); Herbert L. Pottle, *Dawn without Light: Politics, Power & the People in the Smallwood Era* (St. John's 1979); James R. Thoms (ed.), *Call Me Joey* (St. John's 1990); and Harold Horwood, *Joey* (Toronto 1989).

4   *Evening Telegram* 16 May 1949.

5   See Melvin Baker, Janet Miller Pitt and Robert Pitt, *The Illustrated History of Newfoundland Light & Power* (St. John's 1990), 17-40.

6   Ibid., 136-42.

7   Ibid., 143.

8   Ibid., 193.

9   Ibid., 194-8.

10   Ibid., 201-05.

11   Ibid., 235-46.

12   Centre for Newfoundland Studies (CNS), Queen Elizabeth II Library, Memorial University, St. John's, Government of Newfoundland, Dept. of Economic Development, 'Rural Electrification in Canada.'

13   Dominion Bureau of Statistics, *The Canada Year Book 1951* (Ottawa 1951), 554.

14   Baker, Pitt and Pitt, *Illustrated History*, 163.

15   Ibid., 159-60.

16 Power was, however, sold to the owners of the lead and zinc mine opened at Buchans in 1928.

17 *Proceedings of First Session Thirty-First General Assembly of Newfoundland 1957*, vol. 1, 447.

18 *Evening Telegram*, 16 May, 2 June 1949; *Proceedings of Fourth Session Thirtieth General Assembly of Newfoundland 1954*, vol. 2, 2043. In 1953 Hogg became a director of Brinco.

19 Centre for Newfoundland Studies Archives, Queen Elizabeth II Library, Memorial University, St. John's, J.R. Smallwood Collection, COLL-75, 3.23.041, Smallwood to Hogg, 6 March 1952.

20 In 1930 the government of Sir Richard Squires created a Public Utilities Commission empowered to investigate the rates charged to the public for telephone and telegraph service, electricity, and public and private transportation. The commission could also investigate food, clothing, housing and fire insurance charges. The commissioners, Sir William Lloyd, Michael Gibbs, and Charles Hutchings, investigated the price of soft and hard bread and rents in St. John's. After 1931, however, the commission stopped meeting, probably as an economy measure as part of a general retrenchment programme. For the activities of this commission from 12 Aug. 1930 to 13 Aug. 1931 see Provincial Archives of Newfoundland and Labrador (PANL), GN 13/2A, Justice Dept., box 382, file 'Claims of M.P. Gibbs (member Public Utilities Commission) 4 October 1940.' All subsequent GN (Government of Newfoundland) references are to documents in this archive.

21 COLL-75, 3.23.045, Wurtele to Smallwood, 17 March 1950, 5 June 1951.

22 Manifesto of the Liberal Party for the 1951 election (copy in CNS).

23 For the career of Alfred Valdmanis see Gerhard Bassler, '"Develop or Perish": Joseph R. Smallwood and Newfoundland's Quest for German Industry, 1949-1953,' *Acadiensis* 15, no. 2 (1986)): 93-119.

24 GN 13/2A, box 201, file 122, Murphy to Curtis, 1 Dec. 1950; COLL-75, 3.23.036, Murphy to Smallwood, 22 June 1950.

25 Valdmanis wrote Smallwood that 'the new hydro-power shall be considerably cheaper than any power available...[from United Towns Electric] and transmission lines built from Bay d'Espoir should easily reach Gander or Buchans [in central Newfoundland], and also connect with the...Burin and Avalon Peninsulas' (COLL-75, 3.23.039, Valdmanis to Smallwood, 25 Aug. 1950).

26 Ibid., 3.23.040, Uitting (Senior Engineer, Siemens-Schuckertwerke Atkiengesellschaft) to Valdmanis, 1 Nov. 1951, and to Smallwood, 1 Sept. 1952.

27 Baker, Pitt and Pitt, *Illustrated History*, 148.

28 Other companies later joined the original seven. These included C.T. Bowring and Company and the Montreal investment firm of W.C. Pitfield and Company. See Philip Smith, *Brinco: The Story of Churchill Falls* (Toronto 1975).

29 COLL-75, 3.14.020, Pushie to Smallwood, 5 Oct. 1956.

30 Newfoundland Light and Power, *Annual Report Year Ended December 31, 1953* (St. John's 1954).

31 *Canada Year Book 1956* (Ottawa 1956), 557. In 1959 a second turbo-generator was put in service at the steam plant, increasing its total generating capacity to 39,900 horsepower.

32   Baker, Pitt and Pitt, *Illustrated History*, 247-50.

33   Ibid., 247-56.

34   *Newfoundland Journal of Commerce 23* (Dec. 1956): 17; and *Report of the New-foundland Fisheries Development Committee* (1953).35

35   PANL, P7/B/19, box 20, file 'Newfoundland Light & Power - Town of Lewisporte Eel Brook Hydro Electric Development,' 'Conversation held between the Honourable Dr. Rowe and W.A. Reid at 10:15 am Monday, 13 June 1955'; Desbarats to Reid Newfoundland, 15 Feb., 25 March 1954.

36   Baker, Pitt and Pitt, *Illustrated History*, 324.

37   COLL-75, 3.23.033, Smallwood to Curran, 1 March 1954.

38   Ibid., tel., Macdonald to Smallwood, 25 Feb. 1953, with attached note by Smallwood.

39   Ibid., Vardy to Smallwood, 26 May 1953.

40   Ibid.

41   *Proceedings of Third Session Thirtieth General Assembly of Newfoundland 1953,* 671.

42   COLL-75, 3.08.046, Southam to Smallwood, 8 Dec. 1953; 3.23.033, Southam to Smallwood, 24 Feb. 1954; Southam to Curran, 1 March 1954.

43   See Smith, *Brinco,* for the history of that company's efforts to develop Hamilton Falls (later Churchill Falls) in Labrador. See also COLL-75, 3.23.032, Desbarats to McNeill, 16 April 1957.

44   Quoted in Baker, Pitt and Pitt, *Illustrated History,* 335.

45   R.T. Jeffery, 'Report of October 19, 1953 with regard to the matter of Electric Power Supply and Distribution [report prepared for Premier J.R. Smallwood, 1953], ' 1953, pt. II, 4; and *Proceedings of Fourth Session Thirtieth General Assembly of Newfoundland 1954,* vol. 2, 2042-3.

46   'Rural Electrification in Canada.'

47   *Proceedings of Fourth Session Thirtieth General Assembly of Newfoundland 1954,* vol. 2., 2043-4.

48   *Statutes of Newfoundland,* 1954, no. 72.

49   *Proceedings of Seventh Session Thirtieth General Assembly of Newfoundland 1956,* vol. 1, 150.

50   CNS, *Interview of Honourable J.R. Smallwood, Premier of Newfoundland, by Donald Jamieson Esquire, News Commentator on CJON Television...December 22, 1955;* and *Evening Telegram,* 23 Dec. 1955.

51   *Daily News* (St. John's), 2 Feb. 1956.

52   Ibid., 22 Feb. 1956.

53   Evening Telegram, *24 March 1956.*

54   In 1944 the Commission of Government engaged K.G. Chisholm, Chief Engineer with the Halifax office of the Dominion Water and Power Bureau of Canada, to examine the hydro potential of the island of Newfoundland and Labrador. In late 1944 Chisholm recommended that Newfoundland hire a hydro engineer to examine more closely how new hydroelectric sites could be developed (see National Archives of Canada, RG 25 (Records of the Dept. of External Affairs), vol. 2407, file 6704-40, Robertson to Macdonald, 24 Oct. 1944; *Daily News,* 7 Nov. 1944; *Evening Telegram,* 9 Dec. 1944).

55   COLL-75, 3.23.032, 'Newfoundland Power Commission, Programme, 5 Aug. 1956.'

56   Ibid., Desbarats to Smallwood, 1 Feb. 1950. While Smallwood did not imme-
      diately act on this advice, he did find in Desbarats a kindred spirit for his
      economic policies. In Feb. 1950 Desbarats advised the premier as follows: 'it
      now seems reasonable to suppose that with this shortage of power [in Canada
      and the United States], now is the time to try and induce industries to settle
      in Newfoundland' (see ibid., 3.23.032, Desbarats to Smallwood, 1 June 1950,
      with encl. report 'Water Power Potentialities in Newfoundland').

57   Ibid., Desbarats to McNeill, 16 April 1957.

58   Ibid., Desbarats to Smallwood, 16 Oct. 1956. For the town of Burgeo on the
      island's south coast, Desbarats proposed a 150 horsepower diesel-electric unit
      costing over $80,000 with a balanced operating annual budget of $21,000. Each
      of the minimum 250 customers in Burgeo would pay a minimum monthly
      bill of $7.00.

59   Ibid., Desbarats to Smallwood, 24 Oct. 1956.

60   Ibid., 3.14.020, Pushie to Smallwood, 5 Oct. 1956.

61   NLP, *Tie-Lines*, Feb. 1967, 3; Jan. 1980, 16. Stairs was born in 1889 in Dart-
      mouth, Nova Scotia, and joined Montreal Engineering in 1922 as an assistant
      engineer.

62   House of Commons, *Debates*, 1957-58, vol. 4, 3254-81, 3297-308; and *Statutes
      of Canada*, 1957-58, vol. 1, ch. 25, 117-19. See also COLL-75, 3.10.013, Small-
      wood to Diefenbaker, tel., 21 Dec. 1957; Diefenbaker to Smallwood, 21 Dec.
      1957; Smallwood to Diefenbaker, 19 Feb. 1958.

63   COLL-75, 3.10.013, Smallwood to Diefenbaker, 19 Aug. 1958.

64   *Daily News*, 20 March 1958.

65   Ibid.

66   NLP signed on 12 Sept. 1958, United Towns Electric on 4 Nov. 1958, and Union
      Electric on 9 Oct. 1959.

67   *Evening Telegram*, 10 Sept. 1958.

68   In Dec. 1958 Desbarats, now back in private business, told Smallwood that
      some rationalization of the province's power production and distribution
      system was needed. This could be achieved either through the creation of one
      private utility company or through the Power Commission acquiring 51% of
      the common stock of the private utilities (see COLL-75, 3.23.032,Desbarats to
      Smallwood, 21 Dec. 1958).

69   Peter Linegar, 'The Electrification of Rural Newfoundland and Labrador,' in
      Newfoundland and Labrador Hydro, *Outlet*, April-May 1976, 3-5.

70   COLL-75, 3.23.021, annual reports of the Newfoundland Power Commission,
      1959-62.

71   Ibid., 3.23.033, Ryan to Murray, 29 Dec. 1958. See also W.J. Browne, *And
      Now...Eighty-seven Years a Newfoundlander*, vol. 2, 1949-65, of *Memoirs of
      William J. Browne* (St. John's 1981), 352. Smallwood presided at the opening
      ceremony for the Trepassey plant.

72   R.I. McAllister (ed.), *Newfoundland and Labrador: The First Fifteen Years of
      Confederation* (St. John's 1966), 73, 169; Newfoundland and Labrador Power
      Commission, 'Presentation to the Royal Commission on Electrical Energy,'

July, 1965, supplement no. 2, 2-3 (copy courtesy of Leo Cole and Peter Linegar of Newfoundland and Labrador Hydro).

73   Shawmont Newfoundland Engineering, a company incorporated on 2 June 1964 by Shawinigan Engineering Company Ltd. of Montreal and Montreal Engineering, supervised the engineering and construction work.

74   Baker, Pitt and Pitt, *Illustrated History*, 271.

75   Ibid., 269-70.

76   NLP Archives, transcript of an oral interview by William Connors with Aaron Bailey, June 1987, 38-9, quoted in Baker, Pitt and Pitt, *Illustrated History*, 272.

77   COLL-75, 3.23.017, Newbury to Smallwood, 19 July 1966.

78   Joseph R. Smallwood, *I Chose Canada: The Memoirs of the Honourable Joseph R. 'Joey' Smallwood* (Toronto 1973), 342.

79   *Evening Telegram*, 10 Jan. 1930.

Changing Government: the 1971-72 Newfoundland Example*

Peter Neary

NEWFOUNDLAND HAS LONG PROVIDED a rich field of interest for students of constitutional minutiae. The reason for this is not hard to find. In 1842 the colony's elected Assembly and its appointed Legislative Council, both established in 1832, were combined in one chamber.[1] In 1861, only six years after 'responsible government' had been achieved in the colony, the government of John Kent was dismissed from office by Governor Sir Alexander Bannerman.[2] In 1908 a general election produced a tie and a crisis which was resolved only through the action of Governor Sir William MacGregor.[3] In 1919 a motion of no confidence put forward by the minister of finance was seconded by the prime minister and carried unanimously by the Assembly.[4] In 1924, a defeated prime minister, while charged with larceny, entered the legislature and participated in a division in which the government prosecuting him was defeated by one vote.[5] In 1934 Newfoundland gave up 'responsible government' and for the next fifteen years was governed by a commission appointed by the government of the United Kingdom.[6] Finally, in 1949, after her people had voted in two referenda on their constitutional future, Newfoundland became a province of Canada.[7] To the inviting fare which these tasty morsels offer to the appetite of the gourmet of constitutional practice in the British mode, must now surely be added the *chef d'oeuvre* of the Newfoundland politician, the strange and bewildering events of 1971-72.

On 6 October 1971 the thirty-fourth General Assembly of Newfoundland was dissolved and a general election called for 28 October.[8] The previous election had been held on 8 September 1966, over five years before, and had resulted in a sweeping victory for the Liberal administration of Joseph R. Smallwood, who had been premier of the province since 1 April 1949.[9] In 1966 Smallwood and his Liberal party won thirty-nine seats and 61.8 per cent of the popular vote; the Progressive Conservative (PC) party won the remaining three seats and 34 per cent of the popular vote. A master political tactician, Smallwood had always shown consummate skill in the timing of elections. His initial victory at the polls, on 27 May 1949, had come in the first flush of enthusiasm over the recently completed union with

Canada. His subsequent highly successful appeals to the voters—in 1951, 1956, 1959, 1962 and 1966—had given him an extraordinary place in Canadian provincial politics. It represented a startling turn of fortune, therefore, that he should have found himself in the fall of 1971 with all opportunity for electoral surprise lost and with the opposition threatening to appeal to the Crown for dissolution if the government did not.

The root of Smallwood's trouble lay in the manifold discontents which a generation of rapid social and economic change had bred in the Newfoundland people. In the late 1960s these discontents suddenly erupted into a powerful urge for political change—an urge which, in time, the PC opposition was able to exploit. Governments are often like some people: they have a vigorous youth, a prosperous maturity, and then they decline and fall. Arguably, Smallwood's administration fits this pattern. It is impossible, of course, to say exactly when his government entered the final stage, though in retrospect it can be seen that its demise was signalled by a series of electoral reverses. The first of these came on 20 October 1967 when a provincial by-election in Gander district, located in a region which had voted Liberal consistently since 1949, produced a PC victory. The previous month J.W. Pickersgill, Smallwood's man in Ottawa since 1953, had resigned both his portfolio as Minister of Transport and his seat in the House of Commons as member of parliament for Bonavista-Twillingate. Smallwood had been born in this constituency, which, in an earlier generation, had nurtured the populism of William F. Coaker. Pickersgill had made its name synonomous nationally with Liberal hegemony. Few doubted that the Liberals would hold the seat in the federal by-election to be held on 6 November. In 1965 Pickersgill had obtained a majority of 6,426 in a two-way fight. Now, Charles Granger, his successor as Newfoundland's minister in the federal cabinet, managed a majority of only 1,386 over his PC and independent opponents. Then in the federal election which followed in June 1968 Bonavista-Twillingate, along with five other Newfoundland constituencies, resisted the national trend and elected PC members. Since federal and provincial politics were at this time inextricably linked in Newfoundland, Smallwood had met his first general election defeat, albeit at one remove. The long slide downward had begun.

Yet Smallwood was still a formidable opponent. The exercise of power was by now second nature to him and his provincial opponents needed time to prepare themselves to seize the opportunity which had so suddenly come their way. Immediately after the election he reorganized his cabinet and in the autumn of 1969 was able to fight back a formidable challenge to his leadership of the Liberal party by John Crosbie, himself a former minister. But the price of this victory against a member of one of Newfoundland's most powerful families was very great. Smallwood's vulnerability was now plain for all to see and his fate became a provincial obsession. He fought back with all the skill that a lifetime in politics had given him, bargaining above all else for time in which to regain public favour. His efforts, which included the swearing in of five new ministers during the summer of 1971, were characteristically unorthodox and energetic. Yet by the time his hand was forced in October, the Tories, who were now led by Frank Moores, one of the new federal members elected in 1968, and strengthened by John Crosbie, who had joined them in June, were making the government's every act controversial. The electoral contest which followed was bitterly fought and held the attention of Newfoundlanders as had no other election since the referendum of July 1948, which had decided their constitutional future. On 28 October 1971 86.28 per cent of the registered voters went to the polls; this figure was higher than in any preceding election and reflected the sometimes frenetic political activity in the province since 1968. As the votes were cast, anything seemed possible; but the reality of election night and the days following belied even the most bizarre forecasts.

Smallwood listened to the election returns while driving around St. John's.[10] What he heard must have been tantalizing. His party was losing many of the seats it had held in the previous Assembly and was running behind the PCs in popular vote. On the other hand, it was not yet clear who would command a majority in the new Assembly. When the counting stopped in the early hours of 29 October each party had carried eighteen seats and five others were undecided. The remaining place in the forty-two seat House had been taken by Tom Burgess, the leader of the New Labrador Party (NLP), who had been elected in the properous but isolated mining constituency of Labrador West.[11] The final verdict was rendered some seventeen hours after the polls had closed: PCs twenty-one,[12] Liberals twenty, NLP one. One constituency, St. Barbe South, which was to figure prominently in later events, had passed from Liberal to Tory hands on the counting of the last poll.[13] Moreover each party had scored three victories by fewer than 106 votes.[14] By contrast the Conservatives had captured 51.33 per cent of the popular vote to 44.47 per cent for the Liberals.[15]

Clearly, the government had suffered a massive reverse; but if Smallwood was down, he was not yet out, for the result left undecided which party would command a majority in the new Assembly. The Conservatives could lay claim to half the members but if they were to elect a speaker from their own number, twenty government supporters would face twenty-one opposition supporters—twenty Liberals and one NLP. On the other hand the existing Liberal government would, assuming a Liberal speaker, face a House of nineteen government supporters and twenty-two opposition supporters—twenty-one PCs and one NLP. Tom Burgess' position was obviously pivotal: he could not keep Smallwood in power (with his support and a Liberal speaker twenty government supporters would face twenty-one opposition supporters) but he could presumably bring Moores to power by declaring for a Conservative government. With the support of

Burgess the Conservatives could elect a speaker and still outvote the Liberals, twenty-one to twenty.

Burgess, however, was a tricky quantity. Elected as a Liberal (also for Labrador West) in the provincial election of 1966, he had joined John Crosbie and Clyde Wells, another dissident Liberal member, in August 1968, in launching a movement to democratize the party.[16] Later he had announced that he would henceforth sit in the House as a member of a new party he intended to organize, the NLP.[17] But this step did not apparently preclude involvement in Liberal affairs; thus at the time of the 1969 Liberal leadership convention he had supported T.A. Hickman, the Minister of Justice, for the leadership of the party.[18] The basis of support for the party led by the Irish born Burgess himself lay in the frontier discontents of continental Labrador *vis-à-vis* the island of Newfoundland. The NLP's avowed purpose was to achieve social and economic justice for a productive but sadly neglected region. His occupational background was that of an official in the United Steelworkers of America and his reputation was that of a cheeky Irishman, the workingman's Tom.

Given all this, it would be difficult for him to abandon his third party status completely. On the other hand, his present cock of the walk position held out the possibility of great advancement for himself and a hearing for his immense but thinly populated region which the electoral arithmetic of the province might never give it again. In short, his situation was not without hope for either Moores or Smallwood. To Moores, Burgess offered the chance to form a government. To Smallwood, he offered the possibility of a stalemate and time to cast about, with all the resources of government at his command, for fresh support in a political arena where patronage has often proved stronger than principle.

In the weeks following the election Smallwood fought desperately to maintain his position. Politically, the wisdom of his course is arguable; but constitutionally his performance was that of a virtuoso. Smallwood had often been accused of testing the limits of 'responsible government'; now, in his adversity, he ventured onto procedural ground that few had previously trod. His first step was to proclaim his right to continue to govern. With Moores and his supporters clamouring for the government's resignation, Smallwood took the position that the fate of his administration would be decided by the new Assembly.[19] Since the government had been granted supply by the previous Assembly to carry it through until March 1972,[20] the new House need not meet pending the outcome of recounts and any litigation that might arise out of the election. This opening gambit was endorsed by Senator Eugene Forsey, one of Canada's leading constitutional authorities, when he told the St. John's *Evening Telegram*, the newspaper with the largest circulation in the province, that the only constraint on Smallwood was that he call the House together soon. 'I don't know whether it should be days or weeks,' he said, 'but clearly it wouldn't be proper for a minority Party to continue governing without meeting the House [within] a reasonable period of time.'[21] What 'reasonable' meant was anybody's guess. Needless to say, Smallwood sought to give it the broadest possible interpretation. In effect, he took the position that the government need not call the House together until it was absolutely certain who had the right to sit in it.

Daily now the war of nerves between Smallwood and Moores intensified. Indeed, the slanging match about the legitimacy of the government on television, radio and in the newspapers, the *Evening Telegram* in particular, made the election itself seem but a momentary pause in the scabrous donnybrook that had been in progress in the province since 1969. 'The premier's attitude,' the *Evening Telegram* trumpeted on 20 October, 'can only serve to darken his image in defeat still farther. He has already shown himself a poor loser by...trying to turn a heavy rebuff into some kind of triumph.'[22] Smallwood was no ordinary political leader and when his opponents smelled blood they were relentless in their pursuit. Moreover, something more than a mere change of government was on the minds of some of them at least; when justice triumphed, as it surely would, the rascals who had ransacked the province for twenty years would be made to answer for their sins. At one heady moment, Wick Collins, a columnist for the *Evening Telegram*, actually wondered 'what would happen if Frank Moores went and sat in Joe Smallwood's chair in Confederation Building and started to run the government of the province'— in effect, staged a *coup d'etat*.[23] The politicians themselves, however, had better sense. For success they looked to the traditional instruments of their trade: propaganda, patronage, custom and the law. The arrival in St. John's from Labrador City on 29 October of Tom Burgess offered them ample scope for their talents.

With considerable flourish, Burgess travelled from Labrador in the company of John Christopher Doyle, Smallwood's favourite mining promoter and a central figure in the development of western Labrador.[24] Leaving Doyle in Stephenville, he flew to St. John's in a jet owned by Lundrigans, a major local contracting firm, and checked into the capital's Holiday Inn.[25] There, having proclaimed his independence and his determination to get 'the best possible deal for Labrador,'[26] he apparently began receiving all comers. 'Basically,' he told one reporter, 'my inclinations are Liberal but that can not be taken as an indication as to what way I'm going.'[27] Having met with his elected members on 1 November, Moores had this to say about the member for Labrador West: 'We will not make any special concessions to Mr. Burgess in order to obtain his support to form a government, but will approach the problems of Labrador in a manner that is one of fair and equal treatment for all the province...If Mr. Burgess wants to go along with us, that's fine. If he doesn't, then that's his decision.'[28] Faced with this apparent determination, Burgess at once let it be known that the Conservative attitude would not necessarily influence him to go the other way.'[29] He would only decide when the 'time' was right: 'It is not right,' he offered, 'at this particular moment.'

On 1 November also, Smallwood despatched his Minister of Finance, Frederick W. Rowe, one of the defeated Liberal candidates,[30] to Ottawa to represent the province at a meeting of provincial ministers.[31] In undertaking this mission, Rowe announced that his Ottawa engagement would be his last before resigning but his right to represent the province did not pass without challenge.[32] On the general question of what the government now could and could not do Moores stated, again after his initial meeting with his members, that any agreements, deals or borrowings entered into by the Liberal administration after election day would 'be the subject of review' by any future Conservative ministry.[33] 'We will honor appointments within the civil service which deal with the operation of the various departments,' he said. 'However, we will not honor the appointment of any defeated Liberal candidate as a sign of political patronage.'[34]

Smallwood made his next move in Ottawa, whither he had followed Fred Rowe. In the past he had enjoyed great influence in the capital, thanks to his long hold over most of Newfoundland's seats in the House of Commons. But at times, most notably during the strike in the province in 1959 of two locals of the International Woodworkers of America, he had greatly embarrassed some of the national leaders of his party.[35] Newfoundland's sitting representative in the federal cabinet, Donald Jamieson, did not owe his position in his native province to Smallwood.[36] His attitude in the existing crisis, therefore, was crucial. Jamieson could hardly be expected to tie the albatross of the Newfoundland Liberal party around his neck, but if Smallwood and his colleagues were to have any chance of success in their daring enterprise the federal minister's neutrality at least was essential.

On 2 November, the premier and the minister gave separate interviews in Ottawa about events in the province. Smallwood now said that he would resign if impending recounts showed the Liberals in a minority. 'I have no desire to hang on,' the premier said, 'if I do not have a majority.'[37] Jamieson supported Smallwood's stand and said that the best course now was for all concerned to await the results of the recounts.[38] This procedure also had the imprimatur of Senator Forsey who the same day was quoted by the *Evening Telegram* as saying that Smallwood 'would look foolish if he resigned now and then the recounts gave him an extra two or three seats.'[39] Moreover, Smallwood was not required to call the House together before the recount results became known. If, however, he did not have a majority after the recounts, he would have to call the House together as promptly as possible. 'It does not mean,' the Senator said, that 'he would have to interrupt an afternoon nap to do this, but I would think he would be expected to call it, say, within two weeks time, although there could be circumstances like a lot of illness or a major storm in the province which could give reason for a delay beyond that time period.' If the recounts produced a deadlocked

House, Smallwood would be entitled to another dissolution. His right to this would be manifest in the inability of the House, on meeting, to elect a speaker.

The chance of this happening was considerably diminished on 10 November when Moores, having met in Montreal with Tom Burgess, let it be known that the NLP leader would vote with the Conservatives in the legislature.[40] This 'political mixed marriage' was consummated at the St. John's Holiday Inn on 12 November when Moores and Burgess held a joint press conference. Despite offers from Liberal supporters that would make 'James Bond look like a boy scout,' Burgess had decided to support Moores because of the 'reasonable assurance' the latter had given him of a new attitude towards Labrador.[41] Only success in the recounts now stood between Moores and office, for if the election night result were confirmed, the Conservatives would now have twenty-two supporters and the Liberals twenty.

Smallwood meanwhile had taken a short vacation at an undisclosed destination following his Ottawa visit.[42] On his return to the province he announced on 8 November the resignations of six of seven cabinet ministers defeated on 28 October.[43] John Nolan, the Minister of Economic Development, was asked to stay on in the cabinet pending a recount in Ferryland district, where he had lost by only 105 votes. Then, on 11 November, Smallwood announced in a television address that he intended to resign both as leader of the Liberal party and as premier of the province no matter what the outcome of the recounts. To this end a leadership convention would soon be held. 'I shall resign as leader and I will not accept renomination...Should I be Premier then, I'll resign that position a day or so afterwards...If the Liberals have a majority after the recounts we'll stay on in power to meet the House in the coming winter...If the Liberals are in a minority, then I'll go to the Lieutenant Governor...and resign.'[44]

The focus of the crisis now shifted to the courts. Under the terms of the Newfoundland Election Act of 1954 and its amendments, the returning officer for each district was required to complete an 'official count' of the votes.[45] Candidates then had up to ten days to apply for recounts.[46] When completed, these 'official counts' confirmed the standings of election night: twenty-one PCs elected, twenty Liberals, one NLP.[47] Subsequently, petitions for recounts were made as follows:

TABLE 1

Date of Petition	Petitioner	District	Result on Official Count	
Nov. 12	Brendan Howard (PC)	Bay de Verde	William Saunders (L)	1,306
			Brendan Howard (PC)	1,285
			Liberal majority	21
Nov. 12	Trevor Bennett (L)	St. Barbe South	Edward Maynard (PC)	1,756
			Trevor Bennett (L)	1,748
			PC majority	8
Nov. 15	John Nolan (L)	Ferryland	Thomas Doyle (PC)	1,976
			John Nolan (L)	1,871
			PC majority	105
Nov. 15	Walter Hodder (L)	Burgeo & LaPoile	Allan Evans (PC)	2,754
			Walter Hodder (L)	2,671
			Andrew Wells (NDP)	174
			PC plurality	83
Nov. 16	Michael Maher (L)	St. Mary's	G. Ottenheimer (PC)	1,217
			Michael Maher (L)	1,134
			PC majority	83
Nov. 16	George Clarke (L)	Carbonear	Augustus Rowe (PC)	1,828
			George Clarke (L)	1,755
			PC majority	73

Table compiled from the official count as published in the *Evening Telegram* on 13 November and from the records of the Supreme Court of Newfoundland.

The first of the recounts was held on 18 November by Chief Justice Robert S. Furlong of the Newfoundland Supreme Court.[48] It confirmed the election of William Saunders in Bay de Verde and a certificate of election was issued to him the following day. The next recount—that of the votes cast in St. Barbe South—commenced at 10 am on 22 November before Justice H.G. Puddester. The result was sensational: the count could not be completed because the ballots cast in polling station 13 at Sally's Cove,[49] where Mrs. Olive Payne had been deputy returning officer, were missing. These, it now became known, had been burned on election night.[50] Faced with this impasse, Judge Puddester, on 24 November, issued to Melvin Gilley, the returning officer in St. Barbe, the certificate required of the court under section 91 of the Election Act. 'I was unable,' the Judge certified, 'to complete the recount because the votes cast at the said election in polling station 13 in the said District, having been previously destroyed by the deputy returning officer for the said polling station, were not available to be recounted.'[51]

Maynard now pressed Gilley to confirm his election, telegraphing him as follows:

> I now call upon you to transmit immediately to the Chief Electoral Officer the Writ of Election with your endorsement thereon that I have

been elected a Member of the House of Assembly comma a copy of the declaration of my election which you signed and delivered to me at the conclusion of the official count and the other documents which you are now required to send to him by section 78 (1) of the Election Act.[52]

But Gilley had already submitted the writ of election on 24 November, endorsing it to show that the election in the seat was undecided."[53]

When subsequent recounts confirmed all other election night winners, the issue in St. Barbe South became decisive. With no usable certificate of election having been issued there, the standings in the new Assembly now were: PCs 20, Liberals 20, NLP 1, undecided 1. Since Tom Burgess had now agreed to support Moores, the Conservatives could, presumably, control the House with the deciding vote of a Conservative speaker (twenty-one to twenty). On the other hand, the debacle in St. Barbe South meant that Smallwood did not yet have to call the House together, since it was still not clear who had the right to sit in it. Moreover, if the Liberals could get the courts to declare the seat vacant and then carry the subsequent by-election, they would have the same number of members as the Conservatives had with the addition of Tom Burgess (twenty-one each). If the Liberals were then to elect a speaker, they stood to be defeated on the very first vote. But any Conservative government would be faced with exactly the same problem. In the circumstances, Smallwood would have a powerful argument for another dissolution. At the very least St. Barbe South gave him more time to manoeuvre and there was no telling what the prospect of a Liberal by-election victory might touch off by way of movement of elected members from one party to another. The path across the floor was well trodden in Newfoundland and to make the journey before the House had even met was figuratively, not beyond the bounds of possibility. For the Conservatives success in St. Barbe South—whether through the courts or on the hustings—meant power at last; but the prospect of fighting a by-election in a seat they had carried by only eight votes must have been very distasteful to them. It would be like fighting the general election all over again—only this time in a single seat, where the government had a great deal of support and where it could bring the full weight of its influence to bear. With Smallwood threatening to rise phoenix like from his own ashes the Conservatives looked to the Crown and the courts for redress.

On 25 November, Moores released to the press the text of Ed Maynard's telegram to Melvin Gilley.[54] The election in St. Barbe South, he argued, was not null and void until such time as it had been proved so under the procedures of the Election Act and this had not been done.[55] Moores said his party would welcome 'a thorough investigation into the burning of the ballots,' noting that Smallwood had been 'far too confident awaiting the results of the recounts and one cannot help but ask why?' 'We are witnessing,' he ventured, 'a spectacle of a man glorying in the past when the future of our Province is what is important. The hard fact remains that 52 per cent of the people in this Province voted P.C. in this past election and 44 per cent voted Liberal. The hard fact remains that Tom Burgess has openly declared he will be supporting a P.C. government which gives us a clear majority of seats.'

On 30 November Moores addressed a letter to the Lieutenant Governor, E. John A. Harnum, in the same spirit.[56] Reviewing the election results and the magnitude of the turnout at the polls, he attributed the contrast between the popular vote received by each party and the distribution of members elected to 'the present disgraceful distribution of voters in electoral districts in this Province.' With regard to the St. Barbe South situation, Moores claimed again 'that the official count now stands, so that Mr. Maynard of the Progressive Conservative Party is the elected Member for that District.' This situation might change if the Supreme Court granted 'a controverted election petition' but it might be 'many weeks' before 'a final determination' was made on such a petition. With the support he now had from Burgess, Moores argued, the Liberals could not elect a speaker and could not govern even if they ultimately carried St. Barbe South in a by-election. As things stood, the Liberal government was doomed to defeat when the House of Assembly met.

Moores next asserted that 'every modern precedent' indicated that the Liberal administration should resign. He cited three examples: the Nova Scotia election of 1970 following which the PC Smith government had resigned in the face of a result which had given it twenty-one members to twenty-three for the Liberals and two for the New Democratic Party (NDP); the Manitoba election of 1969 following which the PC government of that province had resigned in favour of a New Democrat government which would be in a minority position in the House; and the Canadian general election of 1957 following which a Liberal administration had resigned in favour of a PC minority one. 'In all these instances,' Moores concluded, 'the governments involved accepted the fact that they had lost the support and confidence of the people although no other party received an absolute majority.'

From description and precedent, Moores moved on to advice. Specifically, he submitted 'that the present leader of the Liberal Administration should be called upon to tender his resignation to Your Honour in accordance with the invariable practice in situations where the government party has failed to secure a majority of seats in the Legislature as the result of a general election.' If the premier refused to resign, then the Lieutenant Governor should, in accordance with his discretionary powers, inform him 'that the House of Assembly must be called together within the next week or 10 days so that any claim of the present Administration that it controls a majority of the members of the House of Assembly can be put to the test.' Unless the government could meet the House, appoint a Speaker, and carry on business 'in the traditional manner,' there was no justification for its continuance in office. Moores also informed Harnum that his party took 'the position that no actions of the present government except the transaction of very ordinary routine business, should now be countenanced':

> No vacant offices in the Civil Service should now be filled, no contracts should now be entered into and no obligations should now be undertaken by the rejected Liberal Administration of this Province...the borrowing of money, the issuance of guarantees, the making of appointments and the dealing with the many crises that now affect this Province cannot be undertaken by an Administration that will be defeated as soon as the House of Assembly is called together even were that Administration successful in electing a Member in the District of St. Barbe South if another election were ordered in that District.

Finally, Moores assured the Lieutenant Governor that 'if called upon by you to form a government I will meet the House of Assembly at an early date in the month of December to appoint a Speaker and that my Administration will be in a position to carry on the business of this Province and to have the House of Assembly pass Supply when needed.' For good measure Tom Burgess wrote the Lieutenant Governor the following day to second what Moores had said in his letter. Between them, Moores and Burgess, with the able hand of John Crosbie in the background, had put the opposition case forcefully; but the Conservative leader's arguments were at best controversial. His claim that Maynard was entitled to sit for St. Barbe South until the courts had declared on the disposition of the seat was clearly arguable. Other precedents could be found to counter the ones he had mustered: instances in which governments had stayed in power through facing opposition legislative majorities. Mackenzie King's daring display in 1925-26 was but one example. Moreover, while Moores' analysis of what would happen to the Smallwood government in an evenly divided House was no doubt correct, there was no evidence that he could command the House himself in the same circumstances.

If the situation of an evenly divided House should arise, the question facing the Crown would be the one that had confronted Governor Sir William MacGregor after the Newfoundland tie election of 1908; who should have the right to dissolution? But for the moment this was mere speculation. The Crown, of course, must be guided always in constitutional matters by the facts before it and these were clear enough. Only if the Lieutenant Governor accepted Moores' argument about Maynard's right to sit in the House pending any litigation that might arise out of his election could the Conservative leader form the government that he promised. In the case of St. Barbe South legal remedy had not yet been exhausted and until it was there was no reason for the Crown to act. As for ordering the government to call the House together, Smallwood could still claim that the Assembly ought not to meet until it had been established fully who had the right to sit in it. Accordingly, Harnum's reply on 2 December to Moores' six page typewritten missive could hardly have been more blunt or less promising—or for that matter more constitutionally correct: 'Thank you for your letter of November 30th regarding the matter of the recent election. I have now to tell you that I have referred your letter to my Ministers for their advice.'

The previous day, 1 December, Ed Maynard had sought to have his election validated by applying to the Supreme Court that a writ of mandamus be issued to Melvin Gilley directing him so to endorse the writ of election for the district of St. Barbe South.[57] Then, on 2 December, counsel for Trevor Bennett filed a petition before Justice Puddester calling upon the court to declare the election in St. Barbe South void.[58] While the hearings on these petitions were pending, Moores renewed his efforts to obtain the assistance of the Crown. Thus, in a radio and television address on the night of 2 December, he once more called upon the Lieutenant Governor to intervene, insisting that the Crown had the power either to request the government's resignation or to inform it 'that the House of Assembly must be called together now to resolve this situation.'[59] On 14 December, after Justice Puddester had refused, on 8 December, Ed Maynard's application for a writ of mandamus,[60] Moores appealed to the Governor General, Roland Michener. His letter, he told Michener, was written on the unanimous request of the twenty-one (he counted Maynard as elected) PC members of the House of Assembly and Burgess. The facts of the case were set out in his and Burgess' letters to the Lieutenant Governor and in the latter's letter of reply to him, all of which were forwarded. 'It appears quite obvious,' he continued, 'the Smallwood Liberal Administration has no intention of resigning office. I am most apprehensive His Honour the Lieutenant Governor will not exercise his constitutional responsibilities and dismiss the Smallwood Liberal Administration or alternatively call the House of Assembly into immediate session. I have been asked, therefore, to humbly petition Your Excellency to tender your good advice to His Honour the Lieutenant Governor of Newfoundland and Labrador in hope that he will bring about the resignation on dismissal of the Smallwood Liberal Administration or alternatively call the House of Assembly of Newfoundland into immediate session. The gravity of the constitutional and political situation in Newfoundland is such that I respectfully request Your Excellency's urgent attention to this problem.'

Receipt of this letter was acknowledged on 17 December and the Governor General himself replied on 24 December. Once more Moores had the door slammed in his face:

> In response to your letter of December 14th, 1971, and enclosures (received December 17th), I have given consideration to the request which you made. There seems to be no doubt that as Governor General I have no constitutional right or duty to offer to His Honour the Lieutenant Governor of Newfoundland and Labrador the advice that you requested me to give him with respect to terminating the present

Administration of the Province or calling the Legislative Assembly into session.[61]

Everything now hinged on St. Barbe South and Trevor Bennett's petition, the hearing on which had been set for 5 January. Few cases in Newfoundland history have aroused as much interest and the legal talent on both sides was impressive. Bennett was represented at the hearing by Nathaniel Noel, a former Liberal member of the House of Assembly, and Maynard by James Greene, a former leader of the provincial Progressive Conservative party. Their arguments were heard by Chief Justice Furlong and Justice Arthur Mifflin. Their decision against Bennett and awarding costs to Maynard was filed on 11 January. The essence of Chief Justice Furlong's argument was as follows:

> The law provides the grounds on which an election can be, or more correctly, is to be declared void. These grounds are discoverable either in the [Election] Act or at common law. In a general way they relate and are referable solely, to matters which occur either before the casting of votes or during the actual balloting. The underlying reason for declaring an election void is that is has been established that some conduct on the part of those entrusted with the conduct of the election, has prevented the ballot being conducted properly. I think it is a new concept to hold that what happens after an election has been completed and after a poll has been declared to say that the declared wishes of a majority, no matter how small, of the voters must be set aside and the opponents to begin all over again. To take this position is as unfair as it is illogical. To go further, if the motive for seeking to avoid an election for these post-election irregularities is to prevent abuse, then to throw the whole election in a district open again is to breed corruption and dishonesty. I think that once the result of a vote has been ascertained, and that it has been established that the votes cast by the electors have properly been cast without any taint or corruption or intimidation, then the election must be accepted as the final declaration of the voters...I think the law to be clear: if the election was carried out properly and in substantial manner in the spirit of the Act, and if the voters were able to express their choice clearly and decisively without any obstruction or hindrance an election should not be set aside because of some failure to observe the letter of the Act. This admits of only one qualification, and that is, that if the failure to observe the letter of the Act in the opinion of the election court could have altered the result of the election then it may be set aside. I would add to this that by the result, I mean the ultimate election of one or other of the candidates, and not the number of votes which one received more than another...where the voters had a free and unfettered opportunity to express their choice then the Court should not interfere without being satisfied that there was in fact no true election...I have little difficulty in arriving at the conclusion that this election was properly conducted and there are no grounds upon which it should be set aside and declared void. The electors freely made their choice known, they voted and their votes were counted in all the polling stations in the District, including Polling Station No. 13 at

Sally['s] Cove. The only failure in the mechanics of this election was that a recount of votes was not possible—some of the ballots were destroyed after they had been properly counted. It cannot be over emphasized that the [Election] Act provides for the official counting to be done at the individual polling stations by the Deputy Returning Officers in the presence of the candidates, or their agents, and the result to be recorded and certified by the Deputy Returning Officer in a Statement of the Poll in Form 48. The Act provides for a judicial recount, but where one is not sought then the result certified in Form 48 is the sole measure of the candidate's performance. So with this case; there was no recount; not because one was not sought, but because it was a physical impossibility. Where there is no recount then the Statement of the Poll is the announced result, and this must be so, unless the election be set aside. I have said there are no grounds to set aside the election, and it follows logically that I must say the results at this polling station No. 13 are those shown in Form 48. The Returning Officer for the District has made his official addition and has certified the Declaration of Election (Form 50) with the following result:

> Edward Maynard   1756
> Trevor Bennett   1748

This result must be endorsed on the Writ of Election and it is ordered that the Returning Officer comply with this direction of the Court. The petition must be dismissed, the election of Edward Maynard is affirmed, and a certificate to this effect has been issued for the information of the House of Assembly.[62]

Justice Mifflin also noted that Bennett's petition did not allege 'any wrongdoing before or during the counting of the votes cast for the candidates or before the official addition of the votes by the returning officer from the statements of the poll prepared by the deputy returning officers and the issue of a declaration in Form 50 by the returning officer that Edward Maynard had received the larger number of votes and was therefore declared elected...the mistake was made after the votes were cast, after the poll was closed, and after the votes were properly counted and the official addition of the votes was properly made.'[63] This line of argument led him to precisely the same conclusion as Chief Justice Furlong:

> Such a case is not one in which the election should be declared void; the election was properly conducted up to and including the counting of the votes for each candidate and the preparing of the statement of the poll so far as polling station thirteen is concerned. And there is no suggestion that it was not so conducted so far as any other polling station in St. Barbe South is concerned...A recount 'delays' the making of a return; it does not 'prevent' the making of a return if one can be made. And one can be made if, as in St. Barbe South, the votes have been cast and counted in accordance with the Act but a recount cannot be completed because of an innocent mistake made, after the votes had been counted, not by a candidate or his agent or anyone acting for him but by an election official appointed to have some part in the conduct of the election. To hold otherwise would do a grave injustice to Mr.

Maynard; the mistake was not his; it was made after the votes were counted; there was no irregularity during the holding of the poll. And, not only would it do an injustice to Mr. Maynard but it would do an injustice to the voters of St. Barbe South because they would in effect be disenfranchaised in the election through no fault of any elector or of any candidate. Moreover, not to order a return to be made but to declare an election void under the circumstances would leave the door open to the possibilities of practices which would invalidate any election.

Bennett could presumably have appealed the decision of the Newfoundland court to the Supreme Court of Canada but he did not do so. On the possibility of appeal Senator Forsey told the *Evening Telegram*: 'I won't comment on what I think of such an idea'; 'considering the great public protest,' it would be 'very unwise' for the premier to stay on pending such an appeal.[64] Nor did Smallwood attempt this course: the government, it seemed, now had a certain majority against it in the new Assembly (twenty-two to twenty) and on 13 January Smallwood announced that his government would resign, an intention he carried out on 18 January.

He had maintained himself for so long by invoking the letter of the constitution rather than its spirit. Yet if he had skated on the edge of propriety he had done so in masterly fashion and had never gone over. Moreover, whatever may be thought of the wisdom of his course politically, his daring rearguard action, by testing the limits of 'responsible government,' left behind it some interesting precedents and questions. The first of these involves the calling together of a House after an election. In effect Smallwood successfully defended the proposition that a government faced with an uncertain verdict at the polls need not meet the House until recounts and litigation under the Election Act have made it clear who commands the House, if anyone. In the case of Trevor Bennett's petition the Newfoundland Supreme Court gave precedence to the initial count over a candidate's right to a recount. The Crown seems to have behaved rather differently: in the calling together of the Assembly it gave precedence to proceedings by candidates relevant to the control of the House over the interim verdict of election day. Left perhaps unanswered was the question of the limitations, if any, on the exercise of power by the Smallwood government after the election. When a government clearly has been defeated in an election, custom decrees that, pending resignation, it will limit itself to what Moores liked to call 'very ordinary routine business.' Moores argued throughout that Smallwood's government should limit itself or be limited in the same way but there is no evidence that the Crown expressed an opinion on this matter. Is a government in limbo on the same footing as one about to enter purgatory or worse? It might still well be wondered.

The sequel to Smallwood's resignation was of a piece with what had gone before. On 13 January Tom Burgess had let it be known that his support for the Conservatives was now contingent on the Tory caucus again making public the guarantees which had been given him.[65] One of these guarantees, he later claimed, was a place for him in the cabinet.[66] The same day Burgess stated that he and the Tories would have to reach an agreement by the next afternoon 'or else.'[67] When asked to amplify this remark, he said: 'Or else the country will be into another general election.' On the fourteenth he said that he did not want 'to back Mr. Moores into a corner'[68] but the following day announced that he would be writing to the Lieutenant Governor to revoke the commitment to the Tories he had made in his letter to Harnum on 1 December.[69] His intention now was 'to vote on each piece of legislation and issue as my conscience dictates.' He would not, he said, accept another commitment from the Tories 'if they painted it on the white cliffs of Dover with a tar brush.' Thus when the Moores government was sworn in on the eighteenth, it faced a highly uncertain future in the House. If the Tories were to elect a speaker from their own number, the twenty Liberal members and Burgess could combine to defeat the new administration at will. On 21 January, however, this threat was removed when W.A. Oldford, who had been elected as a Liberal in Fortune Bay, announced that he would not take his seat in the Assembly.[70] Oldford had left the magistracy and been sworn into the Smallwood government as a minister without portfolio on 2 August.[71] On 25 November he had been sworn in as Minister of Supply and Services. He had carried Fortune Bay by 251 votes, his Tory opponent there being H.R.V. Earle, a former Liberal minister who had gone into opposition after the tumultuous Liberal leadership campaign of 1969. In announcing his decision, Oldford said that he had entered politics with a great deal of 'apprehension and reluctance' and wished to return to the magistracy.[72] Commenting on this development T.A. Hickman, now Tory Minister of Justice, said that an application from Oldford for a magisterial appointment would be considered but that the latter's rights under the relevant legislation would 'have to be the subject of fairly careful scrutiny.'[73] Ultimately, this scrutiny produced a favourable verdict and Oldford's passage back to more tranquil waters was completed on 9 February, when he was reappointed magistrate at Grand Falls.[74]

Tranquility, however, was not yet to be the lot of Moores, for three days after Oldford's unusual exit Hugh Shea, who had been elected as a Conservative in St. John's South, announced that he now intended to sit in the House as an independent.[75] Shea, who had been passed over for office, had contested the leadership of the Tory party at the convention which had chosen Moores. His reasoning now was that the district which had elected him was 'so chronically filled with problems' that it had 'to be represented in cabinet.'[76] His action once again put the government in jeopardy; assuming a Conservative speaker, nineteen Tories would face nineteen Liberals and Burgess and Shea when the House opened. The threat facing the new government was made even more explicit on 31 January when both Burgess and Shea announced that they would sit in the House as Liberals.[77] Equally startling, Burgess now also announced that he would be a candidate for the leadership, about to be vacated by Smallwood, of the Liberal party. 'Nobody can deny,' he said, 'that if I were the leader of one of the established parties in essence the rewards that will come to the people of my district as a result of my success will be far greater than me sitting as an Independent.'[78] The NLP was a 'one-shot deal,' to make Labrador the 'focal point of attention.'[79]

The two mavericks were accepted unanimously by the Liberal caucus on 2 February, the day before registration began for the party's leadership convention at the Canon Stirling Auditorium in St. John's.[80] Four leadership candidates presented themselves to the delegates to this convention: Burgess; Edward Roberts, who had served in Smallwood's cabinet; Rod Moores, a twenty-two year old student at Memorial University; and Vincent Spencer, a businessman from Windsor. The first candidate in the field, Steve Neary, who had also served in the Smallwood government, had dropped out on 31 January in favour of Roberts.[81] The latter easily carried the convention on the afternoon of 5 February, winning 564 votes to 82 for Burgess, 14 for Moores and 3 for Spencer.[82]

To say the least, Roberts assumed the leadership of the Liberal party in anomalous circumstances. As things stood, he would, when the House opened, command a legislative majority from the opposition benches. On the other hand he was intimately associated with Smallwood and through him with the electoral reverse of October and the subsequent desperate struggle of the Liberal government to maintain itself in power. Not surprisingly, Roberts chose to play a waiting game. To defeat the government precipitately might bring a further stinging rebuke from the electorate. Yet if the new government faltered, Roberts might find himself in the premier's chair—and without the necessity for a new election. The problem with this strategy was maintaining caucus solidarity: loyalty has never been the most prominent of Newfoundland political virtues and in the spring of 1972, after the actions of Oldford, Burgess and Shea it seemed to be a particularly scarce commodity.

On 19 February Roberts explored the constitutional implications of the existing political balance in a letter to Harnum.[83] Pointing out that twenty-one of those elected in October had said they intended to support the opposition and twenty the government, he informed the Lieutenant Governor that he intended 'to make a public demand that the Administration advise Your Honour to open the House immediately.' 'Until the Administration,' he wrote, 'cause the House to be opened, there is no conclusive way to determine whether the present Administration possess the confidence of the House, in other words the support of a majority of the Members.' The fact that 'the spending authority' approved by the previous Assembly would be exhausted on 31 March was a 'further reason' for immediate action. Next Roberts repeated a commitment he had made publicly on several occasions not to defeat the government 'as long as they act in the best interests of Newfoundland.' While this was 'a matter for judgement,' he assured Harnum that 'we have no intention of seeking the defeat of the government on any matter of confidence involving any issue or question which is not of the gravest and most serious nature. We will not seek to defeat the Administration capriciously or lightly. We are prepared to enable the Administration to organize the House, and to proceed with the normal business including consideration of a request by your Ministers for Supply.' Considering the 'urgent need for a period of political stability in the affairs of the Government of this Province,' the Liberal members would waive 'for the present what many would consider to be our rightful position as a group comprising a majority of the Members of the House of Assembly.' 'We do not seek power,' he asserted, 'we seek to serve the people of this Province.'

Having thus explained the position he would take when the House met, Roberts passed on to a disscussion of the conditions under which the new Assembly might be dissolved. 'My colleagues and I would not presume,' he wrote, 'to advise Your Honour with respect to the constitutional position. Nonetheless, it may not be amiss to set forth our view of the position in Newfoundland, so that Your Honour will have the benefit of this information should it be of assistance to you.' Altogether Roberts dealt with three possibilities: the emergence of an issue 'upon which the Administration will not be able to command the confidence of the House'; advice by the Administration to the Lieutenant Governor to dissolve the House 'even though they may have received the support of the House on any given measure'; and advice for dissolution 'tendered by an Administration which has not even sought to test the House.' While 'the decision whether or not to grant a request for dissolution' was a matter that fell 'within the absolute discretion of the Crown,' there was 'a large and coherent body of precedents and practices' in this regard. The 'persistent theme' running through 'the writings of the authorities' on the subject was that 'an Administration which is defeated by the House on a matter of confidence, or which requests a dissolution even though it has not been defeated, is not entitled to a dissolution if there is a real possibility that an alternative Administration can be formed.'

With this in mind Roberts committed himself as follows:

> The Opposition group in the House of Assembly, twenty-one in number in a House of forty-one, are capable of forming an Administration. We do not seek to do so, and, indeed, as I have said earlier we have taken precisely the opposite position. Nonetheless, if Your Honour invites me to form an Administration I will do so, and will attempt to carry on the business of the Government of this Province. I take this stand because my Colleagues and I believe that the affairs of the people of Newfoundland and Labrador require above all at this time that there be a period of political stability. So strongly do we hold this belief that we are even prepared to foreswear our claim to be the Government. If

the present Administration should spurn our offer to cooperate in an effort to serve the people of Newfoundland, then we would form a Government if Your Honour should invite us to do so...If a request is made for a dissolution, then it is a matter which falls entirely within the discretion entrusted to Your Honour by the constitution. We will have no quarrel with whatever decision Your Honour does make. There will be no criticism of the Crown by the Liberal Party as long as I am Leader. On the precedents, however, we submit that if Your Honour felt it was in the best interests of Newfoundland to reject the request for a dissolution, then you would be exercising your prerogative in full harmony with proper constitutional practice as it has developed in Canada and elsewhere. In these circumstances, if Your Honour should invite me to form an Administration, I would do so. I do not seek such an opportunity, but if the interests of the people of Newfoundland require this, then I will discharge my duty to the best of my ability.

True to his word, the new Liberal leader called a press conference two days later and said it was 'high time for the Crosbie-Moores administration to open the House of Assembly.'[84] The next day Premier Moores, who had for so long pressed Smallwood on the same matter, said that the government intended to call the House together during the first week of March.[85] Then on 25 February he announced that a by-election would be held in Fortune district on 20 March.[86] On 28 February he told a press conference that should his party lose this by-election his government would resign in favour of a new Liberal administration.[87] The initial report of the *Evening Telegram* on this press conference also said that the premier had 'confirmed that the House would not be called until later this month, perhaps as late as 22 March, the first Wednesday after the holding of the Fortune by-election.'[88] But what was stated as fact one day became a 'distinct impression'[89] the next, for on the evening of the 28th the premier announced that the House would meet on the afternoon of 1 March.[90]

In the event, James Russell, the Tory member for Lewisporte, was appointed Speaker, leaving nineteen government supporters to look across at twenty rather than the anticipated twenty-one opposition supporters. The missing member to the right of Mr. Speaker was William Saunders, who had been elected in Bay de Verde and confirmed in his place on a recount.[91] On 28 February he had addressed a letter to the clerk of the House indicating that he would not be taking his seat.[92] His departure did not affect the government's minority position but it ensured that, numerically at least, an administration led by Roberts would, pending the outcome of the by-election in Fortune Bay, be in exactly the same position in the House. In these circumstances Moores approached Harnum for a dissolution on the very evening of the day the House had met. The Moores government had not been defeated in the House; indeed there had been no division there in the brief afternoon sitting.[93] But Moores had gained the advantage by meeting the House successfully, albeit on a single occasion. His advice was accepted by Harnum, leaving the members of the thirty-fifth general assembly with \$259,990.13 in sessional pay for their afternoon's work.[94] In the election which followed the Conservatives carried thirty-four seats and the Liberals eight.[95] Constitutionally at least the good ship Terra Nova had returned to even keel.

NOTES

*This paper was originally published in the *Dalhousie Law Journal*. It is reprinted here, in revised form, with permission.

1   For the details see Gertrude E. Gunn, *The Political History of Newfoundland, 1832-1864* (Toronto 1966), 85-109.

2   S.J.R. Noel, *Politics in Newfoundland* (Toronto 1971), 23.

3   Ibid., 68-76. See also Noel's 'Politics and the Crown: The Case of the 1908 Tie Election in Newfoundland,' *Canadian Journal of Economics and Political Science* 33, no. 2 (1967): 285-91.

4   Noel, *Politics in Newfoundland*, 128.

5   Ibid., 171-2.

6   See Peter Neary (ed.), *The Political Economy of Newfoundland, 1929-1972* (Toronto 1973), 21-2.

7   Ibid., 103-06.

8   *Evening Telegram* (St. John's), 7 Oct. 1971.

9   For a survey of the political history of Newfoundland, 1949-71, see Peter Neary, 'Party Politics in Newfoundland, 1949-71: A Survey and Analysis' in James Hiller and Peter Neary (eds.), *Newfoundland in the Nineteenth and Twentieth Centuries: Essays in Interpretation* (Toronto 1980), 205-45.

10 *Evening Telegram*, 29 Oct. 1971.

11 Ibid., 29 Oct. 1971.

12 Ibid., 30 Oct. 1971.

13 Ibid.

14 In Bay de Verde and Burgeo & LaPoile Liberal candidates had defeated their PC opponents by 21 and 88 votes respectively. In Labrador South Josiah Harvey of the Liberals had defeated Michael Martin of the NLP by 83 votes. Close Conservative wins over Liberals were Carbonear (68 votes), Ferryland (106 votes), and St. Barbe South (8 votes). In accordance with section 78, subsection 3 of the Election Act of 1954 the Chief Electoral Officer, H.W. Strong, published a statistical report on the election in *The Newfoundland Gazette* on 1 Feb. 1972. Except where otherwise noted, all statistical references to the election here are from this source. The St. Barbe South result is marked 'Undetermined (Decision of Supreme Court of Newfoundland)' in Strong's report. The reason for this is evident below.

15 The remainder of the popular vote was divided as follows: NLP, 2.4 per cent; New Democratic Party, 1.73 per cent; Independent, 0.07 per cent.

16 See Hiller and Neary (eds.), *Newfoundland*, 232.

17 Ibid., 235.

18 Ibid.19

19 *Evening Telegram*, 30 Oct. 1971.

20 Ibid.

21 Ibid.

22 Ibid.

23 Ibid., 31 Dec. 1971. 'It is easy to understand,' the same columnist wrote, 'Mr. Smallwood's motive for hanging on. He is drunk with power and has lost all contact with reality. That is why he still thinks he is premier. Now it looks as if some of his cabinet ministers have delusions as great as their master's. They go on burdening the province with new commitments with a kind of Liberal arrogance which points to them being God's Chosen Ones. It is quite amazing that they have the gall to go to Confederation Building to sit in their offices, let alone issue press releases and hold press conferences. They forget that they now rule not as a legal government but as a Liberal Party which has rejected the normal procedures of democracy. In the same way the Nazi Party ruled Germany.'

24 *Evening Telegram*, 1 Nov. 1971.

25 Ibid., 2 Nov. 1971.

26 Ibid., 1 Nov. 1971.

27 Ibid.

28 Ibid., 2 Nov. 1971

29 Ibid.

30 Rowe had been defeated in Grand Falls by Aubrey Senior. Altogether seven ministers had been rejected in the election. On 31 Oct. Smallwood said that the defeated ministers would resign in a 'reasonable and decent interval' (*Evening Telegram*, 1 Nov. 1971). Senator Forsey's view of the matter was that defeated ministers could remain in office for 'eight or nine months or even a year...a year would be considered a reasonable period of time in any kind of respectable jurisdiction' (ibid.). In saying this he had in mind the examples of General A.G.L. McNaughton in the third ministry of Mackenzie King and C.F.G. Masterman in Asquith's Liberal ministry (letter to author, 7 Nov. 1977).

31 *Evening Telegram*, 1 Nov. 1971.

32 Ibid., 3 Nov. 1971.

33 Ibid., 2 Nov. 1971.

34 Ibid.

35 See Hiller and Neary (eds.), *Newfoundland*, 219-23.

36 Jamieson entered the House of Commons as the member for Burin-Burgeo in a by-election on 19 Sept. 1966. He was then successively Minister of Defence Production, Minister of Transport, Minister of Regional Economic Expansion, Minister of Industry, Trade and Commerce, and Secretary of State for External Affairs (*The Canadian Parliamentary Guide*, 1977, 260).

37 *Evening Telegram*, 2 Nov. 1971.

38 Ibid.

39 Ibid.

40 Ibid., 10 Nov. 1971.

41 Ibid., 13 Nov. 1971.

42 Ibid., 9 Nov. 1971.

43 See note 30 above.

44 *Evening Telegram*, 12 Nov. 1971.

45   Deputy returning officers were required by the Act to return their ballot boxes
      to their district returning officer. The box for each poll had to be sealed with
      the ballots, other materials used in the election, and a statement of the poll
      inside in envelopes provided for the purpose (*Statutes of Newfoundland*, 1954,
      no. 79, section 74, 9 and 10, 351). Having received the ballot boxes from his
      deputies, the returning officer was required to open them, take from each the
      official statement of the poll, and 'add together the number of votes given for
      each candidate' (section 75, 2). This process is referred to in the Act 'as the
      official addition of the votes.' When it was completed, the returning officer
      was required to seal each box again 'with a special metal seal supplied to him
      for that purpose' (*Statutes of Newfoundland*, 1964, no. 29, section 75, 4A, 142).
      Thus, the official count did not involve any examination of individual ballots.

46   See *Statutes of Newfoundland*, 1954, no. 79, section 80, 359.

47   *Evening Telegram*, 13 Nov. 1971.

48   Records of Supreme Court of Newfoundland.

49   This is the name given in the *Gazetteer of Canada: Newfoundland* (Ottawa 1983),
      152. Variants in other sources are Sally Cove and Sallys Cove.

50   A magisterial enquiry conducted by Magistrate C.C. Stone of Woody Point,
      Bonne Bay, found that the ballots had been 'inadvertently burnt on election
      night.' Magistrate Stone found no evidence of 'any malicious or wilful intent.'
      'To hold one person up,' he concluded, 'as the object of criticism and suspicion
      in this case seems to be most unfair and undeserving.' Mrs. Payne apparently
      did not realize the ballots had been burnt 'until the night of the recount.' No
      charges were laid as a result of this enquiry (Magistrate Stone's report is
      available in the office of the Chief Electoral Officer, St. John's).

51   For a copy of the certificate see Supreme Court of Newfoundland, 1971, no.
      1601.

52   Ibid., answer filed by William M. Marshall, 17 Dec. 1971. Marshall had been
      elected for the Conservatives in St. John's East.

53   Ibid.

54   *Evening Telegram*, 26 Nov. 1971.

55   Ibid.

56   I am grateful to Frank D. Moores, former Premier of Newfoundland, for the
      use of this letter and his other correspondence following. The Lieutenant
      Governor had previously been sent messages by PC supporters in St. Barbe
      South (*Evening Telegram*, 26 Nov. 1971).

57   Supreme Court of Newfoundland, 1971, no. 1597.

58   Supreme Court of Newfoundland, 1971, no. 1601.

59   *Evening Telegram*, 3 Dec. 1971.

60   Supreme Court of Newfoundland, 1971, no. 1597. Mr. Justice Puddester's
      decision was founded on sections 120, 121 and 135 of the Election Act. Under
      section 120 a petition 'complaining of...no return...may be presented to the
      Supreme Court by a candidate.' Section 121 made this provision: 'whenever
      a petition is presented under this Act complaining of no return, such order
      may be made thereon by the Court as is deemed expedient for compelling a
      return to be made, or the Court may allow the petition to be tried in the manner
      herein provided with respect to ordinary election petitions.' Section 135 (i)
      provided that 'Every election petition shall be tried by two Judges without a

jury.' Citing these provisions, Justice Puddester reached this conclusion: 'Even assuming that the Supreme Court of Newfoundland would have, on general principles, jurisdiction to issue a writ of mandamus directing any official to carry out a duty imposed upon him by the Election Act in connection with an election held under that Act...I am now, after a great deal of study and thought as well before as after the hearing...convinced that mandamus does not lie here because...the legislature of Newfoundland has in its wisdom set up a special court—an election court as I shall call it—consisting of two Judges of the Supreme Court of Newfoundland and has given the election court jurisdiction to deal with, among others, the very question raised here— that of no return—and has also given to the election court power to make the very order I am being asked to make in this mandamus application, that is, an order compelling a return to be made—in effect to grant mandamus.

In my view, therefore, if Mr. Maynard has a specific legal right to be declared the elected representative for the District in the House of Assembly then sections 120 and 121 of the Election Act provide a specific legal remedy for enforcing that right which is no less convenient, beneficial and effectual than a writ of mandamus as such directed to Mr. Gilley would be. Accordingly, I dismiss this application of Edward Maynard for a writ of mandamus...Melvin Gilley, and Trevor Bennett who was given leave to appear and to be heard at the hearing, are both entitled to their costs against Edward Maynard.'

61   Michener could, of course, have intervened on the advice of his ministers. For examples of advice by the Government of Canada to Lieutenant Governors see Eugene Forsey, 'Dominion Status for the Provinces' in his *Freedom and Order* (Toronto 1974), 157-77.

62   Supreme Court of Newfoundland, 1971, no. 1601, 'Judgement of Furlong, C.J.'

63   Ibid., 'Judgement of Mifflin, J.'

64   *Evening Telegram*, 12 Jan. 1972.

65   Ibid., 13 Jan. 1972.

66   Ibid., 17 Jan. 1972.

67   Ibid., 13 Jan. 1972.

68   Ibid., 15 Jan. 1972.

69   Ibid., 17 Jan. 1972.

70   Ibid., 22 Jan. 1972. Oldford's letter to the Clerk of the House is dated 21 Jan. 1972 (I am grateful to Senator G.R. Ottenheimer, Speaker of the Newfoundland House of Assembly, 1975-9, for this information). Oldford was said by the press to have 'resigned' his seat. Technically, of course, this was not correct since he had never been sworn in and taken the seat to which he was entitled. The true meaning of his letter to the Clerk of House, however phrased, was what is said above - that he did not intend to sit.

71   *Evening Telegram*, 26 Nov. 1971.

72   Ibid., 22 Jan. 1972.

73   Ibid.

74   By Minute of Council 137. I am grateful to Anne Hart of the Centre for Newfoundland Studies, Queen Elizabeth II Library, Memorial University, St. John's, for this information.

75   *Evening Telegram*, 25 Jan. 1972. For Shea's own account of this period see his *Shea's Newfoundland Seduced* (New York 1976).

76   *Evening Telegram*, 25 Jan. 1972.

77   Ibid., 1 Feb. 1972.

78   Ibid.

79   Ibid.

80   Ibid., 3 Feb. 1972.

81   Ibid., 1 Feb. 1972.

82   Ibid., 7 Feb. 1972.

83   I am grateful to Mr. Roberts for the use of this letter.

84   *Evening Telegram*, 22 Feb. 1972.

85   Ibid., 23 Feb. 1972.

86   Ibid., 26 Feb. 1972.

87   Ibid., 28 Feb. 1972.

88   Ibid.

89   Ibid., 29 Feb. 1972

90   Ibid.

91   See above table 1.

92   I am grateful to Senator G.R. Ottenheimer for this information. Again, it was said that Saunders had 'resigned' his seat. Like Oldford (see note 70 above), not having accepted his seat he cannot be said to have 'resigned' from it. In practice, of course, not taking a seat in these circumstances had the same effect as resignation.

93   The motion that a select committee be appointed to draft an address in reply to the speech from the throne was carried on a voice vote (House of Assembly, *Verbatim Report*, 1 March 1972). During the afternoon Roberts made the following remark about Saunders: 'May I say though, Sir, a word on behalf of my absent friend and colleague, the hon. the member for Bay de Verde. I am sure he is at home this afternoon watching on the television. He is not well. He has had some illness recently. I know that he is with us in spirit and I understand that in due course he will be with us in person. I am sorry he is not here. Any man who is elected to the House of Assembly should be here and if he could be here he would' (ibid).

94   This figure does not include travel and special allowances. The sessional indemnity at the time was $6,667.67. John Carter, the PC member for St. John's North, refused to accept his sessional indemnity. Oldford and Saunders were, of course, not eligible for the indemnity not having been sworn in as members of the House (I am grateful to the office of the Auditor General of Newfoundland for this information).

95   For the results see *The Newfoundland Gazette*, 6 June 1972.

BIBLIOGRAPHY

Melvin Baker

The scope of this bibliography is the history of Newfoundland and Labrador since about 1800 with special reference to twentieth-century history. The 'Aboriginal Peoples' section ranges more widely in order to give users as much information as possible about a badly neglected topic. Readers should note that the 'Reference Works' and 'General Accounts' sections of this bibliography contain many items relevant to the more specialized headings that follow.

   Current Newfoundland and Labrador bibliography can be followed through 'Recent Publications Relating to the History of the Atlantic Region' in *Acadiensis*; 'Recent Publications Relating to Canada' in the *Canadian Historical Review*; 'Publications and Works Relating to Newfoundland' in *Newfoundland Studies*; and the 'Bibliographie d'histoire de l'Amérique française' in the *Revue d'histoire de l'Amérique française*. Readers may also wish to consult the catalogues and other rich finding aids in St. John's at the Centre for Newfoundland Studies, Queen Elizabeth II Library, Memorial University and the Provincial Reference and Resource Library, Arts and Culture Centre.

Contents

I / Reference Works

Armstrong, Frederick H., Artibise, Alan F.J., and Baker, Melvin, eds. *Bibliography of Canadian Urban History*. Part 1. *The Atlantic Provinces*. Monticello, Illinois 1980.

Barter, Geraldine. *A Critically Annotated Bibliography of Works Published and Unpublished Relating to the Culture of French Newfoundlanders*. St. John's 1977.

Budgel, Richard, comp. *A Survey of Labrador Material in Newfoundland & Labrador Archives*. Goose Bay 1985.

The Canadian Encyclopedia. 3 vols. 2nd ed. Edmonton 1988.

Chang, Margaret, comp. *A Guide to the Government Records of Newfoundland*. St. John's 1983.

Cooke, Alan, and Caron, Fabien, comps. *Bibliography of the Quebec-Labrador Peninsula*. 2 vols. Boston 1968.

Cuff, Robert H., Baker, Melvin, and Pitt, Robert D.W., eds. *Dictionary of Newfoundland and Labrador Biography*. St. John's 1990.

Dictionary of Canadian Biography. 13 vols. to date. Toronto 1966-. A major source for Newfoundland and Labrador biography.

Elliston, Suzanne. *Historical Directory of Newfoundland Newspapers 1807-1987*. St. John's 1987.

Encyclopedia Canadiana. 10 vols. Toronto 1957. Deals comprehensively with many aspects of local history. Covers many Newfoundland and Labrador topics. The 'Newfoundland' entry (vol. 7, 297-320) is by Gordon O. Rothney.

Encyclopedia of Newfoundland and Labrador. 4 vols. to date. Vols 1 (A-E) and 2 (Fac-Hoy), J.R. Smallwood, ed. St. John's 1981 and 1984. Vols. 3 (Hu-M) and 4 (N-R), Cyril F. Poole, editor in chief; Robert H. Cuff, managing editor. St. John's 1991 and 1993.

Fleming, Patricia Lockhart. *Atlantic Canada Imprints, 1801-1820: A Bibliography*. Toronto 1991.

Fowke, Edith, and Carpenter, Carole Henderson, comps. *A Bibliography of Canadian Folklore in English*. Toronto 1981.

Grenville, Nancy, Riggs, Bert, and Thomas, Roberta, eds. *A Guide to the Archival Holdings of the Centre for Newfoundland Studies, Memorial University Library*. St. John's 1989.

A Guide to the Holdings of the City of St. John's Archives. St. John's 1991.

Hamilton, W.B. 'Atlantic Canada.' In J.L. Granatstein and Paul Stevens, eds. *A Reader's Guide to Canadian History*. Vol. 2, *Confederation to the Present*. Toronto 1982, 277-97.

- *Local History in Atlantic Canada*. Toronto 1974.

Hiscock, Philip. 'Newfoundland Folklore and Language: A Bibliography.' *Regional Language Studies... Newfoundland* 12 (1989): 2-56.

Historical Atlas of Canada. Vol. 1, R. Cole Harris, ed., and Geoffrey J. Matthews, cartographer, From the Beginning to 1800. Toronto 1987. Vol. 2, R. Louis Gentilcore, ed., Don Measner and Ronald H. Walder. associate eds., and Geoffrey J. Matthews, Chief Cartographer, *The Land Transformed, 1801-1891.* Vol. 3, Donald Kerr and Deryck W. Holdsworth, eds., Susan L. Laskin, assistant ed., and Geoffrey J. Matthews, cartographer, *Addressing the Twentieth Century.* Toronto 1990.

Hollett, Robert C. 'Linguistic Research in Newfoundland.' *Regional Language Studies...Newfoundland* 11 (1987): 21-30.

Hunter, Isabel, and Wotherspoon, Shelagh, comps. *A Bibliography of Health Care in Newfoundland.* St. John's 1986.

Kemshead, Alison. *Newfoundland: a bibliography of social, economic and political conditions.* Monticello, Illinois 1980.

McManus, Gary E., and Woods, Clifford H. *Atlas of Newfoundland and Labrador.* St. John's 1991.

Mercer, Paul. 'A bio-bibliography of Newfoundland songs in printed sources.' Unpublished MA thesis, Memorial University 1978.

Newfoundland Statistics Agency. *Historical Statistics of Newfoundland and Labrador.* St. John's 1990.

O'Dea, Agnes, comp., and Alexander, Anne, ed. *Bibliography of Newfoundland.* Toronto 1986. An indispensable source. Covers 'printed works relating to Newfoundland from the early voyages of discovery to 1975.'

Ray, Roger B., comp. *The Indians of Maine and the Atlantic Provinces: A Bibliographical Guide.* Portland, Maine 1977.

Riggs, Bert, and Russell, Linda, comps. *An Inventory of the J.R. Smallwood Collection.* St. John's 1985.

Seary, E.R. *Family Names of the Island of Newfoundland.* St. John's 1976.

- *Place Names of the Avalon Peninsula of the Island of Newfoundland.* Toronto 1971.

Smith, Shelley, comp. *Inventory of the Government Records Collection of the Provincial Archives of Newfoundland and Labrador.* St. John's 1988.

Story, G.M., Kirwin, W.J., and Widdowson, J.D.A., eds. *Dictionary of Newfoundland English.* 2nd ed. Toronto 1990.

Story, Norah. *The Oxford Companion to Canadian History and Literature.* Toronto 1967.

Thibault, Claude. *Bibliographica Canadiana.* Toronto 1973.

Thomas, Gerald. 'Le Centre d'études franco-terreneuviennes (CEFT) Memorial University of Newfoundland.' In Rene Dionne, ed. *Quatre siècles d'identite canadienne.* Montreal 1983, 17-32.

Thomas, Roberta, and Wareham, Heather, eds. *A Guide to the Holdings of the Maritime History Archive, Memorial University.* St. John's 1991.

Toye, William, general ed. *The Oxford Companion to Canadian Literature.* Toronto 1983. 'Newfoundland, Writing in' is by Patrick O'Flaherty (548-52).

II / General Accounts

Beck, E. Boyde, Marquis, Greg, Payzant, Joan, and Ryan, Shannon. *Atlantic Canada: At the Dawn of a New Nation.* Burlington, Ont. 1990. The contents include Shannon Ryan, 'Newfoundland, Fishery to Canadian Province,' 7-43.

Brown, Craig, ed. *The Illustrated History of Canada.* Toronto 1987.

Buckner, P.A., and Frank, David, comps. and eds. *The Acadiensis Reader.* 2nd ed. Vol. 1, *Atlantic Canada before Confederation.* Fredericton 1990. Vol. 2, *Atlantic Canada after Confederation.* Fredericton 1988.

Canada and Newfoundland. Vol. 6 of J. Holland Rose, A.P. Newton and E.A. Benians, general eds. *The Cambridge History of the British Empire.* Cambridge 1930. See A.P. Newton, 'Newfoundland, 1783 to 1867,' 422-37, and 'Newfoundland, 1867-1921,' 672-85.

Chadwick, St. John. *Newfoundland: Island into Province.* Cambridge 1967.

Cramm, Frank, and Fizzard, Garfield. *The Atlantic Edge: Living in Newfoundland and Labrador.* 2nd ed. St. John's 1991.

Harvey, Moses. *A Short History of Newfoundland.* 2nd ed. London 1890.

- and Hatton, Joseph. *Newfoundland, the Oldest British Colony: its History, its Present Condition and its Prospects in the Future.* London 1883.

Hiller, James, and Neary, Peter, eds. *Newfoundland in the Nineteenth and Twentieth Centuries: Essays in Interpretation.* Toronto 1980. The contents are: Peter Neary, 'The Writing of Newfoundland History: An Introductory Survey'(3-15); David Alexander, 'Newfoundland's Traditional Economy and Development to 1934'(17-39); Shannon Ryan, 'The Newfoundland Salt Cod Trade in the Nineteenth Century'(40-66); James Hiller, 'Confederation Defeated: The Newfoundland Election of 1869'(67-94); Peter Neary,'The French and American Shore Questions as Factors in Newfoundland History'(95-122); James Hiller, 'The Railway and Local Politics in Newfoundland, 1870-1901' (123-47); Ian McDonald, 'W.F. Coaker and the Balance of Power Strategy: The Fishermen's Protective Union in Newfoundland Politics'(148-80); R.M. Elliott, 'Newfoundland Politics in the 1920s: The Genesis and Significance of the Hollis Walker Enquiry'(181-204); Peter Neary, 'Party Politics in

Newfoundland, 1949-71: A Survey and Analysis' (205-45); and David Alexander, 'The Collapse of the Saltfish Trade and Newfoundland's Integration into the North American Economy' (246-67).

McEwan, Alexander Campbell. 'Newfoundland law of real property: the origin and development of land ownership.' Unpublished PH D thesis, University of London, 1978.

MacKay, R.A., ed. *Newfoundland: Economic, Diplomatic and Strategic Studies.* Toronto 1946. The contents are: R.A. MacKay, 'The Problem of New-foundland'(3-38); R.A. MacKay and S.A. Saunders, 'The Economy of Newfoundland'(39-218); G.S. Watts, 'The Impact of the War'(219-30) and 'Prospective'(231-42); G.S. Graham, 'Newfoundland in British Strategy from Cabot to Napoleon'(245-64); R.A. MacKay, 'Responsible Government and External Affairs'(265-74); A.M. Fraser, 'The French Shore'(275-332), 'Fishery Negotiations with the United States'(333-410) and 'Relations with Canada'(411-83); and A.R.M. Lower, 'Transition to Atlantic Bastion' (484-508).

MacNutt, W.S. *The Atlantic Provinces: The Emergence of Colonial Society, 1712-1857.* Toronto 1968.

Macpherson, Alan G., and Macpherson, Joyce Brown, eds. *The Natural Environment of Newfoundland, Past and Present.* St. John's 1981. Published by the Department of Geography, Memorial University.

Mannion, John J., ed. *The Peopling of Newfoundland: Essays in Historical Geography.* St. John's 1977. The contents are: John J. Mannion, 'Introduction' (1-13); W. Gordon Handcock, 'English Migration to Newfoundland' (15-48); Michael Staveley, 'Population Dynamics in Newfoundland: The Regional Patterns' (49-76); David B. Mills, 'The Development of Folk Architecture in Trinity Bay, Newfoundland' (77-101); Alan G. Macpherson, 'A Modal Sequence in the Peopling of Central Bonavista Bay, 1676-1857' (102-135); Chesley Sanger, 'The Evolution of Sealing and the Spread of Permanent Settlement in North-eastern Newfoundland' (136-51); Patricia A. Thornton, 'The Demographic and Mercantile Bases of Initial Permanent Settlement in the Strait of Belle Isle' (152-83); Frank W. Remiggi, 'Ethnic Diversity and Settler Location on the Eastern Lower North Shore of Quebec' (185-211); Rosemary E. Ommer, 'Highlands Scots Migration to Southwestern Newfoundland: A Study of Kinship' (212-33); and John J. Mannion, 'Settlers and Traders in Western Newfoundland' (234-75).

Matthews, Keith. *Lectures on the History of Newfoundland: 1500-1830.* St. John's 1989.

Neary, Peter, and O'Flaherty, Patrick. *Part of the Main: An Illustrated History of Newfoundland and Labrador.* St. John's 1983.

- eds. *By Great Waters: A Newfoundland and Labrador Anthology.* Toronto 1974.

O'Driscoll, Robert, and Reynolds, Lorna, eds. *The Untold Story: The Irish in Canada.* 2 vols. Toronto 1988. The contents include: Cyril Byrne, 'The First Irish Foothold in North America' (171-4); Kildare Dobbs, 'Newfoundland and the Maritimes: An Overview' (175-94); C.W. Doody, 'The Irish in Newfoundland' (195-201); and Patrick O'Flaherty, 'Growing up Irish in a Newfoundland Outport' (723-8).

Pedley, Charles. *The History of Newfoundland from the Earliest Times to the Year 1860.* London 1863.

Perlin, A.B. *The Story of Newfoundland.* St. John's 1959.

Prowse, D.W. *A History of Newfoundland from the English, Colonial and Foreign Records.* London 1895. Reprinted by Mika Studio, Belleville, Ont. 1972.

Rogers, J.D. *Newfoundland.* Oxford 1911.

Rompkey, Ronald. *Grenfell of Labrador: A Biography.* Toronto 1991.

Rothney, Gordon O. *Newfoundland: A History.* Canadian Historical Association Booklets, 10. 3rd ed. Ottawa 1973.

Rowe, Frederick W. *A History of Newfoundland and Labrador.* Toronto 1980.

Smallwood, J.R., ed. *The Book of Newfoundland.* 6 vols. St. John's 1937-75.

Tocque, Philip. *Newfoundland: As It Was and As It Is in 1877.* Toronto 1878.

Zaslow, Morris. *The Northward Expansion of Canada 1914-1967.* Toronto 1988.

III / Aboriginal Peoples

Armitage, Peter. *The Innu (The Montagnais-Naskapi).* New York 1991.

Bartels, Dennis A., and Janzen, Olaf Uwe. 'Micmac Migration to Western Newfoundland.' *The Canadian Journal of Native Studies* 10, no. 1 (1990): 71-96.

Ben-Dor, Shmuel. *Makkovik: Eskimos and Settlers in a Labrador Community.* St. John's 1966.

Brice-Bennett, Carol. 'Two Opinions: Inuit and Moravian Missionaries in Labrador.' Unpublished MA thesis, Memorial University 1981.

- ed. *Our Footprints are Everywhere: Inuit Land Use and Occupancy in Labrador.* Nain 1977. The contents include: Richard H. Jordan, 'Inuit Occupation of the Central Labrador Coast since 1600 AD' (43-8); J. Garth Taylor and Helga R. Taylor, 'Inuit Land Use and Occupancy in the Okak Region, 1776-1830' (59-81); James K. Hiller, 'Moravian Land Holdings on the Labrador Coast: a Brief History' (83-94); Carol Brice-Bennett, 'Land Use in the Nain and Hopedale Regions' (97-203); and Hugh Brody, 'Permanence and Change among the Inuit and Settlers of Labrador' (311-47).

Budgel, Richard. 'The Beothuks and the Newfoundland Mind.' *Newfoundland Studies* 8 (1992): 15-33.

Dalton, Mary. 'Shadow Indians: The Beothuk Motif in Newfoundland Literature.' *Newfoundland Studies* 8 (1992): 135-46.

Davis, Davena. '"The dayspring from on high hath visited us": an examination of the missionary endeavours of the Moravians and the Anglican Church Missionary Society among the Inuit in the Arctic regions of Canada and Labrador (1880s-1920s).' Unpublished PH D thesis, McGill University 1987.

Dorais, Louis-Jacques. *The Inuit Language in Southern Labrador from 1694-1785*. Ottawa 1980.

Firestone, Melvin. 'Inuit derived culture traits in northern Newfoundland.' *Arctic Anthropology* 29, no. 1 (1992): 112-18.

Gilbert, William. '"Divers Places": The Beothuk Indians and John Guy's Voyage into Trinity Bay in 1612.' *Newfoundland Studies* 6 (1990): 147-67.

Hayson, Veryan. 'Labrador Inuit Land Claims: Aboriginal Rights and Interests v. Federal and Provincial Responsibilities and Authorities.' *Northern Perspectives* 18, no. 2 (1990): 6-10.

Henriksen, Georg. *Hunters in the Barrens: the Naskapi on the Edge of the White Man's World*. St. John's 1973.

Howley, J.P. *The Beothucks or Red Indians: The aboriginal inhabitants of Newfoundland*. Cambridge 1915. Reprinted in Coles Canadiana Collection, 1974.

Inglis, Stephanie Heather. 'The Fundamentals of Micmac Word Formation.' Unpublished MA thesis, Memorial University 1986.

Jackson, Doug. *'On the Country': The Micmac of Newfoundland*. Ed. by Gerald Penney. St. John's 1993.

Kaplan, Susan A. 'Economic and Social Change in Labrador Neo-Eskimo Culture.' Unpublished PH D thesis, Bryn Mawr College 1983.

McGee, H.R., ed. *The Native Peoples of Atlantic Canada*. Toronto 1974.

McGrath, Robin. 'The History of Inuit Literacy in Labrador [1771-1981].' *Newfoundland Quarterly* 87, no. 1 (1991-2): 35-40.

MacLean, Laurie. 'Beothuk Iron - Evidence for European Trade?' *Newfoundland Studies* 6 (1990): 168-76.

Mailhot, José. 'Beyond Everyone's Horizon Stand the Naskapi.' *Ethnohistory* 33 (1986): 384-418.

Marshall, Ingeborg. 'Beothuk and Micmac: Re-examining Relationships.' *Acadiensis* 17, no. 2 (1988): 52-82.

- *The Beothuk of Newfoundland: a vanished people*. St. John's 1989.

- 'Disease as a Factor in the Demise of the Beothuck Indians.' *Culture* 1, no. 1 (1981): 71-7.

- 'Newfoundland Beothuk Illustrated.' *Man in the Northeast* 35 (1988): 47-70.

- _The Red Ochre People: how Newfoundland's Beothuck Indians lived._ Vancouver c.1977.

- _Reports and Letters by George Christopher Pulling Relating to the Beothuk Indians of Newfoundland._ St. John's 1989.

Pastore, Ralph. 'The Collapse of the Beothuk World.' _Acadiensis_ 19, no. 1 (1989): 52-71.

- 'Fishermen, Furriers, and Beothuks: The Economy of Extinction.' _Man in the Northeast_ 33 (1987): 47-62.

- 'Native History in the Atlantic Region During the Colonial Period.' _Acadiensis_ 20, no. 1 (1990): 200-25.

- _The Newfoundland Micmacs._ Pamphlet. St. John's 1978.

- _Shanawdithit's People: The Archeology of the Beothuks._ St. John's 1992.

Patterson, George. 'The Beothiks or Red Indians of Newfoundland.' _Proceedings and Transactions of the Royal Society of Canada_ 9 (1891), section 2: 123-71.

Penney, Gerald, and Nichol, Heather. 'Burnt Knaps: A Micmac Site in Newfoundland.' _Canadian Journal of Archaeology_ 8, no. 1 (1984): 57-69.

Plaice, Evelyn. '"Leemos!" perceptions of ethnic identity among settlers in North West River, Labrador.' _Ethnic and Racial Studies_ 12, no. 1 (1989): 115-37.

- _The Native Game. Settler Perceptions of Indian/Settler Relations in Central Labrador._ St. John's 1990.

Rollmann, Hans.'Inuit Shamanism and the Moravian Missionaries of Labrador: A Textual Agenda for the Study of Native Inuit Religion.' _Études Inuit Studies_ 8, no. 2 (1985): 131-8.

Rowe, Frederick W. _Extinction: The Beothuks of Newfoundland._ Toronto 1977.

Scheffel, David. 'The demographic consequences of European contact with Labrador Inuit, 1800-1919.' Unpublished MA thesis, Memorial University 1981.

- 'The Dynamics of Labrador Inuit Fertility - An Example of Cultural and Demographic Change.' _Population and Environment_ 10 (1988): 32-47.

- 'From Polygyny to Cousin Marriage? Acculturation and Marriage in 19th Century Labrador Inuit Society.' _Études Inuit Studies_ 8, no. 2 (1984): 61-75.

Smith, Philip E.L. 'Beothuks and Methodists.' _Acadiensis_ 16, no. 1 (1986): 118-35.

Speck, Frank G. _Naskapi, the Savage Hunters of the Labrador Peninsula._ Norman, Oklahoma 1935.

Taylor, J. Garth. 'The Arctic Whale Cult in Labrador.' _Études Inuit Studies_ 9, no. 2 (1985): 121-32.

- 'Labrador Inuit Whale Use during the Early Contact Period.' *Arctic Anthropology* 25, no. 1 (1988): 120-30.

- and Taylor, Helga. 'Labrador Inuit Summer Ceremonies.' *Études Inuit Studies* 10, no. 1-2 (1986): 233-44.

Thomson, J. Callum. 'Late Dorset Shamanism at Shuldham Island 9, Northern Labrador.' Unpublished MA thesis, Bryn Mawr College 1988.

Upton, L.F.S. 'The Beothucks: Questions and Answers.' *Acadiensis* 7, no. 2 (1978): 150-5.

- 'The Extermination of the Beothucks of Newfoundland.' *Canadian Historical Review* 58 (1977): 133-53.

Wadden, Marie. *Nitassinan.* Vancouver 1991.

IV / Education

Anderson, George M. 'Vocational Education in Newfoundland: a brief history.' Unpublished MA thesis, University of Alberta 1979.

Andrews, Ralph L. *Integration and Other Developments in Newfoundland Education 1915-1949.* St. John's 1985.

- *Post-Confederation Developments in Newfoundland Education 1949-1975.* St. John's 1985.

Burke, Louis. 'Some Irish Contributors and Contributions to Newfoundland Education in the Last Century.' Unpublished M LITT thesis, University of Dublin 1975.

Crumlish, Michael L. 'The Christian Brothers: A Factor in the Development of Education in Newfoundland.' Unpublished MA thesis, Notre Dame University 1932.

Cuff, Harry A. *A History of the Newfoundland Teachers' Association 1890-1930.* St. John's 1985.

Dunphy, Mary A. 'The History of Teacher Training in Newfoundland, 1726-1955.' Unpublished B ED thesis, Mount St. Vincent University 1956.

Eastman, Wayne D. 'A Historical Analysis of Physical Education in Newfoundland, Canada.' Unpublished ED D thesis, Boston University 1987.

Hamilton, W.B. 'Society and Schools in Newfoundland.' In J. Donald Wilson, Robert M. Stamp, and Louis-Philippe Audet, eds. *Canadian Education: A History.* Scarborough 1970, 126-44.

Hammond, James J. 'A Study of the Administration of Education in Newfoundland, 1949-1973.' Unpublished MA thesis, Dalhousie University 1975.

Lear, Edward James. 'Edward Feild (1801-1876) Ecclesiastic and Educator: His Influence on the Development of Education in Newfoundland.' Unpublished M ED thesis, Bishop's University 1986.

McCann, Phillip. 'Class, Gender and Religion in Newfoundland Education, 1836-1901.' *Historical Studies in Education* 1, no. 2 (1989): 179-200.

- 'The Educational Policy of the Commission of Government.' *Newfoundland Studies* 3 (1987): 201-15.

- ed. *Blackboards and Briefcases: Personal Stories by Newfoundland Educators and Administrators*. St. John's 1982.

McCormack, Sister Mary B. 'The Educational Work of the Sisters of Mercy in Newfoundland, 1842-1955.' Unpublished MA thesis, Catholic University of America 1955.

McKim, William A. ed. *The Vexed Question: Denominational Education in a Secular Age*. St. John's 1988. The contents include: Philip McCann, 'The Politics of Denominational Education in the Nineteenth Century in Newfoundland' (30-59) and 'Denominational Education in the Twentieth Century in Newfoundland' (60-79); and Ronald G. Penney, 'The Constitutional Status of Denominational Education in Newfoundland' (80-101).

MacLeod, Malcolm. *A Bridge Built Halfway: A History of Memorial University College, 1925-1950*. Montreal and Kingston 1990.

- 'Parade Street Parade: The Student Body of Memorial University College, 1925-1949.' In Paul Axelrod and John G. Reid, eds. *Youth, University and Canadian Society: Essays in the Social History of Higher Education*. Kingston & Montreal 1989, 51-71.

Netten, J.W. 'Edward Feild, Protagonist of Denominational Education.' In L.S. Patterson et al., eds. *Profiles of Canadian Educators*. Toronto 1974, 77-94.

Rowe, Frederick W. *Education and Culture in Newfoundland*. Toronto 1976.

- *The History of Education in Newfoundland*. Toronto 1952.

Sheldon, Mary. 'The Establishment of the Denominational School System in Newfoundland with Particular Reference to the Role of the Anglican Church, 1836-1876.' Unpublished MA thesis, University of Toronto 1972.

Teresina, Sister Mary. 'The First Forty Years of Educational Legislation in Newfoundland.' Unpublished MA (ED) thesis, University of Ottawa 1956.

Veitch, N.A. 'The Contribution of the Benevolent Irish Society to Education in Newfoundland from 1823 to 1875.' Unpublished M ED thesis, St. Francis Xavier University 1965.

V / Health and Welfare

Baker, Melvin. 'The Development of the Office of a Permanent Medical Health Officer for St. John's 1826-1905.' *hstc bulletin—Journal of the*

History of Canadian Science, Technology and Medicine 7, no. 2 (1983): 98-105.V / Health and Welfare

- 'Disease and Public Health Measures in St. John's 1832-1855.' *Newfoundland Quarterly* 78, no. 4 (1983): 26-9.

- 'Henry Hunt Stabb and the Establishment of a Lunatic Asylum in St. John's, Newfoundland 1836-1855.' *scientia canadensis* 8, no. 1 (1984): 59-67.

- 'The Politics of Poverty: Providing Public Poor Relief in Nineteenth Century St. John's, Newfoundland' *Newfoundland Quarterly* 78, nos. 1 & 2 (1982): 20-3.

Brown, Malcolm C. 'Public finance of medical and dental care in Newfoundland - some historical and economic considerations.' *Journal of Social Policy* 10, no. 2 (1981): 209-27.

Candow, James E. 'An American Report on Newfoundland's Health Services in 1940.' Document. *Newfoundland Studies* 5 (1989): 221-39.

Dickman, Ilka D. *Appointment to Newfoundland*. Manhattan, Kansas, c.1981.

Fingard, Judith. 'The Relief of the Unemployed Poor in Saint John, Halifax and St. John's 1815-1860.' *Acadiensis* 5, no. 1 (1975): 32-53.

- 'The Winter's Tale: The Seasonal Contours of Pre-industrial Poverty in British America, 1815-1860.' Canadian Historical Association, *Historical Papers*, 1974, 65-94.

FitzGerald, G. Williams N. 'Surgery in northern Newfoundland at the turn of the century.' *Grenfell Clinical Quarterly* 71 (Autumn 1991): 1-9.

Godfrey, Stuart R. *Human Rights and Social Policy in Newfoundland 1832-1982*. St. John's 1985.

House, Edgar. *Light at Last: Triumph Over Tuberculosis in Newfoundland and Labrador 1900-1975*. St. John's 1981.

- *The Way Out: The Story of NONIA 1920-1990*. St. John's 1990.

Kelland, Donald E.J. *The Dr. Charles A. Janeway Health Centre: The First Twenty-Five Years, 1966-1991*. St. John's 1991.

Merrick, Elliott. '1918-1919, The Years of the Flu.' *Newfoundland Quarterly* 80, no. 4 (1985): 27-31.

Nevitt, Joyce. *White Caps and Black Bands: Nursing In Newfoundland to 1934*. St. John's 1978.

O'Brien, Dereck. *Suffer Little Children: An Autobiography of a Foster Child*. St. John's 1991.

O'Brien, Patricia. *Out of Mind, Out of Sight: A History of the Waterford Hospital*. St. John's 1989.

Paddon, Anthony. 'Public Health in Sub-Arctic Labrador 1912-1978.' *Canadian Journal of Public Health* 75 (1984): 356-8.

Paddon, W.A. *Labrador Doctor: My Life with the Grenfell Mission.* Toronto 1989.

Rusted, Nigel. *It's Devil Deep Down There.* St. John's 1985.

VI / Imperial, International and Military

Anglin, Douglas G. *The St. Pierre and Miquelon* Affaire *of 1941.* Toronto 1966.

Baker, Melvin, and Candow, James E. 'Signal Hill Gaol 1846-1859.' *Newfoundland Quarterly* 85, no. 4 (1990): 20-3.

Bassler, Gerhard P. 'Newfoundland's "Dangerous" Internees Who Never Were: The History of Victoria Camp, 1940-43.' *Newfoundland Studies* 5 (1989): 39-51.

- *Sanctuary Denied: Refugees from the Third Reich and Newfoundland Immigration Policy, 1906-1949.* St. John's 1992.

Bercuson, David J. 'SAC vs Sovereignty: The Origins of the Goose Bay Lease, 1946-52.' *Canadian Historical Review* 70 (1989): 206-22.

Brebner, John Bartlet. *North Atlantic Triangle: The Interplay of Canada, the United States and Great Britain.* New Haven 1945.

Brown, Cassie. *Standing into Danger: A Dramatic Story of Shipwreck and Rescue.* Toronto 1985.

Campbell, C.S. 'American Tariff Interests and the Northeastern Fisheries, 1883-1888.' *Canadian Historical Review* 45 (1964): 212-28.

- *Anglo-American Understanding, 1898-1903.* Baltimore 1957.

Candow, James E. 'The British Army in Newfoundland, 1697-1824.' *Newfoundland Quarterly* 79, no. 4 (1984): 21-8.

Cardoulis, John N. *A Friendly Invasion. The American Military in Newfoundland: 1940-1990.* St. John's 1990.

- *A Friendly Invasion II: A Personal Touch.* St. John's 1993.

Cave, Joy B. *Two Newfoundland V.C.s.* St. John's 1984.

- *What Became of Corporal Pittman?.* Portugal Cove, Newfoundland 1976.

Cayley, Charles E. 'The North Atlantic Fisheries in U.S.-Canadian Relations: A History of the Fisheries Problems, their Settlements and Attempted Settlements, with Special Emphasis on the Period since the Establishment of the Dominion of Canada.' Unpublished PH D thesis, University of Chicago 1931.

Chafe, Edward Vincent. 'A New Life on Uncle Sam's Farm: Newfoundlanders in Massachusetts, 1846-1859.' Unpublished MA thesis, Memorial University 1983.

Chafe, Edward W. *Gunners World War II: 166th (Newfoundland) Field Regiment Royal Artillery.* St. John's 1987.

Cullen, Richard. *Federalism in Action: The Australian and Canadian Offshore Disputes.* Sydney 1990.

Curran, Tom. *They Also Served: The Newfoundland Overseas Forestry Unit, 1939-1946.* St. John's 1987.

Davis, D.J. 'The Bond-Blaine Negotiations, 1890-1891.' Unpublished MA thesis, Memorial University 1970.

Day, Douglas. *The Saint Pierre and Miquelon Maritime Boundary.* Durham 1990.

Gilmore, William C. *Newfoundland and Dominion Status: The External Affairs Competence and International Law Status of Newfoundland, 1855-1934.* Toronto 1988.

Gwyn, Sandra. *Tapestry of War: A Private View of Canadians in the Great War.* Toronto 1992.

Gluek, Alvin C., Jr. 'Programmed Diplomacy: The Settlement of the North Atlantic Fisheries Question, 1907-12.' *Acadiensis* 6, no. 1 (1976): 43-70.

Haward, Marcus. 'Intergovernmental Relations and Offshore Resources Policy in Australia and Canada.' *Australian-Canadian Studies* 9, nos. 1/2 (1991): 35-51.

Henderson, Peter A. *Guarding the Gates: A History of Canadian Forces Station St. John's.* Printed by Hawk Duplicating Ltd. 1992.

How, Douglas. *Night of the Caribou.* Hantsport, N.S. 1988.

Hunt, Constance D. *The Offshore Petroleum Regimes of Canada and Australia.* Calgary 1989.

Kenney, Paul F., and Murphy, Tony. 'Wartime Censorship of Photography in Newfoundland.' *Newfoundland Quarterly* 84, no. 3 (1989): 18-24.

McGrath, Judy, ed. *'On the Goose': The Story of Goose Bay.* Goose Bay 1987.

MacKenzie, David. 'Aspects of the Command Problem in Newfoundland, 1941-1942.' *Newfoundland Quarterly* 84, no. 3 (1989): 25-31.

- 'Jeopardised by an International Plan: Newfoundland and the Introduction of the Marshall Plan, 1947-1948.' *British Journal of Canadian Studies* 1, no. 1 (1986), 109-19.

MacLeod, Malcolm. 'Royal Canadian Newfoundland Navy: HMCS PRESERVER operating in Newfoundland-Labrador waters, 1942-1945.' Part 1, *Newfoundland Quarterly* 76, no. 1 (1980): 3-5, 7-10; part 2, *Newfoundland Quarterly* 76, no. 3 (1980), 3-8, 10-11.

Marston, Geoffrey. 'The Newfoundland Offshore Jurisdictional Dispute.' *Journal of World Trade Law* 18 (1984): 335-41.

- 'The Newfoundland Offshore Jurisdictional Dispute - A Postscript.' *Journal of World Trade Law* 19 (1985): 423-5.

Milner, Marc. *North Atlantic Run: The Royal Canadian Navy and the Battle for the Convoys*. Toronto 1985.

Mulock, P.M. 'North-Atlantic Fisheries, 1866-1885: A Study in Canadian and American Relations.' Unpublished MA thesis, Acadia University 1939.

Murphy, Tony, and Kenney, Paul. *The War at Our Doorstep: St. John's During World War Two—An Album*. St. John's 1989.

Nicholson, G.W.L. *The Fighting Newfoundlander: The History of the Royal Newfoundland Regiment*. St. John's 1964.

- *More Fighting Newfoundlanders: A History of Newfoundland's Fighting Forces in the Second World War*. St. John's 1969.

Neary, Peter. 'Alexander Bishop's Account of the Exhumation of the Argentia Cemeteries, August, 1942.' Document. *Newfoundland Studies* 4 (1988): 181-6.

- 'The Embassy of James Bryce in the United States, 1907-13.' Unpublished PH D thesis, University of London 1965.

- 'The French Shore Question, 1865-1878.' Unpublished MA thesis, Memorial University 1961.

- 'Grey, Bryce, and the Settlement of Canadian-American Differences, 1905-1911.' *Canadian Historical Review* 49 (1968): 357-80.

- 'Newfoundland and the Anglo-American Leased Bases Agreement of 27 March 1941.' *Canadian Historical Review* 67 (1986): 491-519.

Reeves, William G. 'The Fortune Bay Dispute: Newfoundland's Place in Imperial Treaty Relations under the Washington Treaty, 1871-1885.' Unpublished MA thesis, Memorial University 1971.

- 'Newfoundlanders in the "Boston States": A Study in Early Twentieth Century Community and Counterpoint.' *Newfoundland Studies* 6 (1990): 34-55.

- '"Our Yankee Cousins": Modernization and the Newfoundland-American Relationship, 1898-1910.' Unpublished PH D thesis, University of Maine 1987.

Robison, Houston. 'Newfoundland's Surrender of Dominion Status in the British Empire, 1918-1934.' Unpublished PH D thesis, University of Chicago 1949.

Stacey, C.P. 'The Withdrawal of the Imperial Garrison from Newfoundland, 1870.' *Canadian Historical Review* 17 (1936): 147-58.

Stewart, Ian M. 'The "Revolution of 1940" in Newfoundland.' Unpublished MA thesis, Memorial University 1974.

Straus, Richard. 'The Diplomatic Negotiations Leading to the Establishment of American Bases in Newfoundland, June 1940-April 1941.' Unpublished MA thesis, Memorial University 1972.

Tallman, R.D. 'Warships and Mackeral: the North Atlantic Fisheries in Canadian-American Relations, 1867-1877.' Unpublished PH D thesis, University of Maine 1971.

Tansill, C.C. *Canadian-American Relations, 1875-1911*. New Haven 1943.

Thompson, F.F. *The French Shore Problem in Newfoundland: An Imperial Study*. Toronto 1961.

Wells, Herb. *Comrades in Arms: A History of Newfoundlanders in Action, Second World War*. St. John's 1986.

Wilson, Theodore A. *The First Summit: Roosevelt and Churchill at Placentia Bay, 1941*. Rev. ed. Lawrence, Kansas 1991.

VII / Newfoundland and Canada: Pre- and Post-Confederation (1949)

Barry, Leo. 'Offshore Petroleum Agreements: An Analysis of the Nova Scotian and Newfoundland Experience.' In J. Owen Saunders, ed. *Managing Natural Resources in a Federal State*. Toronto 1986, 177-89.

Blake, Raymond. 'The Making of a Province: Newfoundland's Integration into Canada, 1948-1957.' Unpublished PH D thesis, York University 1991.

- 'WLMK's Attitude Towards Newfoundland's Entry into Confederation.' *Newfoundland Quarterly* 82, no. 4 (1987): 26-37.

Bridle, Paul, ed. *Documents on Relations between Canada and Newfoundland*. Vol. 1. 1935-1949. Ottawa 1974. Vol. 2 in 2 parts, 1940-1949. *Confederation*. Ottawa 1984.

Browne, G.P., ed. *Documents on the Confederation of British North America*. Toronto 1969.

Brym, Robert J., ed. *Regionalism in Canada*. Toronto 1986. The contents include: J.D. House, 'The Mouse that Roars: New Directions in Canadian Political Economy—the Case of Newfoundland' (161-96); and Ralph Matthews, 'The Nature and Explanation of Regionalism: Some Critiques and Conclusions' (197-205).

- and Sacouman, R. James, eds. *Underdevelopment and Social Movements in Atlantic Canada*. Toronto 1979. The contents include: Steven Antler, 'The Capitalist Underdevelopment of Nineteenth-Century Newfoundland' (179-202); Robert J. Brym and Barbara Neis, 'Regional Factors in the Formation of the Fishermen's Protective Union of Newfoundland' (203-18); and James Overton, 'Towards a Critical Analysis of Neo-Nationalism in Newfoundland' (219-49).

Budgel, Richard, and Staveley, Michael. *The Labrador Boundary*. Happy Valley-Goose Bay 1987.

Channing, J.G. *The Effects of Transition to Confederation on Public Administration in Newfoundland*. Toronto 1982.

Christopher, Brother. 'The Influence of Economic Factors on Newfoundland's Entrance into Confederation.' Unpublished MA thesis, University of Ottawa 1957.

Creighton, D.G. *The Road to Confederation*. Toronto 1964.

Eggleston, Wilfrid. *Newfoundland: The Road to Confederation*. Ottawa 1974.

FitzGerald, John Edward. 'The Confederation of Newfoundland with Canada, 1946-1949.' Unpublished MA thesis, Memorial University 1992.

Forbes, E.R., and Muise, D.A., eds. *The Atlantic Provinces in Confederation*. Toronto and Fredericton 1993. The contents include: D.A. Muise, 'The 1860s: Forging the Bonds of Union' (13-47); James Hiller, 'Newfoundland Confronts Canada, 1867-1949' (349-81); Margaret Conrad, 'The 1950s: The Decade of Development' (382-420); Della Stanley, 'The 1960s: The Illusions and Realities of Progress' (421-59); John Reid, 'The 1970s: Sharpening the Sceptical Edge' (460-504); and E.R. Forbes, 'Epilogue: The 1980s' (505-15).

Gilmore, William C. 'Law, Constitutional Convention, and the Union of Newfoundland and Canada.' *Acadiensis* 18, no. 2 (1989): 111-26.

Harris, Leslie. 'The Labrador Boundary Dispute.' *Newfoundland Quarterly* 87, no. 1 (1991-2): 21-6.

Hayman, Kathryn E. 'The origins and function of the Canadian High Commission in Newfoundland, 1941-1949.' Unpublished MA thesis, University of Western Ontario 1979.

Hiller, Harry H. 'Dependence and independence: emergent nationalism in Newfoundland.' *Ethnic and Racial Studies* 10, no. 3 (1987): 257-75.

Hiller, James. 'The Career of F. Gordon Bradley.' *Newfoundland Studies* 4 (1988): 163-80.

- comp. *The Confederation Issue in Newfoundland 1864-1869: Selected Documents*. St. John's 1974.

Hollohan, Francis. *Albert Perlin: A Biography*. St. John's 1985.

- and Baker, Melvin, comps. *Albert B. Perlin—The Wayfarer: Observations on the National Convention and the Confederation Issue 1946-1949*. St. John's 1986.

Jackson, F.L. *Newfoundland in Canada: A People in Search of a Polity*. St. John's 1984.

- *Surviving Confederation*. St. John's 1986.

Jamieson, Don. *The Political Memoirs of Don Jamieson*. Carmelita McGrath, ed. Vol. 1, *No Place for Fools*. St. John's 1989. Vol. 2, *A World Unto Itself*. St. John's 1991.

Jones, Frederick. '"The Antis Gain The Day": Newfoundland and Confederation in 1869.' In Ged Martin, ed. *The Causes of Canadian Confederation.* Fredericton 1990, 142-7.

McAllister, R.I., ed. *Newfoundland: the First Fifteen Years of Confederation.* St. John's 1966. Includes sections on 'The Land and the People,' 'The Government,' and 'The Economy.'

McCorquodale, Susan. 'Newfoundland: personality, party, and politics.' In Gary Levy and Graham White, eds. *Provincial and Territorial Legislatures in Canada.* Toronto 1989, 166-88.

MacKenzie, David. *Canada and International Civil Aviation 1932-1948.* Toronto 1989.

- 'Economic Union and the 1948 Referendum Campaigns: The View from Washington.' *Newfoundland Quarterly* 83, no. 3 (1988): 24-31.

- *Inside the Atlantic Triangle: Canada and the Entrance of Newfoundland into Confederation 1939-1949.* Toronto 1986.

MacLeod, Malcolm. 'Confederation 1937.' Document. *Newfoundland Studies* 1 (1985): 201-10.

- *Nearer than Neighbours: Newfoundland and Canada Before Confederation.* St. John's 1982.

- *Peace of the Continent: The Impact of Second World War Canadian and American Bases in Newfoundland.* St. John's 1986.

- 'Subsidized Steamers to a Foreign Country: Canada and Newfoundland, 1892-1949.' *Acadiensis* 14, no. 2 (1985): 66-92.

- You Must Go Home Again: A Newfoundland-Canada quarrel over deportations, 1932-1933.' *Newfoundland Quarterly* 78, no. 4 (1983): 23-5.

Mayo, H.B. 'Newfoundland and Canada: The Case for Union Examined.' Unpublished D PHIL thesis, Oxford University 1948.

- 'Newfoundland and Confederation in the Eighteen-Sixties.' *Canadian Historical Review* 29 (1948): 125-42.

- 'Newfoundland's Entry into the Dominion.' *Canadian Journal of Economics and Political Science* 15 (1949): 505-22.

Mitchell, Harvey. 'Canada's Negotiations with Newfoundland, 1887-1895.' *Canadian Historical Review* 40 (1959): 277-93. Reprinted in G.A. Rawlyk, ed. *Historical Essays on the Atlantic Provinces.* Toronto 1967, 242-59.

Neary, Peter. '"A more than usual...interest": Sir P.A. Clutterbuck's Newfoundland Impressions, 1950.' Document. *Newfoundland Studies* 3 (1987): 251-63.

- 'Canadian Immigration Policy and the Newfoundlanders, 1912-1939.' *Acadiensis* 11, no. 2 (1982): 69-83.

- 'Ebb and Flow: Citizenship in Newfoundland, 1929-1949.' In William Kaplan, ed. *Belonging: The Meaning and Future of Canadian Citizenship.* Montreal and Kingston 1993, 79-103.

- 'Great Britain and the Future of Newfoundland 1939-45.' *Newfoundland Studies* 1 (1985): 29-56.

- 'Newfoundland and Quebec: Provincial Neighbours across an Uneasy Frontier.' *Bulletin of Canadian Studies* 2, no. 2 (1978): 35-51.

- 'Newfoundland's Union with Canada, 1949: Conspiracy or Choice?' *Acadiensis* 12, no. 2 (1983): 110-19.

Peckford, A. Brian. *The Past in the Present.* St. John's 1983.

Pickersgill, J.W. *The Road Back: By a Liberal in Opposition.* Toronto 1986.

Rawlyk, G.A., ed. *The Atlantic Provinces and the problems of Confederation.* St. John's 1979.

Rowe, Frederick W. *Into the Breach: Memoirs of a Newfoundland Senator.* Scarborough, Ont. 1988.

Simpson, Jeffrey. *Spoils of Power: The Politics of Patronage.* Toronto 1988.

Smith, F.J. 'Newfoundland and Confederation, 1864-1870.' Unpublished MA thesis, University of Ottawa 1970.

Stanley, G.F.G. 'Further Documents Relating to the Union of Newfoundland and Canada, 1886-1895.' *Canadian Historical Review* 29 (1948): 370-86.

Swain, Hector. *Lester Leeland Burry: Labrador Pastor and Father of Confederation.* St. John's 1983.

Wade, Mason, ed. *Regionalism in the Canadian Community, 1867-1967.* Toronto 1969. The contents include: Gordon O. Rothney, 'The History of Newfoundland, 1900-49: Background Notes' (198-209); Peter Neary and S.J.R. Noel, 'Newfoundland's Quest for Reciprocity, 1890-1910' (210-26); and Peter Cashin, Harold Horwood and Leslie Harris, 'Newfoundland and Confederation, 1948-49' (227-63).'

Waite, P.B. *The Life and Times of Confederation.* 2nd ed. Toronto 1962.

Walsh, Bren. *More than a Poor Majority: The Story of Newfoundland's Confederation with Canada.* St. John's 1985.

Webb, Jeff A. 'Newfoundland's National Convention, 1946-48.' Unpublished MA thesis, Memorial University 1987.

- 'The Responsible Government League and the Confederation Campaigns of 1948.' *Newfoundland Studies* 5 (1989): 203-20.

VIII / Political and Constitutional

Baker, Melvin. 'Absentee Landlordism and Municipal Government in Nineteenth Century St. John's.' *Urban History Review* 15, no. 2 (1986): 165-71.

- *Aspects of Nineteenth Century St. John's Municipal History*. St. John's 1982.

- 'The Government of St. John's, Newfoundland, 1800-1921.' Unpublished PH D thesis, University of Western Ontario 1980.

- 'The Great St. John's Fire of 1846.' *Newfoundland Quarterly* 79, no. 1 (1983): 31-4.

- 'In Search of the "New Jerusalem": Slum Clearance in St. John's, 1921-1944.' *Newfoundland Quarterly* 79, no. 2 (1983): 23-32, 45.

- '"Monopolist Monroe, the Wire-Puller of the West End": The Business and Political Career of Moses Monroe.' *Newfoundland Quarterly* 83, no. 4 (1988): 24-9.

- 'Municipal Democracy on Trial in St. John's, 1888-1898.' *Newfoundland Quarterly* 82, no. 2 (1986): 21-8.

- 'The Politics of Assessment: The Water Question in St. John's, 1844-1864.' *Acadiensis* 12, no. 1 (1982): 59-72.

- 'The Politics of Municipal Reform in St. John's, Newfoundland, 1888-1892,' *Urban History Review* 2-76 (October 1976): 12-29.

- 'The St. John's Fire of July 8, 1892: The Politics of Rebuilding, 1892-1893.' *Newfoundland Quarterly* 79, no. 3 (1984): 25-30.

- St. John's Municipal Politics, 1902-1914.' *Newfoundland Quarterly* 80, no. 2 (1984): 23-30.

- 'William Gilbert Gosling and the Charter: St. John's Municipal Politics, 1914-1921.' *Newfoundland Quarterly* 81, no. 2 (1985): 21-8.

- 'William Gilbert Gosling and the Establishment of Commission Government in St. John's, Newfoundland, 1914.' *Urban History Review* 9, no. 3 (1981): 35-51.

Boswell, Peter. 'Representational Role Style Perceptions of Municipal Councillors in Newfoundland and Labrador.' Unpublished PH D thesis, Carleton University 1983.

Boyle, Christine. 'Newfoundland and Dominion Status.' *Dalhousie Law Journal* 13, no. 1 (1990): 488-93.

Browne, William J. *Memoirs of William J. Browne, P.C., Q.C., LL.D.*. Vol. 1, *Eighty-four Years a Newfoundlander*. 1897-1949. St. John's 1981. Vol. 2, *Eighty-seven Years a Newfoundlander*. 1949-1965. St. John's 1984.

Clark, Richard L. 'Newfoundland 1934-1949: A Study of the Commission of Government and Confederation with Canada.' Unpublished PH D thesis, UCLA 1951.

Cohen, Anthony P. *The Management of Myths: The Politics of Legitimation in a Newfoundland Community.* St. John's 1975.

Copes, Parzival. 'The Fisherman's Vote in Newfoundland.' *Canadian Journal of Political Science* 3 (1970): 579-604.

Courage, J.R. 'The Development of Procedure in the General Assembly of Newfoundland." Unpublished MA thesis, Memorial University 1960.

Coyne, Deborah. *Roll of the Dice: Working with Clyde Wells during the Meech Lake Negotiations.* Toronto 1992.

Cramm, Frank. 'The Construction of the Newfoundland Railway, 1885-1898.' Unpublished MA thesis, Memorial University 1961.

Crosbie, John C. 'Local Government in Newfoundland,' *Canadian Journal of Economics and Political Science* 22 (1956): 332-46.

Cuff, Harry A. 'The Commission of Government in Newfoundland: A Preliminary Survey.' Unpublished MA thesis, Acadia University 1959.

Cuff, Robert H., ed. *A Coaker Anthology.* St. John's 1986. The contents include: Robert Cuff, 'Introduction: The "Noble Endeavour" of William Coaker' (1-2); Robert Cuff, 'A Brief History of the F.P.U.' (3-7); William Ford Coaker, 'The Founding of a Union' (9-16); Catherine F. Horan, 'Sir William Ford Coaker (1871-1938)' (17-28); R.W. Guy, 'Some Reflections on Coaker and his Union' (29-42); J.R. Smallwood, 'The F.P.U. and Its Organizer' (43-7); William Ford Coaker, 'The Bonavista Platform' (49-51); John Feltham, 'The Union in Politics (1908-1919)' (53-70); Gerald Panting, '"The People" in Politics' (71-8); Ian McDonald, 'The Coaker Regulations' (79-86); John Feltham, 'The Union Trading Company and the Commercial Activities of the F.P.U.' (87-101); and Melvin Baker, 'Port Union' (103-12).

Dunn, Christopher. 'Newfoundland and the Constitutional Process.' *Canadian Parliamentary Review* 14, no. 3 (1991): 12-14.

English, Christopher. 'The Development of the Newfoundland Legal System to 1815.' *Acadiensis* 20, no. 1 (1990): 89-119.

- and Curran, Christopher P. *A Cautious Beginning: The Court of Civil Jurisdiction, 1791: Commemorative Essay.* St. John's 1991.

Feltham, John. 'The Development of the F.P.U. in Newfoundland (1908-1923),' Unpublished MA thesis, Memorial University 1959.

Fizzard, Garfield. 'The Amalgamated Assembly of Newfoundland, 1841-1847.' Unpublished MA thesis, Memorial University 1959.

Greene, John P. 'The Influence of Religion in the Politics of Newfoundland, 1850-61.' Unpublished MA thesis, Memorial University 1970.

Gunn, Gertrude. *The Political History of Newfoundland, 1832-1864.* Toronto 1966.

Gwyn, Richard. *Smallwood: The Unlikely Revolutionary*. Rev. ed. Toronto 1972.

Harris, Leslie. 'The First Nine Years of Representative Government in Newfoundland.' Unpublished MA thesis, Memorial University 1959.

Harris, Michael. *Rare Ambition: The Crosbies of Newfoundland*. Toronto 1992.

Hiller, James. 'The 1885 Election in Bonavista Bay: An Anglican Perspective." Document. *Newfoundland Studies* 5, no. 1 (1989): 69-76.

- 'A History of Newfoundland, 1874-1901,' Unpublished PH D thesis, Cambridge University 1971.

- *The Newfoundland Railway, 1881-1949*. Pamphlet. St. John's 1981.

- 'Whiteway and Progress.' *Newfoundland Quarterly* 68, no. 4 (1972): 15-18.

Horwood, Harold. *A History of the Newfoundland Ranger Force*. St. John's 1986.

- *Joey*. Toronto 1989. A biography of J.R. Smallwood.

House, J.D. 'Premier Peckford, Petroleum Policy, and Popular Politics in Newfoundland and Labrador.' *Journal of Canadian Studies* 17, no. 2 (1982): 12-31.

Hoy, Claire. *Clyde Wells: A Political Biography*. Toronto 1992.

Johnson, Jon B. 'The Newfoundland Provincial Election, September 16, 1975.' Unpublished MA thesis, McGill University 1976.

Jones, Frederick. 'Bishop Feild: A Study in Politics and Religion in 19th Century Newfoundland.' Unpublished PH D thesis, Cambridge University 1971.

- 'Bishops in Politics: Roman Catholic v Protestant in Newfoundland 1860-2.' *Canadian Historical Review* 55 (1974): 408-21.

- 'The great fire of 1846 and the coming of responsible government in Newfoundland.' *Bulletin of Canadian Studies* 6/7, no. 2-1 (1983): 61-9.

Kerr, K.J. 'A Social Analysis of the Members of the Newfoundland House of Assembly, Executive Council, and Legislative Council for the Period 1855-1914.' Unpublished MA thesis, Memorial University 1973.

Lewis, Jane, and Shrimpton, Mark. 'Policymaking in Newfoundland during the 1940s: The Case of the St. John's Housing Corporation.' *Canadian Historical Review* 65, no. 2 (1984): 209-39.

McCann, Philip. 'Culture, State Formation and the Invention of Tradition: Newfoundland 1832-1855.' *Journal of Canadian Studies* 23, nos. 1 & 2 (1988): 86-103.

McCorquodale, Susan. 'Newfoundland Plus ça change, plus c'est le même chose.' In Martin Robin, ed. *Canadian Provincial Politics: The Party Systems of the Ten Provinces*. 2nd ed. Toronto 1978, 138-70.

- 'Public Administration in Newfoundland during the Period of the Commission of Government: A Question of Political Development.' Unpublished PH D thesis, Queen's University 1973.

McDonald, Ian. *"To Each His Own": William Coaker and the Fishermen's Protective Union in Newfoundland Politics, 1908-1925.* James Hiller, ed. St. John's 1987.

McLintock, A.H. *The Establishment of Constitutional Government in Newfoundland, 1783-1832: A Study of Retarded Colonisation.* London 1941.

MacWhirter, W.D. 'A Political History of Newfoundland, 1865-1874.' Unpublished MA thesis, Memorial University 1963.

Matthews, Keith. 'The Class of '32: St. John's Reformers on the Eve of Representative Government.' *Acadiensis* 6, no. 2 (1977): 80-94.

- 'The Nature and Framework of Newfoundland History.' In R. Douglas Francis and Donald B. Smith, eds. *Readings in Canadian History: Pre-Confederation.* Toronto 1986, 75-82.

Matthews, Ralph. 'Perspectives on recent Newfoundland Politics.' *Journal of Canadian Studies* 9, no. 2 (1974): 20-35.

- 'The Smallwood Legacy: The Development of Underdevelopment in Newfoundland, 1949-1972.' *Journal of Canadian Studies* 13, no. 4 (1978-9): 89-108.

Mitchell, Harvey. 'The Constitutional Crisis of 1889 in Newfoundland.' *Canadian Journal of Economics and Political Science* 24 (1958): 323-31.

Moulton, E.C. 'Constitutional Crisis and Civil Strife in Newfoundland, February to November 1861.' *Canadian Historical Review* 48 (1967): 251-72.

- 'The Political History of Newfoundland, 1861-1869.' Unpublished MA thesis, Memorial University 1960.

Neary, Peter. 'Changing Government: The 1971-72 Newfoundland Example.' *Dalhousie Law Journal* 5, no. 3 (1979): 631-58.

- 'Clement Attlee's Visit to Newfoundland, September 1942.' Document. *Acadiensis* 13, no. 2 (1984): 101-09.

- 'Democracy in Newfoundland: A Comment.' *Journal of Canadian Studies* 4, no. 1 (1969): 37-45.

- 'J.B. Hope Simpson's account of Sir John Hope Simpson's Newfoundland Career, 1934-6.' Document. *Newfoundland Studies* 6, no. 1 (1990): 74-110.

- *Newfoundland in the North Atlantic World: 1929-1949.* Kingston and Montreal 1988.

- 'The Supreme Court of Canada and "the Bowater's Law", 1950.' *Dalhousie Law Journal* 8, no. 1 (1984): 285-91.

- ed. *The Political Economy of Newfoundland, 1929-1972.* Toronto 1973.

Newfoundland Law Reform Commission. *Legislative History of the Judicature Act 1791-1988.* Newfoundland Law Reform Commission 1989.

Noel, S.J.R. 'Politics and the Crown: The Case of the 1908 Tie Election in Newfoundland.' *Canadian Journal of Economics and Political Science* 33 (1967): 285-91.

- *Politics in Newfoundland.* Toronto 1971.

O'Brien, Patricia. 'The Newfoundland Patriotic Association: The Administration of the War Effort, 1914-1918.' Unpublished MA thesis, Memorial University 1983.

O'Flaherty, Patrick. 'Government in Newfoundland before 1832: The Context of Reform.' *Newfoundland Quarterly* 84, no. 2 (1988): 26-30.

- 'In Search of William Carson.' *Newfoundland Quarterly* 83, no. 1 (1987): 28-34.

- 'The Seeds of Reform: Newfoundland, 1800-1818.' *Journal of Canadian Studies* 23, no. 3 (1988): 39-59.

Overton, James. 'Economic Crisis and the End of Democracy: Politics in Newfoundland During the Great Depression.' *Labour/Le Travail* 26 (1990): 85-124.

- 'Living Patriotism: Songs, Politics and Resources in Newfoundland.' *Canadian Review of Studies in Nationalism* 12 (1985): 239-59.

- 'Progressive Conservatism? A Critical Look at Politics, Culture and Development in Newfoundland.' In Robert Garland, ed. *Ethnicity in Atlantic Canada.* Saint John 1985, 84-102.

Paine, Robert. *Ayatollahs & turkey trots: political rhetoric in the new Newfoundland: Crosbie, Jamieson and Peckford.* St. John's 1981.

- 'The Mastery of Smallwood and Interlocutory Rhetoric.' *Newfoundland Studies* 2 (1986): 191-211.

- 'The Persuasiveness of Smallwood: Rhetoric of Cuffer and Scoff, of Metonym and Metaphor.' *Newfoundland Studies* 1 (1985): 57-75.

- 'Smallwood, Political Strategy, and a "Career" in Rhetoric.' *Newfoundland Studies* 3 (1987): 217-26.

- 'Who's a Spoiler? A Note on the Newfoundland Provincial Election of September, 1975.' *Newfoundland Quarterly* 72, no. 2 (1976): 33-9.

Panting, G.E. 'The Fishermen's Protective Union of Newfoundland and the Farmer's Organizations in Western Canada.' Canadian Historical Association, *Annual Report*, 1963, 141-51.

- 'Newfoundland's Loss of Responsible Government.' In J.M. Bumsted, ed. *Documentary Problems in Canadian History.* Vol. 2, *Post-Confederation.* Georgetown 1969, 241-62.

- '"The People" in Politics.' *Newfoundland Quarterly* 65, no. 4 (1967): 15-17.

Perlin, George. 'St. John's West.' In John Meisel, ed. *Papers on the 1962 Election*. Toronto 1964, 3-18.

Pickersgill, J.W. *My Years with Louis St. Laurent: A Political Memoir*. Toronto 1975.

Plumptre, A.F.W. 'The Amulree Report (1933): A Review.' *Canadian Journal of Economics and Political Science* 3 (1937): 58-71.

Pottle, Herbert L. *Dawn Without Light: Politics, Power & the People in the Smallwood Era*. St. John's 1979.

Powell, C.W. 'Problems of Municipal Government in Newfoundland.' Institute of Public Administration of Canada, *Proceedings*, 1949, 168-82.

Power, Gregory J. *The Power of the Pen: Writings of Gregory J. Power*. St. John's 1989.

Rothney, Gordon O. 'The Denominational Basis of Representation in the Newfoundland House of Assembly, 1919-1962.' *Canadian Journal of Economics and Political Science* 28 (1962): 557-70.

Rowe, Frederick W. *The Smallwood Era*. Toronto 1985.

Senior, Elinor. 'The Origin and Political Activities of the Orange Order in Newfoundland, 1863-1890.' Unpublished MA thesis, Memorial University 1959.

Smallwood, J.R. *I Chose Canada: The Memoirs of the Honourable Joseph R."Joey" Smallwood*. Toronto 1973.

Stanley, G.F.G. 'Sir Stephen Hill's Observations on the Election of 1869 in Newfoundland.' *Canadian Historical Review* 29 (1948): 278-85.

Summers, Valerie A. 'The Politics of Underdevelopment: Resource Policy and Regime Change in Newfoundland.' Unpublished PH D thesis, Carleton University 1988.

Tuck, Marilyn. 'The Newfoundland Ranger Force, 1935-1950.' Unpublished MA thesis, Memorial University 1983.

Vallis, Fred. 'Sectarianism as a Factor in the 1908 Election.' *Newfoundland Quarterly* 70, no. 3 (1974): 17-28.

Wells, Elizabeth A. 'The Struggle for Responsible Government in Newfoundland, 1846-1855.' Unpublished MA thesis, Memorial University 1966.

Winter, Harry Anderson. 'Memoirs of Henry Anderson Winter.' Introduction by A.B. Perlin. Parts 1 and 2, *Newfoundland Quarterly* 72, no. 1 (1976): 15-24; part 3, *Newfoundland Quarterly* 72, no. 3: 17-22.

IX / Religion

Benson, Gerald E. *Out of Our Hearts: Churches of Newfoundland and Labrador*. St. John's 1992.

Blinkley, Marian Elizabeth. 'Bio-cultural implications of outport life: the Anglican parish of Fogo: a case study.' Unpublished PH D thesis, University of Toronto 1981.

Byrne, Cyril J., ed. *Gentlemen-Bishops and Faction Fighters: The Letters of Bishops O Donel, Lambert, Scallan and other Irish Missionaries*. St. John's 1984.

Ford, Augusta. 'The Sisters of Mercy in Newfoundland: their contribution to business education.' Unpublished M ED thesis, Memorial University 1981.

Harris, Michael. *Unholy Orders: Tragedy at Mount Cashel*. Markham, Ont. 1990.

Hawco, James R. 'Change, dependency and the Catholic Church in five Newfoundland communities.' Unpublished MA thesis, University of Alberta 1979.

Hillman, Thomas R., and Kelley, A.R. *Atlantic Canada to 1900: A History of the Anglican Church*. Toronto 1983.

Hogan, Sister Williamina M. *Pathways of Mercy in Newfoundland 1842-1984*. St. John's 1986.

Howley, Michael F. *Ecclesiastical History of Newfoundland*. Boston 1888.

Hubbard, R.H. 'From Rocks and Ice to Leafy Isles: Bermuda's Links with the Dioceses of Nova Scotia and Newfoundland.' *Journal of the Canadian Church Historical Society* 29 (1987): 3-11.

Janes, Burton K. *The Lady Who Came: The Biography of Alice Belle Garrigus*. Vol. 1, 1858-1908. St. John's 1982.

- *The Lady Who Stayed: The Biography of Alice Belle Garrigus*. Vol. 2, 1908-1949. St. John's 1983.

- 'Pentecostalism in Newfoundland: The Early Years.' *Eastern Journal of Practical Theology* 4, no. 1 (1990): 35-43.

Jones, Frederick. 'The Church in Nineteenth-Century Newfoundland.' *Bulletin of Canadian Studies* 5, no. 1 (1981): 25-40.

Lahey, Raymond J. *James Louis O'Donel in Newfoundland 1784-1807: The Establishment of the Roman Catholic Church*. Pamphlet. St. John's 1984.

Mulcahy, Mary. 'The Catholic Church in Newfoundland: The Pre-Emancipation Years.' Canadian Catholic Historical Association. *Canadian Catholic Historical Studies 1985*: 5-34.

- '"Prohibited by Law": The Early Church in Newfoundland.' *Canadian Catholic Review* 2 (1984): 448-54.

Murphy, Terrence, and Byrne, Cyril J., eds. *Religion and Identity: The Experience of Irish and Scottish Catholics in Atlantic Canada.* St. John's 1987. The contents include: Hans Rollmann, 'Religious Enfranchisement and Roman Catholics in Eighteenth-Century Newfoundland' (34-52); and Philip McCann, 'Bishop Fleming and the Politicization of the Irish Roman Catholics in Newfoundland, 1830-1850' (81-97).

- and Stortz, Gerald, eds. *Creed and Culture:The Place of English-Speaking Catholics in Canadian Society, 1750-1930.* Montreal and Kingston 1993. The contents include: Raymond J. Lahey, 'Catholicism and Colonial Policy in Newfoundland, 1779-1845' (49-78); and Terrence Murphy, 'Trusteesiem in Atlantic Canada: The Struggle for Leadership among the Irish Catholics of Halifax, St. John's and Saint John, 1770-1850' (126-51).

O'Neill, Paul. *Upon This Rock: The Story of the Roman Catholic Church in Newfoundland and Labrador.* St. John's 1984.

Parsons, Jacob. 'The Origin and Growth of Newfoundland Methodism, 1765-1855.' Unpublished MA thesis, Memorial University 1964.

Pitt, David G. *Windows of Agates: The Life and Times of Gower Street United (formerly Methodist) Church in St. John's, Newfoundland: 1815-1990.* 2nd. ed., rev. and enlarged. St. John's 1990.

- and Pitt, Marion. *Goodly Heritage: A Centennial History of the Congregation of Wesley United (formerly Alexander Street Methodist) Church, St. John's, Newfoundland, 1884-1984.* St. John's 1984.

Rollmann, Hans. 'Gentlemen-Bishops and Faction Fighters: Additional Letters pertaining to Newfoundland Catholicism, from the Franciscan Library at Killiney (Ireland).' *Canadian Church Historical Society Journal* 30 (1988): 3-19.

Scobie, Charles H.H., and Grant, John Webster, eds. *The Contribution of Methodism to Atlantic Canada.* Kingston and Montreal 1992. The contents include: Hans Rollmann, 'Laurence Coughlan and the Origins of Methodism in Newfoundland' (53-76); and David G. Pitt, 'Methodism and E.J. Pratt: A Study of the Methodist Background of a Canadian Poet and Its Influence on His Life and Work' (218-33).

Story, G.M. *George Street United Church: One Hundred Years of Service.* St. John's 1973.

Winsor, Naboth. 'Methodism in Newfoundland, 1855-1884.' Unpublished MA thesis, Memorial University 1970.

X / Society and Culture

Anderson, David. 'The Development of Settlement in Southern Coastal Labrador with Particular Reference to Sandwich Bay.' *Bulletin of Canadian Studies* 8, no. 1 (1984): 23-49.

Barter, Mary Geraldine. 'A Linguistic Description of the French Spoken on the Port-au-Port Peninsula of Western Newfoundland.' Unpublished MA thesis, Memorial University 1986.

Bassler, Gerhard P. 'Attempts to Settle Jewish Refugees in Newfoundland and Labrador 1934-1939.' *Simon Wiesenthal Centre Annual* 5 (1988): 121-44.

- 'Central Europeans in Post-Confederation St. John's, Newfoundland: Immigration and Adjustment.' *Canadian Ethnic Studies* 18, no. 3 (1986): 37-46.

- 'The Enemy Alien Experience in Newfoundland 1914-1918.' *Canadian Ethnic Studies* 20, no. 3 (1988): 42-62.

- *The German Canadian Mosaic Today and Yesterday: Identities, Roots and Heritage.* Ottawa 1991.

- 'Germans and German Connections in Newfoundland to 1914.' *Newfoundland Quarterly* 86, no. 3 (1991): 18-26.

Bennett, Margaret. *The Last Stronghold: Scottish Gaelic Traditions in Newfoundlanders.* St. John's 1989.

Brookes, Chris. *A Public Nuisance: A History of the Mummers Troupe.* St. John's 1988.

Brown, Cassie. *Death on the Ice. The Great Newfoundland Sealing Disaster of 1914.* Toronto 1974.

Brown, Howard. 'A Study of the Curling Area 1860-1920.' Part 1, *Newfoundland Quarterly* 71, no. 3 (1975): 17-25; part 2, *Newfoundland Quarterly* 71, no. 4 (1975): 17-24.

Butler, Victor. *Harbour Buffett before Nightfall.* St. John's 1982.

- *The Little Nord Easter: Reminiscences of a Placentia bayman.* St. John's 1980.

Byrne, Cyril J., and Harry, Margaret, eds. *Talamh an Eisc; Canadian and Irish Essays.* Halifax 1986. The contents include: John J. Mannion, 'Patrick Morris and Newfoundland Irish Immigration' (180-202); and George Casey, 'Irish Culture in Newfoundland' (203-27).

Carlson, Terry. *The Legacy and the Practice: The John Howard Society in Newfoundland.* St. John's 1991.

Casey, George J. 'Traditions and Neighbourhoods: The Folklore of a Newfoundland Fishing Outport.' Unpublished MA thesis, Memorial University 1971.

Chimmo, William. *William Chimmo's Journal of a Voyage to the N.E. Coast of Labrador during the Year 1867*. William J. Kirwin, ed. St. John's 1989.

Clark, Rex, ed. *Contrary Winds: Essays on Newfoundland Society in Crisis*. St. John's 1986. The contents are: Rex Clark, 'Romancing the Harlequins: A note on Class Struggle in the Newfoundland Village' (7-20); Vince Walsh, 'Stagnant Capital and Mobile People' (21-36); Peter R. Sinclair, 'Saving the Fishery - Again!: The 1981-82 Fisheries Crisis in Newfoundland' (37-55); Gordon Inglis, '"Lawyers, Priests, and Gangsters from Chicago": Factors in the Development of the Newfoundland Fishermen, Food and Allied Workers' Union' (56-75); Elliott Leyton, 'Drunk and Disorderly: Changing Crime in Newfoundland' (76-88); Mark Shrimpton, 'The Big Squeeze: Housing Problems in the City of St. John's' (89-102); W.R. Hynd, 'Oil, Politics, and Social Change: Newfoundland and Alberta Compared' (103-16); J.D. House, 'Oil and the North Atlantic Periphery: The Scottish Experience and the Prospects for Newfoundland' (117-49); James Overton, 'Oil and Gas: The Rhetoric and Reality of Development in Newfoundland' (150-75); and Frederick Johnstone, 'Bones and Bare Cupboards: Dependency, Class and Crisis in the 'New Newfoundland', An Overview' (176-86).

Cohen, Anthony P. 'The Definition of Public Identity: Managing Marginality in Outport Newfoundland Following Confederation.' *Sociological Review* 23 (1975): 93-119.

Davis, Gwendolyn, ed. *Myth and Milieu: Atlantic Literature and Culture, 1918-1939*. Fredericton 1993. The contents include: Elizabeth Miller, 'Newfoundland Literature in the "Dirty Thirties"' (71-6); and David G. Pitt, 'The Challenged Heritage: The Sea as Myth and Milieu in the Poetry of E.J. Pratt' (160-74).

Dawson, Rhoda. 'The Wharves of St. John's, Newfoundland.' *Canadian Parliamentary Review* 15 (Summer 1992): 2-5.

Devine, P.K. *In the Good Old Days: Fishery Customs of the Past*. St. John's 1990. Reprint of articles in *Trade Review*, St. John's, 1915.

Downer, Don. *Uprooted People: The Indian Islands*. St. John's 1991.

Doyle, Marjorie. 'A Biography of Philip Tocque 1814-1899.' Unpublished MA thesis, Memorial University 1986.

Drodge, Janice Ann. 'A heritage portrayed: nationalist theatre in Newfoundland, 1972-1982.' Unpublished MA thesis, Memorial University 1982.

Dunsiger, Jane Catherine. 'A comparative study of narrative accounts of visits home drawn from the immigrant ethnic community in St. John's, Newfoundland.' Unpublished MA thesis, Memorial University 1982.

Fagan, Bonaventure. 'Images of Resettlement.' *Newfoundland Studies* 6 (1990): 1-33.

Feder, Alison. *Margaret Duley: Newfoundland Novelist*. St. John's 1983.

- and Schrank, Bernice, eds. *Literature and Folk Culture: Ireland and Newfoundland*. St. John's 1977. The contents include: William J. Kirwin, 'The Influence of Ireland on the Newfoundland Ballad' (131-45); and Herbert Halpert, 'Ireland, Sheila and Newfoundland' (147-72).

Fizzard, Garfield. *Master of His Craft: Captain Frank Thornhill*. Grand Bank 1988.

- *Unto the Sea: A History of Grand Bank*. Grand Bank 1987.

Forsey, Eugene. *A Life on the Fringe: The Memoirs of Eugene Forsey*. Toronto 1990.

Foster, Gilbert. 'The Divided Heart: Keeping up the "Fince" in Green Bay and Everywhere Else. Structuralism in Newfoundland.' Part 1, *Newfoundland Quarterly* 84, no. 4 (1989): 24-31; part 2, *Newfoundland Quarterly* 85, no. 1 (1989): 24-9.

Fowler, Adrian. 'The Literature of Newfoundland: A Roundabout Return to Elemental Matters.' *Essays on Canadian Writing* no. 31 (1985): 118-41.

Gard, Peter. 'Outport Resettlement 20 Years Later.' *Canadian Geographic* 105, no. 3 (1985): 8-17.

Gilad, Lisa. *The Northern Route: An Ethnography of Refugee Experiences*. St. John's 1990.

Goldstein, Kenneth S. 'Faith and Fate in Sea Disaster Ballads of Newfoundland Fishermen.' In Roger D. Abrahams, Kenneth S. Goldstein, and Wayland D. Hand, eds. *By Land and By Sea: Studies in the Folklore of Work and Leisure Honouring Horace P. Beck on his Sixty-Fifth Birthday*. Hatboro, Pa. 1985, 84-94.

- and Rosenberg, Neil V., eds. *Folklore Studies in Honour of Herbert Halpert: A Festschrift*. St. John's 1980. The contents include: Neil V. Rosenberg, 'Herbert Halpert: A Biographical Sketch' (1-13) and 'The Works of Herbert Halpert: A Classified Bibliography' (15-30); Margaret Bennett, 'A Codroy Valley Milling Frolic' (99-110); Carole Henderson Carpenter, 'Forty Years Later: Maud Karpeles in Newfoundland' (111-24); and Gerald Thomas, 'Other Worlds: Folktale and Soap Opera in Newfoundland's French Tradition' (343-51).

Halpert, Herbert and Story, G.M., eds. *Christmas Mumming in Newfoundland: Essays in Anthropology, Folklore, and History*. Toronto 1990. The contents are: 'Introduction' (2-6); G.M. Story, 'Newfoundland: Fishermen, Hunters, Planters, and Merchants' (7-33); Herbert Halpert, 'A Typology of Mumming' (34-61); Melvin M. Firestone, 'Mummers and Strangers in Northern Newfoundland' (62-75); Louis J. Chiaramonte, 'Mumming in "Deep Harbour": Aspects of Social Organization in Mumming and Drinking' (76-103); John F. Swzed, 'The Mask of Friendship: Mumming as a Ritual of Social Relations' (104-18); Shmuel Ben-

Dor, 'The "Naluyuks" of Northern Labrador: A Mechanism of Social Control' (119-27); James C. Faris, 'Mumming in an Outport Fishing Settlement: A Description and Suggestions on the Cognitive Complex' (128-44); J.D.A. Widdowson and Herbert Halpert, 'The Disguises of Newfoundland Mummers' (145-64); G.M. Story, 'Mummers in Newfoundland History: A Survey of the Printed Record' (165-85); Herbert Halpert and G.M. Story, eds., 'Newfoundland Mummers' Plays: Three Printed Texts' (186-207). Appendices: Clyde E. Williams, 'Janneying in "Coughlin Cove"' (209-15); J.D.A. Widdowson, 'Mummering and Janneying: Some Explanatory Notes' (216-21); and 'The Newfoundland Distribution of the Mummers' Play and Christmas Disguising' (222-9).

Handcock, Gordon. 'Spatial Patterns in a Trans-Atlantic Migration Field: the British Isles and Newfoundland during the Eighteenth and Nineteenth Centuries.' In Brian S. Osborne, ed. *The Settlement of Canada: Origins and Transfer*. Kingston 1976, 13-45.

- 'The West County Migrations to Newfoundland.' *Bulletin of Canadian Studies* 5, no. 1 (1981): 5-24.

Hiscock, Philip Douglas. 'Folklore and Popular Culture in Early Newfoundland Radio Broadcasting: An Analysis of Occupational Narrative, Oral History and Song Repertoire.' Unpublished MA thesis, Memorial University 1986.

Houlihan, Eileen. *Uprooted: The Argentia Story*. St. John's 1992.

House, Edgar. *The Way Out: The Story of NONIA in Newfoundland, 1920-1990*. St. John's 1990.

Jackson, Lawrence. *Bounty of a Barren Coast: Resource Harvest and Settlement in Southern Labrador*. Goose Bay 1982.

Jones, Frederick. 'The Early Opposition to Bishop Feild of Newfoundland.' *Journal of the Canadian Church Historical Society* 16 (1974): 30-41.

- *Edward Feild, Bishop of Newfoundland, 1844-1876*. Pamphlet. St. John's 1976.

- 'John Bull's Other Ireland—Nineteenth Century Newfoundland.' *Dalhousie Review* 55 (1975-76): 227-35.

- 'The Making of a Colonial Bishop: Feild of Newfoundland.' *Journal of the Canadian Church Historical Society* 15 (1973): 2-13.

Kahn, Alison. *Listen While I Tell You: A Story of the Jews of St. John's, Newfoundland*. St. John's 1987.

Kelly, Gemey. *Rockwell Kent: The Newfoundland Work*. Halifax 1987.

Kelly, Ursula. *Marketing Place: Cultural Politics, Regionalism, and Reading*. Halifax 1993.

Kennedy, John. *Holding the Line: Ethnic Boundaries in a Northern Labrador Community*. St. John's 1981.

- 'The Impact of the Grenfell Mission on southeastern Labrador communities.' *Polar Record* 24 (1988): 199-206.

Kirwin, W.J., and Story, G.M., eds. 'J.P. Howley and the Geological Survey of Newfoundland: *REMINISCENCES* of 1868.' Document. *Newfoundland Studies* 7 (1991): 173-201.

Kivlichan, John. 'The Art of Duley's *Cold Pastoral.*' *Newfoundland Studies* 6 (1990): 177-89.

Laba, Martin. 'Narrative and Talk: A Study in the Folkloric Communication of Everyday Conversational Exchange.' Unpublished PH D thesis, Memorial University 1983.

Larson, Eric Hugh. 'Spatial and Temporal Trends in Human Mortality in Newfoundland, 1937-1971.' Unpublished M SC thesis, University of Calgary 1985.

Lehr, Genevieve, and Best, Anita, eds. *Come and I Will Sing You: A Newfoundland Songbook.* Toronto 1985.

Leyton, Elliott, O'Grady, William, and Overton, James. *Violence and Public Anxiety: A Canadian Case.* St. John's 1992. The contents are: 'Introduction' (xiii-xxvii); William O'Grady, 'Criminal Statistics and Stereotypes: The Social Construction of Violence in Newfoundland' (1-106); Elliott Leyton, 'The Theatre of Public Crisis' (109-91); James Overton, 'Riots, Raids and Relief, Police, Prisons and Parsimony: The Political Economy of Public Order in Newfoundland in the 1930s' (195-334); and 'Conclusion' (337-9).

Loder, Millicent Blake. *Daughter of Labrador.* St. John's 1989.

Lovelace, Martin J. 'Literary and Oral Styles in Newfoundland Autobiographies.' *Newfoundland Studies* 5 (1989): 53-60.

Lynde, Denyse, Peters, Helen, and Buehler, Richard, eds. *Proceedings of the Workshop on Newfoundland Theatre Research.* St. John's 1993. The contents include: Denyse Lynde 'Introduction' (vii-ix); Gail Weir, 'Performing Arts Materials in the Centre for Newfoundland Studies Archives' (12-16); 'Discussion' (17-25); Alan Filewood, 'Writing the Mummers Troupe: Historiography and Me' (29-34); Helen Peters, 'A Note on the Text of the Plays of CODCO' (35-41); 'Discussion' (62-70); Paul O'Neill, 'Theatre in Newfoundland: The Beginning' (73-80); John Holmes, 'The London Theatre Company' (81-7); Ches Skinner, 'Newfoundland Amateur Drama - Historical Sources' (88-93); Elizabeth Miller, 'Ted Russell's "Pigeon Inlet": From Radio to Stage to Television' (94-8); Michael Cook, 'Theatre on the Stage and Radio in Newfoundland' (99-105); 'Discussion' (106-12); Ann Anderson, 'The Newfoundland and Labrador Arts Council' (115-16); Andy Jones, 'Plays for Publishing' (117-18); Chris Brookes, 'The Mummers Troupe' (119-27); and 'Discussion' (128-37).

McCann, Larry, and MacMillan, Carrie, eds. *The Sea and Culture of Atlantic Canada*. Sackville 1992. The contents include: Peter Neary, 'American Argonauts: Frederic Edwin Church and Louis Legrand Noble in Newfoundland and Labrador, 1859' (15-46); and Gerald L. Pocius, 'The House that Poor-Jack Built: Architectural Stages in the Newfoundland Fishery' (62-105).

McCarthy, Michael. *The Irish in Newfoundland, 1623-1800*. St. John's 1982.

Macfarlane, David. *The Danger Tree: Memory, War, and the Search for a Family's Past*. Toronto 1991.

MacKinnon, Richard. 'Carriage Making in St. John's, Newfoundland: A Folkloristic Perspective on a Historical Industry.' *Material History Bulletin* no. 27 (1988): 15-26.

- 'Carriage-making in St. John's, Newfoundland: a historical study of the products of a folk industry.' Unpublished MA thesis, Memorial University 1982.

Mannion, John. *Irish Settlements in Eastern Canada: A Study of Cultural Transfer and Adaptation*. Toronto 1974.

- *Point Lance in Transition: The Transformation of a Newfoundland Outport*. Toronto 1976.

Martin, Anne Elizabeth. 'Up-Along: Newfoundland Families in Hamilton.' Unpublished MA thesis, McMaster University 1974.

Matthews, Ralph. *The Creation of Regional Dependency*. Toronto 1983.

- 'The Outport Breakup.' *Horizon Canada* 9 (1987): 2438-43.

- *'There's No Better Place Than Here': Social Change in Three Newfoundland Communities*. Toronto 1976.

Mercer, Paul. *The Ballads of Johnny Burke: A Short Anthology*. Pamphlet. St. John's 1974.

- ed. *Newfoundland Songs and Ballads in print 1842-1974*. St. John's 1979.

Miller, Elizabeth Russell. *The Frayed Edge: Norman Duncan's Newfoundland*. St. John's 1992.

- *The Life and Times of Ted Russell*. St. John's 1981.

Mills, David B. 'The Evolution of Folk Architecture in Trinity Bay.' *Newfoundland Quarterly* 69, no. 3 (1972): 17-23.

Moyles, R.G. *'Complaints is Many and Various but the Odd Divil Likes It': Nineteenth Century Views of Newfoundland*. Toronto 1975.

Narváez, Peter. 'Country Music in Diffusion: Juxtaposition and Syncretism in the Popular Music of Newfoundland.' *Journal of Country Music* 7, no. 2 (1978): 93-101.

- 'The Folklore of "Old Foolishness": The Nostalgic Use of Folklore.' *Canadian Literature* 108 (1986): 125-43.

- '"I've Gotten Soppy": Send-Off Parties as Rites of Passage in the Occupational Folklife of Reporters.' *American Behavioral Scientist* 33, no. 3 (1990): 339-52.

- 'The Protest Songs of a Labour Union on Strike Against an American Corporation in a Newfoundland Company Town: A Folkloristic Analysis With Special References to Oral Folk History.' Unpublished PH D thesis, Indiana University 1986. Available through University Microfilms International, Ann Arbor Michigan, publication no. 86-07-398, 1986.

- ed. *The Good People: New Fairylore Essays.* New York 1991. The contents include: Gary R. Butler, 'The "Lutin" Tradition in French-Newfoundland Culture: Discourse and Belief' (5-21); Barbara Rieti, '"The Blast" in Newfoundland Fairy Tradition' (284-97); and Peter Narváez, 'Newfoundland Berry Pickers "In the Fairies": Maintaining Spatial, Temporal, and Moral Boundaries Through Legendry' (336-67).

- and Laba, Martin, eds. *Media Sense: The Folklore-Popular Culture Continuum.* Bowling Green, Ohio. 1986. The contents include: Peter Narváez and Martin Laba, 'Introduction: The Folklore-Popular Culture Continuum" (1-8); Martin Lovelace, 'Gossip, Rumor and Personal Malice: The Rhetoric of Radio Open-Line Shows' (19-30); Paul Smith, 'Communicating Culture; or Can we Really Vocalize a Brownie?' (31-46); Peter Narváez, 'Joseph R. Smallwood, "The Barrelman": The Broadcaster as Folklorist' (47-64) and 'The Newfie Bullet—The Nostalgic Use of Folklore' (65-76); Michael Taft, 'Of Scoffs, Mounties and Mainlanders: The Popularity of a Sheep-Stealing Ballad in Newfoundland' (77-98); Gerald L. Pocius, 'Holy Pictures in Newfoundland Houses: Visual Codes for Secular and Supernatural Relationships' (124-48); and Neil V. Rosenberg, 'Big Fish, Small Pond: Country Musicians and Their Markets' (149-66).

Neary, Peter. *Bell Island, a Newfoundland mining community 1895-1966.* Ottawa 1974.

- '"Traditional" and "Modern" Elements in the Social and Economic History of Bell Island and Conception Bay.' Canadian Historical Association, *Historical Papers,* 1973, 105-36.

- '"Wry Comment": Rhoda Dawson's Cartoon of Newfoundland Society, 1936.' *Newfoundland Studies* 8 (1992): 1-14.

Nemec, Thomas F. 'The Irish Emigration to Newfoundland.' *Newfoundland Quarterly* 69, no. 1 (1972): 15-19, 22-4.

- 'St. Shotts in Historical Perspective.' *Newfoundland Quarterly* 71, no. 3 (1975): 17-22.

- 'Trespassey, 1505-1840 A.D.: The Emergence of an Anglo-Irish Newfoundland Outport.' *Newfoundland Quarterly* 69, no. 4 (1973): 17-28.

- 'Trespassey, 1840-1900: An Ethnohistorical Reconstruction of Anglo-Irish Outport Society.' *Newfoundland Quarterly* 70, no. 1 (1973): 15-24.

Norman, Agnes, Gallant, Gervase, and Norman, Derek, eds. *Film in New-foundland and Labrador 1904-1980*. St. John's 1981.

O'Brien, Patricia. *The Grenfell Obsession: An Anthology*. St. John's 1992.

O'Dea, Shane. *The Domestic Architecture of Old St. John's*. Pamphlet. St. John's 1974.

O'Flaherty, Patrick. 'Caught in the Nets: Growing up Irish Catholic in Newfoundland.' *Canadian Forum* 65 (March 1986): 6-10.

- *Come Near At Your Peril: A Visitor's Guide to the Island of Newfoundland*. St. John's 1992.

- 'Looking Backwards: the milieu of the old Newfoundland Outports.' *Journal of Canadian Studies* 10, no. 1 (1975): 3-9.

- 'The Newfoundland Irish.' *Newfoundland Quarterly* 86, no. 1 (1990): 20-32.

- *The Rock Observed: Studies in the Literature of Newfoundland*. Toronto 1979.

Oliver, Elizabeth. 'The Rebuilding of the City of St. John's after the Great Fire of 1892: A Study in Urban Morphogenesis.' Unpublished MA thesis, Memorial University 1983.

Ommer, Rosemary E. 'The Scots in Newfoundland.' *Newfoundland Quarterly* 77, no. 4 (1981): 23-31.

- 'Scots Kinship, Immigration and Early Settlement in Southwestern Newfoundland.' Unpublished MA thesis, Memorial University 1973.

O'Neill, Paul, *The Oldest City: The Story of St. John's, Newfoundland*. Erin, Ont. 1975. *A Seaport Legacy: The Story of St. John's, Newfoundland*. Erin, Ont. 1976.

Overton, James. 'Coming Home: Nostalgia and Tourism in Newfoundland.' *Acadiensis* 14, no. 1 (1984): 84-97.

- 'A Newfoundland Culture?' *Journal of Canadian Studies* 23, nos. 1 & 2 (1988): 5-22.

- 'A Whale for the Killing and the Politics of Culture and Ecology.' *Journal of Canadian Studies* 22, no. 1 (1987): 84-103.

Paddock, Harold J., ed. *Languages in Newfoundland and Labrador*. St. John's 1982.

Paddon, Harold G. *Green Woods and Blue Waters*. St. John's 1989.

Paddon, W. Anthony. *Labrador Doctor: My Life with the Grenfell Mission*. Toronto 1989.

Paine, Robert, ed. *The White Arctic: Case Studies from the Labrador Coast*. St. John's 1985. The contents include: Georg Henriksen, 'The Transactional Basis of Influence: White Men Among Naskapi Indians' (22-33); and

James Hiller, 'Early Patrons of the Labrador Eskimos: The Moravian Mission in Labrador, 1764-1805' (74-97).

Peacock, F.W. with Jackson, Lawrence. *Reflections From a Snowhouse*. St. John's 1986.

Peddle, Walter. *The Forgotten Craftsmen*. St. John's 1984.

- *The Traditional Furniture of Outport Newfoundland*. St. John's 1983.

Pike, Kathryn. *The Knights of Columbus in Newfoundland*. Pamphlet. St. John's 1985.

Pitt, David G. *E.J. Pratt: The Truant Years 1882-1927*. Toronto 1984.

- *E.J. Pratt: The Master Years 1927-1964*. Toronto 1987.

Pocius, Gerald L. 'Eighteenth- and Nineteenth-century Newfoundland Gravestones: Self-sufficiency, Economic Specialization, and the Creation of Artifacts.' *Material History Bulletin* 12 (1981): 1-16.

- 'Hooked rugs in Newfoundland: the representation of social structure in design.' *Journal of American Folklore* 92 (1979): 273-84.

- *A Place to Belong: Community Order and Everyday Space in Calvert, Newfoundland*. Kingston and Montreal 1991.

Porter, Helen. *Below the Bridge: Memories of the South Side of St. John's*. St. John's 1979.

Pringle, James S. 'Jewell David Sornborger (1869-1929): An Early Biological Explorer in Newfoundland and Labrador.' *Canadian Horticultural History* 1 (1988): 210-21.

Quigley, Colin. *Close to the Floor: Folk Dance in Newfoundland*. St. John's 1985.

Rapport, Nigel. *Talking Violence: An Anthropological Interpretation of Conversation in the City*. St. John's 1987.

Richling, Barnett. 'Isolation and Community Resettlement: a Labrador Example.' *Culture* 5, no. 2 (1985): 77-86.

- 'Stuck up on a Rock: Resettlement and Community Development in Hopedale, Labrador.' *Human Organization* 44 (1985): 348-53.

- '"You'd Never Starve Here": return migration to rural Newfoundland.' *Canadian Review of Sociology and Anthropology* 22 (1985): 236-49.

Rieti, Barbara. *Strange Terrain: The Fairy World in Newfoundland*. St. John's 1991.

Rompkey, Ronald. 'Elements of Spiritual Autobiography in Sir Wilfred Grenfell's *A Labrador Doctor*.' *Newfoundland Studies* 1 (1985): 17-28.

- 'Heroic Biography and the Life of Sir Wilfred Grenfell.' *Prose Studies* 12 (1989): 159-73.

- 'Philip Henry Gosse's account of his years in Newfoundland, 1827-35.' Document. *Newfoundland Studies* 6 (1990): 210-66.

Rosenberg, Neil V. 'Folksong in Newfoundland: a research history.' In Conrad Laforte, ed. *Ballades et chansons folklorique.* Quebec 1989, 45-52.

- 'The Gerald S. Doyle Songsters and the Politics of Newfoundland Folksong.' *Canadian Folklore canadien* 13, no. 1 (1991): 45-57.

Russell, Kelly. *Rufus Guinchard: The Man and His Music.* St. John's 1982.

Ryan, Virginia. 'Outport and Cosmos: Meaning in *The Way of the Sea.*' *Newfoundland Studies* 5 (1989): 177-202.

Saunders, Gary L. *Rattles and Steadies. Memoirs of a Gander River Man.* St. John's 1986.

Shrimpton, Mark, and Sharpe, C.A. 'An inner city in decline: St. John's, Newfoundland.' *Urban History Review* 9, no. 1 (1980): 90-109.

Sider, Gerald M. 'Christmas Mumming and the New Year in Outport Newfoundland.' *Past & Present* 71 (1976): 102-25.

- *Culture and Class in Anthropology and History: A Newfoundland Illustration.* Cambridge 1986.

- 'The ties that bind: culture and agriculture, property and propriety in the Newfoundland village fishery.' *Social History* 5 (1980): 1-39.

Smith, Marjorie. 'Newfoundland, 1815-1840: A Study of a Merchantocracy.' Unpublished MA thesis, Memorial University 1968.

Staveley, Michael. 'Saskatchewan-By-The-Sea: The Topographic Work of Alexander Murray in Newfoundland.' *Newfoundland Quarterly* 77, nos. 2 & 3 (1981): 31-41.

Steele, Donald H., ed. *Early Science in Newfoundland and Labrador.* St. John's 1987. The contents are: D.H. Steele, 'Introduction' (1-7); J. Malpas and A.F. King, 'Pioneers of Geological Exploration, Mapping and Mining in Newfoundland' (8-28); Alan G. MacPherson, 'Early Moravian Interest in Northern Weather and Climate: The Beginning of Instrumental Recording in Newfoundland' (30-41); H.J. Anderson and M.J. Newlands, 'Pre-20th Century in Chemistry in Newfoundland' (42-8); K.B. Roberts, 'The Training of Newfoundland Medical Men (Abstract)'(49); Malcolm MacLeod, 'Special Six Per Cent. Scientific Aspirations/Achievements Among Pre-Confederation Newfoundlanders Who Went Abroad to Study' (50-62); C.M.T. Woodworth-Lynas, 'Victor Campbell: Newfoundland's Connection with Captain Scott's Last Antarctic Expedition, 1910-1913' (63-84); C. Brice-Bennett, 'Entering a New World. An Exploratory Voyage to northernmost Labrador and northeastern Ungava Bay in 1811 (Abstract)'(85); Frederick A. Aldrich, 'Moses and the Living Water: Victorian Science in Newfoundland' (86-120); F. Elizabeth Johnson, 'Early Contributions of Church of England Missionaries to Newfoundland Natural History' (121-5); John A. Gow, 'Pre-1900 Environmental Microbiology in Newfoundland: Early observations that withstood the test of time (Abstract)' (126); G. Robin

South, 'Pre-Twentieth Century Botany in Newfoundland and Labrador' (127-46); Guy R. Brassard, 'Rev. Arthur C. Waghorne (1851-1900): Newfoundland's first Botanist (Abstract)' (147); B.A. Roberts, 'Merritt Lydon Fernald (1873-1950), his investigations and discoveries in the Newfoundland flora' (148-57); D.H. Steele, 'John James Audubon in Newfoundland' (158-78); and W.A. Montevecchi, 'Trends in Nineteenth Century Ornithology as exemplified by the Research of Peter C. Stuwitz and John Cyrus Cahoon in Newfoundland' (179-99).

Story, G.M. 'Guides to Newfoundland.' *Newfoundland Quarterly* 75, no. 4 (1980): 17-23.

- 'Judge Prowse (1834-1914).' *Newfoundland Quarterly* 68, no. 1 (1971): 15-19, 22-5.

- 'Judge Prowse: Historian and Publicist.' *Newfoundland Quarterly* 68, no. 4 (1972): 19, 22-5.

- 'Newfoundland Dialect: An Historical View.' *Canadian Geographical Journal* 70 (1965): 126-31.

- 'Notes from a Berry Patch.' *Proceedings and Transactions of the Royal Society of Canada* 10, 4th series (1972), section 2: 163-77.

- '"Old Labrador": George Cartwright, 1738-1819.' *Newfoundland Quarterly* 77, no. 1 (1981): 23-31, 35.

- 'The St. John's Balladeers.' *English Quarterly* 4, no. 4 (1971): 50-8.

- '"A tune beyond us as we are": Reflections on Newfoundland Community Song and Ballad.' *Newfoundland Studies* 4 (1988): 129-44.

- 'A View From the Sea: Newfoundland Place-Naming.' In Jean-Claude Boulanger, ed. *Proceedings of the XVIth International Congress of Onomastic Sciences*. Quebec City 1990, 41-58.

Szala, Karen. 'Clean women and quiet men: courtship and marriage in a Newfoundland fishing village.' Unpublished MA thesis, Memorial University 1978.

Taft, Michael. 'The Bard of Prescott Street meets Tin Pan Alley: The Vanity Press Sheet Music Publications of John Burke.' *Newfoundland Studies* 6 (1990): 56-73.

Thomas, Gerald. 'Albert "Ding Dong" Simon: A Tall Tale Teller from Newfoundland's French Tradition.' *Newfoundland Studies* 3 (1987): 227-50.

- 'The Folktale and Folktale Style in the Tradition of French Newfoundlanders.' *Canadian Folklore* 1, nos. 1 & 2 (1979): 71-8.

- and Widdowson, J.D.A. eds. *Studies in Newfoundland Folklore: Community and Process*. St. John's 1991. The contents are: Herbert Halpert, 'Preface' (xi-xvi); Gerald Thomas and J.D.A. Widdowson, 'Introduction' (xvii-xxiii); Diane E. Goldstein, 'Perspectives on Newfoundland Belief Traditions: Narrative Clues to Concepts of Evidence' (27-40); Martin J. Lovelace, 'Animals Kneeling at Christmas: A Belief Topic and its Calendar Context in Newfoundland' (41-52); Gerald Thomas, 'Concepts of Truth and Time in the Mind of a Franco-Newfoundland Storyteller' (53-77); Violetta Maloney Halpert, 'Death Warnings in Newfoundland Oral Tradition' (78-108); David Buchan, 'Sweet William's Questions' (111-25); Kenneth S. Goldstein, 'A Report on Continuing Research into "Treason Songs": A Private Newfoundland Folksong Tradition' (126-53); Neil V. Rosenberg, 'MUNFLA, A Newfoundland Resource for the Study of Folk Music' (154-65); Elke Dettmer, 'Folklorism in Newfoundland' (169-76); Philip Hiscock, 'Folk Process in a Popular Medium: The "Irene B. Mellon" Radio Programme, 1934-1941' (177-90); Peter Narváez, 'Folk Talk and Hard Facts: The Role of Ted Russell's "Uncle Mose" on CBC's "Fishermen's Broadcast"'(191-212); Gary R. Butler, 'Beyond the Text: The Importance of Cognitive Expansion in Folkloristic Anaylsis' (215-26); William J. Kirwin, 'The Rise and Fall of Dialect Representation in Newfoundland Writings' (227-44); J.D.A. Widdowson, 'Lexical Retention in Newfoundland Dialect' (245-58); Gerald L. Pocius, 'Folk Religion and the Ethnography of Literacy: The Image of the Word on Newfoundland Gravestones' (259-86); Roberta Buchanan, '"Country Ways and Fashions": Lydia Campbell's "Sketches of Labrador Life"—A Study in Folklore and Literature' (289-308); and Pat Byrne, '"Tall are the Tales that Fishermen Tell": Manifestations of the Tall Tale Impulse in Selected Examples of Contemporary Newfoundland Writing' (309-28).

Thomas, Gordon W. *From Sled to Satellite: My Years with the Grenfell Mission*. Toronto 1987.

Tizzard, Aubrey M. *Down on the French Shore in the 1940s*. St. John's 1982.

- *On Sloping Ground: Reminiscences of Outport Life in Notre Dame Bay, Newfoundland*. St. John's 1984.

Wareham, Wilfred William. 'Aspects of Socializing and Partying in Outport Newfoundland.' *Material History Bulletin* no. 15 (Summer 1982): 23-6.

- 'Towards an Enthnography of "Times": Newfoundland Party Traditions, Past and Present.' Unpublished PH D thesis, University of Pennsylvania 1982.

White, Marian Frances, comp. and ed. *Not A Still Life: The Art & Writings of Rae Perlin*. St. John's 1991.

Whiteley, Albert S. *A Century in Bonne Esperance: The Saga of the Whiteley Family*. Ottawa 1977.

Whiteway, Louise. 'The Athenaeum Movement: St. John's Athenaeum (1861-1898).' *Dalhousie Review* 50 (1970-71): 543-9.

- 'Newfoundland in 1867.' *Dalhousie Review* 46 (1966-67): 39-62.

Williams, Susan. 'Images of Newfoundland in promotional literature, 1890-1914.' Unpublished MA thesis, McGill University 1980.

Woodford, Paul. *"We Love the Place, O Lord": A History of the Written Musical Tradition of Newfoundland and Labrador to 1949*. St. John's 1988.

Zimmerly, David William. *Cain's Land Revisited: Cultural Change in Central Labrador, 1775-1972*. St. John's 1975.

XI / Women's History

Antler, Ellen. 'Fisherman, fisherwoman, rural proletariat: capitalist commodity production in the Newfoundland fishery.' Unpublished PH D thesis, University of Connecticut 1981.

- 'Women's Work in Newfoundland Fishing Families.' *Atlantis* 2, no. 2 (1977): 106-13.

Benoit, Cecilia M. *Midwives in Passage: The Modernisation of Maternity Care*. St. John's 1991.

- 'Mothering in a Newfoundland Community: 1900-1940.' In Katherine Arnup, Andrée Lévesque and Ruth Roach Pierson, eds. *Delivering Motherhood: Maternal Ideologies and Practices in the 19th and 20th Centuries*. London 1990, 173-89.

- 'Uneasy Partners: midwives and their clients.' *Canadian Journal of Sociology* 12 (1987): 275-84.

Bradbrook, Pauline. 'A Brief Account of the Church of England Women's Association in Newfoundland.' *Journal of the Canadian Church Historical Society* 28 (1986): 92-105.

Campbell, Lydia. *Sketches of Labrador*. Goose Bay 1980.

Colbert, Mary. 'The Portrayal of Outport Women in Selected Twentieth Century Newfoundland Writings.' Unpublished MA thesis, Memorial University 1986.

Dale, Linda. 'A Woman's Touch: Domestic Arrangements in the Rural Newfoundland Home.' *Material History Bulletin* no. 15 (1982): 19-22.

Davis, Dona Lee. *Blood and Nerves: An Ethnographic Focus on Menopause*. St. John's 1983.

- 'The Family and Social Change in the Newfoundland Outport.' *Culture* 3, no. 1 (1983): 19-32.

- 'Occupational Community and Fishermen's Wives in a Newfoundland Fishing Village.' *Anthropological Quarterly* 59 (1986): 129-42.

- 'Women's Experience of Menopause in a Newfoundland Fishing Village.' Unpublished PH D thesis, University of North Carolina 1980.

Forestell, Nancy. 'Times Were Hard: The Pattern of Women's Paid Labour in St. John's between the Two World Wars.' *Labour/le Travail* 24 (1989): 147-66.

- 'Women's Paid Labour in St. John's between the Two World Wars.' Unpublished MA thesis, Memorial University 1987.

- and Chisholm, Jessie. 'Working-Class Women as Wage Earners in St. John's, Newfoundland, 1890-1921.' In Peta Tancred-Sheriff, ed. *Feminist Research: Prospect and Retrospect*. Kingston and Montreal 1988, 141-55.

Giovannini, Margaret. *Outport Nurse*. Janet McNaughton, ed. St. John's 1988.

Goudie, Elizabeth. *Woman of Labrador*. Toronto 1973.

Greenhill, Pauline. '"The Family Album": A Newfoundland Women's Recitation.' *Canadian Folklore* 6, nos. 1-2 (1984): 39-61.

Hubbard, Mina. *A Women's Way Through Unknown Labrador*. St. John's 1981. Reprint of 1908 original.

Kealey, Linda, ed. *Pursuing Equality: Historical Perspectives on Women in Newfoundland and Labrador*. St. John's 1993. The contents are: Linda Kealey, 'Introduction' (1-13); Margot Iris Duley, '"The Radius of Her Influence for Good": The Rise and Triumph of the Women's Suffrage Movement in Newfoundland, 1909-1925' (14-65); Linda Cullum and Maeve Baird with the assistance of Cynthia Penney, 'Women and the Law in Newfoundland from Early Settlement to the Twentieth Century' (66-162); Sharon Grey Pope and Jane Burnham, 'Change Within and Without: The Modern Women's Movement in Newfoundland and Labrador' (163-231); Appendix A, 'Documents: Women's Suffrage,' comp. by Margot Duley (222-9); Appendix B, 'Documents: Women and Law,' comp. by Linda Cullum and Cynthia Penney (230-5); Appendix C, 'Chronology of Laws and Important Legal Changes' (236-8); Appendix D, 'List of Women's Conferences 1975-1988' (239-40); Appendix E, 'Highlights of the Women's Movement in Newfoundland and Labrador 1972-1988' (241-7); Appendix F, 'Documents: The Modern Women's Movement' (248-56).

- and Martin, Gillian. 'Sources on Women in Newfoundland: The Memorial University of Newfoundland Folklore and Language Archive (MUNFLA).' *Culture & Tradition* 8 (1984): 52-71.

Loder, Millicent Blake. *Daughter of Labrador*. St. John's 1989.

Matthews, Anne Martin. 'The Newfoundland Migrant Wife: A Power versus Powerlessness Theory of Adjustment.' In Alexander Himmelfarth and C. James Richardson, eds. *Sociology for Canadians: A Reader*. Toronto 1984, 49-60.

Miller, Ann. 'Narration and life history of a Newfoundland woman.' Unpublished MA thesis, McMaster University 1981.

Nadel-Klein, Jane, and Davis, Dona Lee, eds. *To Work and to Weep: Women in Fishing Economies*. St. John's 1988. The contents include: Dona Lee

Davis, '"Shore Skippers" and "Grass Widows": Active and Passive Women's Roles in a Newfoundland Fishery' (211-29).

Parsons, Linda Ann. 'Passing the Time: The Lives of Women in a Northern Industrial Town.' Unpublished MA thesis, Memorial University 1986.

Penney, Joan. '"The Literature of the Colonized": Feminist Perspective in the Novels of Margaret Duley.' Unpublished MA thesis, Memorial University 1986.

Peyton, Amy Louise. *Nightingale of the North: Georgina Stirling.* St. John's 1983.

Porter, Marilyn. 'Mothers and Daughters: Linking Women's Life Histories in Grand Bank, Newfoundland, Canada.' *Women's Studies International Forum* 11 (1988): 545-58.

- 'Peripheral Women: Towards a Feminist Analysis of the Atlantic Region.' *Studies in Political Economy* 23 (1987): 41-72.

- 'She Was Skipper of the Shore-Crew: Notes on the Sexual Division of Labour in Newfoundland.' *Labour/Le Travail* 15 (1985): 105-23.

- '"The Tangly Bunch": Outport Women of the Avalon Peninsula.' *Newfoundland Studies* 1 (1985): 77-90.

- 'Time, the Life Course and Work in Women's Lives: Reflections from Newfoundland.' *Women's Studies International Forum* 14, no. 1/2 (1991): 1-13.

- '"Women and Old Boats": The Sexual Division of Labour in a Newfoundland Outport.' In Eva Gamarnikow, David Morgan, June Purvis and Daphne Taylorson, eds. *The Public and the Private.* London 1983, 91-105.

Richard, Agnes M. *Threads of Gold: The History of the Jubilee Guilds and Women's Institutes in Newfoundland.* St. John's 1989.

Russell, Dora. *Day by Day: Pages from the Diary of a Newfoundland Woman.* St. John's 1983.

Saunders, Doris. 'Women in Labrador: a Personal Viewpoint.' *Atlantis* 8, no. 1 (1982): 84-8.

XII / Work, Labour and the Economy

Akyeampong, E.B. 'Labour Laws and the Development of the Labour Movement in Newfoundland, 1900-1960.' Unpublished MA thesis, Acadia University 1970.

Alexander, David. *Atlantic Canada and Confederation: Essays in Canadian Political Economy.* Eric W. Sager, Lewis R. Fischer, and Stuart O. Pierson, comps. Toronto 1983. The contents are: 'Introduction' (vii-ix); 'David Alexander: A Reminiscence' (x-xviii); 'Development and Dependence in Newfoundland, 1880-1970' (3-31); 'The Political Economy of Fishing in Newfoundland' (32-43); 'Canadian Regionalism: A Central Problem'

(44-50); 'Economic Growth in the Atlantic Region, 1880 to 1940' (51-78); 'New Notions of Happiness: Nationalism, Regionalism, and Atlantic Canada' (79-100); 'Old and New Money' (101-05); 'The Erosion of Social Democracy in Canada' (106-09); 'Literacy and Economic Development in Nineteenth-Century Newfoundland' (110-43); and 'Convocation Address, Memorial University of Newfoundland, May 1978' (144-8).

- 'The Collapse of the Saltfish Trade and Newfoundland's Integration into the North American Economy.' Canadian Historical Association, *Historical Papers*, 1976, 229-48.

- *The Decay of Trade: An Economic History of the Newfoundland Saltfish Trade, 1935-1965*. St. John's 1977.

- 'Newfoundland's Traditional Economy and Development to 1934.' *Acadiensis* 5, no. 2 (1976): 56-78.

Anderson, David G. 'Government Programmes and the Generation of Employment in Newfoundland and Labrador: Policy into Action.' *British Journal of Canadian Studies* 6, no. 2 (1991): 411-32.

Ashton, John. 'The Lumbercamp Song Tradition in Newfoundland.' *Newfoundland Studies* 2 (1986): 213-31.

- 'A Study of the Lumbercamp Song Tradition in Newfoundland.' PH D thesis, Memorial University 1985.

Baker, Melvin. 'Rural Electrification in Newfoundland in the 1950s and the Origins of the Newfoundland Power Commission.' *Newfoundland Studies* 6 (1990): 190-209.

- Cuff, Robert, and Gillespie, Bill. *Working Men's St. John's: Aspects of Social History in the early 1900s*. St. John's 1982.

- Dickinson, A.B., and Sanger, C.W. 'Adolph Nielsen: Norwegian Influence on Newfoundland Fisheries in the Late 19th-Early 20th Century.' *Newfoundland Quarterly* 87, no. 2 (1992): 25-32, 35.

- and Pitt, Janet Miller. 'Competing for the Limelight: The St. John's Gas Light Company 1844 to 1896.' *Newfoundland Quarterly* 86, no. 2 (1990): 22-7.

- Pitt, Robert D.W., and Pitt, Janet Miller. *The Illustrated History of Newfoundland Light & Power*. St. John's 1990.

Barrett, Gene, and Davis, Anthony. 'Floundering in Troubled Waters: The Political Economy of the Atlantic Fishery and the Task Force on Atlantic Fisheries.' *Journal of Canadian Studies* 19, no. 1 (1984): 125-37.

Bartels, Dennis. 'Markets without Merchants: The Political Economy of the Newfoundland Fishermen, Food and Allied Workers Union's Direct Sales to Bulgaria and Sweden.' *Canadian Journal of Anthropology* 2 (1981): 101-5.

Bassler, Gerhard P. '"Develop or Perish": Joseph R. Smallwood and New-foundland's Quest for German Industry, 1949-1953.' *Acadiensis* 15, no. 2 (1986): 93-119.

Beliveau, John Edward, Cameron, Silver Donald, and Harrington, Michael. *Iceboats to Superferries: An Illustrated History of Marine Atlantic*. St. John's 1992.

Brown, Howard Cecil. 'The Impact of Modernization on a Traditional Regional System: The Case of Inner Placentia Bay, Newfoundland, 1911-1966.' Unpublished MA thesis, Memorial University 1989.

Bryon, R.F. 'Economic Functions of Kinship Values in Family Businesses: Fishing Crews in North Atlantic Communities.' *Sociology and Social Research* 60 (1976): 147-160.

Busch, Briton Cooper. 'The Newfoundland Sealers' Strike of 1902.' *Labour/Le Travail* 14 (1984): 73-101.

- *The War Against the Seals: A History of the North American Seal Fishery*. Kingston and Montreal 1985.

Cadigan, Sean. 'Battle Harbour in Transition: Merchants, Fishermen, and the State in the Struggle for Relief in a Labrador Community during the 1930s.' *Labour/Le Travail* 26 (1990): 125-50.

- 'Economic and Social Relations of Production on the Northeast Coast of Newfoundland, with Special Reference to Conception Bay, 1785-1855.' Unpublished PH D thesis, Memorial University 1991.

- 'Merchant Capital, the State, and Labour in a British Colony: Servant-Master Relations and Capital Accumulation in Newfoundland's Northeast-Coast Fishery, 1775-1799.' *Journal of the Canadian Historical Association*, New Series, vol.2 (1991): 17-42.

- 'Seamen, Fishermen and the Law: The Role of the Wages and Lien System in the Decline of Wage Labour in the Newfoundland Fishery.' In Colin Howell and Richard Twomey, eds. *Jack Tar in History: Essays in the History of Maritime Life and Labour*. Fredericton 1991, 105-31.

- 'The Staple Model Reconsidered: The Case of Agricultural Policy in Northeast Newfoundland, 1785-1855.' *Acadiensis* 21, no. 2 (1992): 48-71.

Candow, James E. *Of Men and Seals: A History of the Newfoundland Seal Hunt*. Ottawa 1989.

Chafe, W.J. *I've Been Working on the Railroad*. St. John's 1987.

Cherwinski, W.J.C., and Kealey, Gregory S., eds. *Lectures in Canadian Labour and Working-Class History*. St. John's 1985. The contents include: David Frank, 'The Struggle for Development: Workers in Atlantic Canada in the Twentieth Century' (135-47); and H. Landon Ladd, 'The Newfoundland Loggers' Strike of 1959' (149-64).

Chisholm, Jessie. 'Organizing on the Waterfront: The St. John's Longshoremen's Protective Union (LSPU), 1890-1914.' *Labour/Le Travail* 26 (1990):
37-59.

Clement, Wallace. 'Canada's Coastal Fisheries: Formation of Unions, Co-
operatives, and Associations.' *Journal of Canadian Studies* 19, no. 1
(1984): 5-33.

- *The Struggle to Organize: Resistance in Canada's Fishery*. Toronto 1986.

Close, David. 'Unconventional Militance: Union Organized Fish Sales in
Newfoundland.' *Journal of Canadian Studies* 17, no. 2 (1982): 3-11.

Coaker, William, ed. *Twenty-Two Years of the Fishermen's Protective Union in
Newfoundland*. St. John's 1984. Reprint of the 1930 original.

Cole, Sally C. 'Cod, God, Country and Family: the Portugese Newfoundland Cod Fishery.' *MAST: Maritime Anthropological Studies* 3, no. 1
(1990): 1-29.

Copes, Parzival. 'The Development of the Newfoundland Fishing Economy.' *Proceedings and Transactions of the Royal Society of Canada* 10, 4th
series (1972), section 3: 309-17.

- 'Fish and the Public Interest: the problem of Newfoundland.' *Canadian
Issues* 3, no. 1 (1980): 103-13.

- *The Resettlement of Fishing Communities in Newfoundland*. Ottawa 1972.

- and Steed, G. 'Regional Policy and Settlement Strategy: Constraints and
Contradictions in Newfoundland's Experience.' *Regional Studies* 9, no.
1 (1975): 93-110.

Crawley, Ron. 'Off to Sydney: Newfoundlanders Emigrate to Industrial
Cape Breton, 1890-1914.' *Acadiensis* 17, no. 2 (1988): 27-51.

Crowley, John E. 'Empire versus Truck: The Official Interpretation of Debt
and Labour in the Eighteenth Century Newfoundland Fishery.' *Canadian Historical Review* 70 (1989): 311-36.

Cuff, Robert. '"On the Cars": Winter Logging on the Bonavista Peninsula
(1911-1949).' *Newfoundland Quarterly* 79, no. 2 (1983): 12-17.

Department of Fisheries and Oceans, Government of Canada. *Independent
Review of the State of the Northern Cod Stock: Final Report*. Ottawa 1990.

Dickinson, Anthony B., and Sanger, Chesley W. 'Modern Shore-Based
Whaling in Newfoundland and Labrador: Expansion and Consolida-
tion, 1898-1902.' *International Journal of Maritime History* 2, no. 1 (1990):
83-116.

- 'Modern Shore-Station Whaling in Newfoundland and Labrador: The
Peak Season, 1904.' *International Journal of Maritime History* 5, no. 1
(1993): 127-54.

- 'A Newfoundland Floating Factory Whaling Expedition.' *Polar Record* 27
(1991): 125-8.

Doel, Priscilla. *Port O'Call: Memories of the Portugese White Fleet in St. John's, Newfoundland*. St. John's 1992.

Driscoll, Jacqueline J. 'Development of a Labrador mining community: industry in the bush.' Unpublished PH D thesis, University of Connecticut 1984.

Economic Council of Canada. *Newfoundland: From Dependency to Self-Reliance*. Ottawa 1980.

Fairley, Bryant O. 'The Struggle for Capitalism in the Fishing Industry in Newfoundland.' *Studies in Political Economy* no. 17 (1985): 33-69.

- and Leys, Colin, and Sacouman, James eds. *Restructuring and Resistance from Atlantic Canada*. Toronto 1990. The contents include: James Overton, "Small is Beautiful' and the Crisis in Newfoundland' (43-77); and Bryant Fairley, 'The Crisis, the State and Class Formation in the Newfoundland Fishery' (171-202).

Fay, C.R. *Channel Islands and Newfoundland*. Cambridge 1961.

- *Life and Labour in Newfoundland*. Cambridge 1956.

Feehan, James, Locke, Wade, Lynch, Scott, and Wernerheim, C. Michael. *Provincial Government Budgetary Policy: An Assessment of the 1991/92 Budget*. St. John's 1991.

Felt, Lawrence, and Sinclair, Peter. 'Home sweet home!: dimensions and determinants of life satisfaction in an underdeveloped region.' *Canadian Journal of Sociology* 16 (1991): 1-21.

Geren, Richard, and McCullogh, Blake. *Cain's Legacy: The Building of Iron Ore Company of Canada*. Sept-Iles, Que. 1990.

Gillespie, Bill. *A Class Act: An Illustrated History of the Newfoundland and Labrador Labour Movement*. St. John's 1986.

Greenwood, Robert. 'The Origins of NAPE: The Civil Service Association during the Commission of Government: 1936-1949.' *Newfoundland Quarterly* 82, no. 1 (1986): 22-6.

Hamdani, Daood Ul Hasan. 'The Role of Public Finance in the Economic Development of Newfoundland, 1949-64.' Unpublished MA thesis, Memorial University 1966.

Handcock, Gordon. 'The Origin and Development of Commission of Government Land Settlements in Newfoundland 1934-1969.' Unpublished MA thesis, Memorial University 1970.

- 'The Poole Mercantile Community and the Growth of Trinity 1700-1839.' *Newfoundland Quarterly* 80, no. 3 (1985): 19-30.

Henke, Janice Scott. *Seal Wars*. St. John's 1985.

Hill, Robert H. *The Meaning of Work and the Reality of Unemployment in the Newfoundland Context*. St. John's 1983.

Hiller, James. 'The Newfoundland Seal Fishery: An Historical Introduction.' *Bulletin of Canadian Studies* 7, no. 2 (Winter 1983/4): 49-72.

- 'The Origins of the Pulp and Paper Industry in Newfoundland.' *Acadiensis* 11, no. 2 (1982): 42-68.

- 'The Politics of Newsprint: The Newfoundland Pulp and Paper Industry, 1915-1939.' *Acadiensis* 19, no. 2 (1990): 3-39.

Horwood, Harold. *Corner Brook: A Social History of a Paper Town.* St. John's 1986.

House, J.D. 'Big oil and small communities in coastal Labrador: the local dynamics of dependency.' *Canadian Review of Sociology and Anthropology* 18 (1981): 433-52.

- *The Challenge of Oil: Newfoundland's Quest for Controlled Development.* St. John's 1985.

- 'Coastal Labrador: Incorporation, Exploitation, and Underdevelopment.' *Journal of Canadian Studies* 15, no. 2 (1980): 98-113.

- 'The Mouse That Roars: New Directions in Canadian Political Economy— The Case of Newfoundland.' In Robert J. Brym, ed. *Regionalism in Canada.* Toronto 1986, 161-96.

- 'Working Offshore: The Other Price of Newfoundland's Oil.' In Katherina L.P. Lundy and Barbara Warme, eds. *Work in the Canadian Context: Continuity Despite Change.* Toronto 1986, 170-89.

- ed. *Fish versus Oil: Resources and Rural Development in North Atlantic Societies.* St. John's 1986. The contents include: J.D. House, 'Fish is Fish and Oil is Oil: The Case for North Sea Comparisons to Atlantic Canada' (129-38); and S.G. Canning, 'Prospects for Co-Existence: Interactions Between the Established Fishery and New Offshore Petroleum Development in Newfoundland' (141-61).

Inglis, Gordon. *More Than Just a Union: The Story of the NFFAWU.* St. John's 1985.

Innis, Harold A. *The Cod Fisheries: The History of an International Economy.* Rev. ed. Toronto 1954.

Joy, John L. 'The Growth and Development of Trades and Manufacturing in St. John's, 1870-1914.' Unpublished MA thesis, Memorial University 1977.

Kimber, Stephen. *Net Profits: The Story of National Sea.* Halifax 1989.

Lamson, Cynthia, and Hansen, Arthur J., eds. *Atlantic Fisheries and Coastal Communities: Fisheries Decision-Making Case Studies.* Halifax 1984. The contents include: R.D.S. Macdonald, 'Canadian Fisheries Policy and the Development of the Atlantic Coast Groundfisheries Management' (15-73); L. Gene Barrett, 'Capital and the State in Atlantic Canada: The Structural Context of Fishery Policy between 1939 and 1977' (77-104);

and Cynthia Lamson, 'Fisheries Assessment and Government Response: The Case of the Newfoundland Inshore Fishery' (105-31).

Leyton, Elliott. *Dying Hard: The Ravages of Industrial Carnage.* Toronto 1975.

Little, Linda. 'Collective Action in Outport Newfoundland: A Case Study from the 1830s.' *Labour/Le Travail* 26 (1990): 7-35.

- 'Plebeian Collective Action in Harbour Grace and Carbonear, Newfoundland, 1830-1840.' Unpublished MA thesis, Memorial University 1984.

Locke, Peter D. 'Coastal Steamer and Branch Railway Line Revenue Competition in the Reid Newfoundland Company.' *Canadian Rail*, no. 419 (1990): 196-201.

- 'Czar of Newfoundland: A Profile of Sir Robert Gillespie Reid.' *Canadian Rail*, no. 419 (1990): 183-95.

McCloskey, William. *Seafarers of the North Atlantic.* New York 1990.

Macdonald, David. *Power begins at the Cod End: The Newfoundland Trawlermen's Strike, 1974-75.* St. John's 1980.

- 'They Cannot Pay Us in Money: Newman and Company and the Supplying System in the Newfoundland Fishery, 1850-1884.' *Acadiensis* 19, no. 1 (1989): 142-56.

McDooling, Jim William. 'The Fishermen: Transition in a Northeast Coastal Community in Newfoundland.' Unpublished MA thesis, University of New Brunswick 1982.

McInnis, Peter S. 'All Solid Along the Line: The Reid Newfoundland Strike of 1918.' *Labour/Le Travail* 26 (1990): 61-84.

- 'Newfoundland Labour and World War I: The Emergence of the Newfoundland Industrial Workers' Association.' Unpublished MA thesis, Memorial University 1987.

MacKenzie, David. 'An Economic and Financial Review of Newfoundland during the Second World War.' Document. *Newfoundland Studies* 8 (1992): 69-89.

MacKinnon, Robert. 'Company housing in Wabana, Bell Island, Newfoundland.' *Material History Bulletin* no. 14 (Spring 1982): 67-71.

- 'Farming the Rock: The Evolution of Commercial Agriculture around St. John's, Newfoundland to 1945.' *Acadiensis* 20, no. 2 (1991): 32-61.

- 'The Growth of Commercial Agriculture Around St. John's, 1800-1935: A Study of Local Trade in Response to Urban Demand.' Unpublished MA thesis, Memorial University 1981.

MacLeod, Malcolm. 'A Death at Deer Lake: Catalyst of a Forgotten Newfoundland Work Stoppage, 1924.' *Labour/Le Travail* 16 (1985): 179-91.

Mannion, John. 'Henry Shea (1767-1830): A Tipperary Trader in Newfoundland.' *Tipperary History Journal* 1 (1988): 182-91.

- 'Irish Merchants Abroad: The Newfoundland Experience, 1750-1850.' *Newfoundland Studies* 2 (1986): 127-190.

- 'The Maritime Trade of Waterford in the Eighteenth Century.' In William J. Smyth and Kevin Whelan eds. *Common Ground: Essays on the Historical Geography of Ireland.* Cork 1988, 208-33.

- 'Migration and Upward Mobility: The Meagher Family in Ireland and Newfoundland, 1780-1830.' *Irish Economic and Social History* 15 (1988): 54-70.

- 'Old World Antecedents, New World Adaptations: Inistioge (Co. Kilkenny) Immigrants in Newfoundland.' *Newfoundland Studies* 5 (1989): 103-75.

- 'The Waterford Merchants and the Irish-Newfoundland provisions Trade, 1770-1820.' In Donald H. Akenson, ed. *Canadian Papers in Rural History.* Vol. 3. Gananoque, Ont. 1982, 178-203.

Martin, Wendy. *Once Upon a Mine: Story of Pre-Confederation Mines on the Island of Newfoundland.* Montreal 1983.

Matthews, Keith. 'Recruitment and Stability of Employment in the British Merchant Marine: the case of C.T. Bowring and Company.' In Rosemary E. Ommer and G.E. Panting, eds. *Working Men Who Got Wet.* St. John's 1980, 77-103.

Matthews, Ralph. 'Federal Licencing Policies for the Atlantic Inshore Fishery and their Implementation in Newfoundland, 1973-1981.' *Acadiensis* 17, no. 2 (1988): 83-108.

- and Phyne, John. 'Regulating the Newfoundland Inshore Fishery: Traditional Values Versus State Control in the Regulation of a Common Property Resource.' *Journal of Canadian Studies* 23, nos. 1 & 2 (1988): 158-76.

Mayo, H.B. 'The Economic Problem of the Newfoundland Fisheries.' *Canadian Journal of Economics and Political Science* 17 (1951): 482-93.

Money and Development: Mobilizing Capital and Organizing for Local Economic Development (A collection of essays). St. John's 1990. The contents are: John Wickham, Richard Fuchs and Janet Miller Pitt, '"Where Credit is Due": A Case Study of the Eagle River Credit Union' (1-63); Peter R. Sinclair, 'The Great Northern Peninsula Development Corporation: An Organizational Framework for Revitalization?' (67-114); and Paul Bugden, Adele Poynter and Anthony McLevey, 'Equity Capital and Economic Development in Newfoundland and Labrador' (117-74).

Neary, Peter. 'The Bradley Report on Logging Operations in Newfoundland, 1934: A Suppressed Document.' Document. *Labour/Le Travail* 16 (1985): 193-232.

- 'Canada and the Newfoundland Labour Market, 1939-49.' *Canadian Historical Review* 62, (1981): 470-95.

Neis, Barbara. 'Competitive Merchants and Class Struggle in Newfoundland.' *Studies in Political Economy* no. 5 (1981): 127-143.

- 'Fishers' Ecological Knowledge and Stock Assessment in Newfoundland.' *Newfoundland Studies* 8 (1992): 155-78.

- 'From Codblock to Fishfood: The Crisis and Restructuring in the Newfoundland Fishing Industry: 1968-1986.' Unpublished PH D thesis, University of Toronto, 1988.

Ommer, Rosemary E. 'Merchant Credit and the Informal Economy: Newfoundland, 1919-1929.' Canadian Historical Association. *Historical Papers*, 1989, 167-89.

- ed. *Merchant Credit and Labour Strategies in Historical Perspective.* Fredericton 1990. The contents include: James Hiller, 'The Newfoundland Credit System: an Interpretation' (86-101); Robert M. Lewis, 'The Survival of the Planters' Fishery in Nineteenth and Twentieth Century Newfoundland' (102-13); David A Macdonald, 'They Cannot Pay Us in Money: Newman and Company and the Supplying System in the Newfoundland Fishery, 1850-1884' (114-28); Patricia A. Thornton, 'The Transition From the Migratory to the Resident Fishery in the Strait of Belle Isle' (138-66); Raoul Andersen, '"Chance" and Contract: Lessons from a Newfoundland Banks Fisherman's Anecdote' (167-82); and Carol Brice-Bennett, 'Missionaries as Traders: Moravians and Labrador Inuit, 1771-1860' (223-46).

Orr, Jeffrey. 'Scottish Merchants in the Newfoundland Trade, 1800-1835: A Colonial Community in Transition.' Unpublished MA thesis, Memorial University 1987.

Overton, James. 'Dirt and Danger, Development and Decency in Newfoundland.' *Canadian Journal of Communication* 12, nos. 3 & 4 (1986): 37-51.

- 'Public Relief and Social Unrest in Newfoundland in the 1930s: An Evaluation of the Ideas of Piven and Cloward.' In Gregory S. Kealey, ed. *Class, Gender, and Region: Essays in Canadian Historical Sociology.* St. John's 1988, 153-66.

- 'Uneven Regional Development in Canada: The Case of Newfoundland.' *Review of Radical Political Economics* 10, no. 3 (1978): 106-16.

Penney, A. R. *A History of the Newfoundland Railway.* Vol. 1, 1881-1923. St. John's 1988.

- and Kennedy, Fabian. *A History of the Newfoundland Railway.* Vol. 2, 1923-1988. St. John's 1990.

Peters, Robert D. 'The Social and Economic Effects of the Transition from a System of Woods Camps to a System of Commuting in the Newfoundland Pulpwood Industry.' Unpublished MA thesis, Memorial University 1965.

Powers, Anne Marie. 'Social Organization in a Newfoundland Fishing Settlement on the Burin Peninsula.' Unpublished PH D thesis, State University of New York at Stony Brook 1984.

Pross, A. Paul, and McCorquodale, Susan. *Economic Resurgence and the Constitutional Agenda: The Case of the East Coast Fisheries.* Kingston 1987.

Reader, W.J. *Bowater: A History.* Cambridge 1981.

Reeves, William G. 'Alexander's Conundrum Reconsidered: The American Dimension in Newfoundland Resource Development, 1898-1910.' *Newfoundland Studies* 5 (1989): 1-37.

Rowe, Francis C. *The Currency and Medals of Newfoundland.* Willowdale, Ont. 1983.

Ryan, Shannon, *Fish Out of Water: The Newfoundland Saltfish Trade 1814-1914.* St. John's 1986.

- 'The Industrial Revolution in the Newfoundland Seal Fishery.' *International Journal of Maritime History* 4, no. 2 (1992): 1-43.

- 'The Newfoundland Cod Fishery in the Nineteenth Century.' Unpublished MA thesis, Memorial University 1971.

- *Newfoundland-Spanish Saltfish Trade: 1814-1914.* St. John's 1983.

- assisted by Drake, Martha. *Seals and Sealers: A Pictorial History of the Newfoundland Seal Fishery.* St. John's 1987.

- and Small, Larry. *Haulin' Rope & Gaff: Songs and Poetry in the History of the Newfoundland Seal Fishery.* St. John's 1978.

- ed. *Chafe's Sealing Book: A Statistical Record of the Newfoundland Steamer Seal Fishery, 1863-1941.* St. John's 1989.

Sager, Eric W. 'The Merchants of Water Street and capital Investment in Newfoundland's Traditional Economy.' In Lewis R. Fischer, and Eric W. Sager, eds. *The Enterprising Canadians: Entrepreneurs and Economic Development in Eastern Canada, 1820-1914.* St. John's 1979, 77-95.

- 'Newfoundland's Historical Revival and the Legacy of David Alexander.' *Acadiensis* 11, no. 1 (1981), 104-15.

- 'The Port of St. John's, Newfoundland 1840-1899: A Preliminary Analysis.' In Keith Matthews and G.E. Panting, eds. *Ships and Shipbuilding in the North Atlantic Region.* St. John's 1978, 19-39.

- *Seafaring Labour: The Merchant Marine of Atlantic Canada, 1820-1914.* Kingston and Montreal 1989.

- with G.E. Panting. *Maritime Capital: The Shipping Industry in Atlantic Canada 1820-1914.* Kingston and Montreal 1990.

Sanger, Chesley W. 'The Dundee-St. John's Connection: 19th Century Interlinkages Between Scottish Arctic Whaling and the Newfoundland Seal Fishery.' *Newfoundland Studies* 4 (1988): 1-26.

- 'The 19th Century Newfoundland Seal Fishery and the Influence of Scottish Whalemen.' *Polar Record* 20 (1980): 231-52.

- 'Technological and Spatial Adaptation in the Newfoundland Seal Fishery during the 19th Century.' Unpublished MA thesis, Memorial University 1973.

- and Dickinson, Anthony B. 'Expansion of Regulated Modern Shore-Station Whaling in Newfoundland and Labrador, 1902-1903.' *The Northern Mariner* 1, no. 2 (1991): 1-22.

- 'Newfoundland Involvement in Twentieth-century Shore-station Whaling in British Columbia.' *Newfoundland Studies* 7 (1991): 97-122.

- 'The Origins of Modern Shore-Based Whaling in Newfoundland and Labrador: The Cabot Steam Whaling Co. Ltd., 1896-98.' *International Journal of Maritime History* 1, no. 1 (1989): 129-57.

- *"They were Clannish as Hell": Origins of Modern Shore-Station Whaling in British Columbia—The Newfoundland Factor.* Halifax 1991.

Scarlett, Maurice. *The Newfoundland Economy, a spatial analysis.* St. John's 1985.

Schrank, William E., and Feehan, James P. 'The Regressivity of Newfoundland's Consumption Tax Structure, 1974-1982.' *Canadian Tax Journal* 32 (1984): 294-309.

- and Roy, N., eds. *Econometric modelling of the world trade in groundfish.* Boston 1991.

Sinclair, Peter R. 'Fisheries and Regional Development: Contradictions of Canadian Policy in the Newfoundland Context.' In S.J. Thomas, L. Maril, and E.P. Durrenberger, eds. *Marine Resource Utilization.* Mobile, Ala. 1989, 105-13.

- 'Fisheries Management and Problems of Social Justice: Reflections on Northwest Newfoundland.' *MAST: Maritime Anthropological Studies* 3, no. 1 (1990): 30-47.

- *From Traps to Draggers: Domestic Commodity Production in Northwest Newfoundland, 1850-1982.* St. John's 1985.

- *State Intervention and the Newfoundland Fisheries.* Aldershot, England 1987.

- ed. *A Question of Survival: The Fisheries and Newfoundland Society.* St. John's 1988. The contents include: Peter R. Sinclair, 'Introduction'(1-19); Rosemary E. Ommer, 'What's Wrong with Canadian Fish?'(23-44); Lawrence F. Felt, 'On the Backs of Fish: Newfoundland and Iceland's Experiences with Fishery-Induced Capital Goods Production in the Twentieth Century'(45-72); Barrie Deas, 'Ownership and Fleet Structure in the Inshore Fisheries of Newfoundland and Northeast Scotland'(75-103); Bonnie J. McCay, 'Fish Guts, Hair Nets and Unemployment Stamps: Women and Work in Co-operative Fish Plants'(105-31); Babrara Neis, 'Doin' Time on the Protest Line: Women's Political Culture, Politics and Collective Action in Outport Newfoundland'(133-53); Peter R. Sinclair, 'The State Encloses the Commons: Fisheries Management from the 200-Mile Limit to Factory Freezer Trawlers'(157-77); J. Douglas House, 'Canadian Fisheries Policies and Troubled Newfoundland Communities'(178-202); Roger Carter, 'Co-operatives in Rural Newfoundland and Labrador: An Alternative?'(203-28); and Peter R. Sinclair, 'Conclusion'(229-34).

Smith, Philip. *Brinco: The Story of Churchill Falls*. Toronto 1976.

Staveley, Michael. 'Migration and Mobility in Newfoundland and Labrador: A Study in Population Geography.' Unpublished PH D thesis, University of Alberta 1973.

- 'Newfoundland: Economy and Society at the Margin.' In L.D. McCann, ed. *Heartland and Hinterland: A Geography of Canada*. Scarborough, Ont. 1982, 214-49.

Steele, D.H., Andersen, R., and Green, J.M. 'The Managed Commercial Annihilation of Northern Cod.' *Newfoundland Studies* 8 (1992): 34-68.

Strong, Cyril W. *My Life as a Newfoundland Union Organizer: The Memoirs of Cyril W. Strong, 1912-1987*. Gregory S. Kealey, ed. St. John's 1987.

Sutherland, John Duff. '"The Men Went to Work by the Stars and Returned by Them": The Experience of Work in the Newfoundland Woods during the 1930s.' *Newfoundland Studies* 7 (1991): 143-72.

- 'Newfoundland Loggers Respond to the Great Depression.' *Labour/Le Travail* 29 (1992): 83-115.

- 'A Social History of Pulpwood Logging in Newfoundland During the Great Depression.' Unpublished MA thesis, Memorial University 1988.

Sweeny, Robert C.H. with Bradley, David, and Hong, Robert. 'Movement, Options and Costs: Indexes as Historical Evidence, a Newfoundland Example.' *Acadiensis* 12, no. 1 (1992): 111-21.

Thornton, Patricia A. 'Dynamic Equilibrium: Settlement, Population and Ecology in the Strait of Belle Isle, Newfoundland, 1840-1940.' Unpublished PH D thesis, University of Aberdeen 1979.

- 'Newfoundland's Frontier Demographic Experience: The World We Have Not Lost.' *Newfoundland Studies* 1 (1985): 141-62.

- 'The Problem of Out-Migration from Atlantic Canada, 1871-1921: A New Look.' *Acadiensis* 15, no. 1 (1985): 3-34.

- 'Some Preliminary Comments on the Extent and Consequences of Out-Migration from the Atlantic Region, 1870-1920.' In Lewis R. Fischer and

Eric W. Sager, eds. *Merchant Shipping and Economic Development in Atlantic Canada*. St. John's 1982, 187-218.

Trump, H.J. 'Newfoundland trade from the Port of Teignmouth in the 19th century.' *Transport History* 9 (1978): 260-8.

Usher, Abbott Payson. 'The Influence of the Cod Fishery upon the History of the North Atlantic Seaboard.' *Canadian Journal of Economics and Political Science* 6 (1940): 591-9. A review of Harold A. Innis, *The Cod Fisheries: The History of an International Economy*.

VanderZwaag, David. 'Canadian Fisheries Management: A Legal and Administrative Overview.' *Ocean Development and International Law Journal* 13 (1983): 171-211.

Weir, Gail. *The Miners of Wabana*. St. John's 1989.

Wright, Guy. *Sons & Seals: A Voyage to the Ice*. St. John's 1984.

Index